The Central Middle East

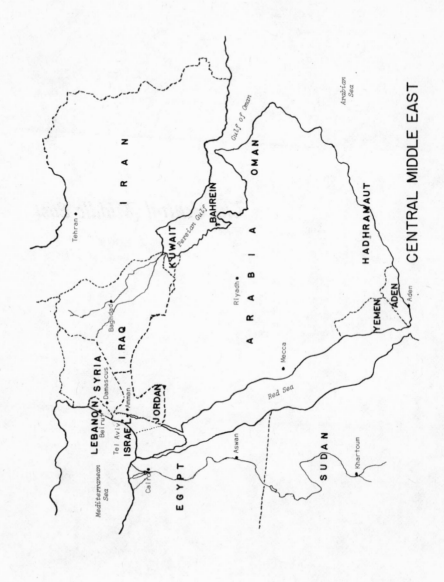

CENTRAL MIDDLE EAST

The Central Middle East

A Handbook of Anthropology and Published Research on the Nile Valley, the Arab Levant, Southern Mesopotamia, the Arabian Peninsula, and Israel

Louise E. Sweet, editor

with a foreword by William D. Schorger
and chapters by Harold B. Barclay, John Gulick,
Robert A. Fernea, Louise E. Sweet, and Alex Weingrod

hraf press
New Haven
1971

Library of Congress Catalog Card Number: 70-148033
ISBN 0-87536-107-2

Printed in the United States of America

Contents

Contributors

Harold B. Barclay
University of Alberta

John Gulick
University of North Carolina

Robert A. Fernea
University of Texas

Louise E. Sweet
University of Manitoba

Alex Weingrod
Brandeis University

ABOUT THE EDITOR

Louise E. Sweet (Ph.D. Michigan) has conducted field research in Syria (1953-54) and the Arab States of the Persian Gulf (1958-59). She has also done archival work in London, spent 17 months in field work in a Druze community in the Anti-Lebanon (1964-65), and spent a summer in research in the Edmonton, Canada, colony from the home village, with return visits to Lebanon (1966, 1968-69). She has recently served as Visiting Professor in the Department of Anthropology at the University of Wisconsin and as of July 1971 is Professor and Head of the Department of Anthropology at the University of Manitoba. In 1969, HRAF Press published *Circum-Mediterranean Peasantry: Introductory Bibliographies*, edited by Louise E. Sweet and Timothy J. O'Leary.

Foreword

This publication results from a project, funded by the American Council of Learned Societies—Social Science Research Council Joint Committee on the Near and Middle East, that I directed for a number of years. The original objective was the preparation of an ethnological survey, by individuals who had personal knowledge of the various regions involved, of the entire Middle East and North Africa. The resulting draft proved, perhaps inevitably, totally unwieldy. The present contributors and I are greatly indebted to Dr. Sweet for getting this portion of the enterprise into print.

William D. Schorger
University of Michigan

Preface

The five chapters presented here survey the cultural diversity and indigenous or introduced institutions of the "heartland" regions of the Middle East: the Nile Valley, the Arab Levant, Southern Mesopotamia, the Arabian Peninsula, and the new industrially-based state of Israel. Each author presents his region within the framework of dominant features of the area under consideration or in terms of themes posed to comprehend the diverse ethnology of the whole. All chapters were written to stimulate further research. Together with the annotated bibliographies appended to each chapter, they provide the serious student of the cultural anthropology of this central sector of the Middle East with an overview of the major regions and socio-cultural types and a guide to the adequacies or inadequacies of the major published research on the area.

All of the chapters and bibliographies, originally composed and compiled between 1960 and 1962, have been updated to 1967 so far as possible, and some additions and revisions have been made for this new issue in 1971.

With profound changes now taking place throughout this central area of the Middle East, the editor and contributors have collectively agreed that the present form of this book is useful as it stands for its "baseline" value in summarizing the data available to the contemporary historical moment. A new synthesis, taking into account the withdrawal of colonial administrators, the establishment of sovereign governing systems, and the introduction and proliferation of international commercial and industrial mechanisms, awaits systematic anthropological study. This has a very small beginning as yet; it is most heartening that scholars of these Middle Eastern countries are themselves moving into such problems. We may hope that the new syntheses and guides may come from them.

For this edition of *The Central Middle East*, the editor and authors are grateful to the staff of the Human Relations Area Files, especially Elizabeth P. Swift, Editor, Timothy J. O'Leary, and Frank W. Moore. Their contributions include editorial and bibliographical work and the addition of a map and an index.

Louise E. Sweet
Editor

Publisher's Note

Originally issued in 1968 as part of the HRAFlex Books Descriptive Ethnography Series (HRAFlex Book M1-001), *The Central Middle East* was so well received by the scholarly community that publication of a regular HRAF Press edition of the book seemed warranted. A few additions and revisions have been made for this new edition.

CHAPTER *1*

The Nile Valley

HAROLD B. BARCLAY

INEVITABLY, in singling out any cultural or geographical area for attention, one is compelled to wrestle with the problem of boundary-making in terms of both space and time. If we are concerned with the larger question of the description of the Middle Eastern cultural area, we are faced with several marginal zones where it is extremely difficult to determine where the Middle East ends and something else begins. Ultimately much of the sorting and categorizing becomes arbitrary and purely for purposes of convenience—what one can adequately deal with in a given context. This problem is especially acute when we attempt to describe one segment of such a major cultural area as the Middle East. If, as I have been given the task to do, we focus on the Nile Valley, it is not difficult to establish a southern limit to such a zone, namely, where Arab Muslim culture ends and the Nilotic tribal cultures begin. For most of Egypt and the Northern Province of the Sudan the decision as to what to include becomes a little more difficult and a little more arbitrary. One is aided here by the degree to which population is almost wholly concentrated in the Nile Valley. Most of the Egyptian oases may be considered as outposts of Arab Nile culture (except Siwa, which because of its strong Berber component is more appropriately dealt with under a discussion of Libya). The various nomadic and seminomadic pastoralists who exploit parts of the desert regions flanking the Nile pose a more difficult problem. On the one hand, they have for centuries trickled into and settled in the Delta area and parts of Upper Egypt, in which case they have been eventually absorbed as part of the mass of fellahin. On the other hand, the cultural ties of those of the Western Desert point to Libya, while those in the east and in Sinai are closely affiliated with the nomadic peoples of Arabia. Still further, the Beja

1

tribes of the northeastern Sudan have undergone a gradual process of Arabization, which has been especially accelerated in the last three quarters of a century. Yet they have a strong cultural affinity with other Hamitic pastoralists of the Horn of Africa, and for large numbers of Beja the Nile Valley and its residents have not had much relevance. Dividing the Nile Valley culturally from the non-Nile Valley becomes most cumbersome in the area from above Kosti to Shendi in the Sudan, because as one moves up the Nile, population becomes more dispersed and less concentrated on the river banks; similarly the contrast between the agrarian economy of the Nile and that away from it becomes less distinct and in some areas nonexistent. The so-called Baggara constitute a belt of cattle pastoralists extending from Kordofan, across Darfur, and eastward to Lake Chad. To include them for detailed discussion here would carry us a long way from the waters of the Nile. The Baggara have close affinity and similarity to Nile Arabs and to the Arabs of northern Kordofan, however, and demonstrate a distinctiveness in their cultural pattern and ecology which deserves detailed and separate consideration. It is further evident that south of Nubia most of the contemporary sedentary Arabs of the Nile were, in the not too distant past, themselves nomadic or seminomadic herders, and that many tribes maintain to this day both a sedentary and a nomadic pastoral section.

The above discussion seeks only to suggest some of the problems at hand. I propose in the limited space available to me to focus primarily on those people who dwell geographically in the Nile Valley and Delta, north of Kosti and Singa in the Sudan. Collateral and peripheral discussion will concern oases dwellers and the Arab camel and cattle nomads flanking the Nile.

The main emphasis in this chapter will be on the rural populace, with, again, a peripheral attention to the city people—in large part because the latter have not received any considerable attention from anthropologists and also because the great majority of the population is rural.

This chapter, finally, will concentrate on the contemporary or recent-contemporary populations. It will commence with a geographical review and from this proceed to a consideration of the ways in which the inhabitants exploit their physical environment and adapt to it. From there, attention is turned to social organization, ideology, and language. A caveat should be entered here. While this discussion commences with the most concrete and proceeds to the most abstract, it is not to suggest that the former is somehow more "real," more "basic," or more "causal" than the latter. Culture as such is the process of making, sharing, and implementing "ideas" which are the product of the dynamic interaction of the "mind" of man with his environment.[1] It is a process of continual modification by man and under the control of man. As such, it is logical to operate from the premise that ecological circumstances, economy, social organization, and ideology are mutually interacting and interdependent forces, although this is not to suggest that they must conform to an organismic or mechanical equilibrium model.

The Nile, one of the major river systems of the world, has for millennia been an instrumental force for cultural uniformity along its banks, particularly where it cuts its path through the Sahara. The ancient Pharaonic culture extended its overwhelming influence from the Mediterranean mouth of the Nile far south into Nubia. Succeeding Coptic Christian and Muslim Arab ways of life have done the same. As the following discussion will indicate, not only has a uniform pattern of a predominantly Arab-oriented Muslim culture evolved throughout the middle and lower reaches of the Nile and its banks but there has been variety within this uniformity as well. Yet neither the uniformity nor the variety is explainable in an oversimplified resort to ecological causality. Certainly, the fact that camel nomadism is replaced by cattle nomadism in the southern extremities of the area is explainable primarily by the physical environment and climate. Nevertheless, cultural and historical factors are also significant, and it is particularly necessary to resort to them in order to understand the persistence of such phenomena as the Nubian and the Coptic Christian enclaves and the development in recent times of such enterprises as the extensive irrigation schemes in the Gizera region.

The intersecting elements of Nile and Sahara are the two most outstanding physical features of this region, and both lend themselves to a correspondingly important cultural significance. The Nile weaves its way through the barren desert as the life-giving artery to an otherwise desolate land. The several sources of the Nile lie in the mountain and lake systems far to the south of its mouth. The Bahr al Ghazal, the Loi and the Jur rivers in southwestern Sudan, and the lake system of Uganda—particularly Lakes Albert and Victoria—all supply water for the White Nile. The mountains of Ethiopia, most significantly the general vicinity of Lake Tana, are the source of the Blue Nile, which contributes 70 per cent of the Nile water. The White and Blue Niles work their separate ways northward from their sources and in the direction of increasingly more arid zones, ultimately joining as a single river at Khartoum. North of the River Atbara no tributary flows into the Nile in its remaining

[1] Rather than employing the above idealist terminology, one could well follow Rapaport and speak of "messages stored in the brain" by way of "dismissing the naturalist-idealist issue as obsolete" (Rapaport 1967).

course of over 1,600 miles to the Mediterranean. From about fifteen degrees north latitude northward, the Nile truly becomes the lifeblood of northeast Africa. Between Khartoum and Aswan are a series of six cataracts, permitting only intermittent river traffic. Between these two cities the Nile banks are characterized by a gradual ascent or, in some cases where the river has eaten away the banks, by steep cliffs of low elevation. In either case, the banks merge into a monotonous, undulating, barren land. Above Aswan, the Nile flows through a flat plain which extends away from the river on either side toward steep, stony cliffs, which in some places rise to 1,800 feet. It was some of these rocky heights across from the present town of Luxor that several Pharaohs utilized as natural pyramid substitutes for their burial places. This region, comprising most of Upper Egypt, is a rift valley constituting a long and deep crack or depression in an extensive plateau. The valley terminates in the Nile Delta beginning below Cairo where the river splits in two main branches: one empties into the sea at Damietta and the other at Rosetta. The Nile region north of Cairo, known as Lower Egypt, is crisscrossed with a multitude of irrigation and drainage canals. In the vicinity from Alexandria to Damietta there are extensive salt marshes and lagoons. Dams are located at Sennar on the Blue Nile, Jebel Awlia on the White Nile, and Aswan on the main Nile. In addition, there are several barrages in the lower part of the Egyptian Nile.

The nature of the topography of the land through which the Nile flows from Kosti to the Mediterranean is, as has been suggested, primarily a level to slightly undulating plain. The southern or Sudanese part is a plateau about 1,000 feet in elevation and interspersed with occasional hills. This plateau is bounded on the west by the highlands of Darfur and on the east by the Red Sea mountains, which form part of the chain that extends from eastern Egypt into Ethiopia. In Egypt these mountains rise to an elevation of 8,600 feet in the Sinai Peninsula, while in the Sudan they are as high as 9,000 feet. For the Western Desert of Egypt, as for the Sudan, the topography is a rolling plain, although at somewhat lower elevations than in the Sudan. Indeed, there are several depressions in the western part of Egypt, the largest of which, the Qattara Depression, reaches a depth of 436 feet below sea level. Other depressions of note are the oases: Siwa, Bahariya, Farafra, Dakhla, and Kharga. Fayum is also technically an oasis, although its main water supply comes from the Nile via an ancient canal. The southwestern corner of Egypt is an enormous sand sea, but elsewhere in western Egypt, outside the Nile Valley, the surface is chiefly rock outcroppings and gravel or stony plains.

The other main physical feature—the factor that makes for the supreme human importance of the Nile—is the desert. Rainfall is at its greatest at the northern and southern extremes of the area and lowest in between. Thus, at Alexandria, on the Mediterranean coast and approximately thirty-two degrees north latitude, rainfall amounts to as much as eight inches a year, while at Aswan, at twenty-four degrees north latitude, it is only a trace. Between Aswan and Dongola, Sudan, nineteen degrees north latitude, rain is extremely rare, and several years may pass without it. South of this latitude rainfall begins to increase, so that at Khartoum, about fifteen degrees north latitude, it is about eight inches a year, and at the southernmost limits of the area, at Kosti, it is over seventeen inches. Most of the region is therefore highly arid, constituting the eastward extension of the Sahara Desert.

From Dongola northward, the rainy season, if it exists at all, occurs in the winter months of December, January, and February. South of this point, the climate is affected by dry northerly and moist southerly winds, which produce rainfall from July through September. Sand and dust storms are another feature of the weather. They may occur in Cairo during the *khamsin*, in March and April, and in Khartoum from April to July.

Temperatures in northeastern Africa are, as would be expected, high throughout most of the year. The greatest extremes are reached at Wadi Halfa, where lows of 34° F. and highs of 120° F. have been reported. From April to November, it is extremely hot and dry in this vicinity. Cairo and Khartoum temperatures are less extreme. The mean minimum for Cairo is 46° F. in January; the mean maximum 97° F. in July. On the whole, temperatures in Cairo are uncomfortable only during August and early September, when the rising Nile increases the humidity. Khartoum temperatures, on the other hand, are much more torrid. Mean minimums reported in January are 61° F., and mean maximums reported in April are 105° F.

One can only be impressed by the degree to which man has altered the physical appearance of so much of the Nile Valley, especially in the vicinity of its lower reaches. In lieu of the idea and the knowledge of hydraulic engineering, the Valley would be a vast swamp of reeds inhabited by a myriad of aquatic fauna (where it was not but a muddy ribbon cutting its course through forbidding desert). The result of the interaction of the collective genius of the human inhabitants with the given ecological circumstances has been a radical alteration of the physical lay of the land and of the composition of the flora and fauna. Thus, the manipulation and control of the waters of the Nile have transformed much of the Valley of the Nile into a garden in which domesticated flora and fauna predominate. Wild game as such can hardly be said to exist, having retreated to less inhabited and civilized zones. Wild plant life is primarily in the form of garden weeds throughout much of the Egyptian Nile.

The unirrigated desert that flanks the Nile sustains only those hardy xerophytic plants that can survive on a minimum of moisture. For much of Egypt's Western Desert literally nothing grows; there is only gravel, rocks, and sand. Elsewhere, certain coarse grasses and thorn scrub cling tenaciously to life. Dwarf mimosa and tamarisk are also to be found, and in the more southerly latitudes of the desert zone varieties of acacia appear. The desert is a refuge for foxes, jackals, jerboas, rabbits, and, in some sections, for an occasional hyena, gazelle, or Nubian ibex. In it, also, are several varieties of lizards and snakes, some of which are deadly poisonous. These reptiles also populate the Nile Valley proper, while rats, mice, and mongoose comprise the wild mammals in that area. The environs of the Nile host countless aquatic birds, e.g. cranes, herons, ducks, kingfishers. Birds of prey, particularly vultures and varieties of hawks, are residents of both desert and sown. Nile waters are rich in fish, of which perch and carp are most important in terms of human consumption. Ubiquitous throughout desert and river valley alike is the multitude of insects and related vermin one would associate with such a climate, including scorpions, mosquitoes, flies, fleas, lice, and grasshoppers. As a result of the gradual desiccation of the area and, particularly, because of human encroachment, all large game have suffered enormously. Once the Pharaohs hunted lions in the desert of Egypt, and probably less than three centuries ago, hippopotamuses wallowed and crocodiles lurked in the Nile as far north as the Delta. The lions and hippopotamuses have vanished, and each year the crocodiles retreat further up the Nile so that they too are now extinct below Aswan.

Most important of the flora and fauna of the Nile Valley has been that associated with man and, indeed, man is in fact the most common mammal of all. The inhabitants of northeastern Africa are predominantly Caucasoid or Mediterranean type. As one moves southward from the Mediterranean Sea, there is an increasing Negroid admixture, so that above Aswan, and particularly in the Sudan, Negroid features are extremely common.

The population map of northeastern Africa reflects geographical and climatic conditions as they have been exploited by human knowledge. In most parts, rainfall is too sparse to permit any concentrated human habitation outside of some major source of water supplied by river or oasis. Of over twenty-eight million people residing in Egypt, twenty-seven million live in the Nile Valley in an area of barely 13,000 square miles, thus giving the Egyptian Nile region over two thousand persons per square mile. Of the remainder, the majority live in the Suez Canal Zone, and about 325,000 in desert governorates having 372,000 square miles. Over 60 per cent of the population reside in the Nile Delta, another 35 per cent in Upper Egypt, 3 per cent in the Canal Zone, and 1 per cent in the desert zones. While all the Egyptian Nile region is one of the most densely populated regions in the world, and certainly the most densely settled area in Africa, some provinces are more thickly populated than others. In Lower Egypt, Qalyubiya (2,700 people per square mile), Al Gharbiya and Al Minufiya (both with over 2,200 per square mile), and, in Upper Egypt, Giza (with over 3,200 per square mile), Sawhaj (with 2,670 per square mile) and Asyut (with 2,300 per square mile) comprise six Egyptian provinces with an excess of 2,000 people per square mile. The extreme density of Giza Province largely results from its proximity to Cairo and from the fact that a great part of its population is thus suburban. Sawhaj Province ranks as the most densely settled in terms of its rural agricultural population.

In the Sudanese Nile area, population is by contrast very sparse. Nevertheless in the Northern Province there is a concentration of settlement along the Nile banks parallel to that in Egypt. Thus, while the Northern Province covers 184,000 square miles and has a population of 1,100,000, over 90 per cent of that population resides on the Nile banks, giving a density of 500 or more persons per square mile, while the desert zones of the province have far below one person per square mile. Indeed, the western half of the Northern Province is completely uninhabited.

From about Khartoum and on up the White and Blue Niles, population becomes increasingly more dispersed and less concentrated on the Nile, reflecting the increased rainfall, along with the correspondingly greater importance of rain cultivation as one proceeds southward.

Settlement Patterns

The typical pattern of the Middle East, with its interdependence of city and village dwellers and nomads, is characteristic of the Nile Valley. Approximately 25 per cent of Egyptians dwell in urban centers of 50,000 people or more, and almost half of these live in Cairo. By contrast, the Arab Sudan (and especially the remainder of that country) has only a small urban population. In the three Arab Nile provinces of the Sudan—Northern, Khartoum, and Blue Nile—a little over 8 per cent of the inhabitants reside in cities in excess of 50,000 population. Furthermore, the largest of Sudanese cities, Umdurman, is hardly equivalent in size to one of the medium-sized Egyptian cities.

The cities of Egypt and the northern Sudan display characteristics common to those preindustrial cities elsewhere in the Middle East that are now being transformed into modern industrial and commercial centers. Cairo, for example, has beside its older quarters a major section of multistoried modern office buildings, department stores, and apartment houses, which would hardly be differentiated from any other major metropolis in the world today.

Over 70 per cent of Egyptians are village and small town dwellers, while in the three Nile Arab provinces of the Sudan this figure is over 80 per cent. Several settlement patterns are observable among the rural sedentary populace. These have been classified for Egypt by Lozach and Hug (1930). First, they identify hamlets of which there are two types: the *'izba* and the *naga'* (Lozach and Hug 1930: 155 ff.). The *'izba* in its original meaning was a provisional encampment in the fields, a meaning still preserved in Upper Egypt (Crary 1949). The more recent meaning of *'izba* is a small village or agricultural colony established by a large-landed proprietor, the inhabitants of which are mainly employed by the owner. These settlements have now, as a result of the agrarian reform program, been transformed into administrative centers for the direction of the land reform, while the inhabitants remain as the cultivators and participants in the program. The *naga'* again has two meanings. An older meaning is close to that of the *'izba*: a provisional camp of Arab nomads. *Naga'* has also come to refer to a small village whose inhabitants are more recently sedentarized Bedawin. The *naga'* is limited to Upper and Middle Egypt (Lozach and Hug 1930: 160).

Besides the hamlet, Lozach and Hug report the large village as a second class of Egyptian rural settlement. Again there are two types of these settlements: the large, compact agglomeration, found in localities away from the Nile banks, e.g. in the Delta; and the polynuclear type, a village strung out along the edge of the desert and cultivated area or composed of a continuous chain of closely adjacent hamlets (Lozach and Hug 1930: 172-75). The polynuclear village is found only in Upper Egypt and in parts of the riverain Sudan. Its linear arrangement reflects the adaptation of settlement to residence on the Nile banks, wherein it is necessary to make use of all available land nearest the river for cultivation by irrigation and yet to maintain a household as close to one's cultivated lands as is possible. Large villages in Egypt have anywhere between 5,000 and 40,000 inhabitants. The *'izba* most usually has from a few hundred to a thousand.

Probably most villages in Sudan are properly considered as hamlets, being isolated clusters of houses, often having less than a thousand people. A polynucleated village strung along the Nile between desert and cultivation is common, especially north of Khartoum, but such villages tend to be much smaller in their population than those in Egypt. Hamlets and villages in the central Sudan can be located away from the Nile and thus, like those of the Nile Delta, they may have a compact rather than a linear form, with cultivation possible all around the settlement. In contrast to Egypt, any compact settlement in the Sudan which reaches a population of 3,000 or so is usually considered more in the nature of a town, in which a substantial minority of the population are engaged in crafts and commerce.

Neither Egyptian nor Sudanese villages have any particular order to them in terms of internal physical layout. On the whole, Egyptian villages are highly congested and cluttered; narrow paths and streets wind between house compounds. In the Delta region, the predominant house form is a mud brick, rectangular, flat-roofed structure, which may be one or two-storied or, on occasion, three-storied. The frequency of multistoried dwellings results from the attempt to maximize space in the Delta for cultivation purposes. The first floor includes a guest room, a court where various household activities are carried out and animals are stabled at night, an oven off the court, and one or more storerooms. The second floor is the sleeping quarters of the family. The flat roofs are used for storing fodder, manure cakes for fuel, and other items. Beehives are also placed on roof tops. This type of house is common in other parts of Egypt as well. However, in Upper Egypt, particularly among the Kanuz in the Nubian area, there are houses with vaulted roofs, and some areas have houses with cupolas. The latter have also been located in certain 'izbas of Lower Egypt (Lozach and Hug 1930: 96-101). In villages bordering on the desert in Egypt and Nubia, houses are often made from blocks of stone instead of mud. Dwellings of fired brick are owned by more prosperous farmers in most areas. Where these alternative materials are used, houses are built in the same pattern as those made of mud brick. Huts of straw are built in the fields in parts of Middle and Upper Egypt among those villagers who spend most of the winter living in the fields pasturing stock and harvesting grain (Lozach and Hug 1930: 76).

Nubian and Sudanese villages are more frequently spread out and are more roomy and neat than those of Egypt. Such differences are in part, at least, related to population density. The predominant style of house along the main Nile of the Northern and Khartoum Provinces of the Sudan is a single-storied, mud brick, flat-roofed structure, usually consisting of one room. Most families have two or more of these houses, all of which are enclosed by a wall of mud or thorns, thus constituting a compound. The mud wall is most widespread in the Northern Province and is common among the more prosperous farmers of the rest of the riverain area. Houses occasionally have a sloping thatch roof extending over the front door, which serves as a porch. As one proceeds above the Main Nile, on the Blue and White Niles, the so-called Sudanese-type house becomes characteristic. This is a cylindrical, one-room hut, with a thatch cone roof. Among the Nile villages the cylindrical base is made of mud, while in Kordofan it is made of thatch, like the roof. The cylinder-cone type of house once had a much wider geographical distribution. A hundred years ago, it was the prevailing house form as far north as Berber on the Main Nile. Gradually, from Wad Medani northward, it has been replaced by the rectangular form, and while most houses are made from mud brick, an increasing number are constructed of fired brick, especially in areas of heavier rainfall. Where there are ten to fifteen inches of rain a year, a flat-roofed mud hut is not exactly a practical dwelling.

In most of the settlements in the Nile Valley today there is at least one shop, which supplies necessities such as sugar, coffee beans, flashlight batteries, spices, tobacco, oil, and kerosene. Larger villages have several shops and also maintain a carpenter, barbers, tailors, shoemakers, and midwives. Some have professional water carriers. In Egypt, many have pottery kilns for manufacturing fired bricks. The flour mill is a common feature of a considerable number of Egyptian communities, although it is found in only the major villages of the Sudan. Larger villages in the Gezira in the Sudan have beer houses, identified by white flags, while in Egypt some have one or more coffee houses.

The third major type of settlement pattern in the Nile Valley is that associated with the nomads, the smallest population segment numerically, yet the one that exploits the most extensive land area. In Egypt there are hardly more than 100,000 nomadic Bedawin, 75 per cent of these being in the Sinai Peninsula. The nomad population is numerically more important in the Sudan. Thus 8 per cent of the Northern Province is nomadic, including a large number of Beja tribesmen east of the Nile and Arabs who roam close to the Nile banks in the southern part of that province. In Khartoum Province, 10 per cent of the population has been classed as nomadic, while in Blue Nile Province the figure is 7 per cent (Philosophical Society of Sudan 1958: 57).[2] Nomadic settlements are composed of small populations, which may vary in size over the course of the year, according to seasonal demands of the livestock. Thus, the settlements of Bedawin camel herders of the Egyptian desert are dispersed into small clusters of a half dozen or so tents or households in the winter, when there is a greater abundance of food, and con-

---

[2] Roushdi Henin has estimated the nomadic population of the northern Sudan to be much greater than indicated in the 1955/56 Census (Henin 1966: 145-57).

sist of a larger number of families in the summertime, when it is necessary to concentrate around wells and other permanent sources of water. A local encampment among Kababish and Baggara is known as a *fariq*, a term also used by Sudanese sedentaries for a small hamlet. A *fariq* has a stable core of agnatically-related kinsmen, but also may include other relatives, families of clients, and, until a very few years ago, slaves. Among the Humr, a Baggara tribe, the *fariq* consists of two main parts, each related to a different economic activity. The *'azzaba*, composed mainly of bachelors, is a group which often goes off with the cattle; whereas the *tagaliva* consists of houses, household goods, and people who remain with these goods (Cunnison 1954: 56). In the Humr encampment, the huts are arranged in a circle, so that stock are corraled within it at night. They are also milked in this area (Cunnison 1960: 310).

The common dwelling of the Egyptian Bedawin is the black tent, but Arab nomadic populations in the Sudan live in a variety of other types of dwellings. A few live in the cylinder-cone Sudanese style house made of thatch. The Kababish build small huts by first constructing a framework of slender poles, over which they lay camel hair mats (Seligman and Seligman 1918: 117). Many Baggara, or cattle nomads, live in huts of similar construction, but use mats made of bark. In general, the houses of Sudanese nomads are either hemispherical or cylindrical in shape and are constructed with hair, bark, or skin mats.

Agriculture

Agriculture is the bulwark of the economy of the Nile Valley. Land is by far the major natural resource, and agricultural products are both the chief exports and the greatest portion of the national production of Egypt and the Sudan. Outside the towns, only a small minority are engaged in nonagricultural pursuits, and these are chiefly handicraft and commercial occupations servicing the farm population. On a national scale, agriculture claims a majority of the population. In the Arab-dominated areas of the Sudan, over 80 per cent of those gainfully employed are classed as farmers, farm laborers, shepherds, or animal owners by the 1955/56 Sudan Census (percentage derived from figures in the ninth interim report, *First Population Census of Sudan, 1955/56*, Republic of Sudan 1957/58). In Egypt, about 60 per cent of those gainfully employed are in agriculture (Encyclopedia Britannica, Inc. 1966: 197). It should be emphasized that the vast majority of these agricultural peoples are no longer subsistence farmers, but are today dependent on one or more cash crops and so have been wedded to the international market economy. Agriculture is based upon both livestock rearing and crop cultivation. Among the sedentary population, livestock in much of the area are maintained to provide power for cultivation activities, but domesticated animals are also important as suppliers of protein, especially milk, which is consumed as a liquid, as cheese, or as clarified butter. In Egypt, ducks and chickens are common fowl, and pigeons are considerably important, particularly as providers of manure. Honey bees are also common in most villages in Egypt. By comparison, poultry and bees are rarities in the Sudan.

From Alexandria to Aswan, the most important livestock to the fellahin are the water buffalo (*gamusa*), goats, sheep, and donkeys. The *gamusa* is used as a draft animal on plow and water wheel and provides milk with an extremely high butterfat content. The camel is of little importance to the Egyptian peasant. A few more prosperous farmers in a village may own horses, which are paraded about on festive occasions. Recent livestock statistics report 1,588,000 cattle, 1,397,000 buffalo, 1,578,000 sheep, 723,000 goats, and 157,000 camels (*Britannica World Atlas* 1966: 193). When one considers that these are divided among some three million peasant and approximately 20,000 nomad families, the extremely limited livestock ownership in Egypt will be more appreciated. Few Egyptian fellahin own more than one buffalo or cow, one or two sheep or goats, and a donkey. A large percentage have no animals at all. This pattern of livestock ownership extends southward among the Nile dwellers of the Northern Province of the Sudan, especially among the Nubians. It is in the central Sudan that livestock takes on a paramountcy unknown in the north.

Above Aswan and in the Sudan, as in Egypt, sheep, goats, and donkeys are of primary importance among sedentary peoples. The buffalo, on the other hand, is absent, and cattle are far more numerous, especially among Sudanese Arabs. Above Khartoum, this is particularly so, since, for one thing, many sedentaries in this area are only one or two generations removed from a more seminomadic pastoral way of life. As a result of the greater pastoral orientation in the Sudan, extensive sections of the Nile flanks are grazing lands, a point of sharp contrast with Egypt, where every available acre of the Nile Valley and Delta is cultivated. As in Egypt, the camel is less frequently found among farmers. By contrast it is the most important beast for nomadic peoples from the Mediterranean coast to as far south as about fourteen degrees north latitude. Sudanese nomads, such as the Kababish of Kordofan and the Shukriya of Kassala Province, maintain extensive herds of camels, but also have numbers of goats and sheep. In the rainy season, herds associated with a given local group are pastured freely within the tribal domain, but in the driest weather encampments are established beside wells (Seligman and Seligman 1918: 117).

Beginning in central Kordofan and in Blue Nile Province southward, cattle replace camels, which are less well adapted to the moister climate of these latitudes. The Baggara, or cattle nomads, in Kordofan during the dry season move to the south along the Bahr al Ghazal, where they pasture their cattle until the beginning of the rainy season. Before the beginning of this century, the Baggara took advantage of this movement to raid neighboring Dinka and other Negro tribes for slaves and cattle and to hunt elephants and other big game. It is, in fact, through this process that the Baggara acquired their unique pastoral habit. Originally camel nomads, in moving into the damper climate they replaced their camel herds for cattle stolen from the Nilotic herders of the south, after finding the camel unsuited to such an environment. When the rainy seasons begin, the Baggara migrate northward toward central Kordofan, where they graze their stock and cultivate modest crops of millet. In an earlier day, they traded their slaves and ivory to northern buyers during this season. Horses are more important and more common among this group than in any other in the Sudan. Among other things, they are used in hunting giraffe and are ridden by men in moving camp. Cattle are the basic livestock and chief source of wealth. They provide milk, meat, and hides and act as beasts of burden in the regular movements of the local camp. Bulls are also ridden, usually by women (Tothill 1948: passim).

Throughout the central and southern Blue Nile Province are semi-nomadic peoples who reside from July to December in small villages no different in appearance from those of the sedentary population. They pasture their cattle, goats, and sheep and cultivate a rain crop of sorghum in the vicinity of the village. The sorghum is harvested in November or early December, after which the herds are moved close to the river, accompanied by nearly all the villagers. Temporary camps are established by the river, and the herds are pastured until the approach of the rainy season, at which time they again return to the village (Culwick 1951: 30).

Rain cultivation, or dry farming, has an extremely circumscribed distribution in northeastern Africa. As we might expect, the most extensive rain cultivation is in the central Sudan. This form of agriculture occurs with considerable risk and more as an incidental activity as far north as the sixteenth degree of latitude. It is only further south, in Blue Nile Province and in central Kordofan, that it is possible to depend upon it entirely. Inhabitants along the Nile banks from Khartoum southward engage in both rain cultivation and in limited irrigation farming. Rain cultivation involves neither tillage of the soil nor fertilization and is, in fact, a form of shifting cultivation. After the soil has been adequately moistened with early rains, seeds are planted with the aid of a dibble (*saluka*). Once planted, the sorghum and millet are not further tended until the time of harvesting.

Irrigation agriculture supplies by far the overwhelming proportion of agricultural produce, and all the agriculturalists of Egypt and the Northern Province of the Sudan are completely dependent upon it. The Nile is not only the single factor that saves Egypt, particularly from being as inhospitable a land as present-day Libya, but it also floods at an opportune time. Due to the summer rainy season that characterizes the Ethiopian highland source of the Blue Nile, the high Nile or Nile flood period in Egypt occurs in August and September, the driest part of the year. Several types of irrigation are utilized. There is a limited amount of irrigation from underground water sources, mostly provided at the oases, but this is of the most minute significance compared to water taken from the Nile.

The river waters are utilized in river bank or *jirf* cultivation, basin agriculture, and perennial irrigation schemes. River bank agriculture is of very minor importance in terms of the contribution to the total economy, but it is widely practiced from Aswan up the Nile. Following the receding of the flood waters of the Nile, the resultant muddied river banks are planted in sorghum, millet, beans, tomatoes, melons, and maize. The ground is not prepared for sowing, and planting is accomplished with the *saluka*, as in rain cultivation. As the season proceeds, the soil eventually dries out, and it is sometimes necessary to introduce artificial irrigation to supply water. The banks are often very steep and, thus, this practice, particularly in Nubia, gives the appearance of terrace farming (see Tothill 1948).

Basin agriculture was the prevailing irrigation system in Egypt until the mid-nineteenth century. It has now largely been replaced by a system of perennial irrigation. Nevertheless, there are still approximately a million acres, or about 40 per cent of the cultivated land of Upper Egypt, which employ this method of irrigation (Ghonemy 1951: 56). With the completion of the High Dam near Aswan, 70 per cent of this basin land will be converted to perennial irrigation, and the total cultivated area in Egypt will be increased by some 1,300,000 feddans (Gadalla 1962: 99). Such expansion has become an absolute imperative for Egypt, since population has expanded so much faster than the amount of cultivated land that the ar a of cultivated land per capita in the fifty-year period between 1897 and 1947 declined from 0.52 feddans to 0.31 feddans (the population increased from nine to nineteen million people, while cultivated land increased from 5,100,000 to 5,800,000 feddans) (Gadalla 1962: 29).

Various small areas in the Northern Province of Sudan, totaling 100,000 acres, also depend on basin irrigation (C. B. Tracey and J. W. Hewison, in Tothill 1948: 744). In this system, low-lying lands adjacent to the river are divided into rectangular areas and surrounded by banks. At the beginning of the Nile flood (August in Upper Egypt), water is admitted into the basins, where it remains during the flood season. Today, in Upper Egypt it remains for forty days (Ghonemy 1951: 56). The river silt settles out and acts as fertilizer while excess water is drained off, after which the land is prepared and planted. Basin irrigation, like river bank agriculture, allows for only one crop a year except for lands immediately beside the river, where lift irrigation machinery may be employed.

Perennial irrigation is made possible by systematic control of the waters of the Nile. Four storage dams, a series of barrages, and 25,000 kilometers of canals allow for a regular year-round flow of irrigation water supplying the entire Delta and over 60 per cent of the cultivated lands of Upper Egypt (Issawi 1963: 127). Water is taken from the canals and floods and fields by free flow or mechanical means. The latter include the *saqiya* or Persian water wheel, the *shaduf*, and the *tambur* or Archimedean screw, in addition to gasoline pumps, which Issawi reports numbered 15,000 fifteen years ago (Issawi 1954: 100). Water is distributed to individual farmers by the government free of charge. "The distribution of water, a highly complicated operation, is managed by the government engineers with great skill and equity" (Issawi 1954: 101). In parts of the Sudan, private operations pump water directly from the Nile and so provide for almost year-round irrigation. The only important area of perennial irrigation, however, is the government-operated Gezira-Managil scheme, in Blue Nile Province.

Perennial irrigation allows for two and, in some places, three crops a year. Thus, while the cultivated area in Egypt is hardly six million acres, the cropped area is over nine million. Where there is perennial irrigation, lands are plowed, fertilized, and smoothed before planting. The traditional plow is the Arab type, with one handle and no wheel, and is made entirely of wood except for a metal point. It is drawn by yoke of bulls, cows, or buffaloes. In Egypt almost indispensable as an agricultural implement is the short-handled hoe or *fass*.

Since animal manure is widely used as a fuel in Egypt, it serves as a fertilizer only to a limited extent. Silt cleaned from canals and, in Upper Egypt, certain kinds of soils taken from the cliffs serve as fertilizers. Within the last generation chemical fertilizers have come into increasing prominence in both Egypt and Sudan. The growing of beans and ber-seem, a type of clover, constitutes an integral part of the Egyptian crop rotation system. Berseem is harvested during the winter season between the cotton and grain crops and, while essentially a green manure, is also a major source of livestock feed.

Throughout the Nile Valley, especially in the Delta of Egypt, in Mid-dle Egypt, and in Blue Nile Province of the Sudan, the most important and most widespread cash crop is cotton. Introduced on a large scale in Egypt in the early nineteenth century and carried to the Sudan by Turko-Egyptian rulers, it is today the chief export of both Egypt and Sudan.

Maize ranks next to cotton in Egypt, where within the last century it has replaced millet as the peasant's staff of life. Wheat, the traditional crop of ancient Egypt, is today definitely secondary to maize. These two cereals are of little importance in the Sudan, where sorghum and millet are the staples.

Dates are the principal fruit in Egypt and Nubia, but below Atbara, where the rainy season appears in July, date growing is not productive. In Upper Egypt, sugarcane and onions are important cash crops. Other significant crops in Egypt include rice, barley, figs, and several varieties of beans. Sesame and gum Arabic are the cash crops of the sedentary populations of central Kordofan in the Sudan. Citrus fruits and bananas are grown in both countries, but they are of greater consequence com-mercially in Egypt, where vegetable production is also sufficiently large to support a canning industry.

Land Tenure

Largely as a result of regulations adopted in the nineteenth century by Muhammad Ali and his successors, Egypt became a nation with a small number of large landholders and a multitude of peasant land-owners, most of whom could claim only an infinitesimal amount of land. Baer (1962) has delineated the process that culminated in this state of affairs. The large landholdings arose through the granting or the sale by the state of extensive blocks of land to various notables, the acquisition of village lands by political machinations, and the establish-ment of family *waqfs*, or endowments, so that estates would not be fractionated as a result of Islamic inheritance regulations. The small fellah holdings appeared after 1871, when the fellahin were, in effect, granted the right to purchase from the state the lands they cultivated (Ayrout 1945: 35 ff.; also Baer 1962).

In 1956, less than 14 per cent of the land was divided among 72 per cent of the landowners, no one of which had as much as one feddan. These minute holdings are continually increasing, having more than doubled in number during the period 1913-56. Another 22 per cent of landowners, owning from one up to five feddans, possessed 24 per cent of the land. At the other extreme, a total of 12,000 landowners of fifty or more feddans (0.4 per cent of all landowners) owned over 30 per cent of the land (statistics derived from Issawi 1954: 126 and Berger 1962: 239-40).

Following the revolution of 1952, the new regime undertook measures to rectify this situation. A 200-feddan limit was placed on land ownership, with a provision of 100 feddans for a man's wife and each of his sons. In 1961 this limit was reduced to 100 feddans (Berger 1962: 229). Excess lands were expropriated by the state, with compensation to former owners, and distributed to the fellahin. The latter farm their plots through cooperative organizations and make annual payments to the government in order to buy the land. Because of fairly good management and cooperative organization, production did not fall as it did in some similar agrarian reform programs. Thus far about 950,000 feddans have been seized by the government, 450,000 having been taken in 1952 on the initiation of the program (*Statistical Handbook of The United Arab Republic, 1962-65* 1966: 44). The extent to which the whole program has altered the fundamental pattern of land tenure in Egypt is uncertain. Fragmentation of holdings still continues, and the large landless rural proletariat has in no sense benefited by the program. Agrarian reform is, after all, reform. It places an effective upper limit on the size of landholdings, but it does not dispense with the basic mechanism that produces inequitable holdings. It is still possible for a small number of individuals to build modest estates and for increasing numbers to join the ranks of the landless agrarian populace. In addition, there is a strong tendency for a government under agrarian reform to become merely a substitute landlord. In any case, the agrarian reform, as Warriner has written: "... means a real gain for the majority of the fellahin, either by giving them protection as tenants, or by giving them secure status as cooperative farmers" (Warriner 1962: 48).

Since most cultivators own extremely small plots, it is necessary to rent land. Ghonemy reports that in 1939, 24 per cent of the land was rented out, while in 1948-49 the figure was 60 per cent (Ghonemy 1951: 30). Obviously, a proportionate increase from 1949 to the present is not possible. Yet the fact remains that despite the agrarian reform, the majority of all cultivators in Egypt are still renters (Warriner 1962: 196). The agrarian reform program sought to reduce rents, but the "most general benefit conferred by the reform is no longer the reduction of rents, but this greater degree of security" provided by the extension of existing tenancy contracts (Warriner 1962: 197). The most common form of land rental is on a cash basis, wherein an oral agreement is made to pay a fixed amount of money for use of land for a specified period, usually a year (Ghonemy 1951: 36). Standing rental, where the tenant pays a fixed amount of one or more crops, is also practiced. Among small tenants, share renting is common. Here the landowner may supply everything (seeds, animal power, fertilizer, land and tax payments) except the labor and thus receive four fifths of the crop. Should the tenant pay for the seeds and fertilizer, his share is one third, and if he also pays the tax, his share increases to one half (Ghonemy 1951: 39). A similar type of tenancy prevails in the Sudan.

The land tenure problem in the Sudan is by no means as acute as it is in Egypt. However, fractionation is severe in many parts of the Northern Province (see Tothill's study on land fractionation on the Nile at Merowe [Tothill 1948: 210-21]). Elsewhere there seems to be an abundance of land. Most of the inhabitants along the Nile are freehold farmers cultivating river banks and small irrigated holdings. In some areas, such as on the White Nile around Ed Dueim and Aba Island and on the main Nile just north of Umdurman, rather extensive private "pump schemes" have been established. These schemes have developed largely through the acquisition of lands by religious leaders and city merchants who invest in gasoline-driven pumps and irrigate large tracts of land, employing numbers of laborers and renters. The government maintains several irrigation projects throughout the country, but mostly along the Nile. The largest of these is the Gezira-Managil scheme in Blue Nile Province, which is devoted primarily to the production of cotton. The land of the scheme, now approaching a total of two million acres, is rented from its owners by the government for a small sum and divided into tenancies deemed adequate to support a man and his family. Each operator is a tenant on the government project. He may also be an owner of land rented by the government. Indeed, preference is given to prior landowners by the government in distributing tenancies. The government supplies the water through an elaborate system of irrigation canals, the market for cotton, and the agricultural advisors, and, in return, takes a percentage of the profit of the cotton crop. The crop rotation, planting, plowing, and fertilizing are regulated by the government. Other government schemes are operated according to a similar pattern, but on a much smaller scale.

Another type of landed property in Sudan is communal land found outside the riverain area.

The Kordofan village is typical of communal holdings in areas where there is a light sandy soil requiring frequent changing of plots suitable for gum-trees. Within the village lands each villager has the right to cultivate. If he leaves the village the land occupied by him is allotted to someone else. There is not inheritance according to Mohammedan Law. Land in excess of the requirements of the village may be allotted by the sheikh to strangers. The area allotted to a man is supposed to be no more than he can work ... [A. R. C. Bolton in Tothill 1948: 190].

A pattern of village communal landholdings was characteristic of Egypt before the nineteenth century, but the land was not the property of the village. Rather, all cultivated Egypt was essentially the grand estate of the ruling elite, and communal village land arrangements were primarily a device for distributing land for cultivation to the peasant tenants.

Among the nomads, land is tribal property or, in modern times, government property to which the several tribes have use rights. A tribesman has the right to graze his cattle on his own tribe's land. Any stranger in Kordofan must first obtain permission to graze, although he has the right to standing water in an area " ... but the right to open up a well in a well-field is often restricted to the particular group living in the vicinity or normally grazing in the area" (A. R. C. Bolton in Tothill 1948: 190).

Muslim rules of inheritance are applied in full or in part over most of the Nile Valley and its vicinity. As noted in the Kordofan example above, in places where land is communal property, Islamic law is not applied. In other localities, such as in the Nile Valley of Egypt and in parts of the Northern Province of Sudan, where fractionation has greatly enhanced land value, various circuitous means are applied to avoid passing land on to women in particular. Brothers may request their sisters to sign over their share of the land, or they may become the guardians of sisters' lands and use them for themselves. In the Sudan and, formerly, in Egypt, where it is now illegal, a father might endow his property as a family *waqf*, in which case the land could not be subdivided among heirs but remained an indivisible unit as long as descendants lived. In the riverain Sudan, especially in Nubia, land is registered in an individual's name, and after his death the holding is not divided by his heirs unless they quarrel (Barclay 1964: 32; Crowfoot 1918: 121; and A. Kronenberg, personal communication).

Egyptian fellahin pay a land tax, as do some Sudanese cultivators. However, it is becoming more common for the latter to pay a tax based on a fixed percentage of gross value of a crop (H. A. L. Tunley in Tothill 1948: 199-201). In the Sudan as well, there are taxes on irrigation machinery and on livestock.

Villages were in the past more self-sufficient than they are now, in part because necessities were simpler and fewer; but even today, in a moderate-sized settlement of two thousand or more inhabitants, the peasant will find most of his needs. For other trading purposes, he may periodically visit the markets (*suqs*) and shops of the larger nearby towns or the rural marketplace. The latter is a weekly affair, named after the day on which it is held. Thus, Tuesday market occurs every Tuesday in a customary place, often at the edge of a village in an open space which is owned, in Lower Egypt at least, by an individual who collects a sum from each merchant—the amount varying according to what a person has for sale. The market owner is its director and pays a tax to the central government. Beside peasant sellers who peddle livestock, vegetables, and eggs, there are professional merchants who travel from *suq* to *suq*. Sometimes trade is by barter, especially in the spring and summer before the sale of the cotton harvest. Markets serve as places where scribes, religious curers and diviners offer their services, and in the Sudan the *'umda* often attends to settle minor disputes (Trimingham 1949: 21). More usually in the latter country the market is a meeting place for sedentary and nomadic peoples.

Money lending is a ubiquitous element of the rural economy and often entails the taking of interest at outrageous rates. Since interest charges are technically prohibited by Islam, money lenders usually resort to circuitous means to obtain such income. For example, money may be lent by giving less than is actually written in the loan agreement. It is common in the northern Sudan to advance money against a future crop, in which case the lender specifies the quantity of produce that is to be paid him at the harvest time, anticipating the price of the crop so as to assure himself of a substantial profit, i.e. interest (Wilmington 1955).

In Egypt, there have been government programs for relatively cheap agricultural credit as well as cooperative societies for purchasing seeds, fertilizers, and the like. These facilities are mainly patronized by more prosperous farmers and neglected by the poor—those who would most benefit by them. However, in the large estates now managed by the government under the agrarian reform program, all participating farmers are organized into cooperative societies for marketing crops, purchasing agricultural machinery and supplies, crop storage and transport, and the cultivation and management of lands and irrigation canals. Such cooperatives, it should be borne in mind, are not true cooperatives based on voluntary membership and managed by the membership, but are instead collective organizations managed by government officials and involving compulsory membership (Warriner 1962: 42).

In addition to regular commercial transactions, various formalized systems of mutual aid and reciprocity are worthy of note. In Egypt, for instance, payments in the form of a part of the crop are made to certain village specialists. If a family has had occasion to employ the services of a barber, an undertaker, or a carpenter during the year, he appears at the time of the harvest to receive a specific share. Similar payments to the *mu'azzin* may be made, but they are apparently voluntary obligations, which some observe and others do not (Barclay 1966: 150). *Nuqta* occurs in Egypt and in parts of the Sudan, although its distribution in the latter country is unknown to this writer. *Nuqta* is a money gift made to a bridegroom, a bride or her mother, and to newly-circumcized boys. It is made with the expectation that it will be reciprocated under approximately similar circumstances. Gifts also called *nuqta* are made by guests to the barber who circumcizes the boy or places *hinna* on the groom and to any entertainers who might be hired for a wedding (Barclay 1964: 250-51). In Egypt, all nonmoney gifts made to a bride, a groom, a woman with a newly-born child, or a boy on his circumcision are specifically distinguished from *nuqta*, the money gift (Barclay 1966: 150).

The cost of providing refreshment to the visitors who come to extend their condolences at a funeral are supported by friends and relatives. The bridegroom in the riverain Sudan is expected to make countless payments to various individuals during the course of the wedding celebrations. These payments are known as *haq*. For example, he must pay *haq al wazira*, a gift to the assistant to the bride, and *haq al mushatta* as a gift to the bride's hairdresser (Barclay 1964: 260).

A Note on Nonagricultural Industries

The cities and small towns of the Nile Valley function as major commercial and service centers for a predominantly agrarian population. Manufacturing varies from the small-scale, traditional craftsman's shop to large modern factories, producing the variety of goods essential for an industrialized society. Modern industrialization is far more sophisticated and highly developed in Egypt than in Sudan. The most fundamental change in Egyptian industry in the past decade has been the introduction of Arab socialism, under which an extensive program of nationalization has been pursued, particularly since 1961. "Manufacturing and mining are overwhelmingly under government ownership or control," as is public transport, banking, and insurance (Issawi 1963: 63). In rural areas, there is a limited development of some cottage industries, e.g. rugs, basketry, and Egyptian "antiquities."

Primary industries, such as mining and fishing, are of only minor import. There is some fishing activity in the saline swamps of Lower

Egypt, in the Red Sea, and in parts of the Nile. Petroleum is the chief mining activity.

Finally, it is necessary to mention the economy of remittances that is essential to the inhabitants of Nubia. Land resources are so limited in this region that men must emigrate to find employment, usually in the major cities and particularly in Cairo, where they find employment as servants, cooks, and doorkeepers. Periodically they send funds to their families which they have left behind in Nubia (Kronenberg 1964).

Political Organization

In Egypt, the Nile in its desert surroundings has provided a natural context for maintaining a highly centralized state organization, even under preindustrial technological conditions. For thousands of years the Egyptian Nile has been a relatively consolidated and centralized political entity, and on the whole it may be said that power has traditionally emanated from the Nile banks and extended east and west into the desert wilderness. Political integration is further enhanced in Egypt by its ethnic homogeneity. Ninety-eight per cent of the population are Arabic-speaking Egyptians.

At the national level, Egypt is a centralized republican regime, whose leaders describe it as an Arab socialist society. Within the past decade and a half Egypt has undergone several basic political transformations. First, in 1953 the country was officially changed from a monarchy to a republic. A short-lived union with Syria from 1957-61 brought several modifications in the republican regime, and additional basic political reforms were introduced again in 1962.

Egypt is divided into twenty-five governorates, and the administration of each is under the executive arm of the central government, which appoints the local governors. Each governorate has a council composed of members elected from the several subdivisions (sing., *markaz*) of the governorate. Election is by popular vote from a list approved by the central government and favoring those who are members of the National Union, the political party organization founded by Gamal Abd Al Nasser. This council is responsible for maintaining law and order, public health, elementary education, and agricultural well-being. Each *markaz* is administered by a *ma'mur*, who is responsible to the governor and is assisted by local police chiefs.

At the local level, the chief executive of a village has traditionally been the *'umda* (mayor) who is responsible to the *ma'mur*. In 1960 the Egyptian government adopted regulations aimed at reforming both city and village administrations, in which the latter would be directed by councils appointed by the governor (Berger 1962: 94). Such councils have a head, appointed ex-officio members, two members who are active members of the Arab Socialist Union, and other members who are elected by secret ballot from among members of the Arab Socialist Union (*Statistical Handbook* 1966: 260). The Arab Socialist Union is the political organization established by the present regime which has as its chief aims a "bridging of the gap" that exists between the government and the masses and a making clear to the people "that the government is nothing but the expression of the masses' free will" (*Statistical Handbook* 1966: 261). Under the old system, the *'umda* was usually the most important man of the village as well as the richest. He had considerable leeway in administering the village's internal affairs, and often gained a reputation for ruling with an iron hand. He was presumably elected by popular choice from among those men in the village who owned ten or more feddans of land and invariably was a son or some other member of the retiring *'umda's* family. Once the *'umda* held office for life, but this was changed under Abd Al Nasser to a ten-year term. The mayor served without a salary, the prestige of the position having been deemed sufficient payment. The duties of the *'umda* were to entertain notables on visiting the village, oversee the watchmen, settle minor disputes, maintain order, report diseases and epidemics, and record births and deaths. Assisting him were one or more *shaykh al balad*, each representing a quarter of the village. These were respected men who, until the Revolution, were expected to own five or more feddans of land. They advised the *'umda* and informed him of public feeling.

Each village has its *ghaffirs*, or watchmen, who are assigned to discourage violence. There is usually a telephone operator, who maintains communication with the local police station and also may assume the responsibility of recording births and deaths. A village also often has a *ma'zun*, a recorder of marriages and divorces, and a *sarraf*, or tax assessor and collector. These two officials may serve for two or more villages (Barclay 1966: 162 ff.; also H. Ammar 1954: 61, 80; Ayrout 1945).

The Sudan, in contrast to Egypt, is culturally far less homogeneous. As it now exists, it is a creation of European imperialism, its present boundaries having little relation to cultural or geographical reality. The much greater rainfall in the central Sudan enhances the possibilities for human exploitation of the area, and thus secondary foci of power have appeared in the past outside the Nile Valley. The largest ethnic group, the Arabic speakers, constitute barely 50 per cent of the population, and the remainder is divided among a host of smaller groups.

The Republic of the Sudan was created in 1956 out of the Condominium of the Anglo-Egyptian Sudan. For two years it functioned as a parliamentary republican system, which ended in a military coup d'etat, and for six years thereafter the Sudan was ruled by a military clique headed by General Ibrahim Abboud. In late 1964, the country, in what may be considered a most unusual *civilian* coup, returned to parliamentary rule. It has since experienced additional coups and political instability.

The administration of the Sudan is not greatly different in structure from that of Egypt. The country is divided into provinces, with a governor appointed by the central government and assisted by a council of advisors. Until 1961 the provinces of the Sudan were subdivided into districts administered by commissioners—a continuation of the old British pattern. This administration has now been abolished. Rural councils, composed of members elected from the *'umudiyas* of the district and chaired by an appointee of the Minister of Local Government, are increasingly being established. They have the power of local taxation, administration of public health and veterinary services, and education, but all these activities are ultimately subject to the Ministry of Local Government. Most of the Sudan has been divided into *'umudiyas*, nearly all of which include several settlements. The area is administered by an *'umda* with the assistance of *shaykhs*.

The *'umda* and *shaykhs* are presumably elected from among the local populace, and the election is approved by higher authorities in the central government. The *'umda* and his shaykhs settle minor disputes, keep law and order, and assess and collect taxes. In most parts of the northern Sudan (except Khartoum Province) *'umudiyas* are consolidated into *khatts*; each is headed by a *shaykh khatt*, who is responsible for passing tax money gathered by the *'umdas* on to the central government. In areas where tribal organization is still strong—mainly among the nomadic peoples—the tribal heads are the local political officers administering nazirates which are composed of a number of *'umudiyas*.

Both Egypt and the Sudan maintain a system of secular courts. In addition, the Sudan retains Shari'a courts, which have jurisdiction in cases of Muslim marriage and divorce, inheritance, and guardianship. Egypt abolished her religious courts in 1955.

We have been concerned so far with a skeletal presentation of the formal government system. A consideration of the distribution of power in the Nile Valley at the local village and tribal level must also take into account the role of the segmentary lineage principle of organization. Indeed, the dynamics of the situation are most appropriately considered as a conflict and competition between the more acephalous principle of the segmentary lineage system and the centralized, more autocratic, principle of republicanism and monarchy, so that each is a limiting factor of the other. In the village, particularly in Lower Egypt, the segmentary lineage system has, however, at least in modern times, been of minor importance. Tribal nomads, on the other hand, have held more tenaciously to this system, but even they could not be characterized as employing it in the purer or more ideal type sense, as applies, for example, in the case of the Tiv or the Nuer. The general trend in recent years is distinctly toward the ultimate elimination of the segmentary lineage system from the political scene, as the centralized republican regimes approach a monopoly of power and authority.

In the rural community, a vigorous attempt is always made to settle disputes between members of the same lineage or family within the respective kin group and under the mediation of its senior member. In addition, interlineage disputes have often been submitted to mediation by Arab councils (*haq*). When a quarrel arises involving members of two or more lineages, prestigious and acceptable neutrals from other lineages are invited by the disputants to attempt to settle the matter. Such men confer with each of the parties involved and suggest a solution which the disputants are morally bound to accept (see, e.g., H. Ammar 1954: 58-60; Barclay 1966: 165-66). This procedure has been especially prevalent in Upper Egypt, but it remains a question as to how widespread it is today.

Lineage and family affiliations play other important roles in local politics in the formation of specific factions and alliances. Ordinarily, village factional lines are drawn on a lineage basis, so that the faction in power includes the lineage of the *'umda* and allied lineages. In this way, dual organization in the village sometimes appears.

Social Stratification[3]

The Nile Valley shares with other areas of the Middle East and with other agrarian societies many common elements of social stratification. Both Egypt and the Sudan possess dominant elites, whose power and wealth far exceeds that of the great mass of the populace. To a considerable extent the status system of the nomads parallels that of the sedentary population but has been largely independent of it, and today, especially, nomad elites must submit to the authority of the nation state.

The sedentary world, incorporating the mass of the population, has its center of power and wealth in the city. It is here that the elites identified with the national state reside: the landed aristocrats, the intelligentsia, and the military and bureaucratic elites. These elites together

---

[3] A substantially similar view of Middle Eastern social stratification has already been presented by Van Nieuwenhuijze (1965).

have many of the attributes of an upper class: a segment of the population with approximately similar access to wealth and power and similar style of life, social interaction, and awareness to some degree of common interests. On the other hand, the group is itself internally segmented into special interest groups or competing and conflicting elites, each of which has interests that take priority over any "class" loyalty. Two elites are especially deviant, since they are more open and able to recruit from the less privileged elements of society: These are the military and the intelligentsia. Since both derive part of their clientele from outside the aristocracy, they include people with experience and backgrounds in another perspective on the world and with previous loyalties outside the aristocracy, which they do not always dismiss on rising to the top. Thus the military and the intelligentsia can be "unreliable." They might too readily identify on certain issues with the wrong "class." This has, of course, been the condition with regard to the intelligentsia in many societies. But the intelligentsia are the weakest element in the upper echelon of society. A military elite, on the other hand, has control of the physical might in the land and, thus, can pose an effective threat to other elites. It can even use its power for purposes of social amelioration, as numerous examples in the Middle East, including Egypt, testify. However, such an apparently worthwhile pursuit need not arise out of any social concern, but rather may be a device by which the military seeks to weaken the power of its competitors, especially the landed aristocracy, by strengthening the poor.

The elites of the Sudan have a slightly different composition than those of Egypt. Thus, the leaders of the major religious brotherhoods (sing., *tariqa*) and of the Mahdiya sect, many of whom are likewise wealthy landowners and influential with the national government, are significant elements of the upper echelons of Sudanese society, whereas their counterparts in Egypt are not. This, of course, is another way of saying that the religious emphasis in the two countries is different, despite their common profession of Sunni Islam. In the Sudan, the religious brotherhoods and the Mahdist sectarians still influence the masses, while in Egypt these brotherhoods are rapidly losing any prestige they once had. Sudanese elites are different from those of Egypt in another respect as well. Social stratification in Egypt has developed within the context of a high degree of ethnic homogeneity and an overwhelming sedentary population closely tied to urban centers which have functioned as the sources of centralized political administration. Political uniformity and centralism have, as we have said, long characterized Egypt, and this situation has been enhanced by the unity of the Nile. In the Sudan, by contrast, there has been no sense of peoplehood or of any uniform social structure. Rather, there have been different cultural and geographical foci of power and influence. Because of their greater education, sophistication, and control of power, the Arabs have been the culturally and politically dominant segment of the population, and in modern times the most powerful of the Arab elites have been centered in the cities of Khartoum and Umdurman. Nevertheless, because of the power of the several tribes, different and autonomous elites are to be associated with them. While in Egypt the tribal people have comprised for some time only an infinitesimal part of the population and one which is politically subject to the centralized authority of the city, in the Sudan the situation is different. The tribes have a high percentage of the population, and their elites in varying degrees compete with the elites centered in the major urban communities and those that are closely identified with the national government of the Sudan. Thus, in the Sudan, within the upper echelons of society, the tribal chiefs are a far more important element than they are in Egypt. But as the Sudan becomes politically more integrated in the course of time, it will also eventually become more integrated in terms of its system of social stratification.

To sum up, the elites in Egypt and the Sudan do not form a single unitary social class, but potentially competing interest groups. The top echelon holds the reins of power, but for some within it this power is largely manifested in wealth (the landed gentry); whereas for others it lies in physical force (as with the military elite or the government bureaucracy). These different segments tend to be interrelated, but they can and sometimes do act autonomously.

Aside from these national elites the city is home also for a middle segment of the population, composed of independent merchants and craftsmen. One would not call it a middle class, however, primarily because it lacks a common sense of self-identity and self-interest. The mass of city dwellers are propertyless wage workers, today free to sell their labor and, hence, very broadly a proletariat.

The rural sedentary population is far less differentiated than the urban. In Egypt the landed aristocracy is composed of absentee owners, who dwell in the urban centers and use their villas in the villages largely as summer vacation houses. While the members of the aristocracy obviously impinge upon the village social life, they are essentially outside it, having, among other things, few kin ties with the villagers. This group of city-dwelling absentee owners includes those owning a hundred feddans of land and more and a large segment of those having from fifty to a hundred. A second category includes the wealthy peasants. These individuals are permanent residents within the village. Having invariably been derived from the fellahin, they are involved in the local network of kinship. From this group the village notables have largely been drawn. Many in this category are holders of from fifty to a hundred feddans, but, especially today, a large number have from twenty to fifty feddans of land. Both the landed aristocrats and the wealthy peasants acquire incomes wholly or in part from letting out land and are also the chief employers of wage labor. A third category is that of the prosperous peasants who cultivate their own holdings of from five to twenty feddans, often hire wage labor, and occasionally rent out land to tenants. In the fourth category are the small holders owning from two to five feddans. They include owner-operators who only occasionally hire labor and frequently rent additional lands from others. A fifth category includes those who own infinitesimal amounts of land (under two feddans) and resort to rental of additional lands or part-time employment for wages. Finally, there are the landless, who largely engage in wage labor and along with a segment of the very small landowners constitute what may roughly be called a rural proletariat, a group which according to the 1937 census constituted over a third of the agricultural labor force (Ghonemy 1951: 30).[4] This group is certainly no smaller in its percentage today. I have referred to these various economic segments as categories rather than as social classes, because I do not believe the term "class" is entirely appropriate. First, they are purely economic categories, and while the major variables of the class concept—wealth, power, and style of life—tend to correlate, there is some independent variation, especially between power and wealth. Secondly, village life, traditionally, has been in innumerable respects autonomous from urban life. The city-dwelling absentee landlords, as noted above, are essentially outside the village social life and not part of the *village* system of stratification. They constitute one of the national elites and a part of the upper stratum of urban society. The individuals who may be identified as fully integrated with the village social context include a broad spectrum in terms of landowners, from a large segment of the wealthy peasants down to wage workers. Nevertheless, true social class differentiation *within* the village has not developed because of various crosscutting factors. Most important of these is kinship. Village patrikin groups include within them individuals of differing degrees of prosperity. The poverty-stricken wage worker is not necessarily completely alienated from the wealthy "kulak," because the two may be "cousins," i.e. members of the same lineage and so obligated to one another in a variety of

---

[4] The above categories are largely based on Imam Selim's classification (1950: 196 ff.).

ways. The religious brotherhoods, far less so today than formerly, also perform a similar crosscutting function, so that the same *tariqa* has members from different economic strata and also different kin groups. Furthermore, life in the village in many ways discourages extremes of differentiation, with the emphasis on communal sharing and participation and the negative sanctions against what are deemed excessive displays of wealth and position. Villages are usually sufficiently separated or socially isolated from one another that a development of a national class of peasantry or a rural proletariat is inhibited. The individual indentifies strongly with his own village and kinsmen and often looks upon those in other villages with considerable suspicion. The intensity of identification is such that it largely precludes any full consciousness of common "class" condition with others of similar economic position in other villages. Then, too, one might say that even the poorest peasant believes "in the system" to the extent that he holds that differences between men are inevitable; that it is right that some should be wealthy and powerful so long as certain equalizing factors are recognized by those in power, such as the equality of worth of the individual, and so long as he has some feeling that he has a "chance" in the system. This is not to suggest that the Egyptian peasant, for example, has any affection for his master. On the contrary, he has a longstanding and deeply ingrained distrust and veiled hostility toward him, which, however, has only rarely been expressed in revolt. Distrust and hostility are derived in large part from the peasant's belief that his master has gone beyond the rules of the game. The master has been *unduly* oppressive and *unduly* exploitive.

Conditions are, of course, changing. Thus, the religious brotherhoods have lost their effectiveness in Egypt. The lineage system is breaking down as state centralization and control increase and as greater numbers of people no longer expect any inheritance of land in worthwhile amounts, so that they have no real vested economic interest in agnatic kin or in the village. Population grows at a rate greater than the expansion of arable land, and this increases the numbers of landless wage workers and of wage workers who are losing these crosscutting ties of kinship and religion. Couple these factors with the improved communications and transportation, which mean that the peasants are more aware of the wider world around them, are exposed to new ideologies, and acquire greater expectations, and one has a set of factors which, operating in concert, are ingredients for evolving a full class awareness in the classical Marxist sense. On the other hand, to develop class consciousness and class conflict, Marxism assumes an ever-increasing degradation of the "masses"—the acceleration of a perceived gap between the owners and the owned. Several intervening factors have frequently tended at least partially to invalidate this theory. One has been the introduction of ameliorative reforms by the established elites, so as to reduce the gap and blunt budding feelings of resentment and hostility. Another has been the increased efficiency of production which has allowed owners to amass fortunes without the necessity of grinding the "masses" further and further into poverty. Rather than acquiring a class consciousness and spirit of class war, the economically less well-off, particularly where they attain a degree of prosperity because of the improvements in production, tend to endorse the ethic and weltanschauung of the elites and strive to emulate them. Agrarian peoples invariably do not wish to dispense with the principle of landed proprietorship. On the contrary, they wish to participate in it so that turning a peasantry into a body of self-sustaining and independent landed proprietors usually makes for a solid conservative force. Finally, throughout that part of the world presently or formerly the object of exploitation by the modern industrial nations, conflict arises on a dimension different from that of classical Marxism. Thus, in Egypt as elsewhere, internal strife between landed aristocrats and peasants or between capitalists and wage-workers is inhibited by the conflict, real or imagined, that pits Egyptians against Euro-Americans. Much of the resentment and hostility which might otherwise be directed against landlords, etc., is syphoned off against the "imperialist," a phenomenon which has the added "merit" of unifying the nation behind the ruling elite. In effect, what becomes valid in the Marxist theory is the truism that those who perceive themselves as being oppressed will develop hostility toward those whom they believe are the oppressors; out of this a dialectic process occurs in history—certainly not an idea that is original with Marx. Rather than common classes of peasantry and rural proletariat, what has meaning for the Arab villager is his awareness of those groups that are primarily of a face-to-face nature, which he can, so to speak, embrace as a significant unit.

It is necessary to mention yet another well-known feature of Middle Eastern society which has relevance to the question of social stratification, namely, the existence of unassimilated endogamous minority ethnic-religious groups, wich adamantly persist and create in the Middle East the elements of a pluralistic society. Most important of these groups in Egypt are the Copts. In the Arab Sudan, it is the West Africans. They may have their own elites, some members of which stand above certain of the majority group, but not with the highest echelon of society. From one point of view they, as a group, are viewed as inferior to the majority group; from another perspective some of the minority belong, in the case of Egypt, to the landed gentry or the military elite and, thus, are superordinate over members of the majority group.

The important criteria for ranking in village, town, and nomad camp alike include male sex, seniority in age, wealth and authority, and membership in a prestigeful family or lineage—especially one claiming descent from the Prophet or a noted religious personage. Personal qualities, too, are important, such as hospitality, generosity, religiosity, bravery, strength, and honesty. In the Sudan, Arab descent is paramount in claiming higher status, and associations with religious power are more prestigeful than in Egypt. In Sudanese villages, also, descendants of slaves are considered a distinct strata beneath the "freemen" (Barclay 1964: 128). Sedentarized Bedawin of Egypt consider themselves to be so much superior to all of their fellahin neighbors that they prohibit the marriage of their daughters to men of the fellahin villages (Barclay 1966).

These several considerations mean that Middle Eastern social stratification is a rather diffuse system. There is a distinct ranking, with specific elites which can roughly be viewed as a sort of "open" ruling class, but mobility is difficult. There are broad strata and wide differences between the extremes. One way to elucidate the dynamics of such a system at the intergroup level may be in terms of a conflict theory along lines suggested by Proudhon. That is, the opposition of different segments produces intergroup conflict and may also lead to that ongoing equilibrium which for the Middle East has been called the mosaic pattern (see, e.g., de Lubac 1948: 140-65).

Kinship Groupings

Kinship is a cornerstone of the rural community. In the broadest sense of the word, the tribe is the largest possible kinship group, although it is, of course, also, and more significantly, a political, territorial entity. The tribe remains a kin group to the extent that ideally it is believed that all members of the tribe are patrilineally descended from a common ancestor, after whom the tribe is named. In fact, most tribal members do not know their genealogy and many have no such relationship to the tribe. In most of Lower Egypt, tribe has no meaning. In Middle and Upper Egypt, the term has a limited significance and more so among the sedentarized descendants of Bedawin nomads, some of whom have sentimental attachments to a given tribe to which they are affiliated, and still recognize a tribal leader who, nevertheless, has no authority. The tribe has no role in political administration in Egyptian villages.

All Arabs of the Sudan and the Nubians claim tribal affiliation. This is strongest and functionally most significant among the nomads and least among sedentaries, particularly those of the Nile. Tribal intermixture in the past century has been so extensive that nearly all villages of the Nile consist of mixed groups. Often there is one tribe that is dominant in a village or constitutes the core of the community, but tribal organization has definitely broken down in the face of an organizational network of tribally mixed village communities tied to a centralized government.

The tribal structure is, broadly, of the segmentary lineage type and is best perpetuated among pastoral nomads. Tribes, such as the Humr Baggara of the Sudan or the Sa'ada Bedawin of Egypt, have an initial division into two major sections. These sections are again segmented into a number of subsections and the subsections each into a number of lesser units, which in turn are subdivided still further. Each segment comprises a number of individuals who are presumably patrilineally descended from the apical ancestor after whom the segment is often named and who is presumed to be a patrilineal descendant of the apical ancestor of the next more inclusive segment. Segments are combined to form larger ones, which include individuals who are presumably more remotely related than are individuals within a specific segment. The segmentary system is supposed to correspond to paternal kinship affiliation, so that ideally all the members of a tribe believe they are descendant from a common ancestor. The members of one of the major sections of the tribe are more closely akin to each other than to those in the other section, since each claims descent from two separate descendants of the tribal founder. Within the major sections, members of subsections claim closer kinship to others in their own subsection than to those of other subsections of the same section. Finally, at the smallest segmental level are the closest kin, constituting an extended family grouping. Social distance and mutual aid are important to the segmental pattern, so that obligation and esprit de corps are strongest within the minimal segment, comprising the closest kin, and least in relation to the largest segment. Activation of one's obligation as a member of any segment occurs with complementary opposition—when any segment to which one belongs is threatened and opposed by a complementary segment, i.e. a division at the same level of segmentation. There is a relation between segments and residence, so that all or most members of a major section pasture flocks in an area associated with that section, and those of the other section have their own area. The local encampment, the group that herds together and migrates together, is roughly comprised of members of one lineage segment, although most such camps contain outsiders such as affines or distant and paternal kin or clients. Cunnison has pointed out that for the Humr Baggara, tribal organization can be outlined as a typical segmentary lineage pattern, but in fact in its day-to-day operation this pattern is highly modified by the organization of political alliances and the institutionalization of formal political offices, which tend to ignore and even cut across the segmentary pattern (Cunnison 1966). Again, this is to suggest the point that was mentioned previously in this chapter that the political dynamics of the Middle East may be better understood in terms of a competition or conflict between the principles of the segmentary lineage system and those of centralized republican or monarchical government.

The segmentary structure of Nile society frequently reflects a moiety structure, as in the case of the Humr Baggara and the Sa'ada Bedawin mentioned above. The most extensive description of dual organization among sedentary villagers is 'Ammār's report on Aswan Province (H. 'Ammār 1954: 44-47). He reports a major division of villages of the province into two main sections, at least one of which, the Ja'afra, he describes as being further subdivided into two segments, those of the east bank of the Nile and those of the west bank. Again, within these segments is apparently a further bifurcation. The villages of the east bank, for example, comprise the five villages of North Silwa on the one hand and the five villages of South Silwa on the other. Further, within the village there is a dual division, the members of each claiming descent from two brothers and residing in separate quarters. Members of the different village moieties traditionally regard one another with some degree of hostility and believe that they have different personality characteristics. 'Ammār, in describing the local village political structure prior to the recent reforms in Egypt, states that each moiety in the village is represented by a shaykh who assists the *'umda* (H. 'Ammār 1954: 61).

Dual organization throughout the Middle East has been briefly reviewed by Raphael Patai in his *Golden River to Golden Road* (1962). He refers to reports, mostly by nineteenth century writers, of dual organization in both Lower and Upper Egypt. Aside from summarizing 'Ammār's observations on Silwa, Patai does not demonstrate any other meaningful contemporary significance for the moiety in the Nile Valley (Patai 1962: 226-34).

Moiety organization in Egypt and in the Sudan has, of course, its historical roots in the dual division of ancient Egypt and among the Arabs of the Arabian Peninsula. But, then, one should not expect such a mode of organization to be in any way unusual in the Nilotic region, where so much of life is oriented to the river: people are either upriver or downriver or on the east bank or the west bank. What we need to know is the contemporary distribution and importance, if any, of this principle.

On the whole, kinship organization in the Nile Valley village lacks the elaborate levels of segmentation preserved among the nomads, primarily because, as has already been suggested, the political-territorial functions associated with the larger, more inclusive segments are assumed in the village by other institutions—by village and national government. Yet in the village, distinct patrikin groups are readily observable, and these are best conceived as agamous patrilineages, the members of which are able to establish their patrilineal kinship to one another through a known apical ancestor, who usually lived from four to six generations before, and after whom the group is named. In Egypt, due to the operation of patrilocal residence, there is a tendency for a given quarter of the village to be predominantly inhabited by those in one lineage and, thus, for the quarter to be identified with that lineage. Within it the lineage usually maintains a guesthouse, which is used for the celebration of festive occasions, Ramadan recitations of *Qur'an*, entertainment of guests, and as a general meeting place for kinsmen. In Egypt the lineage head (*kbir al 'ayla*) is its most prestigious member, which usually means he is its oldest member. Traditionally the *kbir al 'ayla* was able to exert a considerable amount of power, acting as a patriarch among patriarchs.

The lineage is not a corporate group economically, since no property is attached to it other than the guesthouse. In a sense, Nubia represents a slight variation to this generalization. Here irrigated holdings are technically owned by individuals who, because of the segmental process and inheritance, are agnates and neighbors in land ownership. Thus, a single block of land in the vicinity of a village is composed of separate lots, each owned by members of the same lineage. In interlineage relations, land is individually owned, but from the intralineage point of view such land holdings are viewed as "belonging" to the lineage. Prior to the individual land registration in the Sudan in 1907, it would probably be more correct to say that the lands did belong to the lineage and that individual members within the group thereby had usufruct rights (Kronenberg and Kronenberg 1963 and personal communication). Throughout the Nile Valley, the lineage may be viewed to some extent as a corporate unit politically, in that each member is duly obligated to support his fellow lineage mates in a crisis, such as a feud. When one member of the lineage is attacked, it is conceived as an assault upon the entire lineage, and the whole lineage of the attacker is held collectively responsible. The lineage in this sense is viewed as a single body, enduring in time beyond the life of any of its members. This role of the lineage has been weakened in the past few decades, particularly in Lower Egypt, and one likely reason for this is suggested in Stirling's discussion of the Turkish lineage (Stirling 1960). He argues that the only function specific to the lineage alone is as a feuding group. Lineage members contribute labor and financial aid to each other, but this is not a feature unique to the lineage alone, since an individual also engages in mutual aid with other kin and neighbors who are outside his patrilineage. Thus, wherever feuding persists, the lineage remains strong, and where it disappears, the lineage no longer has any distinctive function and hence becomes markedly weak. The decline of this feuding role results from the strengthening of central government authority, coupled with a greater interest in internal village affairs by the central government. It may also be enhanced by the accelerated emigration from the home village—especially to the cities—of younger men, leading to a dispersion of the effective fighting force, so that implementation of a feud is made more difficult.

In the Sudan, likewise, the agamous patrilineage persists, but among the Nile sedentaries there has occurred a considerable mixing of populations, which was particularly increased during the Mahdiya (1881-98) and again in more recent times. This mixing has contributed to the development of a sense of village rather than lineage loyalty and has hence weakened the lineage. Village endogamy appears to continue as the general rule, but there is widespread intertribal and interlineage marriage within a village, an additional factor which can only serve to weaken the divisive quality and feuding role of the lineage. In sum, lineage organization today has little meaning throughout much of Lower Egypt. Its role has more importance among sedentary Arabs of the Sudan and among the Nubians and Upper Egyptians.

The family is a residential kin group which may be viewed as a segment of a lineage, since if not all the members of the family belong to one lineage, at least the household head and the children of the family do. Throughout rural Egypt, the joint extended family formed around a senior male and his married sons is common. Upon marriage, the son brings his bride to live in a part of his father's house. In recent years there has been a tendency away from such behavior. Due in part to the extreme overpopulation in villages and the resultant lack of land, sons leave their home villages for larger cities in order to obtain work, or leave the parental home to live in another part of the village for lack of room in that house (see Adams 1957). All of this apparent increase in neolocal residence weakens the old patriarchal structure of the family, as does the fact that a son no longer becomes dependent upon his father for employment or inheritance of a piece of land. Wherever, as in the traditional pattern, patrilocal residence prevails, the father can exert his authority, and his wife tends to act as a tyrant over her sons' wives, who are comparative strangers in the family household. In a compound or extended family, the several nuclear segments—each consisting of an individual married man, his wife, and his unmarried children—constitute distinct functioning units. Matters of concern to the entire extended family are dealt with by the paternal head and the adult males. Such affairs primarily deal with lands cultivated by the family group and general maintenance of the compound. Each nuclear unit has its own problems and possesses some autonomy in dealing with them. At this level, the husband is senior and ultimate judge. An extremely young husband, however, may accept a considerable amount of advice from his father and elder brothers in the administration of his newly-established family unit.

From Aswan Province southward along the Nile there is initially a kind of uxori-patrilocal residence—in the house of the wife's father—until the birth of the first child. Thereafter it may be neolocal or patrilocal or may continue in the uxorilocal pattern. The temporary residence in the wife's father's house followed by patrilocal residence is characteristic of the Arabic-speaking population of Aswan Province, while among the Nubians such practice is more often followed by neolocal residence. Among the Arabic population of the riverain Sudan, initial uxori-patrilocal residence is likewise the rule, but there appears to be a great deal of variation after this. Culwick suggests that in the Gezira, temporary matrilocal residence is followed by patrilocal residence (Culwick 1951: 13-15). In brief observations made in a Gezira village northwest of Wad Medani, this writer found that both a prolonged uxori-patrilocal residence and a pattern of initial uxori-patrilocal residence followed by neolocal residence were not uncommon (Barclay 1965). In a village suburb of Khartoum he found that neolocal residence was most frequent, but that uxori-patrilocal residence was far more widespread than patrilocal (Barclay 1964: 137-144).

In the nomad encampment, the tent constitutes the domestic household and is frequently closely associated with neighboring tents in the camp to comprise an extended family grouping. Whereas among Bedawin the general pattern is one in which the newly married pair take up residence in the camp of the husband's father and near his tent, among the Baggara the situation is different. For the Humr, at least, the woman owns the tent and the segment of a camp circle associated with a common extended family can include both married sons and married daughters of the founder (Cunnison 1966).

The following remarks are to be viewed as a most general outline of the major kinship roles among Nile Valley villagers. The pervading themes of kinship relations in the Nile Valley stress seniority of age, of generation, of male sex, and of the patrilateral bond. The oldest male, the father, is the head and supreme ruler of the family. While he is the ultimate decision-maker in matters of concern to the whole family, he is expected to listen to the counsel of his adult sons and on occasion of his wife as well. Respect for one's father is a central and fundamental tenet of kinship relations. Throughout the Nile Valley, this respect is symbolized by such behavior as a son remaining standing in the presence of his father unless invited to be seated; it is further symbolized by the son's avoidance of smoking before his father and of placing a hand upon him. Often a son greets his father by kissing his hand. Of a limited importance in the domestic power structure is the wife of the family head. On some occasions, where the senior male has died and left an aging widow, it is the eldest woman in the family who fills this role. In Egypt she is usually the holder of the keys to the family stores and is the family "treasurer" and keeper of important documents. To her belongs the absolute reign of the kitchen—power and authority of the male stops at the kitchen door. This means not only that the senior woman determines meal preparation but also that she is a guardian and matron of the women of the house. In Egypt, where patrilocal residence is the practice, it is under her iron hand that the luckless bride falls on marriage to be ordered about as a menial and only to graduate to a better position with the passage of time and the arrival of still younger women within the family fold. The public behavior of women in all acts which reflect on the honor of the lineage, however, remains the province of the woman's male agnates. A brother is responsible for his sister in the same way as a father is for his daughter. The ultimate dictators of a girl's life are her father, her brothers, and her father's brother's sons (sing. *'ibn amm*). The primary concern of these individuals for the girl is for her honor. These men must prevent her from committing dishonorable acts and prevent others from dishonoring her in any way. All such behavior revolves around the concept of *'ar*, or shame, and requires that brothers prevent their sisters from appearing in undesirable places, from marrying men objectionable to them and from engaging in untoward behavior to other men. The men may have the power, but the women's behavior is the gauge that largely determines the reputation or honor (*sharaf*) of the lineage.

Relations between a father and his children can generally be described as austere and removed; those between a mother and her son are more often sentimental in character. For more distant collateral kinsmen, a halo effect operates, so that a more compassionate and informal relationship exists in connection with maternal kin, while with those related through the father, the behavior is more stern and distant. Relations between grandparents and grandchildren are less severe than those between parent and child, and, as in many other parts of the world, grandparents are often accused of spoiling the children.

Throughout the Arab Sudan and parts of Upper Egypt, there are avoidance rules. That a man should avoid his mother-in-law and not look at or speak to her has been reported for the Kababish (Seligman and Seligman 1918: 126), the riverain Arabs (Barclay 1964: 208; Trimingham 1949: 179), and for some of the Kordofan sedentaries (Seligman and Seligman 1918: 129). The bridegroom in Aswan Province in Egypt avoids both his parents-in-law (H. 'Ammār 1954: 197). Both Reid and Culwick have reported mother-in-law avoidance by the bride for White Nile Arabs (the Hassaniya) and the Gezira area (Culwick 1951: 15; Reid 1930). Such restrictions have begun to break down, however.

Marriage

While there are declared preferences for FaBrDa marriage, only a minority of marriages are actually contracted with this person. Cunnison reported that for three surras[5] among the Humr Baggara 10 per cent of marriages were with FaBrDa and another 20 per cent were with other members of the same surra (Cunnison 1966: 89). This writer found in a suburban village of Khartoum that among seven lineages over the last three generations, 25 per cent of marriages were with FaBrDa, and that for extant marriages in the village as a whole (which included a large population of recent immigrants) 11 per cent were with this cousin (Barclay 1964: 120).

Fifty years ago, Seligman and Seligman found nineteen out of sixty Kababish marriages to be with FaBrDa (Seligman and Seligman 1918: 138). There are no available figures for Egyptian villages. In a Pyramids village in Giza Province this writer reported that in one year (1956), nineteen of twenty-eight marriages were between members of the same lineage (Barclay 1966: 215). As in other parts of the Arab world, there is a tendency to consider any female related agnatically to ego as a bint 'amm or FaBrDa and, thus, to be a preferred marital mate. Other preferences are for FaSiDa and other paternal relatives. In the Sudan there is some indication that MoBrDa is a desirable mate (Barclay 1964: 120). A high proportion, if not a majority, of marriages in Egypt and the Sudan are between kinsmen, and it is likely that the overwhelming majority of marriages are among residents of the same village.

While there are no available statistical data on divorce, it is fair to hypothesize that a rather high percentage of marriages are so terminated.

[5] The surra is a patrilineage of approximately seven generations in depth and is identified with a specific camp (Cunnison 1966: 58 ff.).

This writer found in a village near Khartoum that at least one of every five marriages had ended in divorce (Barclay 1964: 124).

Polygyny has become a rarity in Egypt, although it is far more common in the Sudan. In the latter country, for example, in the Northern Province, 9.3 per cent of married males had more than one wife. Nearly all of these had two wives (Sudan, Republic of, 1957-58: ninth interim report, 54). Among the Christian minorities, polygyny is, of course, prohibited, and divorce is a rarity, if only because the Oriental churches recognize few grounds for dissolving a marriage.

In both Egypt and the Sudan there are rather elaborate wedding festivities. In the former there are two important days: *al laylit al hinna* and *al laylit al dukhla.* Entertainment, noisy processions, feasts for guests, and a ceremonial application of henna to the hands and feet of the bride and groom in separate rites usually take place on the first day. On the *laylit al dukhla*, the bride herself is taken in procession to her husband's house. In Lower Egypt, the groom leads an evening procession to his bride, and a widespread practice is to deflower her with his forefinger wrapped in a handkerchief. For the assembled guests the ecstatic climax to the festivities occurs when the bloodstained handkerchief is displayed by the groom from the front door of the house.

The wedding among Sudanese riverain Arabs is more complex. It differs from the Egyptian patterns in four major respects: (1) the bride remains in her father's house and the groom then comes to her; (2) on the *laylit al dukhla* the girl is not deflowered, but dances before her future husband wearing a leather girdle (*rahat*), from which the future husband is expected to pull seven thongs, possibly symbolic of a breaking of the hymen; (3) prior to the *laylit al dukhla* and, in some areas, following that evening, there is a *jirtig* ceremony, at which ornaments known as *jirtig* aimed to protect against the forces of evil are placed upon the bride and groom by women relatives; (4) there is no demonstration of the accomplished act of defloration, perhaps because the operation of infibulation effectively insures virginity in a girl (Barclay 1964: 243 ff.).

A mock battle between the families of the bride and groom constitutes a part of the wedding celebration in Aswan and among the Nubians (H. 'Ammār 1954: 194-95; Herzog 1957: 91).

Child Rearing

H. 'Ammār has thus far presented the fullest description of child rearing for this area (1954). The first major period of a child's life is that roughly from birth to age seven, when it is believed the child cannot be taught or trained to any extent. There is little disciplining and considerable indulgence, especially for boys. Toilet training is of a casual nature, and children are not weaned before their first year, and in some places, e.g. the Gezira, they may be two years old. This apparently can result in a more difficult learning experience. Not long after a child is weaned, he may be placed in the care of an older sister. Gradually he enters the world of his peers, so that by age three or four he is running around with age-mates in small gangs. Indulgence is sharply curtailed at this time, particularly if the child is a girl, and if the mother has given birth in the meantime. At age seven, the child undergoes a significant transformation from a life of considerable freedom to one of subjection to rigid discipline. He now comes more under the rule of his father, who until this time has left the child-training process primarily in the hands of the women of the house. Boys are expected to adopt the ways of men, to become *mu'addab*, or polite, and girls are expected to act like ladies. Children also gradually assume more adult responsibilities. Even before this age, girls between five and eight are given such household assignments as taking care of younger children. At a later age they help clean the house, feed small animals, and run errands. By the time they have reached puberty they participate in all household tasks, including cooking and baking. Indeed, much of the burden of work in a house may fall upon the younger girls. By age seven, boys are involved in minor agricultural tasks, such as tending the family goats, driving the bulls on the *saqiya*, and directing irrigation waters into farmlands. At a slightly later age, they begin to participate in planting and harvesting activities. In Upper Egypt, boys are trained by age twelve to collect clay from the cliffs, which is used as a fertilizer (H. 'Ammār 1954: 29). About this time they learn to operate the *shaduf*. One becomes a full-fledged farmer in Upper Egypt when he reaches about seventeen and is allowed to sow seeds and distribute fertilizer on the farm (H. 'Ammār 1954: 29).

At age seven, as well, formal education begins in the schools. Until the advent of the European system of education, schools were only for boys, and their curriculum was primarily religious in nature. In the course of three or four years, the student might memorize a considerable part of the *Qur'an*, but only a few ever learned to read or write. In the past three decades, there has been an attempt to extend into the rural areas a more secular education, modeled on European lines, so that in Egypt today most young children, including girls, are within easy access of schools providing this type of education. Modern schooling is far less advanced in Sudan, actually having gotten underway only since independence (1956).

Religion

Eighty-five per cent of the population of Egypt and 99 per cent of the inhabitants of the three Sudanese provinces of Northern, Khartoum, and Blue Nile are Muslims. The remainder are predominantly Christians associated with a variety of sects. There are probably 10,000 Jews, chiefly in Cairo.

Christianity is confined to a small part of the Egyptian population and to foreigners of European and Lebanese background. The indigenous Arab and Nubian population of the Sudan is entirely Muslim. Of the Roman Catholics, who number approximately a quarter of a million in the area, about half are Egyptian Copts converted to Rome and organized in the Coptic Catholic Rite. The remainder are foreigners, chiefly Italians, but also including Lebanese, Armenians, and Greeks, and nearly all dwellers in the large urban areas.

Most Protestants are organized in the Coptic Evangelical Church of Egypt (150,000 members). Like the Roman Catholics, the Protestants draw their indigenous support from converts from the Coptic Orthodox population of Egypt. They are largely an urban, "middle-class" population.

The Greek Orthodox Church, approximately coterminous with the Greek community in Egypt and Sudan, is also an urban population. The Armenian Orthodox Church is confined to a segment of the small Armenian community, located mainly in Cairo.

The Coptic Orthodox Church, comprising a community of four million individuals, represents the ancient Egyptian Christian Church. While it has long been closely allied with the Ethiopian state church, the latter has evolved certain beliefs and rituals which are divergent from those of the Egyptian church. Both denominations, however, adhere to the Monophysite doctrine. The Coptic Church is headed by a patriarch and has a hierarchical structure similar to that of other Oriental churches. On the whole, the priesthood is very poorly educated. From its inception the Coptic Church has been closely associated with the development of monasticism, particularly of the contemplative type. There are still a few monks residing as recluses in lonely desert outposts, often in caves. The church liturgy is long and complex and utilizes the ancient Coptic language, along with some Arabic. Baptism of infants by complete immersion is also practiced. The Copts are the only minority religious sect with any considerable rural following. On the basis of the 1947 census in Egypt the majority (57 per cent) resided in four Upper Egyptian Provinces of Minya, Asyut, Sawhaj, and Qena. Sixteen per cent lived in Cairo. Copts comprised one quarter of the population of Asyut, one fifth of the population of Minya, 16 per cent of Sawhaj, and 10 per cent of Qena. Several villages in these provinces are completely Coptic in population. Villages scattered throughout the extent of Egypt, from the Delta to Aswan, have minorities of Copts. On superficial examination, rural Copts differ little from their Muslim countrymen except in religious affiliation. In the village the only external signs of Coptic inhabitants is the presence of a church, but one should not be misled thereby into minimizing the difference that does exist between Muslims and Copts. Behind the external similarities this difference between church and mosque symbolizes distinctive points of contrast in terms of personality and various nuances of social organization. Some indication of the latter has been given by Wakin, who reported on a government study of an Upper Egyptian village in which a minority were Copts. A Coptic family obtains protection from Muslims against other Muslims by attaching

> ... itself to a Moslem family known as 'the Arab protector of the Christian family' and the Moslem family assumes the duty of avenging the murder of any member of the Coptic family. The avenging Moslem family not only murders in retaliation, but also becomes liable to the counter-retaliation in the chain reaction of revenge that goes on for decades in Upper Egyptian villages. The Copts assist their protector by providing guns and money, but never take a direct part in the revenge. In case of conflicts between Moslem families, the Copts act as carriers of news as well as suppliers of guns and money, but they always remain on the outside [Wakin 1963: 77].

If a member of the protector family murdered one in the Coptic family, no revenge was demanded. Further, there was not found any case in which a Copt killed a Muslim (Wakin 1963: 78).

As with similar minority groups, the Copts have learned to survive by learning how to accommodate to the Muslim majority. Certainly the Copts' position as members of a frequently insecure minority group for fourteen centuries has had its marked effects on the individuals involved. What is more, as Copts—as Christians, rather than Muslims—they have adopted a different attitude toward suffering and "weakness." These are, then, examples of the causal effect of ideology on social organization and personality.

Islam

The Muslims of the Nile Valley are of the Sunni persuasion.[6] They adhere to one of three *madhhabs*, or legal schools: Lower Egypt or the

---

[6] There are a few Syrian and Yemeni immigrants, some of whom may technically be Shi'a, but there is no organized Shi'a community as such.

Delta is traditionally Shafi'i, while Upper Egypt and the Sudan are traditionally Maliki. The third *madhhab*, the Hanafi, was supported by the former Turkish rulers of these lands and finds adherents in Lower Egypt. Except under special circumstance, Hanafi law is officially applied in the Shari'a courts of Sudan, although the population itself adheres to the Maliki school in their private rituals. In Egypt, too, Hanafi law has had a place of special privilege within the religious courts, which have, however, now been abolished. For the ordinary layman these schools have been meaningful primarily in defining specifically religious rituals, such as the minor differences that occur in the *salat*, the regular daily prayer.

As in other parts of the world, the Sunni community is very loosely organized. The *'ulama*, or religious scholars, dwell in the major cities and are attached to the large mosques and the theological seminaries. They stand at the top of the religious hierarchy, but the connection between them and the village religious leaders is of a most tenuous nature. They are not involved in the appointment or overseeing of the village prayer leader (imam), nor do they have anything to do with the administration of the small rural mosques. Each village is an autonomous religious community, whose senior male members assume responsibility for maintaining the religious edifice and for appointing the imam and any other religious functionaries who may be required. The imam is most frequently unpaid and makes a living as a teacher in the *Qur'an* school, or as a maker of religious charms or a reciter of *Qur'an*. He may also support himself by a nonreligious occupation, such as shopkeeping or farming. On occasion, usually at the end of Ramadan, he receives a gift from some of the more prosperous villagers. As imam, his duties are to lead the prayers in the mosque five times each day and particularly at Friday noon, at which time he is expected to read a sermon. In the case of numerous smaller villages, especially in the Sudan, the mosque has no formal officials. The Friday prayer or any other prayer is led by any important community leader who may be present; no sermons are delivered.

Within the Nile Valley there is a great range in the elaborateness of mosques. None, of course, approach the grandeur of city mosques, but most of those in Egypt have a minaret, are painted inside, and are sometimes decorated with calligraphy. Frequently they are built of stone or fired brick. Those in the Sudan are, by comparison, extremely modest; they are plain, unadorned, mud-brick, one-roomed buildings without minarets. The interiors are bare. In some places there is no structure at all, but rather an area marked off by stones. In Kordofan, mosques, like village houses, are constructed of thatch.

In addition to functioning as a house of prayer five times each day and as the place for the regular Friday congregational services, the village mosque has other functions, religious and secular. It may serve as the meeting place of a religious brotherhood (*tariqa*) or for a *Qur'an* school (called a *khalwa* in Sudan and a *kuttab* in Egypt). Religious rites connected with the celebration of the Prophet's birthday, a saint's day, or services in connection with the fast month of Ramadan and the Great Feast (Al 'id al Kbir) may be held at the mosque. These services include recitations of biographies of the Prophet (*mawlid*), repetitions of sacred words or phrases accompanied by rhythmic bodily movements (*zikr*), chanting of hymns, and recitation of *Qur'an*. The latter is an especially common practice in Egypt for almost any occasion. In connection with certain mosque activities, such as the commemoration of a death, there is a distribution of food. The mosque and its environs are also a center for secular activity. It is a place to rest, a meeting place for friends to sit and chat, and even a meeting place for formal discussion of community affairs. (In parts of the Sudan, the latter is viewed as profane activity and is therefore conducted outside the mosque, at the front door.)

The formal Islam of the mosque, with its belief in the unity of an all-powerful and merciful God, the prophecy of Muhammad, the holiness of the *Qur'an*, and the ritual obligations of prayer, fasting, almsgiving, and pilgrimage, is still important in the daily life of the villager in one way or another. But these represent only one aspect of the total religious life. Several cult groups and various magical beliefs and practices also play their role. One of the most prevalent types of cult is the mystical brotherhood (*tariqa*), whose leaders teach a special discipline or path (also *tariqa*), designed to lead the practitioner into a state of holiness and unity with God. Numerous such organizations are still active throughout Egypt and the Sudan. They are, however, in a general state of decline, especially in Egypt. In villages in both countries only a small minority actually become full-fledged members of any *tariqa*. On the other hand, a far greater number do receive the initial induction as a *talib* or initiate. A *khalifa*, or local leader of a *tariqa*, may serve an area covering several villages and hamlets or his activities may be confined to a single community. In any case, the *khalifa* acts as master of ceremonies for the weekly services of his brotherhood and initiates young men into the organization, training them for the different stages of membership. Each *tariqa* has its own religious service, which includes prayers, litanies, and a *zikr* peculiar to the brotherhood.

In many cases, *tariqas* serve as a counterforce to the mutual hostility resulting from strong lineage and village identification by inculcating a feeling of brotherhood among members who nevertheless belong to different villages or kin groups. On the other hand, a given *tariqa* can become associated with a specific lineage, village, or tribe, and so operate to enhance divisiveness. In the Sudan the *tariqas* are politically more powerful than in Egypt, some having become associated with specific political parties.

The Mahdiya in the Sudan is a religious organization similar to, but distinct from, the *tariqas*. It is more in the nature of a sect, such as the Wahhabiya in Saudi Arabia, and, like the latter, it seeks a return to the primitive Islamic community. It has been an influential force in Sudanese politics and still has hundreds of thousands of supporters throughout the country, especially in the Central Sudan.

In both Muslim and Coptic communities there is a cult of saints, in which certain individuals are venerated. In fact, in some sections of Egypt, Copts and Muslims alike accept the same person as a saint. The tombs of numerous holy men dot the Egyptian and Sudanese countryside. Pilgrims visit the tombs in order to make specific requests and vows of sacrifice. The saints are believed to have special powers to cure disease and bring good fortune. Often a given holy man is recognized for his ability to cure a single illness.

The only universally observed saint's day is the Mawlid al Nabi, Muhammad's birthday. Both in the Sudan and in Egypt, villagers hold commemorative services of varying degrees of elaboration. *Mawlids* and *Qur'an* may be recited and the *zikr* performed. Muhammad, however, is not held to have had supernatural powers, and he is not appealed to for aid.

Many Egyptian villages have a patron saint whose birthday is honored each year with festivities not unlike those of the Prophet's birthday. In some villages these anniversaries celebrate the presumed birthday of the man, while in others a special day may be set after the cotton harvest, when more money is available. These are likewise occasions for many marriages and circumcisions, it being believed that such days are especially efficacious. Annual celebrations honoring saints in the Sudan occur in the vicinity of the saint's tomb and on the anniversary of his death. On all saints' days, the *tariqas* are active participants.

In Egypt and the Sudan a saint cult is often related to a *tariqa* in the common veneration of a given holy man. The latter may have been the founder of a local branch of a *tariqa* or one of its special devotees. Further, the cult is also related to curing in that it is in part concerned with attempts to overcome disease. The living curer is always a potential saint. He need only demonstrate that he is honored by God with special powers in order to obtain popular canonization. Healing is also associated with the *tariqa* in that a *khalifa* may prepare remedies to bring good health. Specifically, curing involves the preparation of charms or the performance of special rituals. In both, the *Qur'an* is important, since the charms usually include verses written from *Qur'an* and a common ritual performance entails drinking the water that has washed the holy verse from a slate. Other aids are employed as well: cabalistic signs, Arabic letters, and incense. Curers may seek to diagnose through divination in which the use of the *Qur'an* is common. Blackman reports that in Upper Egypt women "magicians" hold séances by which they seek to consult with familiar spirits to diagnose and prescribe for a patient (Blackman 1927: 183 ff.).

Of more peculiar interest in the Nile Valley is the *zar* cult, an exclusively women's club which is mainly centered in the cities, but which has diffused to some extent into the rural hinterland. The *zar* is basically part of a larger African religious complex, which involves the belief in possession by spirits (*zar*), the practice of inducing trance states in religious ceremonies, and the practice of making blood sacrifices to appease the spirits. The *zar* cult is probably a relatively recent innovation in Egypt and Sudan, having been introduced in the last century, possibly from Ethiopia. However, beliefs in spirits of various kinds have been a traditional part of the religious systems of the peoples of this area. *'Afarit* (plural) are spirits who inhabit the underworld, and some of these are classed as devils or *shayatin*. Spirits dwell in stones, trees, wells, and houses. There are also spirits of the Nile, which in the Sudan have traditionally been appeased at different points in the rites of birth and marriage. Besides a belief in a personal soul (*ruh*) there is a belief in *qarin*, which in Egypt refers to the individual's double—a spirit which accompanies the individual and is an exact replica of him. On occasion it can do him harm. Blackman compares the *qarin* concept to that of the ancient Egyptian *ka* (Blackman 1927: 288). The belief in black magic is found throughout the Nile Valley, but this writer knows of no one who has actually observed its practice.

The "evil eye," symbolizing the evil power of envy, is another type of supernatural belief that is widespread in Egypt and Sudan. Among Muslims, foreigners and Christians may bear the "evil eye," and sometimes old men are said to have it. But in actuality no one can say for sure where the "eye" lurks at a given moment. Thus, it is always necessary to protect one's self against it. A child should not look attractive, but left dirty so that the "evil eye" will not notice it. Charms and blue beads may be worn; anything blue-colored is especially effective.

There is little data on the extent and intensity of belief in the various kinds of spirits and in the "Evil Eye." One might surmise that it is strongest among the least educated, and this includes the great majority of women and elderly, rural men. It is also likely that this is one aspect of religion which has been most effectively weakened by the advances of secularization. It should be made clear, incidentally, that beliefs in *'afarit* and other spirits as well as the "Evil Eye" are shared by both Muslims and Copts.[7]

Artistic Expression

Cairo, above all, possesses an impressive collection of artistic forms. The delicate and intricate design of the Mamluk-style mosques and the powerful architecture of the great mosque of Ibn Tulun rank among the masterpieces of the world. The beauties of Egyptian craftmanship in gold, copper and brass, and woodwork are today largely appreciated by tourists. In contrast to such art developments, largely commissioned as they were by rulers of state and the wealthy, the "embellishment of existence" cannot be considered a strong point with the rural populace of the Nile Valley. Certainly, the reason for the paucity of art is not to be explained entirely by economic deprivation, since across the Mediterranean, Greek and Slavic peasants and even the neighboring Arabs of the Levant have developed highly respectable traditions in dance and costume, among other things. It is more likely that the Muslim ideology, combined with the intense poverty, have been effective in dampening developments in the artistic realm. Islam in general has frowned upon dancing, garish attire, and on depicting the human or other living forms. Thus, painting, drawing, and sculpture have never been of much significance in the Muslim Nile Valley. Art expression has focused on architecture, which is limited to those with adequate financial resources—thus, more often state enterprises—or it has found expression in calligraphy, literature, and music.

The most impressive architecture in an Egyptian village, and frequently in a Sudanese village also, is the mosque, or possibly the tomb of some holy man. In Nubian villages, a house is frequently decorated with a china plate over the door. These plates are brought by the men on their return from Cairo, where they work as cooks and servants. Throughout Nubia, the outer walls of houses, especially around the doorway, are painted with elaborate designs. In Egypt, the front wall of a house belonging to one who has gone on a pilgrimage to Mecca is painted with a large design, which typically portrays the great mosque of Mecca with a railroad train or boat moving in its direction. A creed

[7]This description of Islam summarizes materials gathered primarily from the following sources: H. 'Ammār (1954); Barclay (1963, 1964, 1965, 1966); Blackman (1927); Lane (1908); McPherson (1942); el Tayib (1955-56); Trimingham (1949); Zenkovsky (1949, 1950).

or verse from the *Qur'an* is written beside the painting. In the Sudan, such elaborate decorations are not made, although religious verse may be painted on the doorway of the house. Or part of the latter may be merely painted green, the color symbolizing the Prophet.

"*Mawlid* dolls," manufactured of sugar and brightly decorated with colored paper, are sold during the Mawlid al Nabi (Prophet's birthday) throughout Egypt and much of the Sudan. Some of these dolls are figures taken from folklore; others are representations of mosques.

Wearing apparel is often decorative. In Nubia and Sudan skull caps are crocheted for men, and throughout the entire area women wear gold and silver jewelry, which is as much a bank or means for storing wealth as it is for decoration. The basketry of Nubia and Sudan is sometimes elaborately designed by dying the fibers in various colors and plaiting them in patterns. Pottery, however, is unembellished.

The written literature significant to the rural populace is almost entirely of a religious nature, and while used by the villager or nomad, it does not ordinarily originate with him, but with urban teachers and scholars. Thus, the most common piece of written literature is the *Qur'an*; others include the litanies (*ratib*) of religious brotherhoods, biographies of the Prophet, hymns, and certain prayers. Almost any other literature utilized by the rural population is of an oral nature. Proverbs are the most common and are widely employed in everyday speech. Folktales are the second most important type of oral literature. In most villages, there is at least one person who has a great store of tales, which he recounts to interested audiences. In Egypt the storyteller apparently has traditionally a kind of semiprofessional status. Although he pursues a trade, he also tells tales for a small sum (Blackman 1927: 268). In the Sudan most tribes have legendary histories and a special folklore. Secular songs—especially "romantic" love songs—riddles, and nursery rhymes constitute other important types of oral literature (see Hillelson 1935).

Instrumental music is primarily composed to accompany songs, hymns, tales, or dances. Drums, tambourines, reed horns, and the *rababa*, an ancient, one-stringed instrument, are common. In recent years, Western instruments such as the violin and the guitar have become popular in many areas; and in numbers of Egyptian villages there are both semiprofessional "balady" bands, playing the traditional instruments, and semiprofessional brass bands.

Throughout the Nilotic Sudan and Egypt, the common dance is a solo and is designed either for women or for men. The dances of the latter are apparently a survival of a form of ancient Arab war dance. In Egypt there is truly no dance which would be considered proper for a lady to perform in public. This is not the case further south among

Arabs along the Sudanese Nile, where there is a special solo dance which every girl should learn so as to perform before the men on festive occasions. The Baggara contrast with the Nile dwellers in possessing a circle dance in which both men and women participate together. The religious brotherhoods have produced a variety of rhythmic movements to be performed in their congregational devotions, and these must be considered as distinct dance forms.

Language

Over 97 per cent of the people in the Nile Valley area are native speakers of Arabic. In Egypt the only non-Arabic speakers are the European immigrant minorities and the Kanuz-speaking Nubians. In the Arab Sudan, there are scattered numbers of migrants from the south of the Sudan who retain their native speech and a larger group of approximately a quarter million in Kordofan, Blue Nile, Khartoum, and Northern Provinces who are speakers of West African languages. Speakers of Nubian languages (Kanuz, Mahas, Sukkot, and Dongalawi), which are classified in the Sudanic family, are concentrated in the area between Aswan and Dongola. In the Sudan section, they number close to two hundred thousand, and in Egypt, about fifty thousand.

The Arabic dialects can be approached from several different angles. First, there is the ubiquitous distinction between the colloquial speech used in ordinary conversation and the literary Arabic, a modernized version of which is used in radio broadcasting and highly formalized occasions such as university lectures; while *Qur'anic* Arabic is the language of religious ritual. Secondly, within the colloquial speech, differences arise which are a result of specific sociological factors. Thus, the educated who are the equivalent of the upper stratum of society contrast with the unlettered. Among the uneducated in the Nile Sudan, sex differences are important dialectically. Certain words are exclusively parts of women's vocabulary and are never uttered by men. And finally, there is the dimension of geographical variation. Very roughly, Egypt has been divided into two major dialect areas—Lower Egypt and Upper Egypt. This is not a satisfactory classification, however, since there are apparently major pockets in Lower Egypt—Sharqiyah Province, especially—where the dialect is more akin to that of Upper Egypt. In addition, in both areas there are numerous important subdialect areas. Hillelson has pointed to some of the unique characteristics of the Arabic in various parts of the Sudan. One can, in fact, broadly differentiate a riverain dialect, a dialect of the Baggara, and one for central Kordofan (Hillelson 1935: Introduction).

In plain fact, the dialect geography of Arabic speakers of northeastern Africa has hardly been explored, and a great deal remains to be done in the scientific analysis of the language of this area. The reader interested in Egyptian Arabic should consult Richard S. Harrell's *The Phonology of Colloquial Egyptian Arabic* (1957).

Conclusion

The Nile Valley region specifically is roughly divisible into five cultural-ecological zones: the Delta, Upper Egypt, Nubia, the Arab Sudanese Lower Nile, and the Arab Sudanese Upper Nile. The Delta region is characterized by a most intensive cultivation, which is enhanced by perennial irrigation. Land is cultivated all around the village, so that the village has a compact and concentrated form. In addition, the demand for land encourages multistoried buildings to conserve space. The Delta is both the cotton and the rice bowl of Egypt. Lineage structure here is extremely weak, and tribal organization nonexistent. The rural population is overwhelmingly Muslim; non-Muslim minorities are concentrated in urban centers. Urbanization is the most extensive in the Delta, and over three quarters of the Nile's city dwellers reside here. Upper Egypt tends more to linear and polynucleated types of settlement, because of the pattern of living along the outer edges of cultivated land flanking the Nile. Upper Egypt, beginning just upriver from Cairo, is the center for extensive sugarcane and onion production; while perennial irrigation is of primary importance, much of the land is managed by means of basin irrigation. Here the rural populace have a reputation for conservatism. Lineage structure retains a more important role, and in many areas tribal background is still remembered; especially is there a noticeable conservatism in the role and status of women. In much of Upper Egypt, there is a persistent pattern of temporary uxori-patrilocal residence. A large minority of the rural population is Coptic Christian.

Nubia, a third zone of importance, is ecologically a continuation of Upper Egypt. A distinctive feature of Nubia is that its agricultural productivity is inadequate for the size of the present population, so that Nubian men leave their home villages and obtain work in major cities in an attempt to accumulate adequate funds to send home. Countless hamlets and villages in Nubia consist of a population which is 60 to 70 per cent female, the small male population being preponderantly under eighteen years of age or over sixty. Those who remain behind cultivate the small gardens along the river banks. Nubia is further distinguished for its retention of the Nubian language, its distinctive house styles, and conservatism relating to the role of women.

Up the Nile from Nubia to Khartoum and beyond is the area of the Sudanic Arab people. Distinguishing cultural features among them include the practice of temporary, uxori-patrilocal residence, infibulation of girls, facial scarification for both men and women, and marital rites centering around the *rahat* and the *jirtig*. Dress also differs from that of the Egyptian peasant, in that the common outer garment for both men and women is a kind of wrap-around known as a *tawb*. Sudanese sedentaries preserve more of a tribal structure and have a strong pastoral orientation. Besides keeping herds of goats, sheep, and cattle, they cultivate sorghum and millet—in contrast to Egypt, where maize and wheat are staples—and their diet is as much one of porridge as it is of bread. In the northern arid parts of this area the house form is a rectangular, single-storied building made of mud brick, and the settlement pattern is one of scattered hamlets, particularly of a linear type, almost wholly along the Nile, and dependent on Nile irrigation. South of Khartoum and entering the Gezira region, there is greater rainfall and patterns of settlement, of cultivation, and of house form change. Here, particularly at the southern extremities, rain cultivation is of considerable importance. There is a predominance of the cylinder cone or Sudanese type of dwelling; settlements which are located away from the Nile banks are concentrated and compact, with cultivated land and pasture surrounding them. The number of nomadic and seminomadic peoples increases in importance and cattle, rather than camels, are the mainstay of such a way of life. Here, too, tribal identification is more intense. Although in both Egypt and the Sudan Sunni Islam prevails, among Sudanese Arabs the religious fraternities, or Sufi orders, are of much greater significance; the indigenous Mahdiya sect, which claims the allegiance of a large proportion of Sudanese, lends a distinctive contrast to the religious ideology of Egypt.

Most of these characteristics also apply to the region of central Kordofan, which deviates primarily from the riverain region in that millet is the staple crop rather than sorghum, and gum Arabic and sesame are more important as cash crops. Also, peripheral to the Nile Valley itself are the oases of the Western Desert of Egypt. These oases—Kharga, Dakhla, Bahariya and Farafra—are culturally distinguished from neighboring Upper Egypt chiefly by their dependence upon subterranean water resources and the production of dates.

Finally, the open desert impinges upon the Nile Valley throughout most of its length, and it remains the realm best exploited by camel nomads.

Potentialites for anthropological research throughout the entire Nile Valley and its environs are numerous. The bare handful of community studies in Egypt have hardly scratched the surface in that country; this is even more true in Sudan. Ethnographic surveys are fully in order to provide some idea of the relative distribution of numerous cultural traits and complexes that now, more often than not, one must guess as being typical of this or that region. The dynamics of kinship, the changes in structure in kinship groupings, the effects of government irrigation schemes and agrarian reform legislation, the entire problem of sedentarization of nomadic and seminomadic peoples, the extent and intensity of magico-religious beliefs and practices represent only a partial listing of the kinds of urgently needed research. The main question is: Will the prevailing regimes in the United Arab Republic and the Republic of Sudan at least see their way clear not to hinder legitimate research undertakings?

THE NILE VALLEY:
AN ANNOTATED BIBLIOGRAPHY

1. EGYPT

Al Abd, Salah
1946   *The Egyptian village,* unpublished M.A. thesis, Chapel Hill, University of North Carolina. 111 pp.; tables, maps.

This thesis, by an Egyptian government social worker, is concerned with rural economics and the author's particular attempts to improve living conditions in villages in Manufiya Province. There is a brief, superficial coverage of housing, land distribution, irrigation, diet, and health, and a general description of village layout. The author reports constructing and distributing a questionnaire in the villages, but he furnishes none of the results of the survey.

Abou-Zeid, Ahmed M.
1963   "Migrant labour and social structure in Kharga Oasis," in *Mediterranean Countrymen: Essays in the Social Anthropology of the Mediterranean,* Julian Pitt-Rivers, ed., Paris and La Haye, Mouton, pp. 41-53.

Abou-Zeid attempts to demonstrate the extent to which social structure in this oasis has been altered by the constant emigration of workers from Kharga to the Nile Valley. The village communities of the oasis are briefly described.

1965   "Honour and shame among the Bedouins of Egypt," in *Honour and Shame: The Values of Mediterranean Society,* Jean G. Peristiany, ed., London, Weidenfeld and Nicolson, pp. 243-59.

The author explores the concepts of *sharaf* (honor) and *'ar* (shame), the various dimensions of their meaning, and the roles they play in social control and as a code of morality among Bedawin of the Western Desert of Egypt.

Abu El. Ezz, M. S.
1953   *The northern part of Aswan Province, Upper Egypt,* unpublished Ph.D. thesis, Durham University, U.K. Vol. 1: viii, 329, and xiii pp.; vol. 2: maps, graphs, and photographs.

The following information is taken from Coult's annotated bibliography of the Egyptian fellah (1958: 130-31): "This

53

thesis is based upon field work conducted during the summers of 1951-52. . . . Considerable use is made of national statistics as well as firsthand data, however. . . .

"This study is divided into 4 parts, the first of which concerns the usual topics of physical geography. Of the second, outlining the demographic features of the area, the chapter on marital conditions stands out. . . .

"Among the usual subtopics of agriculture, discussed in Part 3, are those of occupational structure and land tenure. . . . Detailed studies of land use in 'Ezbet el-Manshiya', typical of the 'izbah type, and Silwah Baḥarī, of the peasant agriculture type, emphasize geography, topography, irrigation, communications, population, and the labor potential. The account of the latter provides a little information supplementing Ḥāmid 'Ammār's more social psychological study. In Part 4, the influences of physical environment, social structure, economic structure, agricultural revolution, and ethnic origin of the settlers upon the various types of settlements are explained."

Abu-Lughod, Janet L.
1961   "Migrant adjustment to city life: the Egyptian case," *American Journal of Sociology 67*: 22-32; map.

A study of village migrants to Cairo, this article notes that migrants from the same village tend to settle in the same area of the city so as to form small subcommunities, that migrants must make certain important changes in their way of life in the city, and that adjustments are facilitated by mutual aid groups developed among immigrants. Among the latter are the various village benevolent societies organized throughout Cairo.

1966   *The ecology of Cairo, Egypt: a comparative study using factor analysis*, unpublished Ph.D. dissertation, Amherst, University of Massachusetts. 446 pp.

According to the dissertation Abstract, the thesis contributes a case study of a major Middle Eastern city and seeks to "test the applicability of a factor analytic variation of social area analysis to a city at an earlier stage of demographic and economic development than the American and European cities to which these methods have hitherto been applied." The censuses of 1947 and 1960 constitute the raw data for the research.

1969a   "Testing the theory of social area analysis: the ecology of Cairo, Egypt," *American Sociological Review 34, 2*: 198-211.

An article based on a major segment of the author's Ph.D. thesis reported above (1966).

1969b "Varieties of urban experience: contrast, coexistence and coalescence in Cairo," in *Middle Eastern Cities*, Ira Lapidus, ed., Berkeley and Los Angeles, University of California Press.

Adams, John Boman
1957 "Culture and conflict in an Egyptian village," *American Anthropologist 59*: 225-35.

This is an attempt to explain various cliques and factions within a Lower Egyptian village and their members' attitudes toward the Abd Al Nasser regime on the basis of their earlier experience in the social structure and their present position within it. Of particular importance is the authoritarian and hierarchical nature of the family, the equalitarianism of the peer group, and changing kinship and authority patterns.

'Ammār, 'Abbās M.
1942 "A demographic study of an Egyptian province (Sharqiya)," *London School of Economics and Political Science, Monographs on Social Anthropology 8*. 96 pp.; illus., maps, graphs.

'Ammār analyzes Egyptian census data covering the censuses from 1882 through 1937 in Sharqīya Province. Population increase in various districts of the Province in terms of immigration and emigration, birth and death rates, sex ratios, age categories, marital conditions, divorce and reasons for divorces, are investigated. A socioeconomic survey conducted in 1939 provides information concerning households and their relation to economic conditions. Finally, soil problems and future population distribution are dealt with.

'Ammār, Hāmid M.
1954 *Growing up in an Egyptian village: Silwa, Province of Aswan*, London, Routledge and Kegan Paul. xix, 316 pp.

Hāmid 'Ammār's work stands at the forefront of anthropological studies on the Egyptian fellahin. Primarily concerned with socialization and enculturation processes in his home village in Aswan Province, he discusses birth, infancy, and early childhood training; sibling and peer group behavior; aims and methods of socialization; children's games, play, and tales; the period of adolescence and preparation for marriage; and formal educational systems. Attention is also paid to village economics, agriculture, kinship, and community structure. The village is considered in relation to the concept of the folk society and the broader question of sociocultural change. Appendixes include life histories, proverbs, riddles, kinship terms, Coptic and lunar calendars, and data on standards of living. This is an indispensable work for the ethnographer of Egypt. (Reprinted, 1967, New York, Octagon.)

Awad, Mohamed
1954   "The assimilation of nomads in Egypt," *Geographical Review*
       44: 240-52; map and photographs.

       This paper contains a brief review of major nomadic move-
       ments in the past history of Egypt, but its primary thesis is
       to outline five stages in the assimilation of nomads to seden-
       tary life. These stages, each briefly described, are: absolute
       nomadism, partial nomadism, partial assimilation, advanced
       assimilation, complete assimilation. A map indicates the geo-
       graphic distribution of these stages in Egypt.

Ayrout, Henry Habib
1945   *The fellaheen* (Hilary Wayment, trans.), Cairo, K. Schindler.
       179 pp.; illus., glossary. (First published in France in 1938.
       A new translation, *The Egyptian Peasant*, updated and re-
       vised by the author, was published in 1963 by Beacon Press,
       Boston.)

       Like Hāmid 'Ammār's work, Ayrout's book represents one of
       the classics on the Egyptian fellahin. Ayrout is a Jesuit mis-
       sionary priest who has spent most of his life among the rural
       peoples of Upper Egypt and, therefore, has come to know
       them more intimately than most anthropologists could ever
       expect to know a people. *The fellaheen* attempts to present a
       general picture of the peasant without concentrating on any
       single area or village. It is not based on ethnographic field
       research as such, but upon years of personal contact supple-
       mented by some data from published sources. The book
       covers most of the areas found in an ethnography. Consider-
       able space is devoted to what in essence amounts to specula-
       tions on the psychology of the fellah. His unchanging char-
       acter and the isolation of the village are greatly overempha-
       sized. This book is useful where it presents factual data;
       where it seeks to interpret, it is of more questionable value.

Baer, Gabriel
1962   *A history of landownership in modern Egypt 1800-1950*,
       London, Oxford University Press. xiii, 252 pp.; maps, tables,
       appendixes.

       The development of private ownership of land after the es-
       tablishment of Muhammad Ali's dynasty is described. Baer
       provides the background for the formation of large estates
       and the mass of tiny landholdings. He also discusses the dif-
       ferent types of landed domains and views on agrarian reform
       prior to the 1952 Revolution.

1969   *Studies in the social history of modern Egypt*, Chicago, Uni-
       versity of Chicago Press. xx, 259 pp.

Balls, William Lawrence
1915   *Egypt of the Egyptians*, London, Sir Isaac Pitman & Sons.
xvi, 266 pp.; illus.

> Balls, author of other books on Egypt, presents a general sur-
> vey of Egypt of which only certain chapters are of any rele-
> vance to the anthropologist. Chapter V may be of interest in
> dealing with the harnessing of the Nile and describing irriga-
> tion and the over-all pattern by which water is supplied for
> perennial irrigation. Chapter VII describes traditional agricul-
> tural technology and systems; while Chapter VIII is a general
> coverage of the fellahin, and is of little value. The remainder
> of the book gives a history of Egypt and a general, super-
> ficial description of the country.

Barclay, Harold B.
1966   "Study of an Egyptian village community," *Studies in Islam*
3: 143-66, 201-26.

> This is a report on field research during the summer of 1958
> in a Giza Province village near Cairo. The inhabitants con-
> sider themselves "Arabs," as distinct from fellahin, their an-
> cestors having been sedentarized Bedawin. The article surveys
> the social and religious organization of the community. Brief
> attention is paid to the role of the tourist guide.

Berger, Morroe
1962   *The Arab world today*, Doubleday, Garden City, N.Y. 480
pp.; map.

> Berger has ordered the data from a number of sociological,
> anthropological, and social psychological studies on Egypt,
> Iraq, Jordan, Lebanon, and Syria into an insightful survey of
> contemporary Arab culture and personality. He briefly re-
> views the Islamic background of the Arab world, describes
> the several aspects of social life, and pays particular attention
> to the personality and values of the Arab, the Arab "ideol-
> ogy," the current military regimes, and the urban sociology
> of the Arab world. Approximately half of the material pre-
> sented directly relates to Egypt, and the author's experience
> in the area has been primarily with that country.

1970   *Islam in Egypt today: social and political aspects of popular
religion*, Cambridge University Press (forthcoming).

Berque, Jacques
1957   *Histoire sociale d'un village égyptien au xxème siècle*, Paris
and The Hague, Mouton. 87 pp.; illus., maps.

> The large (36,000 pop.) village of Sīrs Al Layyān, Manūfīya
> Province, is all too briefly surveyed in one of the rare ethno-
> graphic monographs of Lower Egypt. Based on two years res-

idence in the village, it contains most of the materials usually covered in an ethnographic report. The general theme of the work is cultural change in this century. The data presented are useful and that it is not a more extended and detailed monograph is to be regretted.

Blackman, Winifred S.
1927   *The fellāhīn of Upper Egypt: their religious, social, and industrial life to-day with special reference to survivals from ancient times*, London, George C. Harrap. 331 pp.; illus., glossary.

Blackman, who obtained a diploma in Anthropology at Oxford, spent several years in Egypt, and this well-known book represents a product of these years. Like Ayrout, her descriptions are not confined to any one village or area. The book is especially unique in that, being written by a woman who spent much of her time talking to and observing the peasant women of Upper Egypt, it is able to present a more than usual amount on the woman's world view. *The Fellāhīn of Upper Egypt* concentrates in the main on magical beliefs and practices, the cult of saints, and the rites of passage. Like so many such works, it describes magical practices and beliefs, but gives no indication of the extent to which they are accepted. There are also chapters on village industry, ornamentation, and agriculture. This is certainly one of the more useful works on rural Egypt. (Reprinted in 1968, London, Cass; New York, Barnes and Noble.)

Coult, Lyman H.
1958   *An annotated research bibliography of studies in Arabic, English, and French of the fellah of the Egyptian Nile, 1798-1955*, Coral Gables, University of Miami Press. v, 144 pp.; map, glossary.

This is an indispensable tool for the ethnologist of Egyptian village life and has been invaluable in the preparation of this bibliography. Bibliographic references are categorized as general reference works, secondary analyses, travel and description, records of professionals serving the village, autobiographical accounts, reports by trained Egyptians, short field trips, and advanced studies. The description of many of the latter are one to two pages in length. There is both an author and a subject index, a list of sources covered, and a map indicating all places mentioned in the text.

Crary, Douglas D.
1949   "Irrigation and land use in Zeiniya Bahari, Upper Egypt," *Geographical Review 39*: 568-83, illus., maps.

Crary, a professional geographer, did field work in Zaynīya Baharī, an Upper Egyptian village of 5,000 people just north of Luxor. He describes the three types of irrigation systems used in this village: basin, perennial, and lift systems. These are each related to crop cycle, and there is a brief discussion of settlement pattern and house form.

Fakhouri, Hani
1968 "The Zar cult in an Egyptian village," *Anthropological Quarterly 41, 2*: 49-56.

Describes Zar practices in a village suburb of Cairo. Claims a decline in the Zar cult as a result of improved education, higher income, and the provision of medical services by industrial employers.

Fernea, Robert A., ed.
1966 *Contemporary Egyptian Nubia*, 2 vols. *HRAFlex Books MR 8-001.*

This reviewer has not had an opportunity to read this work. It is a collection of papers written by social anthropologists who engaged in a team investigation of Egyptian Nubian villages between 1963 and 1966.

Fernea, Robert A., and John G. Kennedy
1966 "Initial adaptations to resettlement: a new life for Egyptian Nubians," *Current Anthropology 7*: 349-54.

These two American anthropologists, drawing upon their extensive field work in the area, discuss cultural changes of Egyptian Nubians resulting from relocation as a result of the construction of the High Dam.

Gadalla, Saad M.
1962 "Land reform in relation to social development, Egypt," *University of Missouri Studies 39*, Columbia, University of Missouri Press. xiii, 139 pp.; map, tables.

Gadella's book presents the results of field research undertaken in 1956-57 in the Egyptian Delta. There is a brief review of the land tenure situation prior to the reform and an outline of the law itself, followed by an analysis of the effects of the law on three estates, one each in Daqahliya, Behariya, and Kafr el Shaykh Provinces. The author uses three matched *waqf* estates as controls against which changes effected by land reform can be examined.

Ghonemy, Mohamed Riad
1951 *A study and analysis of farm tenancy in Egypt*, unpublished M.A. thesis, Knoxville, University of Tennessee. vii, 159 pp.; maps.

Ghonemy's thesis, based primarily upon the analysis of government statistics, presents data concerning the extent of farm tenancy, types of tenancy, rental costs, land values, and taxation. There is also a limited amount of information regarding agricultural practices.

Hamdan, G.
1952   *Population of the Nile Mid-Delta: past and present; a study of dialectical integration in regional ecology*, 2 vols., unpublished Ph.D. thesis, University of Reading, U.K., Vol. *1*: 192 pp.; Vol. *2*: 379 pp.

According to Coult (1958: 128), Hamdan's thesis "contains . . . much material primarily culled from secondary sources. . . ." although he did devote three months visiting "perhaps 100 villages." The author ". . . attempts to explain several basic characteristics of the Egyptian peasantry by integrating aspects of demography, geography, and cultural history." The work summarizes ". . . the population of the Mid-Delta during the major historical periods since 7000 B.C." It provides a history of systems of landownership and discusses settlement patterns.

Holt, Peter M., ed.
1968   *Political and social change in modern Egypt; historical studies from the Ottoman Conquest to the United Arab Republic*, London, Oxford University Press. 400 pp.; illus.

Papers presented at a conference at the School of Oriental and African Studies on the history of modern Egypt.

Issawi, Charles P.
1954   *Egypt at mid-century; an economic survey*, rev. ed. of *Egypt: an economic and social analysis*, London, Oxford University Press under the auspices of the Royal Institute of International Affairs. xiv, 289 pp.; tables.

Issawi reviews the economic changes in Egypt from 1798 to 1952. Relying on data from the 1937 and 1947 censuses, his book summarizes occupational and population characteristics, distribution of income, consumption patterns, agriculture, industry, trade and finance, and future socioeconomic trends. It offers, therefore, background economic information on Egypt as a whole.

1963   *Egypt in revolution: an economic analysis*, London, Oxford University Press. xiv, 343 pp.; tables.

Egypt in revolution is essentially an updating of Issawi's *Egypt at mid-century*, covering similar topics with the addition of a discussion of Arab Socialism.

Klunzinger, Carl B.
1878 *Upper Egypt: its people and its products. A descriptive account of the manners, customs, superstitions, and occupations of the people of the Nile Valley, the desert, and the Red Sea coast with sketches of natural history and geology* (translated from the German), London, Blackie; New York, Scribner, Armstrong. xv, 408 pp.

Klunzinger, a German, spent several years on the Red Sea coast as an Egyptian government sanitary physician. He has provided descriptions primarily of small town life in Upper Egypt and in Al Qusayr on the Red Sea. Such varied items as markets, crafts, food habits, public baths, coffee shops, beer shops, dancing girls (Ghawāzi), and houses are portrayed. Observations are made on local administration, taxation, and on certain Coptic customs. For Al Qusayr, there is material on fishing, pearl fishing, and the Meccan pilgrimage. Village life is discussed to some extent. There is a chapter on "popular beliefs" and "superstitions" and another on the Ababdah. This work is one of the best nineteenth-century sources on Egypt.

Lane, Edward William
1908 *An account of the manners and customs of the modern Egyptians*, Everyman's Library, No. 315, London, J. M. Dent & Sons. xxxii, 630 pp.; drawings.

A description of life in Cairo during the first half of the nineteenth century, this classic work is of utmost significance to the anthropologist. After being trained in Arabic language and literature, Lane took up residence in Cairo, where he lived for several years as a native. His data were acquired according to such typical modern anthropological techniques as the use of the native language and participant observation. While Lane was not a professional anthropologist, his book is, in fact, a remarkably comprehensive and objective ethnography of Cairo. It ranks along with the works of Hamed Ammar, Ayrout, Berque, and Blackman as the best in Egyptian ethnography. *An account of the manners and customs of the modern Egyptians* focuses on the Muslim community, although there are short supplements on the Copts and Jews of the city.

Lane-Poole, Stanley
1884 *Social life in Egypt, a supplement to picturesque Palestine, a description of the country and its people*, London, J. S. Virtue. vi, 138 pp.; illus.

The most important feature of this book is the number of

steel and wood engravings of Cairo, rural Egypt, the Bedawin, and the Suez area, portraying life in Egypt after the
midnineteenth century. Such topics as town and country life,
Islam, and European innovations are briefly discussed. Material on agriculture and on the Ababdah are taken from
Klunzinger, and a description of a Coptic wedding is from L.
Oliphant's *Land of Khemi*.

Leeder, S. H.
1918 *Modern sons of the Pharaohs: a study of the manners and
customs of the Copts of Egypt*, London, Hodder and Stough-
ton. xvi, 355 pp.; illus.

Leeder is mainly interested in magico-religious beliefs and
practices and in the rites of passage of Egypt's ancient Christian minority. His associations have apparently been chiefly
with the more well-to-do urban Copts, and, thus, his descriptions often appear biased in favor of this group. Nevertheless,
the work is helpful in its rather detailed descriptions of the
rituals of the Coptic Church and in its observations on the
church organization. The author, unlike many Europeans
who have written about the Copts, is objective and fair to
both Muslims and Copts. A major theme of the book is the
high degree of similarity between the members of the two
religious groups.

Lichtenstadter, Ilse
1952 "An Arab-Egyptian family," *Middle East Journal* 6: 379-99.

This article is based upon field work in a village in Gīza Province, near Cairo. The village is one of a number in this vicinity originally settled by Bedawins from the Western Desert.
The various relationships among family members are described. There is a discussion of marriage and of education,
and attention is paid to changing values in connection with
family relationships and marriage.

Lozach, Jean
1935 *Le delta du Nil: étude de géographie humaine*, Le Caire, E. &
R. Schindler, pour le Société Royale de Géographie d'Égypte.
303 pp.; 13 plates, maps.

In this geographical study of Lower Egypt, the author covers
a multitude of different subjects in brief form, including
geography, people, use of the Nile, agriculture, and communications. He distinguishes two regions: the heart of the Delta
and the Lower Delta. Both regions are described in terms of
the rural habitat: settlement patterns, village layout, and
house construction. Village life is dealt with only briefly.
This material covers much of that dealt with in the earlier

work by Lozach and Hug. Examples of land reclamation in the Lower Delta by large landowners are presented.

Lozach, Jean, and G. Hug
1930   *L'habitat rural en Égypte*, Le Caire, Imprimerie de l'Institut Français d'Archéologie Orientale de Caire, pour le Société Royale de Géographie d'Égypte. xxiii, 215 pp.; maps, illus.

A study in human geography, this is most valuable in its presentation of materials on geographical regions, settlement patterns, house forms, and village layout. The authors explain the settlement patterns as a result of historical, economic, social, and political factors. Part One, by Lozach, concerns Lower Egypt and Part Two, by Hug, describes Middle and Upper Egypt. Data were acquired from extensive responses to a questionnaire circulated throughout the country. In addition, some material was gained by visits to villages.

McPherson, Joseph W.
1941   *The moulids of Egypt*, Cairo, Nile Mission Press. xiv, 351 pp.; illus., maps.

This compendium of the Coptic and Muslim saints' days in Egypt is primarily limited to those in the cities and to those observed by the author, at one time head of the secret police in Egypt. McPherson describes both the sacred and profane activities at the *mawlids* (*moulids*) and indicates the place for a given *mawlid* and the time of the year in which it is observed.

Mohsen, Safia K.
1967   "The legal status of women among Awlad 'Ali," *Anthropological Quarterly 40, 3*: 153-66.

A summary of the position of women in this nomadic tribe of the Western Desert of Egypt, among whom Safia Mohsen did anthropological field research. The paper points up the woman's lack of power, but also indicates that women do "... enjoy a number of significant rights. But it is only through their forfeiting certain of these rights that they are able to maintain the others."

Murray, George W.
1935   *The sons of Ishmael; a study of the Egyptian Bedouin*, London, George Routledge & Sons. xv, 344 pp.; illus., maps.

The author spent twenty-five years working in the Egyptian deserts and presents here the ethnographic data which he collected over those years. The nomadic peoples of the Red Sea region, Sinai, and the Western Desert are described. Attention is also paid to the Bedawin in the Nile Valley and the Ababdah and Beja of southeastern Egypt.

Nelson, Cynthia
 1968 "Changing roles of men and women: illustrations from Egypt," *Anthropological Quarterly 41, 2*: 57-77.

   Examples from Egyptian novels, a very brief presentation of a couple of cases with which the author is personally familiar, three letters to a columnist in an Egyptian weekly magazine, etc., all of which aim to show the changing sex roles in Egypt.

Ross, Mary, Mona Khoury-Schmitz, and Zeinab Hefnawy
 1954 *Preliminary report on visits to 23 families in Agbour Soughra*, Cairo, FAO (mimeographed). 85 pp.

   Coult reports that families in this Lower Egyptian village were interviewed " . . . primarily for the purpose of obtaining information about the food of poorer families and its preparation" (1958: 108). Methodological problems are discussed and the village and a neighboring *'izba* are described. These descriptions are apparently rich in information on food habits and domestic economy and include details on child rearing and family relations.

Saint John, Bayle
 1852 *Village life in Egypt: with sketches of the Saïd*, 2 vols., London, Chapman and Hall. Vol. *1*: xxiv, 296 pp.; Vol. *2*: xii, 299 pp.

   Scattered throughout this traveler's report are numerous items of anthropological interest: settlement patterns, house types, food, work of men and women, a little on child rearing practices, discussion of conscription and use of corporal punishment by officials, religious activities, and general remarks on Cairo as a city. There is a brief description of Saqqara village, and about a third of Volume *2* comprises stories and anecdotes told by town and rural dwellers.

Saleh, Mohammed
 1922 *La petite propriété rurale en Égypte*, thesis for doctorate in Political Science and Economy, University of Grenoble, Grenoble, Joseph Allier. 127 pp.

   While primarily interested in demonstrating the positive significance of the small proprietor, the author gives some brief attention to agricultural practices and reviews forms of land ownership from Pharaonic times to the present. He discusses techniques for classifying landowners, various methods for exploiting the land, and other materials relevant to agricultural economics.

Selim, Imam
 1948 *General relationship between the size of the farm and rural*

life with reference to the Lower Nile Valley region and the Southeast region of the United States, unpublished M.A. thesis, Chapel Hill, University of North Carolina. viii, 149 pp.

In this thesis Selim reviews briefly the history of land tenure and irrigation in Egypt and presents statistics from Egyptian government sources on number and size of farms and on land ownership. He discusses factors affecting farm size and outlines social class divisions, chiefly according to land ownership, although supplementary social characteristics are also mentioned.

1950 *Planned rural community for the Nile Valley*, unpublished Ph.D. thesis, Chapel Hill, University of North Carolina. v, 310 pp.

While this thesis is primarily concerned with community planning for Egypt, it does contain some information of value to the anthropologist. There are descriptions of village houses, general village layout, and agriculture. The question of social classes is considered, but this, like the cursory discussion of some other aspects of social structure, often appears artificially forced into an American sociological conceptual framework.

Tignor, Robert L.
1966 *Modernization and British colonial rule in Egypt, 1882-1914*, Princeton, N. J., Princeton University Press. xi, 417 pp.

Tignor focuses on government as an instrument of change, arguing that the British administration had, on the whole, a modernizing effect upon Egypt. Modernization is here employed as an analytic tool. Among other things, Tignor shows that the Marxist notion of imperialist and colonialist exploitation is overly simplistic and distortive when applied to Egypt.

Wahba, Raphail
1963 "Cairo," in *The New Metropolis in the Arab World*, Morroe Berger, ed., New Delhi, Allied Publishers, pp. 23-38.

Half of the article is a brief survey of the history of Cairo. The remaining half considers the modern city, its growth, increase in population, and industrialization.

Wakin, Edward
1963 *A lonely minority: the modern story of Egypt's Copts*, New York, William Morrow. ix, 178 pp.; photographs.

This book, written by a journalist who spent some time in Egypt, concentrates on the Copts' role as a minority religious community in Egypt. It is often colored by a highly pro-Coptic bias, but nevertheless contains some interesting observations, especially as it seeks to portray a Coptic view of the Coptic position. Materials are also presented on the internal problems and politics of the Church and on contrasts between Muslims and Copts.

Walker, John
1934　*Folk medicine in modern Egypt, being the relevant parts of the Tibb al-Rukka or Old Wives Medicine of 'Abd al-Rahmān Ismā'īl*, London, Luzac. 128 pp.; illus.

This is a translation by Walker of those parts of the *Tibb al-Rukka* which deal with magical and related cures and the conception of disease by the unsophisticated. There is also material on the various kinds of curers.

Warriner, Doreen
1962　*Land reform and development in the Middle East: a study of Egypt, Syria and Iraq*, 2d ed., London, Oxford University Press, under the auspices of the Royal Institute of International Affairs. xii, 238 pp.; tables, maps.

Although this entire volume is eminently relevant to any discussion of the Arab world, Chapter I, the short Conclusion, and the longer Postscript are concerned with Egypt. There is a review of the nature of land tenure in Egypt prior to the Revolution, particularly in relationship to problems of population and agricultural productivity. This is followed by a description and analysis of the land reform program initiated by the Abd Al Nasser regime. In addition, there is a brief description of the Liberation Province experiment.

Winkler, Hans Alexander
1934　*Bauern Zwischen Wasser und Wüste; Volkskundliches aus dem Dorfe Kiman in Oberagypten*, Stuttgart, Verlag von W. Kohlhammer. xi, 214 pp.; illus.

This ethnographic study is based on two months' residence in the village of Kiman, between Qena and Luxor, and in the vicinity of Gift (Koptos) during the Spring of 1932. A German-speaking villager was Winkler's chief informant and interpreter. The usual ethnographic categories are covered, although only scant attention is paid to political and kinship structure, and religion and social stratification are neglected. Since Winkler's main interest is folkloric, about a quarter of the work describes games and records various types of folk songs. A large part of the remaining portions deal with technology and economics. One chapter records the *Weltbild* of his chief peasant informant, in which the latter's history of the world is recorded.

2. SUDAN

Anderson, J. N. D.
1950 "Recent developments in *Shari'a* law in the Sudan," *Sudan Notes and Records 31*: 82-104.

After presenting some background data on Muslim law, Anderson considers the modern movement for Sharī'a reform in Egypt. He then deals with the extent to which this movement has been effective in the northern Sudan, particularly as compared to Egypt. Finally, he makes suggestions about possible future developments.

Asad, Talal
1964 "Seasonal movements of the Kababish Arabs of Northern Kordofan," *Sudan Notes and Records 45*: 48-58.

1970 *The Kababish Arabs: power, authority and consent in a nomadic tribe*, London, C. Hurst.

Barbour, Kenneth M.
1961 *The Republic of the Sudan; a regional geography*, London, University of London Press. 292 pp.; illus., maps, diagrams, tables.

This lecturer in geography at the University College in London describes the physical geography of the Sudan and then turns to a consideration of its human geography. Finally, he deals with the specific regions within the country. Much of the material presented summarizes the 1956 census of the Sudan.

1964 "North and south in the Sudan: a study in human contrasts," *Annals of the Association of American Geographers 54, 2*: 209-26. Maps, tables.

Uses the 1955/56 census of Sudan to show the wide contrast between the northern six and southern three provinces of Sudan, particularly in regard to birth rates, reproduction rates, death rates, and infant mortality.

Barclay, Harold B.
1963 "A Sudanese religious brotherhood: Al-Ṭarīqa Al-Hindīya," *Muslim World 53*: 127-37.

The history, organization, and ritual of the Hindīya Tarīqa of the Sudan are described, and the *tarīqa* is contrasted with the more ecstatic brotherhoods.

1964 *Buurri al Lamaab, a suburban village in the Sudan*, Ithaca, Cornell University Press. xx, 296 pp.; map, photographs, diagrams, tables.

This work is based on anthropological field research in a village of 2,400 inhabitants on the edge of Khartoum. It covers most of the usual topics of an ethnography, although more attention is focused on the kinship structure and religion than on other topics. The question of cultural change is considered throughout, and an appendix provides a listing of kinship terms.

1965   "Notes on a village in the Jazira area of the Republic of Sudan," *Muslim World 55*: 46-57.

A sketch of the historical background, social strata, and kinship groupings is presented.

Burckhardt, John Lewis
1819   *Travels in Nubia*, London, John Murray. xcii, 543 pp.

Burckhardt, a well-known traveler, presents a useful general picture of Nubia and the Nile area from Aswan to Shendi in the period 1813-14. Data are presented on the crops grown, agricultural systems employed, house types, flora and fauna, dress, women, and slavery. There are descriptions of the various riverain towns through which the author passed. (Reprinted in 1968, London, Gregg.)

Crowfoot, J. W.
1918   "Customs of the Rubātāb," *Sudan Notes and Records 1*: 118-34.

Crowfoot, a frequent contributor to the ethnology of the Arab Sudan, reports data acquired from a Rubātāb *shaykh* on the life cycle, the role of women, household management, the cult of the holy man, marriage, and various rites of passage.

1922   "Wedding customs in the Northern Sudan," *Sudan Notes and Records 5*: 1-28.

This article describes wedding preparations and arrangements and the various rituals of the wedding itself as practiced among the sedentary Arab riverain population of the Northern Province.

Culwick, Geraldine Mary
1951   *Diet in the Gezira irrigated area*, Khartoum, Sudan Survey Department. vii, 228 pp.; map, tables.

In this survey of nutritional problems in the Gezira Scheme area, much of anthropological interest is offered throughout. There is a brief description of village social life, but the focus is on food preparation and processing, consumption habits, and etiquette and other customs associated with eating and drinking. The author obtained most of her information from a year's residence in northern Gezira villages.

Cunnison, Ian
1954 "The Humr and their land," *Sudan Notes and Records 35, part 2:* 50-68.

This article is based on anthropological field research among the Messiriya Humr, a Baggara tribe in southern Kordofan. There is a description of the general social structure, including the tribal organization, subdivisions and segments, with an emphasis on the local encampment.

1960 "The Omda," in *In the Company of Men: Twenty Portraits by Anthropologists*, Joseph B. Casagrande, ed., New York, Harper and Bros., pp. 309-31.

Again drawing on his rather lengthy field experience with the Messirīya Humr, Cunnison portrays an *'umda* of one of the tribe's sections. The main theme concerns the struggle of the *'umda* through the course of a year to maintain his position and protect himself against his opponents. Material on Baggara attitudes and values and men's and women's activities is also presented.

1966 *Baggara Arabs: power and the lineage in a Sudanese nomad tribe*, Oxford, Clarendon Press. xiv, 236 pp.; maps, photographs, diagrams.

This is the first extensive social anthropological account of an Arab nomad tribe of cattle pastoralists or Baggara. Cunnison undertook extensive field work among the Humr of southwestern Kordofan Province between 1952 and 1955. The first quarter of the book is concerned with an ecological description: the role of cattle in the tribe, migratory patterns or cycles, general land use, the household, and the nomad encampment. In line with its major theme, the remainder of the book deals with the lineage and tribal structure and marriage patterns as they relate to the distribution of power and in light of the ecological background. Details of a blood feud, blood-money transaction, and peacemaking are presented.

Hamilton, J. A. DeC.
1935 *The Anglo-Egyptian Sudan from within*, London, Faber and Faber. 307 pp.

Most relevant to the anthropologist in this collection of essays by various authorities on the Sudan are J. A. Reid on the Arab camel nomads, W. D. C. L. Purves' social survey of the Northern Province, S. Hillelson's article on religion, and L. F. Nalder's article on folklore and fable. Other articles concern the Beja, the Baggara, and southern Sudanese. Since the book was written with the aim of helping British officials administering the Sudan to understand the Sudanese, much of the material presented is of a superficial nature.

Ḥasan, Yūsuf Faḍl
1967   *The Arabs and the Sudan: from the seventh to the early sixteenth century*, Edinburgh, Edinburgh University Press.

Herzog, Rolf
1957   *Die Nubier*, Deutsche Akademie der Wissenschaften zu Berlin Volkskundliche Forschungen, Band 2, Berlin, Akademie-Verlag. 218 pp.; map, illus.

Die Nubier is one of the few ethnological studies of the Nubians. It is primarily concerned with culture historical problems, about a quarter of the book being devoted to the question of Nubian origins. Nubian speech and dialects, social organization, agriculture and economy, and some of the more recent factors of culture change are discussed. Kinship and family are given only cursory attention, and religion and magic are hardly mentioned. The anthropologist interested in Nubian social organization will find the work disappointing. Herzog depends on extensive use of secondary sources and observations on two trips to Nubia, each of less than two months' duration. A twenty-four-page bibliography would appear to present a near exhaustive listing of Nubian materials.

Hill, L. G.
1968   "Hababin village economy," *Sudan Notes and Records 49*: 58-70. Map.

Hill describes the basic economic systems of a small Arab tribe in northern Kordofan. Probably of chief interest is the brief discussion of gum Arabic collecting. The article also indicates why, from an economic point of view, Hababin prefer animal husbandry.

Hill, Richard L.
1939   *A bibliography of the Anglo-Egyptian Sudan, from the earliest times to 1937*, London, Oxford University Press, Humphrey Milford. xii, 213 pp.

The bibliography is divided into several major parts, of which those of interest to the anthropologist are agriculture, anthropology, archeology, economy, geography, health, history, language, law, religion, and sociology. Unhappily the entries are not annotated. Hill's bibliography, along with el Nasri's bibliography (1962) and the survey appearing in each issue of *Sudan Notes and Records* since 1937, provide a most exhaustive listing of publications on the Sudan.

Hillelson, S.

1935   *Sudan Arabic texts, with translation and glossary*, Cambridge, University Press. xxiv, 218 pp.

In the introduction, Hillelson, long a member of the Sudan Civil Service, discusses the phonology and grammar of Sudanese Arabic. The remainder of the book comprises sample riddles, folk tales, anecdotes, nursery rhymes, verse, and prophecies collected from various parts of the Northern Province, Gezira, and Kordofan. Each item, where in colloquial speech, is presented in transliterated Arabic and accompanying translations. There are, also, examples of literary Sudanese Arabic. The texts, thus, demonstrate dialectical variations in Arabic over the country as well as the variety of literary expression, while at the same time they provide much data on the life-ways and thoughts of the Sudanese Arabs.

Kennedy, John G.

1967a   "Mushahara: a Nubian concept of supernatural danger and the theory of taboo," *American Anthropologist 69, 6*: 685-702.

Mushahara refers to the supernatural dangers which threaten an individual, particularly at periods of such crises as pregnancy and childbirth. Kennedy describes *Mushahara* beliefs and rituals among the Kanuz Nubians of Aswan Province, Egypt. He suggests that Freudian, evolutionary, and functionalist explanations of taboo are all helpful in explaining *Mushahara*, but, nevertheless, leave something to be desired. He then attempts to further clarify taboo theory.

1967b   "Nubian Zar ceremonies as psychotherapy," *Human Organization 26, 4*: 185-194.

As in the above article, Kennedy again presents results from researches among Egyptian Nubians during 1963-65. He outlines the theory and purpose of the Zar, describes the Zar ceremony, and seeks to account for its effectiveness in treatment. He seems to be unaware of the several previous studies of the Zar cult.

Kronenberg, Andreas, and Waltraud Kronenberg

1963   "Preliminary report on anthropological field-work 1961-62 in Sudanese Nubia," *Kush 11*: 302-11.

1964   "Preliminary report on anthropology field-work in Sudanese Nubia, 1962-63," *Kush 12*: 282-90.

1965a   "Preliminary report on the anthropological field-work in Sudanese Nubia, 1964," *Kush 13*: 205-12.

1965b "Parallel cousin marriage in mediaeval and modern Nubia, Part 1," *Kush 13*: 241-60.

1965c "Die Bevölkerung im Stauseegebiet Sudanesisch-Nubiens," *Paideuma 11*: 119-24.

These several reports are the results of research conducted intermittently between 1961-64 in the lower part of Sudanese Nubia by the Austrian anthropologists, A. and W. Kronenberg, under the sponsorship of the Sudan Antiquities Service. The reports provide brief summaries of lineage and other kinship groupings, locality groupings, land tenure, preferred marriage, problems of migration, and voluntary associations of Nubians in cities. Cultural historical questions relevant to Nubia are also considered. The article in the journal *Paideuma* is a summary in German of the materials published in the *Kush* articles.

Lampen, G. D.

1933 "The Baggara tribes of Darfur," *Sudan Notes and Records 16*: 97-118.

While dealing with Baggara tribes considerably removed from the Nile Valley, this article is germane to any consideration of the Baggara people. It briefly reviews locality groupings, economic activities, home life, and marriage. Of particular interest is the brief description of the Baramba society, a somewhat unique example of a voluntary association within a nomadic pastoral society.

Lebon, John H. G.

1965 *Land use in the Sudan*, The World Land Use Survey (Monograph 4), Geographical Publications Ltd., Bude, Cornwall. xiii, 191 pp.; illus., maps, diagrams, tables.

The British geographer, Lebon, has presented a worthy sequel to Tothill's *Agriculture in the Sudan* and Barbour's *The Republic of Sudan: A Regional Geography*. The first third of the book reviews the usual physical geographical topics. The major part of the work discusses land use according to eight land use types and concludes with a summary of the Sudan's major problems in this area. There is a good summary of the patterns of nomadic movement.

MacMichael, Harold A.

1912 *The tribes of northern and central Kordofan*, Cambridge, University Press. xvi, 259 pp.; illus., map.

MacMichael has here written a general history of northern and central Kordofan, emphasizing the period since 1821. The various Arab tribes are dealt with, as are the non-Arab peoples of the region. Aside from the historical account, little ethnographic information is presented. Furthermore, much of the material in this work is apparently later incorporated into MacMichael's *A History of the Arabs in the Sudan*. (Reprinted in 1967, London, Cass; New York, Barnes and Noble.)

1922   *A history of the Arabs in the Sudan*, Cambridge, University Press, 2 vols. Vol. 1: xxii, 347 pp.; vol. 2: viii, 488 pp.; map.

MacMichael's study is of fundamental importance to the student of the ethnology of the Northern Sudan. It is far more than an ordinary history of the Arabs in the Sudan, since it includes a rather extensive treatment of the non-Arab groups of the Northern Sudan, a history of Arab movements throughout that country, and descriptions of the background and relationships of the various Sudanese Arab tribes. Volume Two presents translations of several native manuscripts which are chiefly genealogical in nature. There is also a native historian's account of the Fung kingdom and the Turkish rule and extensive extracts from the *Tabakāt wad Dayfulla*, a book of biographies of the Sudanese Muslim saints. (Reprinted in 1967, New York, Barnes and Noble.)

el Nasri, Abdel Rahman

1962   *A bibliography of the Sudan, 1938-1958*, London, Oxford University Press, on behalf of the University of Khartoum. x, 171 pp.

This bibliography continues, up to 1958, Hill's *Bibliography of the Anglo-Egyptian Sudan from the Earliest Times to 1937*.

Philosophical Society of Sudan

1958   *The population of Sudan*, Philosophical Society of Sudan, Khartoum. 96 pp.; maps, illus.

The Population of Sudan is a collection of papers dealing with different population problems and drawing on data provided by the 1955-56 census of Sudan. Of particular interest to the anthropologist are K. J. Krotki, "Demographic Survey of Sudan," R. A. Henin, "Modes of Living in the Sudan" (urban, rural sedentary, and rural nomadic), H. E. Wachter, "Size of Households in Sudan," D. B. Climenhaga, "Seasonal Migration and Tribal Nomadic Movements in the Sudan," and J. H. G. Lebon, "Population Distribution and Land Use in Sudan."

Randell, John R.

1958   "El Gedid—a Blue Nile Gezira village," *Sudan Notes and Records 39*: 25-39. Illus.

The primary focus of this article is geographical. Randell concentrates on a description of the physical setting of the village, its history, and some recent developments.

1966   "Patterns of settlement in the Manaqil Extension to the Sudan Gezira Scheme," *Sudan Notes and Records 47*: 88-103. Maps, figure.

Randell, of the Geography Department at the University of Khartoum, discusses fundamental changes in distribution of population and settlement patterns resulting from the introduction of irrigation into the Manaqil area. Among other things, irrigation resulted in the expansion of population into the unpopulated southern part of the Manaqil and provoked the growth of "micro-urban" settlements. The article describes historical background, original settlement patterns, house type, water supply, and recent settlement pattern.

Seligman, C. G., and B. Z. Seligman
1918   "The Kababish, a Sudan Arab tribe," in *Harvard African Studies 2*; *Varia Africana 2*: 105-85. Map, illus.

"The Kababish" is a result of ethnographic research conducted in the winter of 1911-12 for the Sudan government and is one of the very few ethnographic reports on an Arab camel nomad people in the Sudan. Its brevity makes it rather superficial in coverage, but data are presented on tribal organization, clientship, slavery, blood revenge, tribal movement, marriage and kinship, inheritance, technology, warfare, songs, and legends.

Sudan, Republic of,
1957-58   *First population census of Sudan 1955/56*, Khartoum, Minister of Social Affairs, Population Census Office.

The first census of the Sudan has been issued in nine interim reports. The census data, presented according to "census areas," provide statistics for age, sex, language spoken in the home, highest school attended, tribe, nationality, main occupation, marital status, number of wives, crude birth and death rates, number of children of females past child bearing. Except for places classed as towns, the census was obtained by sampling techniques. The interim reports are rather awkward to use, in that the census areas are not grouped systematically. Thus, the fourth report concerns twelve census districts scattered over seven of the nine provinces. The ninth report is a summary according to province, and another report gives total population with a sex breakdown for *'umudivas*. In the tribal census, the classification of Arab tribes is not too helpful.

El Tayib, Abdulla
1955-56   "The changing customs of the riverain Sudan," *Sudan Notes and Records 36*: 146-58; *37*: 56-69.

El Tayib, a Sudanese member of the faculty of the University of Khartoum, here seeks to record what he believes are the fast-disappearing customs of the riverain Arabs of the Northern Province. In the first part, published in the 1955 issue of *Sudan Notes and Records*, he describes birth and the accompanying magical-religious rites, recording folk sayings, incantations, etc. In the second part, published in 1956, he reports on rituals surrounding the hair and the milk teeth of the child. There is a brief note on scarification, but the bulk of his article describes games and records folk stories.

Tothill, John D., ed.
1948   *Agriculture in the Sudan*, London, Oxford University Press. xviii, 974 pp.; illus., maps.

This important work includes the contributions of several British authorities on agriculture in the Sudan. Various topics related to agriculture, such as animal husbandry, vegetation, geology, crops, etc., are considered and the agriculture of each province is then investigated separately. There is, therefore, detailed information on agricultural systems, government and private irrigation schemes, technology, animal husbandry, and land tenure systems, in addition to scattered bits of additional cultural information about the peoples of the area. The historical background of Sudanese agriculture and its connections with that of Egypt are surveyed.

Trimingham, John Spencer
1949   *Islam in the Sudan*, London, Oxford University Press. x, 280 pp.; map.

Canon Trimingham, Anglican missionary in Sudan for a number of years, has undoubtedly written one of the most useful single books on the Northern Sudan for the anthropologist. There is a general outline of the culture of the sedentary Arab population and some remarks on the Baggara and the Beja. The body of the volume, of course, concerns Islam: the traditional system of orthodox Islam, the modern organization of the 'ulama, festivals, the cult of saints, the Mahdīya and Mahdist movement, the tarīqas, and the animistic influences in Sudanese Islam. (Reprinted in 1968, London, Cass; New York, Barnes and Noble.)

Wilmington, Martin W.
1955 "Aspects of moneylending in Northern Sudan," *Middle East Journal 9*: 139-46.

Wilmington discusses means by which merchants and landowners make loans to farmers in the form of advances against the next crop. He points out the numerous services which are actually extended to the borrower by lenders.

Zenkovsky, Sophie
1945 "Marriage customs in Omdurman," *Sudan Notes and Records 26*: 241-55.

Zenkovsky describes the numerous rituals performed by Arab women in connection with preparation for marriage and the actual wedding in Sudan's largest city.

1949 "Customs of the women of Omdurman," *Sudan Notes and Records 30*: 39-46.

In this article, Zenkovsky deals with pregnancy, childbirth, and early child care, focusing on the magico-religious rites associated with Omdurman Arab women at these times.

1950 *"Zar* and *Tambura* as practiced by the women of Omdurman," *Sudan Notes and Records 31*: 65-81. Illus.

The Zar ceremony as performed in Omdurman is outlined. Two types are reported: the "Zar Bori" and the "Tambura." Installation of the *shaykha* or Zar priestess, yearly sacrifice, and celebration of the *mawlid* are also described.

OTHER REFERENCES

Encyclopaedia Britannica, Inc.
1966 *Britannica World Atlas International*, New York, Praeger.

Harrell, Richard S.
1957 *The phonology of colloquial Egyptian Arabic*, New York, Program in Oriental Languages, Publications Series B, Aids No. 9, American Council of Learned Societies. 90 pp.

Ḥasan, Yūsuf Faḍl
1967 *The Arabs and the Sudan: from the seventh to the early sixteenth century*, Edinburgh, University Press. v, 298 pp.

Henin, Roushdi A.
1966 "A Re-estimation of the nomadic population of the six Northern provinces," *Sudan Notes and Records 47*: 145-47.

Lubac, Henri de
  1948   *The un-Marxian socialist: a study of Proudhon*, London, Sheed & Ward.

Nieuwenhuijze, C. A. O. van
  1965   *Social stratification and the Middle East. An interpretation*, Leiden, E. J. Brill. viii, 84 pp.

Patai, Raphael
  1962   *Golden river to golden road*, Philadelphia, University of Pennsylvania Press.

Rapaport, Anatol
  1967   "Have the intellectuals a class interest?" *Our Generation 5*: 31-49.

Reid, J. A.
  1930   "Some notes on the tribes of the White Nile Province," *Sudan Notes and Records 13*: 149-209.

Statistical Handbook of the United Arab Republic, 1962-65
  1966   Cairo, Central Agency for Public Mobilization and Statistics.

Stirling, A. Paul
  1960   "A death and a youth club: feuding in a Turkish village," *Anthropological Quarterly 33*: 51-75.

CHAPTER 2

The Arab Levant*

JOHN GULICK

Introduction

The Arab Levant consists of the western and northwestern agricultural areas of Syria, of the "west bank" and "east bank": the hilly regions of Jordan, and Lebanon in its entirety. In other words, it constitutes most of the western part of the Fertile Crescent, which for several millennia has been ecologically characterized by agricultural villages and commercial towns and cities. After the Islamic conquest in the seventh century A.D., the population of the area became almost entirely Arabic-speaking. Hence the term "Arab" Levant.

If this chapter were being written twenty years ago, the territory of what is now Israel north of Beersheba would also be included in the Arab Levant, although the Negeb, being nonagricultural, would not have been included. The former area would have been described as inhabited primarily by Arab villagers and town- and city-dwellers, plus a much

*This chapter was planned, and most of it was written, in 1960. Its topical structure is not entirely what the author would have preferred, but it was adopted in conformance with the requirements of the original project of which the chapter was only one part.

In 1961 and 1963, a few small revisions were made in the text, and several new items were added to the annotated bibliography. In fact, substantive material is included in some of the annotations which does not appear in the text. The text and the bulk of the bibliography were typed in 1963, and the opinions of the author expressed therein reflect his thinking in 1963. They may subsequently have been modified.

The Addendum, pp. 135-36, brings the chapter up to date as of October 1967. It does not attempt directly or systematically to revise any material in the main text.

smaller number of seasonally migrant Arab herders, plus a relatively small number of urban and farming enclaves of European Jews. The almost complete dislocation of Arabs from, and eradication of Arab culture in, the territory of western Palestine that accompanied the establishment of Israel has virtually reversed the situation, there now being only relatively small Arab remnants in the area. Consequently, "Arab Palestine" cannot be formally included in our consideration of the Arab Levant. References will be made from time to time, however, to earlier studies in Arab Palestine and to more recent studies of Arabs in Israel when they seem relevant to matters concerning the Arab Levant generally. Our description of the natural habitat of the area will include the territory of Israel.

If this chapter were being written a hundred years ago, much of the eastern border of the Arab Levant would have been located further west than it is now. This shift would have been particularly noticeable in the "east bank" area of Jordan and on the northern plains of Syria. During the past century and more, there has been a steady expansion of agricultural settlements in these areas, and therefore, by definition, an expansion of the Arab Levant eastward. As we shall see, however, this "border" can hardly be conceived of as a sharp, arbitrary line like the political borders of Israel. Much of the agricultural expansion has been accomplished by the sedentarization, in part or in whole, of nomadic tribes of herders. Although there is a considerable amount of literature on the nomadic tribes as such, we shall not consider them as social groups, but only insofar as sedentarization and desert fringe herding are relevant to the predominantly agricultural Arab Levant. Consideration of nomadic culture, as it has occurred in the Negeb and in eastern Jordan and Syria, can more appropriately be encompassed in consideration of the Arabian Peninsula (see Chapter 4 on the Arabian Peninsula).

The Syrian Jezirah has also been undergoing agricultural settlement, but we shall not consider this, since the Jezirah can more appropriately be included in the Mesopotamian area.

In the northern frontier region of Syria, Turkish cultural influences become increasingly strong. We shall take note of these, as well as some other non-Arab cultural influences there, since the fact is that this is a region of transition from one culture area to another, which is only rather arbitrarily indicated by the existence of national boundaries. By the same token, we shall give some consideration to the territory of Alexandretta, even though it was ceded to Turkey in 1938.

Small in size, the Arab Levant has one of the longest recorded histories of any area in the world. It is a history which has often had momentous effects on other areas, and it is, in an entirely functional sense, a part of the present-day culture of the area itself—as the Zionists' claim to the territory of Palestine plainly attests. The anthropologist must take cognizance of this aspect of Levantine culture, and he will often have difficulty in assessing the limits of necessity in this connection. Indeed, the sociocultural anthropologist, a newcomer in the scholarly world generally, is most particularly so in regard to the Arab Levant, which has long been an area of highly specialized interest to historians, archeologists, theologians, and linguists of various kinds and is also of major interest to certain economists and political scientists. Most of these scholars are likely to remain more expert in certain aspects of Levantine culture than the anthropologist is likely to become. These are humbling facts, which may partly account for the rather small number of anthropologists who have attempted, and are now attempting, to do field work in the area.

Of the vast amount of scholarly literature on the Arab Levant, relatively little has a frame of reference which is directly useful to the anthropologist, and the bulk of this anthropologically relevant material was not produced by professional anthropologists. Yet this material constitutes "the anthropology of the Arab Levant," and an adequate review and assessment of the latter should include attention to the nature of the source material as such as well as to its content. While the annotated bibliography at the end of this chapter is intended to serve this function, its itemized nature tends to diffuse certain general points to such a degree that they may become invisible. These points will, therefore, be stated here at the outset of the chapter.

With some exceptions, the anthropologically relevant source materials on the Arab Levant tend to fall into three general categories which, in roughly chronological order, are as follows:

(1) Works whose authors were primarily interested in finding in the contemporary culture of the area traits which are parallel to, or apparently identical with, those mentioned in the Old or New Testaments;

(2) Works whose author's interests were pragmatically related to the political and economic policies of the French Mandatory regime in Syria and Lebanon and the British one in Palestine and Transjordan;

(3) Works by North American, and some British, sociologists, psychologists, anthropologists, and other behaviorally-oriented social scientists.

The studies that were carried out in the Biblical tradition date from the latter part of the nineteenth century and were mostly made before World War I. This literature is quite extensive, and much of it is travelogue and not particularly useful. However, it also includes some of the major classics of the area, notably the works of Dalman, Jaussen,

Musil, and von Oppenheim. In the same tradition and of comparable scale, but dating from the early Mandate period, is the four-volume village study by Hilma Granqvist. These works focus their attention on what is now Israel and Jordan, though some of them also range more widely. They are conspicuous for their thorough and meticulous attention to ethnographic detail, much of which is presented to the accompaniment of Biblical citations. A considerable amount of this material was not published until some time after the studies were made, as for example in the cases of Dalman, Granqvist, and von Oppenheim.

Under the aegis of the French Mandate of Syria and Lebanon, two important types of study were produced. One is a series of studies in human geography which pay particular attention to such ecological matters as the distribution of water, land use and land tenure, and to some extent settlement patterns. Perhaps their major limitation from the anthropological point of view is that they consist of topical surveys of the region, supported by specific examples, to be sure, but lacking in the intensive analysis of more limited horizons that so often is particularly useful to anthropologists. Having accepted this limitation, one can, however, readily perceive that these works of Weulersse, Latron, Thoumin, and others have great relevance to the anthropology of the area. The other French series consists of ethnographic studies of "special" peoples and of urban communities in the region. Primary data on such groups as the 'Alawites, Druzes, and Yazidis, for example, are provided by them. Besides being scholarly works per se, these studies reflect the political concern that France had with the ecological potential and the cultural heterogeneity of its Mandated territory.

The British Mandate of what was then Palestine and Transjordan produced socioeconomic surveys which provided some of the most reliable quantitative materials on land tenure and population for the entire region, but they are now almost entirely obsolete. Also produced under the British Mandate was a series of studies by such authors as Ashkenazi, Epstein, Patai, and Shim'onī. Recurrent in these studies are such subjects as the political organization of Arab Palestine, the relative degrees of stability of the nomadic and seminomadic tribes of Palestine and Transjordan, the question of the extent to which the sedentary Arab populations of Palestine and Transjordan at that time were of relatively recent nomadic origin, the potentialities of various parts of the Arab Levant for intensified agricultural settlement, and the cultural relationships between the Jewish and Arab sectors of the population of the Mandate. While clearly related to some of the issues of concern to the Zionist movement, these studies contain a wealth of ethnographic and ethnological material.

The studies by American and British behavioral scientists include some which were made in the 1920s, but most of them have been made since the end of World War II. Notable among them are several anthropological village studies, sociological and social psychological surveys of various kinds, and one study of personality-in-culture. For various reasons, most of this research has been done in Lebanon, but important work has also been done in Syria, and research is currently being carried out in Jordan. Much of this work is descriptive, and necessarily so. While in some cases the descriptive material is presented in terms of theoretical models which have been developed from research in other culture areas, there has been, so far, very little testing of hypotheses. Serious gaps in descriptive material remain, and they need to be filled by strategically placed field studies. In the opinion of the author of this chapter, the situation is also ripe for studies whose purpose would be to test, or at least to explore, certain functional hypotheses of general applicability as well as relevance to the Arab Levant itself.

Since the foundations of the anthropology of the Arab Levant are well, though not completely, represented in the above corpus of literature, certain difficulties in the survey of the subject become readily apparent. One is that the "ethnographic present" spans a period from early in the twentieth century to the present. Another is that the various significant contexts of the subject—Lebanon, Syria, Jordan, Arab Palestine, villagers, city dwellers, herders, "special ethnic" groups, and the various analytic elements of culture (e.g. kinship organization, community organization, culture-in-personality, etc.)—are not by any means given equivalent attention throughout this period. Instead, we have to put together, for example, an analysis of culture-in-personality in a particular village at a particular time, a survey of land tenure practices in a subregion at another time, or an analysis of the relationships between particular farmers and particular herders at a certain time (when the main body of material about the herders as such dates from a considerably earlier period), and so on.

Still another difficulty is the fact that the period during which these varied and specialized studies were made has been one of momentous cultural changes in the area, changes which are documented largely in terms of economics, politics, and demography, rather than anthropology. Consequently, although we can be sure, for example, that the city of Nablus of today is very different from the Nablus of the 1920s, when Jaussen described it, we cannot describe the present city in comparable terms because no comparable present study exists. Is Jaussen's study therefore to be ignored because it is partly out of date? The same question could be asked in regard to all the other anthropologically relevant studies that were made not so recently in the Arab Levant. A consistent affirmative answer would result either in obviating the writing of much of this chapter or in tediously couching nearly every paragraph of it in terms of provisos concerning discontinuities in time and place.

Fortunately, these difficulties are somewhat reduced by two facts: First, the earliest studies tend to concentrate upon tribal nomadic groups as such and upon Arab Palestine, both of which are, for different reasons, peripheral to our primary concerns. Second, several of the most recent studies in themselves take cognizance of various trends in culture change, and so this subject can be incorporated at appropriate points in our presentation.

The sections which follow will, insofar as is possible given the facts considered above, outline the anthropology of the Arab Levant as it is at the present time. Serious gaps in knowledge will be indicated primarily in terms of research which needs to be done.

Habitat

The anthropologist's contention that the natural habitat of a culture must often be the base line upon which other levels of analysis are founded could hardly be better supported than by the case of the Arab Levant. Many aspects of Arab Levantine culture, including historical events, cannot be adequately comprehended unless the habitat is taken into account. The topographical and climatological features of the area are, for anthropological purposes, rather simple in outline, and yet cultural features of considerable complexity are, in part, elucidated by an understanding of them. It should be noted at the outset that certain effects of thousands of years of human occupation, notably soil erosion, are for the present-day inhabitants virtually as much a part of the natural environment as are such features as mountains and rainfall. The location of this habitat—constituting as it does a juncture between northeastern Africa, Asia Minor, the Arabian Peninsula, and Mesopotamia—is another characteristic to which there have been highly significant cultural adaptations.

From Aqaba in the south to Alexandretta in the north extend two roughly parallel ribbons of plateaus, hills, and mountains, which are separated from each other by a series of narrow valleys. Between the western chain of highlands and the Mediterranean Sea runs an intermittent coastal plain, which in two places (the Plain of Esdraelon in northern Israel and the Plain of Akkar, which is divided between northern Lebanon and Syria) extends eastward sufficiently to give access to the interhighland valley system. In other places (especially in the north), it is so narrow as to be interrupted by mountainous spurs which are washed by the sea. From the eastern highlands, relatively level plains extend eastward to the Euphrates and southeastward into the Arabian Peninsula. The elevations of the two highland systems and of the valley system between them vary greatly in relation to sea level and in relation to each other in east-west profile.

From May through October, there is almost no precipitation whatever in the Arab Levant. From November through April, moisture-laden westerly winds prevail across the Mediterranean; condensation is particularly great in the cold upper elevations of the western highlands, and precipitation there is heavy. The storm tracks are such that moisture is more abundant in the northern half of the region than in the southern.

Precipitation abruptly decreases immediately east of the western highlands and, except in a few locations where the eastern highlands to some extent increase it, it decreases steadily from there to a minimum point in the interior plains. The latter are desertic, or at best semidesertic, and these conditions extend to some degree into portions of the interhighland valley system. The zone in which annual rainfall averages between 10 to 15 inches is the zone in which agriculture and pastoralism as basic subsistence technologies are in particularly unstable balance. It is, therefore, in this zone that cultural configurations begin to shift from those of the Arab Levant to those of the desert.

Some of the features of the above outline must now be examined in greater detail. While the same geological rift system runs from Aqaba to Mount Hermon, visible evidence of it is not noticeable until some miles south of the Dead Sea. In general, the Negeb is a plateau averaging in elevation from 1,000 to 2,000 feet above sea level. Rainfall is minimal, and the area is essentially desertic. The interhighland valley system of the Arab Levant begins south of the Dead Sea, where the elevation drops from over 1,000 feet above sea level to 1,300 feet below sea level at the shore line of the Dead Sea. Simultaneously, the highlands of Judaea and Samaria to the west and of the Kingdom of Jordan to the east rise to an average of 3,000 feet above sea level. While the highlands receive a relatively great amount of rain, the valley receives very little, and summer temperatures there are especially high. The drainage of the highlands of Judaea and Samaria flows westward, both above and below ground, contributing to the relatively great amount of moisture in the adjoining coastal plain, which was, in fact, created by the alluvial deposits of this drainage. The eastern highlands also generally drain westward, as, for example, in the case of the Yarmouk River, which feeds the Jordan. The Jordan is initially created by run-off from the Sea of Galilee, whose surface is 686 feet below sea level. The Sea of Galilee is, in turn, fed by the southward run-off from Mount Hermon and the adjacent northward highlands, where precipitation is quite heavy.

This sector of the interhighland valley system—the "Jordan Trough" —is thus a paradoxical region. Though it receives very little rainfall, it contains large bodies of water which derive from exotic sources. These bodies of water are landlocked and do not, in turn, provide water for any other region. The Jordan Trough is, in effect, a vast sump into which large amounts of water are poured but from which water escapes only by evaporation. The rate of evaporation is so great that the water of the Dead Sea is too saline to be potable, and the Jordan is flanked on both sides—except on its immediate banks, where there is dense tropical vegetation—by extensive and sterile mineral flats (the "Ghor").

The highlands that border the Jordan Trough east and west consist primarily of thick layers of limestone and sandstone, as in fact do the highlands of the Arab Levant generally, with one important exception. This exception is the plateau of the Hawran, which fans out east and southeast of the Sea of Galilee. The plateau averages 1,000 to 2,000 feet above sea level except at its point of culmination in the Jabal Druze, which attains 5,000 feet. This is a region of desolate lava flows and volcanic cones, but also of rich volcanic soils. Because of the low elevation of the Plain of Esdraelon and the relatively low elevation of the highlands of Galilee, a considerable amount of windborne winter water passes over these regions and is deposited on the Hawran and the Jabal Druze, which consequently have greater rainfall than the adjacent regions to their north, east, and south.

North of the Plain of Esdraelon and the Sea of Galilee, the elevations of the highland and valley systems rise rapidly. Mount Hermon reaches 9,200 feet above sea level and hence receives a maximum amount of rain and snow even though it is part of the eastern highland system, but the considerably lower Anti-Lebanon Mountains receive far less. Drainage from the Anti-Lebanon Mountains is nevertheless sufficient to contribute water to al-Biqa' (the Lebanese segment of the valley system) and to produce several short rivers, of which the Barada is the most important, which flow eastward into the desert. The transition from the Jordan Trough to al-Biqa' is precipitous, and it has such rough terrain that the valley system is, in effect, interrupted at this point, from which the traveler descends into the Biqa'. The gently undulating floor of al-Biqa' averages 3,000 feet above sea level, and drainage from the valley consists primarily of two rivers, the Orontes flowing north and the Litani flowing south and then sharply west into the sea.

Mount Lebanon is the climax of the highland system of the Arab Levant. It attains 9,000 to 10,000 feet above sea level at two points, and its average elevation is higher than that of any other segment of the region's mountains. It is also the most extensive area of maximal precipitation, both rain and snow depending on the elevation. Like the highlands of Judaea and Samaria, Mount Lebanon's drainage is primarily westward toward the Mediterranean, but because of its greater altitude and precipitation, the effects of its drainage are distinctive. While the western slopes of Samaria are considerably gullied in comparison to those of Judaea, the western slopes of Mount Lebanon exhibit deep gorges cut by the several short rapid streams that flow into the sea. The swiftness of these precipitously falling streams has minimized alluvial deposition, and so the coastal plain is for the most part very narrow. However, between the elevations of 3,000 and 5,000 feet Mount Lebanon has a zone of springs that are created by downward seepage from above, and these have created well-watered pockets of land at high altitudes which do not occur elsewhere. There is considerable subterranean as well as surface drainage, and so the region is one of caves and underground rivers as well as of sheer cliffs and waterfalls.

A geological fault north of Mount Lebanon helps to form the Plain of Akkar, but the western highland system resumes in the form of the Jabal Ansariyah, a rough plateau whose crest has an average elevation of about 4,000 feet. This northernmost segment of the western highland system is matched on the east only by the Jabal Zawia, whose elevation does not exceed 2,000 feet. Between the latter and the Anti-Lebanons, which diminish to nothing in the north, there is no eastern highland system at all, but rather the Plain of Homs, into which the Biqa' opens. The Orontes, however, flows northward, its course cut deep below the surface of the plain, until it reaches the region between the Jabal Ansariyah and the Jabal Zawia (the Ghab), where swampy conditions prevail. There the river makes a 180-degree westward turn and empties into the sea.

It must not be inferred from any discussion of the drainage of its terrain that the Arab Levant is a moist, humid region. Except in the sense of contrast with the desert, it is quite the contrary. During the long summer, the entire region is hot and dry. After the summer harvest, the cereal-producing plains—such as Sharon, al-Biqa', and the region between Homs and Aleppo—appear to be quite as barren and desiccated as the desert itself. While the temperatures are less in the higher elevations of the mountains, the impression of general desiccation is present here also, accentuated by the prevalence of naked rocky outcrops, marl, and karst, and alleviated only in a minor way by patches of vineyard and orchard. In the lowlands, occasional watercourses and places where water is conserved convey the sense of oases.

It appears to be certain that much of the highland area of the Arab Levant was, in early historic times, covered by a mixed forest of conifers, oaks, and other hardwoods. This natural cover has been completely destroyed—except for a few minuscule groves—by human action. In consequence, there has been massive soil erosion, to which much, though not all, of the rocky outcrop terrain can be attributed. Even the soil that remains tends to be filled with a seemingly inexhaustible supply of small stones. Erosion has been further aggravated by the grazing of sheep and goats throughout the region.

While the location of this habitat is in itself not a cultural datum, the ways in which human beings have taken advantage of it may appropriately be discussed at this point. In brief, the Arab Levant provides a bridge of well-watered and not impassable terrain between the western Mediterranean and Mesopotamia and between Asia Minor and Mesopotamia, on the one hand, and between Egypt and the Arabian Peninsula, on the other. It has therefore been a constant highway for travelers between these latter areas. North-south travelers along the eastern border of the eastern highlands are offered frequent sources of water and no serious natural obstacles. Access from this route to the seacoast is provided in the region of Aleppo, in the Akkar, by the mountain passes between Beirut and Damascus, and in the plain of Esdraelon, whence passage into Egypt through the plain of Sharon is easy. East-west travel across the desert is accommodated at the same points, which, in turn, provide access to the sea. It is for these reasons that there is a series of seaports along the Levantine littoral and another series of inland trading cities and towns along the desert fringe. The highland areas have tended to be bypassed by travelers and conquerors, and yet at the same time they include some of the best watered and most defensible locations in the region. Consequently, they have attracted the settlement of several subcultures, which for various reasons have, at one time or another, been fugitives from social groups more powerful than themselves. In short, the habitat of the Arab Levant has provided various opportunities, responses to which have resulted in subcultures which have tended to be particularly insular and self-contained.

Material Culture: Technology

A. Exploitive

The exploitive technology of the Arab Levant is involved primarily in food production. The area has little in the way of exploitable natural resources. As mentioned earlier, the original timber was long ago exploited to the point of extinction. The existing natural tree growth is largely scrub and is widely used for firewood and charcoal, but is not suitable on a large scale for construction or manufacturing purposes. There are no important mineral resources aside from stone and mud, which are used locally for building purposes. Although the Arab Levant adjoins the largest petroleum reserves in the world, no important discoveries of this nature have been made in the area. There are some inconsequential deposits of asphalt and lignite in Lebanon. The exploitation of phosphates in the Ghor and of potash in various desert locations could be greatly augmented. Salt is extracted in commercial quantities from the sea by means of shallow evaporation pans, which are quite numerous along the seashore.

Of the various means of Levantine food production, fishing has received the least attention. It is, in fact, a quite neglected subject, from the point of view both of technology and of social organization. Although there is some fishing in inland bodies of water—the Sea of Galilee being a classic case in point—most of it would appear to be done in the Mediterranean. Fishing is a specialty of some persons in otherwise agricultural villages along the littoral, and fleets of fishing boats have home ports in each of the seaport towns and cities. The lack of efficient preservation techniques has undoubtedly been one of the limiting factors in this matter. Tinned fish is imported into the Arab Levant from northern Europe and Japan and is a secondary staple item in the diet of many people, especially in the urban and relatively urbanized agricultural areas.

Agriculture, accompanied nearly everywhere by the raising of sheep and goats, is the primary mode of food production. Animal husbandry, aside from the herding of sheep and goats, consists of the custodial care of oxen, camels, and donkeys, which, despite the highly significant recent diffusion of automotive power, are the traditional and still most widely encountered agents of traction and transportation.

Agricultural techniques vary according to the crops involved: wheat and barley; orchards (figs, olives, apricots, and citrus fruits being the most important types) and vineyards; small gardens producing lentils, peas, tomatoes, cucumbers, melons, and potatoes; cotton, apples, bananas, and the silk-producing mulberry, which at various times have been developed primarily as commercial crops. Each of these crops is particularly common in certain, though not all, parts of the Arab Levant, owing in part to the topographic and hydrographic characteristics of the region. This will be considered further in the next section.

Various authors have devoted considerable attention to the farming tool kit, although perhaps Dalman, Mesnil du Buisson, and Thoumin have dealt with the matter in the greatest detail. Standard tools are the wooden plow, with a simple iron share and no mold-board; a spike-har-row; a threshing sledge set with sharp stones; iron hoes, sickles, spades, and pruning shears; wooden rakes and pitchforks; and circular threshing floors of packed earth or flagstones. Descriptions of these items recur from all parts of the region, together with comments that this tool kit is hardly distinguishable from that used in Roman times, if not earlier—a comment which can be extended to mason's and carpenter's tools also. While some Western agricultural experts have cast a jaundiced eye at these unmechanized tools, others have pointed out that the plow, for example, is virtually indispensable in the small, irregularly shaped, ter-raced fields, and that it may also be better adapted than a deep-cutting "modern" plow to use in certain plains areas where only a thin layer of topsoil covers hardpan. Mechanized farming implements—such as tractors and harvesters—have been introduced only in some plains areas, and for the most part they are financed by absentee entrepreneur-landlords who, socioeconomically, are generally considered to be as anachronistic as their capital investments are up to date.

In the highland areas—most especially in Lebanon—terracing is an essential adjunct of farming technology. Terraces create small tiers of level ground in very precipitous topography, in many parts of which farming would otherwise be impossible. Terracing is also a deterrent to further erosion. The vertical walls are made of stone—usually dry-laid—and require considerable skill in construction as well as constant main-tenance.

Although the Arab Levant is generally a dry-farming area, irrigation techniques are employed in some localities where water is particularly abundant but within narrow limits. The Ghoutah of Damascus is un-doubtedly the most extensive of these, and the French human geogra-phers devoted particular attention to the system of canals, sluice gates, and timing devices that are used to guide and apportion the flow of water in this and other smaller oases in Syria. Along the middle course of the Orontes, where the river has cut far below the surface of the plain, water is raised from the former to the latter by containers set in the circumferences of enormous wooden wheels, which are turned by the force of the stream.

Industrial technology has been applied to some extent to the problem of irrigation and water control. Fuel-powered pumps are now used in various regions where—rather ironically—marshy conditions prevail during the winter, and drainage operations are underway in the Ghab. In the Kasmie district of the southern Lebanese littoral, a system of concrete ditches now distributes water to otherwise dry sections between the rivers, and there are some similar canals along the littoral north of

Beirut. However, really large-scale irrigation and hydroelectric power schemes—such as the Litani Project in southern Lebanon and the highly controversial plans for diverting the waters of the Jordan and the Yarmouk—are at present merely schemes for the future. To date, industrial technology has only partially supplemented the traditional irrigation technology; it has certainly not transformed it. Wells, springs, and storage cisterns are still the primary sources of water for human and animal use in most settlements except in some of the larger towns and cities, where water piped under pressure is available.

The technology of herding has been described largely in the literature concerning nomadic tribes of the desert and desert fringe, which are at most only peripherally relevant to the Arab Levant. Sheep and goat herding in the village context varies somewhat in terms of division of labor, and this will be considered later. Sheep and goats are primary sources of meat and milk in the Arab Levant.

B. *Processing*

Food processing. Domestic cooking is now done almost everywhere by means of the kerosene-burning Primus stove, an importation from Sweden, or by gas bottled under pressure. These methods have largely replaced the traditional masonry stove, in which brushwood or charcoal was used as fuel. However, charcoal braziers, which serve as heaters in the chilly winter, are also used for boiling coffee and broiling meat. Boiling, frying, and roasting are the chief applications of heat; baking is employed largely in the making of bread, which is an extremely important part of the diet. In most of the Arab Levant, the discoid "flaps" of bread are made in ovens which are generally operated on a communal basis, though they may be privately owned. However, in some highland districts and among seminomadic peoples, bread is made by applying the dough to a heated hollow hemispherical utensil made of iron (*saj*).

Grain mills and olive presses are very widely distributed on a village basis. Water-power is used where it is available, chiefly in the highlands —otherwise, animal and human energy are used. At the present time, there is a growing tendency to substitute machine-driven mills and presses for the traditional implements.

Food preservation techniques are rudimentary. Perhaps the most important is the fermentation of milk to make *laban* and cheese. Meat is consumed as soon after slaughtering as possible. Relatively imperishable bulk items—like grain, olive oil, and dried peas—are stored in earthenware and basketry containers. Refrigeration plays a noticeable part in food processing only in some sectors of the population of some urban centers.

Cloth and clothing. Spinning and weaving at the domestic level have been eliminated through culture change. The desire on the part of Western European powers to make the Arab Levant a market for their textiles was an important factor in their political interest in the area, and this desire was long ago realized. While some cloth is made commercially in urban centers, most of the cloth that is used (primarily for clothing) in the Arab Levant is imported. It is made up into clothing, however, almost entirely in the Levant.

Neither the economic nor the symbolic aspects of Levantine clothing styles have been adequately analyzed by anyone. The few specialized studies of the subject have been motivated primarily by the desire to record the styles that have been to some extent displaced by European ones, and these are chiefly of descriptive historical interest. The symbolic aspect of the subject is of particular significance to anthropologists, since it is related to attitudes toward group identities and probably also to attitudes toward culture change. In saying that it has not been adequately analyzed, we do not mean that the subject has been ignored, but simply that it has not been given the specialized and extensive study it deserves. A number of observers have made keen observations of some aspects, but these have been ancillary to other interests.

Housing and shelter. With the exception of the plains area south of Aleppo, the basic traditional house style of the Arab Levant is a one-story structure, with one or two rooms and a flat roof of packed earth and clay. On this theme there are a number of regional variations. In the plains areas, mud brick is the predominant material, and the houses often have walled enclosures attached to them. In the highlands, stone is the predominant material, and the houses usually stand alone, without an enclosure. However, where highland houses are built on slopes, as they often are, they may be adjoined by an additional structure whose roof is on the same level as the floor of the main house. This lower structure provides additional storage space and shelter for animals in the winter. Where sufficient timber is available, the earth roof is supported by beams; otherwise, it is supported by masonry arches or vaults.

In the plains south of Aleppo, a number of villages consist of houses whose roofs are conical domes, constructed by an ingenious combination of the corbel and keystone principles. Used singly, the dome limits the size of the room below, but the domes are also built in rows and clusters, thus allowing for more space beneath.

In the Hawran, stone houses with pitched roofs—conveying a startling but fleeting European impression—occur along with the flat-roofed type.

These houses—with their thick walls and either thick or elevated roofs—provide a considerable amount of insulation from summer heat, although the practice of sleeping outdoors under brush shelters in summer is common. In winter, the houses are reasonably snug as long as the roofs are kept in repair. The earth roofs require constant repacking by means of stone rollers. If, for some reason, the roof is not properly maintained, the house itself may fall rather rapidly into ruins, and ruined houses are of commonplace occurrence in the villages of the Arab Levant.

During the two or three decades preceding World War I, another type of house was erected quite widely in the Arab Levant, especially in the western highland areas. This is a multiroom, sometimes two-story, stone house with a hipped or pyramidal roof covered with flat red tiles. Such houses are usually furnished with glazed windows fitted with wooden casements of European design. Pointed arches, either in the tops of the windows or in open arcades, are characteristic embellishments. These houses are frequent and conspicuous enough to be considered "typical" in some sections—especially in Lebanon—but they are outnumbered by the more traditional ones. Reflecting European influences, the building of these houses was accomplished by the introduction of European styles in household furniture, which are now common in households in the western Levant but much less so in the eastern plains.

Details of the construction and design of these various house styles have engaged the attention of the French human geographers in particular.

Since World War I, many of the tile roofs have been replaced by flat concrete roofs, and newer houses with the same basic floor plan and the flat concrete roof are very numerous. The most recent development is the construction of rather modernistic "villas" of southern European design, which depart noticeably from the simple rectilinearity of the older styles. These are very much in the minority except in places where urban influence and affluence are concentrated. The use of concrete has increased tremendously in recent decades, and the manufacture of cement is an industry of growing importance.

The above remarks have been made with villages primarily in mind. With the exception of the earth roof style, the other types of houses occur also in larger towns and cities, but there are still other types of domestic architecture in the urban communities which have not been given very much systematic attention. Studies of urban architecture have tended to concentrate on structures of monumental and/or historic interest, such as mosques, madrasahs, and churches. Sauvaget's study of Aleppo (1941) is a notable example of this.

However, two very recent studies have approached the subject from other points of view. Chéhabe-ed-Din (1960) discusses the present-day architectural patterns of Beirut in terms of human ecology, and Gulick (1963) has given consideration to these same patterns in Tripoli, Lebanon, in terms of community behavior and attitudes.

The erection of multi-storied, modernistic apartment houses in many Levantine cities affords some interesting examples of selective diffusion. While the apartments are often very spacious by North American standards and are furnished with electricity and plumbing fixtures, screens are rare, despite the prevalence of flies. Central heating is also rare, and in the winter, rooms are often heated by means of traditional charcoal braziers or imported kerosene heaters. Much hand labor is involved in the construction of these buildings.

Crafts. Not very much attention has been paid to the technological aspects of utilitarian crafts in the Arab Levant, although Bazantay's study (1936) of artisans in Antioch and Crowfoot's study (1941) of weaving techniques are important contributions. Chief among them are: tailoring, cabinet work and furniture making, sheet-metal work, shoemaking and leather work, and pottery making. These crafts are concentrated in the bazaar, or suq, areas of the towns and cities, and it is primarily in this context that they have been considered. The products of these crafts compete with ready-made importations, but the prices of the latter are generally prohibitive for many people in the area.

Social Organization: Economic Structure

The Arab Levant is an area of village-based food production and of goods processed in towns and cities whose populations are fed by village products. Production, distribution, and consumption in the area can hardly be considered seriatim, but rather in multiple interrelationships with each other. This economic structure has existed for a long time, and while entrepreneurs have also been active in the area for a long time, the problems of capital formation in the modern industrial sense are only beginning to be felt indigenously.

Wheat and barley are grown—sometimes in both winter and summer crops—chiefly in the open plains and in the more extensive valleys. While they are to some extent grown in the highland areas, as crops they are usually secondary to orchard and vineyard products, and these grains must be imported in order to feed the highland population. On the national level, this means, for example, that Syria can export wheat while Lebanon must import it. On the whole, the grains and the orchard and vineyard products are produced by the individual farmer in surplus over and beyond his own needs of subsistence, but the means and conditions of distribution vary.

Olives, grapes and figs, and other fruits, when they are not eaten in the natural state, are transformed into oil, "preserves" of various kinds, and (among Christians) wine. To some extent, the farmer may sell such products directly in the small stores in his village, but this market is small and quickly saturated. He is more likely to sell his surpluses to middlemen in nearby towns, whence they are distributed in towns and cities. Transportation may be provided by either the farmer or the middleman. In either case, the farmer's earnings are subject to market fluctuations of which he is keenly aware, although they are beyond his control. He is, furthermore, frequently in debt to the middleman who has advanced him money in anticipation of delivery of his produce. The management of money, even in small amounts, is familiar to the highland peasant, especially in the western littoral. It is, therefore, not unheard of for some farmers to develop small shops of their own, and a small proportion of these constantly expand their successes into the urban sphere. This is one of the ways in which the complex social interchange between villages and cities takes place.

The cereal plains farmer is very likely to distribute his surplus in the form of shares paid in kind to the owner of the land which he works, and thus he is often less involved directly in commercial affairs. Before proceeding further, it should be noted that the "cereal plains" region includes sections, particularly along the rivers, where orchards of fruits and nuts (especially the pistachio) are cultivated. It is also primarily in the cereal plains that cotton has become an important commercial crop in the past two decades.

This brings us to the matter of land tenure, in which there happens to be a general correlation of types with certain topographical features and with predominant types of crops—a contrast, in general, between the inland plains and the highland areas, especially of Lebanon and Syria.

Arab Levantine land tenure has been studied in detail from the economic, historic, and juridical points of view. For the anthropologist, the works of Weulersse, Latron, Thoumin, and Warriner are virtually indispensable, and Granott's study of Arab Palestine is useful to the extent that it may be generalized to other areas. *Mulk* lands are parcels which are owned on an individual basis. *Miri* tracts are lands which were at one time crown lands of the Ottoman Empire and which subsequently have been made over to individual landlords or have become state lands of the new states which succeeded the empire. The variety and complexity of these subsequent arrangements are very great. *Waqf* lands are religious endowments, both Christian and Muslim. *Musha'* lands are owned communally by individual villages.

Waqf lands are scattered throughout the area and usually provide support for religious functionaries, although there is some concern that these lands are often not used to best advantage.

Mulk holdings are concentrated in the Lebanese highlands and in the Jabal Ansariyah. This means that in these areas the individual farmer tends to have maximum control over the land that he works. This has not always been the case, however. In Lebanon, the Shihab and Jumblatt lineages, for example, until fairly recently, held large "feudal" estates, which were broken up largely by the purchase of small tracts by individuals. A factor here is the greater availability of money to the mountain farmer. Another element (Latron 1936: 72) is the type of contract known as *al-mugharasah*, whereby the farmer who develops an orchard may acquire over a number of years title to some of the orchard itself. Another factor, probably, is that these mountain farmers belong to sect groups which historically have been resistant to centralized controls of any kind.

At the village level, *musha'* tenure has been characteristic of the cereal plains and of the highland regions east and west of the Jordan. Theoretically, *musha'* means that each of the male heads of household owns a share of the lands that are held by the village as an organization, and that periodically there is a reallocation of parcels to the members of the village on the basis of their shares, presumably for the purpose of equitably distributing the use of more and less desirable lands. In practice, while local operations do take this form superficially, the cases are rare indeed in which individual villages actually own their own land. Many *musha'* villages are on *miri* land, which means, in fact, that they are actually controlled by city-dwelling landlords who acquired title by various means. In other cases, *musha'* villagers have made over the title to their land to city-dwelling influential patrons with whom they have a client relationship, one which they hope may give them political protection of various sorts, but which is likely to reduce them simply to the status of tenants of an absentee landlord.

In these same areas there are also absentee-owned villages, in which the yearly round of tasks may be coordinated by the owner's agent in a manner reminiscent of *musha'*, but where, in fact, the farmers are under short-term contracts to the owner rather than holding even a theoretical share in the holdings of the village itself. Under these conditions, the farmer's residential stability is by no means assured, and there is some evidence of village-to-village mobility, a phenomenon which may have some implications in regard to social organization apart from economics.

In the desert fringe regions of Syria and Jordan, which are generally east of the older sedentary villages but which have been sedentarized

during the past century, much of the land is owned de facto by seminomadic shaykhs. Some of these shaykhs have established themselves in
the cities, and operate very much in the same style as city-dwelling landlords who have no nomadic traditions.

There is no question but that absentee landlordism is a major element
in landholding, but exact quantitative assessments of its over-all dimensions are lacking. At the village level, we do know that it ranges from
the ownership of part of a village by one or more landlords to the ownership by a single landlord of large blocks of territory containing scores
of villages. The latter situation, as exhibited in the region of Homs and
Hama, has been given particularly close attention, from the economic
point of view, by Doreen Warriner.

The fact that *musha'* is so closely associated with absentee ownership
does not mean that the two are theoretically synonymous. Latron seems
to feel that independent *musha'* villages were once the basic type of
community in the area, but his conclusion would definitely seem to be
that this true community has been eroded by the assertion of individual
family interests, by intervillage mobility, by the fragmentation of
holdings, and most certainly by the loss of independence through client-
age (Latron 1936: 238).

The British attempted to reduce the amount of *musha'* and associated
absentee landlordism in their Mandate, and they achieved some success,
particularly west of the Jordan. The French, though certainly concerned
about absentee landlordism, seem to have devoted most of their ameliorative efforts to the reduction of excessive fragmentation of holdings.
Throughout the Arab Levant, a man's property (if he has any) is inherited equally by his sons, with great fragmentation as a result—a result
which is not always offset by sales, trades, or the marriage of patrilateral
parallel cousins.

Water rights and water apportionment are issues of vital importance
which are obviously related to land use and land tenure. Information on
this subject, which was of paramount interest to the French human
geographers, deals chiefly with the traditional community-level aspects.
Of adaptations to the new large-scale commercial irrigation developments
we know very little.

In general, the issue is important everywhere in the Arab Levant, but
it becomes greatly intensified in those areas where water is the scarcest,
and it is to the latter areas that the French geographers devoted most of
their attention. In Jabal Ansariyah and Mount Lebanon, however, the
shawi, or water warden, is a recognized functionary in the villages that
have distributable water, often stored in open tanks. Nevertheless, one
has the impression that in these relatively well-watered areas disputes

over fair shares, over the precise measurement of those shares, and over ultimate control of sources are less frequent and less intense than they are in the more desertic regions. In the latter, at any rate, competition for water is keen, and the social and technical devices for coping with this competition are correspondingly complex. Attention to the subject has been concentrated in the *ghouta* of Damascus and in the smaller *ghoutas* that lie northeast of Damascus along the eastern fringe of the Anti-Lebanon mountains. These are spring- and stream-fed oases in a semidesertic area. The Damascus irrigation system consists of six major canals which lead off from the Barada River. From each of these, water is redistributed by systems of small dams, sluice gates, and subsidiary channels. There is no over-all control of the system, but for each dam and set of sluice gates (*repartiteurs de l'eau*, as the French would call them), there is a commonly accepted temporal cycle according to which the water is made available to the dependent plots in turn. Water distribution in the other *ghoutas* is accomplished in very much the same way, except on a smaller scale. It seems to be universally true in the *ghoutas* that the sources of the water are regarded as being inalienable from each section of land. When a section of land is sold, it is sold automatically with a share of water. Water disputes turn primarily around the way in which shares are distributed (which becomes especially complicated when several villages partake of the same source), rather than around the right to have shares at all. This situation is not, however, found universally throughout the Arab Levant. Cases have been reported from various locations in Syria and Jordan in which ownership of the water source itself is held or claimed by a particular individual or party. Latron deals with this matter at some length, and he concludes (1936: 172-73) that, generally, where the sense of community is particularly strong (by which he probably means where true *musha'* conditions prevail or where extended kinship organization is particularly strong) water rights are inalienable from the land. Where "individualism" prevails, however, various arrangements occur, always operated in favor of the most influential party or individual at the time, though modified by the expectation that he who controls the water source will share the water he does not need with others. While this conclusion, coming as it does from a highly authoritative source, merits our respect, it is not wholly satisfactory, since it rests on certain concepts of social relationships whose definitions are none too clear as far as the Arab Levant is concerned. "Individualistic" orientations are present in the Arab Levant, as recent studies in contrast to earlier ones show. However, this "individualism" exists in a context of extended kinship groups, however idealized they may be. The two cannot, at least in the state of our present knowledge, be dichotomized. This matter will be treated more fully in a later section.

Sheep and goat herding is an important adjunct of agriculture in all parts of the Arab Levant. However, herding cannot be regarded solely in terms of a technical specialty, and it has not been so regarded in the literature. It has also been regarded as a diagnostic trait of a culture which is different from that of the villages, namely the culture of the desert tribes. One sometimes senses in the literature the notion that where herding is particularly prominent among the villages, "tribal" culture is correspondingly strong—the extreme of this notion being that the Arab Levantine peasant is basically a sedentarized nomad. Actually, prehistoric, historic, and contemporary facts are susceptible of differing interpretations and can easily be manipulated by nominalistic extravagance. Some of the most ancient village sites in the world are located in the Arab Levant. Postdating these sites are a series of known settlements of sedentarized areas by previously nomadic herders who subsequently became farmers, as well as cases of the expansion of farmers into areas previously occupied by nomadic herders, and also the reverse—the displacement of farming from certain areas by nomadic herders. Extensive areas of the Arab Levant have many times experienced the ebb and flow of the two ecologies, and in the plains of northern Arab Palestine, in the hills east of the Jordan, and in the plains of northern Syria, to cite three examples, there definitely are villages whose inhabitants have known nomadic origins. Furthermore, contemporaneously, nomadic bands have customarily pastured their flocks around and among these villages at certain seasons of the year, primarily the summer. In other areas, notably northwestern Syria, Mount Lebanon, and the hills west of the Jordan, sedentary settlements have apparently been continuous since the beginning. Here there are villagers who have no known nomadic origins (which, of course, does not in itself prove that they had no nomadic ancestors or that their ancestors have all been farmers since the Neolithic period). Under the circumstances, it seems to this writer rather pointless to suggest, as has been done, that sheep and goat herding, extended kin groups and some other traits in these villages necessarily are vestiges of a "tribal" (i.e. nomadic) past. Rather, the situation can better be looked upon this way: Farming and herding are both very ancient in the area. They appear to have developed together symbiotically. In the well-watered hills, farming has tended always to predominate, with herding as a technical adjunct; whereas east of the Arab Levant, where farming is impossible because of the aridity, herding predominates. In the very irregularly bordered intermediate zone, social groups specializing in one or the other ecology have always interpenetrated each other, and, in addition, there has always been a tendency for individuals or groups to be "converted" from one ecology to the other. This conversion has been made possible by the fact that despite the negative stereotypes in terms of which farmers and herders view each other at any given time, their techniques are symbiotically related and furthermore they share certain nonecological patterns, such as patrilineal kinship. Owing to the latter, farmers and erstwhile herders settling together in a new village—as has happened very frequently since 1800 in the desert fringe area—have few conceptual problems to overcome, at least in the matter of basic kinship organization and related phenomena. Knowing that given a unilineal principle of kinship organization a people can relatively easily organize kinship groups which range greatly in extensiveness depending on their needs, we do not need to rely on imputed nomadic origins to account for the presence of widely ramified kin groups or on imputed sedentary origins to account for more restricted ones. In the desert fringe area there are groups of villages, each of which is inhabited by a section of a recently nomadic tribe, so that the whole can indeed be regarded as a "tribal" group consisting of localized sedentary sections. But not all herders become sedentarized in this fashion, and similar "tribal" localizations occur in other areas, the Jabal Ansariyah, for example, whose people have been farmers for a very long time.

While what we have just said may seem to be a digression, though presaging the section on kinship organization, the point is that as far as the Arab Levant is concerned, the relationship of herding to farming can best be understood in technological terms.

Herding in the well-watered hills is generally a specialty of some villagers. A frequent arrangement is that certain villagers, as individuals or families, take care of the animals that are owned by the other villagers, who are primarily farmers. In such cases the status of shepherd is one of several specialties, along with carpentry, masonry, and so on. However, in some areas, especially in the high villages of Lebanon, which are blanketed by snow in winter, the shepherds must practice a type of transhumance in winter, accompanying their flocks to the interior or coastal lowlands for several months. Technologically this operation suggests a strong resemblance of these people to the "tribal" herders of the desert, who also make seasonal migrations. But the resemblance is superficial. The highland village shepherds are specialists in husbandry in an otherwise strongly agricultural context, and in their winter quarters they take up residence in lowland villages. Somewhat further east, in the Biqa' for example, village-owned flocks may be cared for not by village specialists but by nomadic herders who are hired to do the job. Such herders may sometimes eventually become farmers. Alternatively, farmers in the plains villages may not own any flocks at all, but obtain their meat and milk from seasonally adjacent nomadic groups in exchange for cash, agricultural products, grazing rights on village territory, etc. In the present periphery of the Arab Levant, the desert fringe of Syria and Jordan, where villages are common, many of whose inhabitants are sedentarized herders, the herding components of the ecology may still be interrelated with nomadic herding. For example, if such a village is located in an area which has been in the normal zone of summer pasturage of a nomadic tribe, the herds of the village will naturally remain in the village during the summer. But in winter, when the nomadic herders migrate southeastward, some of the villagers with their flocks will migrate with them and, during the winter, live in nomadic style. The desert fringe villages, from northern Syria to southern Jordan, represent a remarkable variety of ecological and cultural patterns: predominantly sedentary origins and ecology; primarily sedentary, but with an important segment of people of nomadic origins—Adra northeast of Damascus, for example (Thoumin, 1933: 621-41); predominantly nomadic in origin, with the village representing a former tribal section; and primarily nomadic in origin but not a sectional block and including a scattering of people of sedentary origin—Tell Ṭoqaan, south of Aleppo, for example (Sweet 1960). The latter village illustrates even further complexities in the fact that its agriculture has become mechanized under the aegis of urban landlords. While the conceptualization of the area in terms of contrasts between herders, villagers, and city dwellers is a useful one for heuristic purposes, the fact is that many representatives of these "types" are intricately involved with each other, and this is nowhere better illustrated than in the desert fringe of the Arab Levant. While Sweet's study is the primary anthropological one for this zone, we should also mention de Boucheman's study of Sukhnah (1937). Although this small town lies beyond the agricultural zone, midway in the desert between Tadmur and Deir-ez-Zor, and is not therefore in the Arab Levant, its ecology is involved in the Arab Levant. A certain amount of gardening is done by its inhabitants, who are of nomadic origin, but they derive their cash income from desert products such as potash, which they market in the desert fringe of trading towns and cities of the Arab Levant. There are resident colonies of Sukhniotes in most of these towns.

While villagers and herders produce the Arab Levant's food and some of the raw materials for manufactured articles such as clothing, furniture, and leather goods, the processing and the control of money are town- and city-centered. To the extent that city dwellers control the circulation of money among the peasants and herders—and this extent is considerable—the cities dominate the hinterland. We have also suggested

that this occurs in the contexts of absentee landlordism and the extension of credit. In addition, town- and city-based agencies also levy taxes,
a reflection of the political dominance of the larger centers as well.

In regard to processing and trade, towns, cities, villages, and herders
are all involved in a complex network of outlets. With the decline of
handicrafts and the great increase of industrially produced articles, the
villagers are primarily receivers of processed goods. Small, locally owned
shops are characteristic of Arab Levantine villages. They provide outlets
for locally produced foodstuffs, but more importantly for processed
items which have been transported from towns or cities and possibly
even imported. Items such as kerosene, flashlight batteries, matches, and
various relatively imperishable condiments are typical. The economics of
these small enterprises, of which there may be several in one village, has
not received the attention it deserves. Peddlers, operating out of towns
and cities, may also bring certain goods to villages and herders, as well
as offering certain services such as knife sharpening and retinning brass
vessels. Other services, such as carpentry and masonry, are often provided by local village specialists, although in some villages a considerable
number of men export such services to other communities besides their
own.

Processing, however, seems to be concentrated in towns and cities,
which are also centers of trade. Here, groups of specialists manufacture
their respective goods, which are then distributed by various means
through regions of various sizes. Smaller towns may have predominant
specialties, such as tanning and leatherwork, for which they are widely
known. Large cities like Aleppo and Damascus are also well known for
certain specialties, but the variety of products made in such places is
always great. The organization—spatial, social, and economic—of town
and city processing specialists is also a largely neglected subject, despite
its great importance in the culture of the Arab Levant. Weulersse's study
of Antioch (1934), though somewhat dated, is a notable contribution to
the matter.

The locale of urban trade and processing, the *suq*, has long impressed
foreign observers of the Arab Levant and of the Middle East generally.
The *suqs* of Aleppo and Damascus, with their labyrinths of covered
streets occupied in turn by various specialists, perhaps most conform to
the traditional image of the "oriental bazaar," but the same effect on a
smaller scale recurs in other places, and while Beirut's large and important *suq* area more resembles a European business district physicially, its
organization and functions are the same as those of *suqs* elsewhere in
the Arab Levant. These functions include not only the production of
utensils, furniture, textiles, pottery, and luxury items but also wholesale

and retail buying and selling of foodstuffs. Furthermore, at the present time and always in the past, the largest *suqs* have served the function of being the primary distribution points of imported items, and thus they are places of specific cultural change. The *suqs* of the Arab Levant have recently been given some attention in these terms by Dalton Potter (1955).

The economic organization of the Arab Levant conveys, perhaps above all else, a sense of constant movement of people and goods. While over longer time spans there have been the successive dominances of herding and farming in the desert fringe and the migration of villagers to the cities, there are also, every year, seasonal movements: the westward migration of nomadic herders into the Arab Levant in the spring and their departure into the desert in the fall; the downward movement of highland shepherds (and even of some highland villages in their entirety) in the fall and their return in the spring; the transportation of harvested crops to the towns and cities in the summer. Lastly, there is the virtually daily movement of herders and villagers to and from the towns and cities for commerce and entertainment. Inasmuch as the Arab Levant has so often been characterized as being static and stagnant, it is well to keep these indisputable facts of mobility in mind. They are reflected even in the histories of what might be thought of as the most stable element in the situation, the peasant village in other areas besides the desert fringe. Nearly all of the studies of such villages that have been made note that all or most of the component families do not have traditions of having been in their present locations since time immemorial, but rather of having moved to them from some other region or village, the time of the move being anywhere from three centuries earlier to very recently.

Social Organization: Social Structure

A. Kinship and Marriage

The subject of kinship and marriage occupies a rather prominent place in most of the anthropologically relevant literature on the Arab Levant. There are two reasons for this. One is that the Levantine Arabs are very conscious of their own patterns of behavior and expectations in this area of life. They think in genealogical terms, they have innumerable proverbs and exhortations concerned with kinship and marriage, and formal cognizance of the subject is taken in their legal codes and religious precepts. It is, therefore, a subject on which it is easy to get them to talk, especially since they are a highly verbal people anyway. The second reason is that it is a standard and basic subject of anthropological inquiry.

As a result, the data on kinship and marriage are numerous, although there are some serious ethnographic gaps. Another result is that the earlier, and also some of the more recent, observations on Arab Levantine kinship and marriage are in the process of critical re-evaluation by some anthropologists. This development, which is only beginning to gather momentum, is due to the greatly increased number of field studies which have been made by anthropologists, coupled with certain conceptual developments in anthropology generally.

Older sources, sometimes using each other for reference, convey this impression of Arab Levantine kinship and marriage:

> Descent is strongly patrilineal, consistent with the completely depressed social status of women. The basic family unit is the patrilocal, patriarchal, extended family, often linked to a larger lineage. For the Muslim majority, polygyny is permitted and patrilateral parallel-cousin marriage is preferred, hence both may be presumed to be frequent. Where monogamous nuclear families as independent units occur, they are due to urban influences. Among Christians, neither polygyny nor patrilineal parallel-cousin marriage is permitted, but the Christians are a small minority. The social status of women is better among Christians than among Muslims, but it is not good by twentieth-century European and North American standards.

This has been the general picture of the situation, amplified of course by many details and examples. While a number of the component statements are literally true, many of the implications that have been drawn from them are of questionable validity, and in a number of instances it is questionable how generalizable some of the statements really are. Recent thinking on the social structure of the Arab Levant would not appear to be headed toward the goal of demolishing this picture in toto, but rather of modifying it critically, for it would appear that its origins probably lie in the literal acceptance by foreign observers (equipped with various ethnocentric biases) of statements by Arab Levantines of their rationalizations of various normative patterns. Such statements can be assumed to be at some variance with behavioral reality, and the latter is often obscured in many studies.

All cultures provide means of accommodating the various inescapable differences between the sexes. One means of accommodation is by avoidance and segregation of social spheres, and if a cross-cultural scale of intensity in this matter were to be constructed, Arab Levantine culture would undoubtedly rate high on it. Such an arrangement need not be disadvantageous to the women, but if, as in the Arab Levantine case, it is coupled with patriliny, the formal power structure is in all probability going to be vested in the men. The Arab Levant's patriliny is a local manifestation of the universal association in Asia of patriliny with both peasant agriculture and pastoralism. From the point of view of anthropological analysis, it is better to look upon the status of women in the Arab Levant as being an aspect of a very complex cultural configuration, rather than as a phenomenon which, regardless of context, must be changed. Perhaps it ought to be changed, but changes in it will necessitate other, possibly prior, changes in the social structure and values system.

Indexes of the low status of women which are frequently cited begin with the explicit preference for boy babies over girl babies. There seems to be ample support for this in the literature. However, it is not clear to what extent this is conventional verbalism, as opposed to being sincerely motivated. Functionally, the preference is consistent with the desire to augment the membership of patrilineal kin groups, but it is not clear from the literature whether it can be validly interpreted as a denigration of women as such. Recent evidence, which will be discussed more fully in a later section, suggests that Arab Levantine parents tend to be explicit about their differential preferences among their children in general, of which this could be a specific instance. But the fact that this phenomenon, if it is truly general, could have profound effects on the adult personality must also be kept in mind.

Preferential marriage to the patrilateral parallel cousin, arrangement of marriage by the parents, the payment of "bride price" (Arabic: *mahr*), and polygyny have all been cited in the context of the low status of women. Patrilateral parallel-cousin marriage is a formal ideal among the Muslims, but the actual evidence—largely from village studies and surveys—shows that only a small minority of such marriages actually occur. Rather than viewing it as the central focus of marriage selection, this writer is in agreement with Millicent Ayoub that it should be regarded as "but the most extreme example of the more general configuration of preferential endogamy" (M. Ayoub 1959: 274). This writer has himself explored the dimensions of such preferential endogamy (Gulick 1955: 170, passim), attempting to show that the basic pattern obtains among the Christian Arabs, among whom first-cousin marriages are forbidden, as well as among the Muslims.

The confusion of verbal normative statements with objective behavioral facts leaves the matter of actual parental controls in mate selection very unclear. At one extreme is the image of a girl's arranged marriage to a man she hardly knows, and whose face she has not seen, owing to the segregation of unmarried males and females. Accompanying this there is a considerable body of folklore—stories, poems, and songs—revolving around the theme of secret love affairs and elopements. Where there is smoke, there is some fire. However, there is no evidence which indicates the actual frequency of such extreme forms of marriage arrangement, although individual cases are cited in the literature. If endogamous marriages, variously defined, are accepted in the culture, and if extended kin groups are significant in the culture, and if marriages are regarded in part as being exchanges between such groups (all of which appear to apply), it is clear that mate selection is not a matter of completely free individual choice. Gulick encountered statements of a preference for the latter, and a considerable number of instances of it, among one group of Lebanese Christian villagers, but these people had been exposed to Westernized urban influences to what is probably an unusual degree in the Arab Levant. It is hardly satisfactory to say that the majority of marriage arrangements probably lie between the two extremes, but in the absence of a sufficient number of reliable data, we have no choice in the matter.

Agreement on the amount of *mahr* is a part of the prewedding negotiations between the families. It is not conceived of as a purchase of the bride, but as part of an exchange. Descriptions of weddings are numerous in the village literature, and the same general patterns are recurrent among both Christians and Muslims. The ritual clearly symbolizes the separation of the bride from her natal family and her formal transfer to her husband's family: a procession to the bride's house, a ceremonial observance there, another procession escorting the bride to the groom's house, with a further ceremonial observance there. There are various symbolic expressions of the loss to the bride's family which the marriage entails. For this, *mahr* is a symbolic compensation. If the marriage is between patrilateral parallel cousins, the amount of *mahr* may be considerably reduced (Daghestani 1932: 22), but rather than considering this as an inducement to arranging such marriages in the first place, as Daghestani and others do, we can perhaps understand it more clearly when we recognize that in such marriages the social loss is minimal. The bride leaves her nuclear family, but she does not leave her extended family.

Among Muslims, *mahr* payments are standard, but the available material does not make it clear to what extent the payment is essentially a token, on the one hand, or a major economic transaction, on the other. Reports of cases of both have been made, but with no quantification. Daghestani (1932: 26) notes wide variations in the amount, but it is not clear whether this is due to attitudes toward the payment (token vs. major transaction) or to differing degrees of affluence, which could vary independently of each other.

Mahr (or *naqd*) has been reported among Christian Arab Levantines, but with qualifications. Chémali (1915-16: 917) and Safi (1917-18: 135) note its occurrence among Lebanese Maronites. More recently, among the same general population, Williams (1958: 32) notes no *mahr*, but says that the groom deeds some property to his bride. Zarour (1953: 436) says that in Ramallah, West Jordan, Greek Orthodox Arabs have paid *mahr* until very recently. Gulick (1955: 82) did not find *mahr* among Greek Orthodox in one coastal Lebanese village. These findings suggest a change among the Christians, but we do not know if there is a significant difference between the Muslims and the Christians in this respect. At least in the Greek Orthodox cases, the change may be due to Western urban influences.

In this connection, an important warning is in order. The literature on the Arab Levant is very careless in its references to "urban influences" and like phrases. Daghestani frequently mentions special urban characteristics, but, typically, he never makes it clear whether he is referring to Western-oriented or to non-Western-oriented people in the city. For example he says (1932: 13) that in the cities, the prospective bride is always consulted by her parents in regard to mate selection. Is this due to Western influences among the city people? We have no way of knowing, and this ignorance and lack of clarity is most unfortunate, since it makes far more difficult the task of discovering whether or not there are significantly different social patterns between city dwellers and villagers *apart from* Western influences. Since Western influences are now strong, especially in the cities, this issue may no longer be susceptible of ready clarification, although research on it needs to be done and would certainly be profitable. In the meantime, there is no available material upon which comparisons between Western-oriented Muslims and Christians could be made.

In no culture where plural marriages are permitted are any but a small proportion of the marriages actually plural. The Arab Levant is no exception, but there is remarkably little concrete information on the subject. A government survey made in 1945 of five Muslim villages in Arab Palestine revealed that 10.6 per cent of the married men had more than one wife and that nine tenths of these had two wives. Only 0.2 per cent of the men had the maximum of four wives permitted by Islam (Palestine, Government of, 1945-46). We do not know whether these figures are representative of the Muslim villagers of the Arab Levant generally. One would suspect that the proportion of maximal polygynous marriages would be higher among wealthy Muslims, but there are no data to support or refute this. Churchill's survey (1954: 5) of a sample of almost 2,000 households in Beirut revealed, startlingly enough, only two cases of polygynous marriages. It is not known, unfortunately, what proportion of the households were Muslim.

Let us now consider the kinship groups, which are the larger context in which marriage occurs. First of all, there is some material on the size of households in Lebanon and Jordan. Churchill's Beirut sample had an average of 5.76 persons per household (Churchill 1954: 4). The 1952 Census of Housing in Jordan showed an average of 5.70 in 'Amman and a range of averages of from 5.48 to 6.57 in the other cities and principal towns of Jordan. The Arab Palestine village survey gave an over-all average of 6.4 persons, the range being 5.2 to 7.4. The median village had 6.1 persons per household (Palestine, Government of, 1945-46: 432). A survey of eight Shi'ah villages in the southern Lebanese littoral revealed an over-all weighted average of 6.6 persons, the range being 5.5 to 8.3, and the two median villages having averages of 6.1 and 6.8 persons per household (Gorton et al. 1953: 8). There is a consistency in these figures which suggests that they may well be representative of the larger population of Lebanon and Jordan. There are no comparable data for Syria. While the average city household appears to be somewhat smaller than the over-all average village household, there are a few villages with averages about the same as the cities. In other words, the city-village contrast is not very great, and, as a matter of fact, a survey of thirteen villages in the central Biqa' shows an over-all average household size which is slightly smaller (5.5 persons) than Beirut's (Churchill 1959: 3). Religious differences are, however, an important countervariable in this matter. Prothro (1961: 45) and Yaukey (1961: 29) find that in Lebanon, village nuclear families among both Muslims and Christians are larger than their urban counterparts; but they also find that while urban Muslim families are only slightly smaller than village families, the village -urban difference among Christians is much greater.

On the basis of these samples, the average Arab Levantine household is certainly larger than the average household in the United States, whose size is approximately 3.5 persons—an average which is somewhat lowered by the one- and two-person households which appear to be unusual in the Arab Levant. Apart from this, however, what can be deduced about the composition of Arab Levantine households from their size? Patai (1956a: 256), in reference to Lebanon (though he makes the same references to Syria and Jordan elsewhere), says that the large average size is "a concomitant of the extended family system," the extended family, in this view, being the "typical" family in the area. The present writer believes that available data show not only that this deduction is unwarranted but that the whole depiction of the "typicality" of the extended family must be re-examined and cleared of the serious ambiguities in which it has been couched. The fact that the average Levantine household is nearly twice as large as the average United States household is not prima facie evidence of the prevalence of the extended family in the former, as opposed to the nuclear family in the latter. Let us take one case in point. In the Lebanese Greek Orthodox village studied by Gulick, the average household size was 6 persons, well within the ranges cited above. Of the 87 households, only 2 were inhabited by extended families, and these were explicitly temporary arrangements. This study (Gulick 1955: 48-49), which is one of the few that provides a precise tabulation of household composition, indicates that the large size of the households is not at all due to the prevalence of extended families, but rather to the larger number of children per married couple than occurs in the United States and also to a tendency which is probably greater than in the United States for unmarried young men and women to continue to live with their parents until they are married and for older widowed or separated persons to live with either their grown children or adult siblings. Numerically, in this village, the nuclear family is the typical residence unit, frequently augmented by additional personnel.

Fortunately, we need not rely on this one study to make our point. In 1950 Hadchite, a highland Maronite Lebanese village, had 96 households, of which 78 were inhabited by nuclear families, 9 by nuclear families plus additional relatives, and 9 by extended families which were considered to be temporary (Williams 1958: 13). In Hawsh al-Harimah, a Sunni Muslim, absentee-owned village in the Biqa', Herbert Williams and Ralph Kepler Lewis found that of the 124 households only 6 were inhabited by extended families. All the rest were nuclear. In a village in Galilee, Israel, two thirds of whose population is Sunni Muslim and one third Christian, Rosenfeld (1958: 1129) found 275 households, of which 205 consisted of nuclear families, and 44 of which were fully or nearly fully extended families. In Tell Ṭoqaan, a village south of Aleppo which has strong pastoral traditions, Sweet (1960: 165) counted 56 household compounds, of which 14 were inhabited by extended families. In "Kallarwan" (pseudonym for a predominantly Druze village in central Lebanon), there are 171 households, 18 of which are extended (or at least stem) families, and 106 of which are nuclear families, the remainder being variations of simple nuclear families (M. Ayoub 1957: 14). Prothro's sample comprised people two thirds of whose households were nuclear families, with most of the remainder being nuclear families with patrilateral adjuncts, such as father's sibling, uncle or aunt, and sometimes parent (Prothro 1961: 45).

No clear-cut conclusion can be drawn from these findings. The figures from Rosenfeld's village and from Tell Toqaan *suggest* that extended families may be more prevalent in Muslim or predominantly Muslim villages, but, on the contrary, Hawsh is reported to have a smaller proportion of extended families than is Hadchite. Gulick's findings, at the one extreme, could be accounted for in terms of urban influences, and Tell Toqaan, at the other, in terms of pastoral influences, whatever those "influences" may be. Realization that household arrangements are changeable and that we have no information on the financial status of these families should make us hesitant to try to prove any points with these figures.

With these cautions duly recognized, we nevertheless have a diversified village sample which shows that the nuclear family is overwhelmingly the most frequent type of residence unit. This fact, which cannot be attributed to Western urban influences, has been completely obscured in the earlier studies.

The reason for the prevalence of nuclear families having been obscured is probably that earlier observers were greatly impressed with the fact that, regardless of the structure of the residence units, there is a definite system of sentiments which favors the recognition and maintenance of larger kinship aggregations. There are also serious tensions within sibling groups, which can result in the opposite tendency for the encouragement of independent nuclear families. Rosenfeld, in the article cited (1958), deals in one way with these counteracting tendencies, and Gulick (1955), Victor Ayoub (1955), and Murphy and Kasdan (1959) have all dealt with it in somewhat larger contexts. It is a highly complex issue, which requires the interweaving of data on, and interpretations of, social and psychological sets. The subject has yet to be done full justice, but a start has been made. The matter of sentiments will be discussed further in a later section. We turn next to the composition of larger kinship units, which can be viewed in terms of the territorial dimensions of social organization.

B. *Territory*

In all of the villages that have been studied in the Arab Levant, the members of the majority of households are linked to larger patrilineal kin groups. The least extensive link is that between adult brothers, and the next is that between adult brothers and an aged father (the extended family). Beyond the extended family may be patrilineages, which vary greatly in size. From the data at hand, there appear to be no significant differences between Christians and Muslims in this respect. For the most part, the lineages are traced to different ancestors who are believed to have come to the site from various other places, but there are occasional instances in which all or most of the ancestors of a village's lineages are said to have been brothers or cousins. Villages dominated by a single lineage occur, for example, among the Hawrani Druzes (Bouron 1930: 295), but this situation appears to be unusual. There is a general tendency for lineage-endogamous marriages to be preferred and frequent, and there is a general tendency for the houses occupied by each lineage to be clustered together. All the village studies, however, note that these are tendencies, noticeable, but by no means without exceptions. In general, the lineages are not corporate bodies, but rather, given the definition of kinship as being patrilineal, aggregations of recognized kinsmen among whom mutual aid and tokens of loyalty are expected. In at least three villages—Munsif, Lebanon (Gulick 1955), Hawsh, and Tell Ṭoqaan —there are, in addition to the lineages, a number of nuclear families, mostly recent migrants, which are not linked to any larger kin groups in the village even though they may well be linked to such groups elsewhere. Peripheral from the point of view of the established lineages, the occurrence of such families has probably always been characteristic of Arab Levantine villages. The lineages themselves seem to have been descended from such families in the past.

In many instances, the lineages do not seem to extend beyond a particular village. But there are some cases in which they do—in which, in other words, lineage X in village A is a segment of a larger lineage in villages B and C. Cases of this sort were reported from Arab Palestine in which the *khirbah*, "branch" or "daughter" village, was apparently frequent, having been established by the relocation of people from another village (Shim'onī 1947: 234). Shim'onī also notes (1947: 259-60) that some lineages had a regional (i.e. intervillage) distribution and that some attained protective or coercive dominance over others. Villages which represent segments of larger kin groups are also found in the recently sedentarized areas of the Syrian desert fringe. In Mount Lebanon, in the past, there were several large and influential lineages among the Maronites and the Druzes. The Ayoubs (see M. Ayoub 1959: 267) note that each of the two internally segmented lineages in "Kallarwan" was affiliated with a much larger Druze kin faction. Among the 'Alawites in Jabal Ansariyah, Weulersse (1940: 328) noted that there were four confederations of lineages, each occupying distinct, though discontinuous, blocks of territory. The ultimate in genealogical extension in the Arab Levant is the claim, reported from some sections, of affiliation with either the Qaysite or Yamanite factions of Arabia. This seems to have been particularly noted in Arab Palestine and in what is now West Jordan, where it made possible certain at least sentimental linkages between villagers and seminomads. The 'Alawites claimed Yamanite affiliation.

These data do not permit us to generalize as much as we should like, but we can be certain of one thing. Given a unilineal principle of descent, the Arab Levantines exhibit all levels of segmentation and expansion of social units, the organization of groups at such levels being one of the properties of unilinearity. The system allows for the shifting through time and variable fortunes of the extent of any given descent group, and it has clearly done so in the history of the Arab Levant. At any given time such as the present, we have, however, no way of knowing how many people participate actively in lineal groups which transcend individual village boundaries. Wider extensions and participation seem to be due either to socioeconomic dominance or to relatively recent relocation, but these are only impressions, and there are known exceptions. The whole issue needs a great deal more careful study and, above all, concrete evidence.

Some attention has been paid to the Arab Levantine kinship terminology, which is, of course, but a variant of that used by Arabic speakers elsewhere. Davies (1949) provides two paradigms, one obtained from a Christian Arab living in what is now Israel, the other from a Muslim from Damascus. They do not vary significantly from each other nor from paradigms which are included in other sources. The consanguineal system is of the Sudanese type, which means that it makes possible the individual designation of all statuses with maximum economy. However, two patterns are observable in it. The base terms are morphologically paired by gender in one-to-one correspondence with the sex of the referent. In effect, there are basic roots for father's sibling, mother's sibling, sibling, and child, each of which has a masculine and feminine form. The uniqueness of the terms is therefore somewhat reduced. Secondly, there are derived terms, most of which are formed by prefixing "son (of)" or "daughter (of)" to a base term. These can be reduplicated to indicate successive generations. Thus, while the system literally applies a unique term to each status, it also emphasizes individual descent lines, and this may be of functional significance for the kinship structure itself, which involves various levels of segmentation and aggregation. The affinal system includes terms which show some "classificatory" usages. These have been analyzed to some extent by Gulick (1955: 115-20) and more extensively by M. Ayoub (1957, chap. II), both of whom emphasize the functions of various terms in reflecting certain extensions of kinship conceptions to nonkinship situations and the emphasis on kin group endogamy.

The territorial dimension of the kinship structure is seen most clearly in village sections, in villages as wholes, and in regional blocks of villages. Of kinship organization in the cities, we have virtually no information. This is a serious ethnographic gap. We can deduce that most urban households are probably nuclear families, but this tells us nothing about the types of relationship which obtain between them. We know that many city dwellers preserve village ties, and so possibly they tend to preserve village-type kinship organization, but this is supposition only.

Our territorial focus now shifts from kinship to other types of organization or aggregation. One is the division of each of the Arab Levantine countries into political districts and provinces. These divisions are links in the juridical and police systems of the countries, but we are not aware of any anthropologically relevant analyses of them, and so we pass on to the territorial distribution of religious aggregations.

The great majority of Arab Levantines are Sunni Muslims, but other religions are well represented in the area, and to some extent there are territorial blocks of them. 'Alawites and Isma'ilis predominate in the Jabal Ansariyah, although many of the latter have recently been moving eastward into the plains. Maronites are concentrated in northern Mount Lebanon. Druzes are concentrated in the southern half of Mount Lebanon and, by recent migration, in the Hawran. Mitwalis are concentrated in the southern plains of Lebanon. There are smaller enclaves of such religions as Greek Orthodox and Greek Catholic in all three of the Arab Levantine countries. Lastly, there is a small enclave of Yazidi villages west of Aleppo (Lescot 1938a: 201).

Within the larger blocks, there are villages which are internally homogeneous in religion and surrounded by other villages of the same religion (e.g. Hawsh, Hadchite, Tell Ṭoqaan). On the other hand, in central Lebanon, in northwestern Syria, and in Jordan, villages of one religion which abut villages of other religions are frequently encountered. Internally, furthermore, there are cases of villages in which the established lineages belong to one religion but where there are also peripheral families belonging to another (e.g. Munsif). There are also cases of villages in which there are well-established lineages belonging to two or more different religions. Examples of the latter are Bishmizziin, Lebanon, which is predominantly Greek Orthodox but has well-established groups of Muslims and Maronites (Tannous 1943); "Kallarwan," which is predominantly Druze but has a well-established Maronite section; and Ma'lula, Syria, which has a Greek Catholic and a Greek Orthodox section with a scattering of Muslims (Reich 1937).

"Mixed" villages of this sort are known from the examples cited, but the frequency of such villages is not known. At any rate, they suggest, on a very small scale, the socio-territorial structure of Levantine cities insofar as the latter is known. Levantine cities are known to be divided into named sections or quarters (Arabic: *ḥara, muḥallah,* or *ḥayy*). In earlier periods, these were often separated from each other by walls, and they appear to have formed subcommunities. To what extent they can be said to constitute subcommunities, in any meaningful sense, in the large modern cities, as opposed to smaller towns, is not known. Patai, in the three HRAF Subcontractor's Monographs on Syria, Lebanon, and Jordan that he edited (1956), lists and briefly describes the quarters in Damascus and Aleppo (*Syria 1*: 347-60), Beirut and Tripoli (*Lebanon 1*: 234-39, 245-56), and 'Amman (*Jordan*: 274-77). Primarily, the quarters are defined in terms of the religion that is predominant among their inhabitants. Thoumin (1931) describes the Christian and Kurdish quarters in Damascus in terms which certainly convey the impression of subcommunities, as does Weulersse in his description of Antioch (1934).

The census-type surveys of Arab Levantine cities which have been conducted in the 1950s by Charles W. Churchill, of which only the Beirut survey has yet been published, provide data of unique importance. There is, however, a vital need for "anthropological" studies which would closely analyze the actual social relationships which occur in these cities.

C. *Social Stratification*

It has been customary to characterize the Arab Levant's population as falling into two classes, defined primarily by occupation and relative wealth: a huge class of what is called the "masses," composed of farmers, small shopkeepers, and wage laborers—all very poor; and a small class of notables who wield the political power, control most of the wealth, and are supported either by agricultural revenues or large-scale trade. Latron (1936: 225) states the case in terms which are very similarly stated in many other sources.

In general, the class contrasts are most noticeable in the cities and towns, for in many villages representatives of the notables are hardly ever present, let alone the notables themselves. However, this is by no means always the case, and it is possible, actually, that in the majority of villages the existence of the notable class is continually felt in the presence of landlords' agents or in houses which are owned and occasionally occupied by the landlords. There are certainly cases of this. Arab Levantine attitudes toward social class differences are confusingly and unsystematically presented in the literature. One theme is the equalitarian one, which asserts the equal value of all men regardless of class. Another theme stresses considerable hostility and tension between the classes. In the latter connection, Peters (1956) has contributed a valuable description of how, in a southern Lebanese Shi'ah village, social class tensions are expressed and to some extent worked out by ritual means.

The Levantine peasants are extremely conscious of social class differences and of their vulnerability to the political and economic power of notables, and there appears to be no doubt that many of them attempt (a few successfully) to become wealthy and powerful themselves. Nevertheless, the two-class characterization appears to be a gross oversimplification. Statistical surveys in the Lebanese Biqa' have shown conclusively that there is considerable occupational and class diversity even in absentee-owned peasant villages (Armstrong and Hirabayashi 1956: 429). Perhaps the major complication, however, is that the influence of Western-style occupations and professions has produced aggregations of people who fit neither of the two traditional categories. To refer to the former as a "new and growing middle class," as is frequently done, supplies a label but contributes nothing in the way of understanding.

The subject calls for intensive analysis, since it is related not only to the social organization aspect of Arab Levantine culture but also to the agents of cultural change in the area. A stimulating start in this direction is Daniel Lerner's analysis (1958) of the surveys which were conducted in 1950-51 by the Bureau of Applied Social Research of Columbia University. The surveys were conducted in six Middle Eastern countries, three of which are the Arab Levantine countries, and gathered questionnaire responses generally on degrees of political awareness and on exposure and reactions to the mass media of communication. The responses were analyzed into three "types"–traditional, transitional, and modern. Lerner makes the serious error, in this writer's opinion (see his review in the *American Anthropologist 61* [1959]: 135-38), of interpreting these as being personality and societal types. If, on the other hand, one reads "transitional" and "modern" as a new type, or new types, of social class, some useful insights into the subject may be gained. In regard to the relative influence of this new class in the Arab Levant, Lerner's rank order of modernity, from most to least modern, is: Turkey, Lebanon, Egypt, Syria, Jordan, Iran (Lerner 1958: 90).

Political Structure

This section does not deal with political structure in the sense of political parties and formal governmental institutions, for these topics are the special concern of specialists other than anthropologists and lie beyond the scope of this chapter. We are concerned, rather, with the prevailing sentiments and forces of group action and with the characteristic roles of power, authority, and influence which may be played by certain individuals.

As in the matter of kinship and marriage, the literature on this subject abounds in what are apparently very generalized idealizations and stereotypes, together with what appear to be contradictions.

A. Local Groups

For the great majority of Arab Levantines, the village is the primary local group. To what extent the *haras* of towns and cities constitute meaningful local groups for their inhabitants is not known. Consisting of a more or less compact cluster of houses and garden plots surrounded by fields and orchards, and having definite, though sometimes disputed, boundaries, the Arab Levantine village is a clearly definable unit.

Tannous (1944b), writing generally, notes that villagers are customarily highly conscious of their community identity and are intensely loyal to each other and cohesive in their villagewide behavior. Gulick employed the concept of village cohesion in his village study (1955) and subsequently surveyed the then available village-relevant literature from the Arab Levant in terms, inter alia, of village cohesion (see Patai 1956: *Lebanon 1*: 136-209; *Syria 1*: 253-319; *Jordan*: 206-49). His rather tentative conclusion, which he would now state more definitely, is that "village cohesion" is actually a congeries of behavior patterns and verbal expressions, that these *are* exhibited under certain circumstances, but that their intensity can be greatly modified by various factors. As Gulick has attempted to show (1955, Part II, and see also Victor Ayoub 1955 and Murphy and Kasdan 1959), "in-group" behavior in the area, of which "village cohesion" is one type, can at certain times be very intense, but it is situationally cued and situationally variable. Situations defined as being defensive (e.g. when strangers, especially government officials, are present; when there are boundary, water, or personal disputes involving other villages, etc.) are those which primarily cue villagecohesion behavior, which appears in such forms as verbally asserting the village's superiority in various respects, protecting native fugitives from justice, and carrying on longstanding feuds with other villages. Apart from defensive situations—and also ritual occasions—which are attended by most of the villagers, "village cohesion" is not in evidence. In fact, except in such situations, the members of a village are frequently divided against each other—as in the case of kin-group feuds and the frequently reported tendency for villagers to polarize into two opposed factions. The dual factions may be cued by kinship or political differences. This is the situation which appears in general to be true of villages in which communitywide cohesion, when it does occur, is likely to be very intense; and these are probably for the most part villages which are homogeneous in regard to religion and whose component lineages are limited to the individual village. Villages in which persons representing different religions are well established, for example "Kallarwan" (V. Ayoub 1955) and Ma'lula (Reich 1937), apparently rarely, if ever, exhibit communitywide cohesion. Tannous, in fact, refers (1944b) to such villages as being "double," essentially two separate communities in one location. Villages whose lineages have extravillage ties we should expect also to give minimal expression of village cohesion, but we lack any conclusive instances of this.

Having recognized the relativity of "village cohesion" as a behavioral phenomenon, we find that the reported role of the titular head of the Arab Levantine village, the mukhtar, is never one of power, but usually one of only formal authority, such as keeping required records, and of influence only given the requisite personality and kinship ties of the individual.

Within the village, the extended family appears to be the most constantly important group larger than the nuclear family, of several of which, of course, it is an aggregation. The extended family is significant to some extent economically and most certainly in terms of sentiments, although, as we have shown earlier, it is usually not a residential or commensal unit. Before proceeding further, we should make the points that not all Arab Levantines participate in extended families, that not all extended families are actively involved in larger lineages, and that the larger lineages vary greatly in size.

Because of the nature of the human life cycle, the extended family necessarily occurs in various phases: (1) A man and wife (or wives), their unmarried children, and their first-married son and his nuclear family of procreation. (2) A man and wife and all of their sons, married and with their nuclear families, the daughters having married out. (3) A group of brothers, their parents having died, with their own nuclear families. There are obviously other intermediary phases, but these are the most useful ones in terms of which to think. Given the preponderance of nuclear family residence in the Arab Levant, the reality of the extended family as a social unit lies in the sentiments which the members have concerning each other and in economic ties, which are inevitably present in phase (1), but which may or may not be continued in phases (2) and (3).

The older literature, which generally confuses the phases or ignores all phases except the second, generally states that the sentiments are of the utmost loyalty, that all real property is owned in common, and that mutual assistance is the rule; it generally states further that the extended family is ruled by the grandfather or the eldest competent male, in a thoroughly authoritarian way. Recent evidence indicates that there are countertendencies to each of these characteristics, which in many instances may actually prevail. In fact, the older depiction may be in large part an idealization. Lacking sufficient quantitative evidence, we do not know how frequently the traditional depiction is actually acted out as opposed to merely being stated as a model image. Reports of it for the most part are general statements rather than specific cases. On the other hand, there are now available reports of specific cases in which the model situation does not occur or occurs only partially.

Curiously, the widely-reported Arabic saying, "I am against my brother, my brother and I are against our cousin, and I, my brother, and our cousin are against the stranger," has rarely been taken fully at its face value, and yet in it the Arabs very succinctly state what appear to be fundamental realities in the situation. These realities, however, the Arabs themselves often verbally contradict with other sayings.

Rosenfeld has recently adduced concrete Muslim village evidence of (a) how the extreme poverty of the father necessitates the sons' setting up independent nuclear families and (b) how various inequities in work loads relative to nuclear family responsibilities make adult brothers unwilling to work jointly (Rosenfeld 1958: 1130 ff.). Victor Ayoub (1955: 51) notes that in "Kallarwan" it is frequently only the involuntary inability of recently married sons to make sufficient money independently that leads them to continue participating in an economic extended family. Rosenfeld again (Rosenfeld 1958: 1133) seems to feel that it is primarily economic factors, rather than psychological ones such as personality conflicts, which tend to disperse the extended family.

The present writer feels that there is sufficient evidence to indicate that psychological conflicts may be equally important in the matter. First, the type of jealousies and resentments which are involved in factor (b), above, are hardly, in themselves, economic. And if, as the traditional model would have it, there actually were extremely strong solidary sentiments among brothers (rather than mere verbalizations of them), the emotional reactions to economic inequities would be successfully counterbalanced more than they are. Second, several sources report the intense jealousies which tend to occur among *salafat*, the wives of brothers, and the conflicts between mothers-in-law and their daughters-in-law, even when they are living, as most of them do, in independent commensal units. Attempts at close cooperation in the extended family, even short of common residence, tend to multiply and exacerbate these tensions. Third, the rule of equal inheritance among sons creates a strain among brothers to divide their patrimony, but the difficulties in making the division often induce the brothers to postpone it, perpetuating for a while the "common property" aspect of the extended family, but hardly in a spirit of unity. Eventually the property is always divided, but not always amicably, one result being the extreme fractionation of land-holdings that typifies the Arab Levant generally. Were division of property to be held in abeyance for several generations, the result would be lineages which hold property in common. No examples of this are provided in the literature. Fourth, Herbert Williams (1958: 28 passim) and Millicent Ayoub (1957: 118 ff.) report that as children, brothers characteristically fight bitterly despite the fact that they also form close playgroups. Williams, in particular, feels that sibling rivalry, a certain amount of which normally occurs everywhere, is deeply imbeded by various child-training practices. If these conflicts are not resolved, they will tend to be perpetuated into adult life. If these findings, which come from two villages in Lebanon—one Maronite and the other predominantly Druze—are generalizable to the Arab Levant, it would appear to be highly probable that the structural and economic elements of fusion and fission in the Arab Levantine extended family are reinforced, if not ultimately caused, by well-entrenched emotional factors. On this view, the many expressions of group solidarity would be regarded as compensatory acts not always in fact mirrored in other types of behavior.

Evidence seems clear that the senior competent male of the family (either extended or nuclear) is formally regarded as being the head of the family. But the older notion that he is a patria potestas is not supported in concrete cases. Again, there has apparently been a confusion of conceptual models and behavioral realities. Even Touma, who generally perpetuates the widespread stereotypes of Arab Levantine kinship, writes: "All members of the family, even the collaterals with their descendants, stay united under the influence of a master of the house, the grandfather, the father, the paternal uncle, the older brother, the mother sometimes. We have used the term influence in preference to that of authority, for the head of the family is not a chief. Rather, he is the symbol of family unity. People respect him. They pay attention to his advice and his acts." (Touma 1958: 100—translation ours). It is interesting that quite independently of Touma, Victor Ayoub makes the same distinction between influence and authority in this connection. He says (1955: 51) that while the head of the family theoretically has absolute control, he does not in fact exercise it. For one thing, the mother's influence over the children is very strong (an impression which Williams also has concerning the Maronites). Once married, a son is no longer under his father's authority, and he may or may not continue to be under his influence.

It could be argued that these findings among Maronites and Druzes, to which Gulick would add his impressions of Greek Orthodox, are not characteristic of the Muslim majority, who are more patriarchal in fact as well as theory. This may be true, but more specific Muslim material must be adduced before the matter can be set forth definitely. If Rosenfeld's findings (1958) are any indication of the general situation among Muslim villagers, the burden of proof is certainly on the proponents of there being greater Muslim patriarchy.

De facto village leaders are almost always also heads of families, and the way in which they perform their former roles seems to be an extension of the latter. Generally speaking, Arab Levantine lineages do not have formal chiefs who have recognized authority. Lineage leadership, where it occurs, inheres in certain member individuals who have gained influence wider than their immediate nuclear or extended families. Their influence may be due to imponderable "personality factors," or to unusual wealth, or to the ability to mobilize physical force (i.e. sheer power).

The most extensive analysis of these wider aspects of Arab Levantine leadership patterns is Victor Ayoub's study of "Kallarwan" (1955), although Emrys Peters' two papers (1956 and 1963) bear on the same subject, as did field work in northern Syria by Alan Horton in 1954, the results of which are available, but not yet published (Horton 1961). It remains to be seen to what extent Ayoub's findings and their wider implications are generalizable.

The Druze population of "Kallarwan" is divided into two endogamous sibs, which Ayoub calls tertiary lineages. Each has several hundred members, and, as noted earlier, each represents a Druze faction of regional proportions. Each tertiary lineage is segmented into three secondary lineages, each of which is segmented into a number of primary lineages. The primary lineages consist of the patrilineal descendants of a common great-grandfather; in other words, they are the next level of organization beyond the extended family, and they consist of both extended families and independent nuclear families (V. Ayoub 1955: 46 ff.). Of these hierarchical segments, only the tertiary lineages have formally elected heads (of whom more anon).

At each level there are informal gatherings of family heads, each level being actually a larger or smaller aggregation of families. One of the major functions of such groups is to resolve disputes by arbitration (*waasṭa*), and the pattern of arbitration follows the lineage level structure. A dispute which divides a primary lineage will be arbitrated by a *waasṭa* party (usually three or four men) of a different primary lineage but from the same secondary lineage (V. Ayoub 1955: 135). In the midst of a dispute, the embattled individuals can count on the support of the members of their immediate level—the defensive in-group principle at work. The pattern operates at all levels, so that, for example, a dispute between members of two different secondary lineages could (a) rally each secondary lineage as a whole and (b) be arbitrated by a *waasṭa* party representing the tertiary lineage. The pattern that Ayoub describes fits precisely the model outlined by Gulick (1955, Part II) in more general terms.

Since any embattled segment can theoretically resort to armed force (i.e. exercise power), and since the contending forces may each be able to rally equal forces, *waasṭa*, Ayoub feels, is a functional prerequisite if open conflict is to be avoided. The *waasṭa* party has no authority but eventually influences the contending parties to reconcile their differences.

While the ultimate sanction in "Kallarwan" (as in other villages) could be the mukhtar's calling in the district constabulary or even a unit of the Lebanese army, this resort to force is rarely if ever made, and there is a definite preference for settling disputes within the kinship structure of the village rather than taking them before extravillage courts of law (V. Ayoub 1955: 82 passim). These phenomena are indications of the primacy of kinship loyalties over nonkinship ones, of the suspicion (generally well founded) that official government agencies will not settle disputes impartially, and of the emphasis on localization of social activities within the village. The present writer would hypothesize that "Kallarwan" is representative of most other Arab Levantine villages in these respects.

B. *Regional Political Systems*

On the subject of regional political systems we can only project outward from the village and the city contexts, for no thorough study of the matter as a whole has been made. Districts defined by the definite direction of political influence that may occur in them appear to fall into three types: (1) Religious blocs, which may, for example, elect legislative representatives on a religious basis—characteristic of Lebanon in particular. (2) Areas which are economically controlled by large landowners. These may exert pressures on the appropriate government agencies in such villagers' interests as tax relief or protection from nomadic groups—in return for which the landowner, or persons representing him in the regional or national structure, are given bloc support by the villagers. (3) Districts in which extensive kin groups can marshall enough support to make their numbers felt.

These types are not mutually exclusive. "Kallarwan," for example, would seem to participate in the first and third types simultaneously. On several occasions, apparently, the heads of one or the other of the tertiary lineages have been elected to the Lebanese parliament (V. Ayoub 1955: 75). They were not elected by "Kallarwan" alone, but by the bloc votes of Druzes in the district who belonged to the same faction. Such direct "links" between the village, the regional, and the national levels of political structure probably never occur in some villages, but, on the other hand, "Kallarwan" is not unique in this respect.

In conclusion, we should like to hazard the guess, which is inspired largely by Ayoub's work, that in the Arab Levant, the following tend to be recurrent "political" patterns at all levels, from the household to the nation: There are recognized statuses, which theoretically carry formal authority. There is, however, a strong tendency to minimize the power and influence of formal authority figures by the informal exertion of influence, using kinship and religious identities as levers and backed up, if necessary and where possible, by economic pressures which can approach the effectiveness of sheer power. Resort to physical force by either formal authorities or the agents of informal influence tends to be avoided, since it is not controllable by any means except counterforce. As much as possible, arbitration and negotiation, often very lengthy processes, are used instead.

There would be no point in making such very general, abstract, and unsubstantiated remarks if it were not for two facts. One is that there is evidence, piecemeal and localized though it may be, that there may be some validity in them. The second is that it is customary in many circles to accuse the Arab Levantines of being incapable of "making democracy work," even though they have the institutional trappings of Western European democracy. A more objective and insightful view of the situation may be gained if, in comparison to the above portrayal of Arab Levantine political patterns, we view "Western democracy" this way: There are more formal authority figures, and every possible precaution is taken to insure that influence—clearly defined and circumscribed—is vested in them rather than in informal agents. Influence which relies on kinship and religious identities is explicitly frowned upon, and resort to physical force is legitimized only by the action of certain formal authorities and must always be satisfactorily accounted for. The differences between the two systems are related to widely divergent cultural histories and systems of values. They certainly cannot be accommodated, if accommodation is desirable, by polemics.

Enculturation, Education, and Personality Structure

A. *Enculturation*

There are several descriptions—some brief and partial, others quite exhaustive—of beliefs and practices surrounding conception, prenatal care, routines at birth, and early child training. Granqvist's descriptions (1931-35, 1947, 1950) of these matters as they occurred in the 1920s in Artas, a Muslim village in what is now western Jordan, are probably the most exhaustive. Father Chémali's descriptions inform us on the same subject among Lebanese Maronites earlier in the century. There are a number of other descriptions scattered in the literature. These sources, though often highly detailed, lay great emphasis on the ritual aspects of this area of life and little or no emphasis on what would today be considered more important: the developmental dynamics involved.

We shall not repeat such details here, since the original sources are readily available and are noted in the bibliography. Suffice it to say that among both Muslim and Christian samples earlier in this century, ritual devices centering around the feeling of great supernatural danger to both mother and child, both before and for some time after birth, were very numerous. In terms of anthropological theory, this should hardly be surprising, for this is a culture in which children are valued highly because of their roles in kin groups and also in which infant and maternal mortality rates have been very high. More recent observations—impressionistic though they are—suggest that at least among the Western-influenced people there has been great attenuation of those ritual procedures.

Among the more recent studies that have been concerned with the matter in terms of developmental dynamics, those of Herbert Williams (1958) and Millicent Ayoub (1957) are notable. As indicated before, these are studies of Lebanese Maronite and Druze villagers. Prothro's recent monograph (1961) is the most comprehensive coverage to date. All of this material is from Lebanon, and there is no comparable material from either Syria or Jordan. However, the Prothro study, which was based largely on interviews with mothers in clinics, has the great value of sampling three religious aggregations (Sunni Muslim, Greek Orthodox, and Armenian Orthodox) residing in villages, in towns, and in the city of Beirut. Relatively Westernized and non-Westernized persons are both represented.

Among the highland Maronite villagers of Hadchite, it would appear that babies and small children are still enveloped in a ritual world of amulets and charms protecting them from harm, including that of the Evil Eye, very much as Chémali described a half a century ago (Williams 1958: 22). Children are freely breastfed until they are one-and-a-half to two years old, but there is generally a very abrupt weaning process and a clear-cut displacement of the weaned child by a younger sibling. In-fants are given much physical affection, but after weaning they are shifted from the mother to various part-time nurses, often siblings who are openly resentful of their charges. The sharp change from mother-nurturing to rather hostile caretakers is seen as perpetuating emotional overdependence on the mother and stressing sibling rivalry. Boys are openly preferred to girls as offspring. While children are stated to be highly valued by parents, they are also clearly a burden and a source of marital quarrels. Much of the enculturation process—outside of formal education—is delegated to age-mates, very frequently siblings and cousins. A constant admonition is the concept of 'aib (shame)—shame particularly to the family consequent upon improper behavior. Sanctions are the withholding of family approval and immediate corporal punish-ment, violent resistance to which is expected and frequent (Williams 1958: 25-30). A comment by Tannous (1944a: 8) is of interest here. He says that in enculturation, the child is constantly admonished by the concept of sharaf (honor), honor of the family in particular. 'Aib and sharaf are clearly opposite sides of the same coin, but in the encultura-tion process, which of them is the most stressed in general? Are there any consistent patterns in the Arab Levant in this connection? Prothro (1961: 94) finds that the use of shaming is typical and that it often accompanies invidious parental comparisons of siblings thus fostering sibling rivalry. He also finds that positive reinforcements are less used than they are among American parents (Prothro 1961: 104). The earlier literature, incidentally, gives details on the various bogeymen—often hardly distinguishable from the Muslim jinn—with which children are frightened.

Ayoub's orientation toward child training is related to her primary interest in kin groups. She finds that among the Druzes of "Kallarwan," enculturation is strongly bounded by kinship ties, both in terms of the agents of enculturation and the behavioral expectations which they im-part (M. Ayoub 1957: 120). While brothers' playgroups are frequent and brotherly solidarity is idealized, quarrels between brothers are so fre-quent as to be proverbial. Younger children are teased a great deal by older boys and young men, and threats of castration are common. Pun-ishments are both verbal and physical. Sisters grow up in an atmosphere of dependence on their brothers, which is projected into adult life. Despite the formal authority of the father, children seem most likely to support the mother in quarrels between the parents (M. Ayoub 1957: 107 ff.). The accounts of Williams and Ayoub appear to be complemen-tary, in some instances corroborative, and in no instances contradictory.

Both authors agree that sex education is rarely received from the parents, and Williams stresses that it is virtually nonexistent among the girls. This should perhaps not be surprising, considering the very uneasy accommodation with sexual matters which both Christianity and Islam, of which the Druze religion is an offshoot, have made. Ayoub notes that the relationship of a child with his mother's brother tends to be an affectionate one. He is a person with whom there are no formal obligations, who can be turned to, nevertheless, for emotional support in times of trouble. The existence of this matrilateral tie, which is consistent with Gulick's finding of a limited bilateral emphasis among Greek Orthodox villagers (Gulick 1955: 132, passim), deserves more investigation in the Arab Levant. Its occurrence is quite to be expected on the basis of recent thinking on formally unilineal kinship systems in general.

In conclusion, Prothro (1961: chap. 9 et passim) sees among the Lebanese a general emphasis on food indulgence, coupled with severe restrictions on sexual indulgence. He also finds relatively early and decisive toilet training and relatively late and stressful weaning. He emphasizes that the adult Lebanese personality is decidedly not "anal." Lebanese mothers do not generally encourage independence in their children. However, he finds that occurrences of the encouragement of independence, coupled with the use of positive reinforcements, are present in significant proportions among these sociocultural groups, which are noted for their high level of achievement.

B. *Formal Education*

The Arab Levantines are the rather direct inheritors of the oldest literate tradition in the world. In their own terms, from the religious point of view, they are *ahl al kitab*, people of the book, whether they be Christian or Muslim. That most of them are illiterate in no way contravenes the symbolic importance of this tradition among them.

Until the relatively recent diffusion into the Arab Levant of school systems and curricula modeled along European lines, formal education was limited very largely to boys' schools, whose primary purpose seems to have been training in reading and writing so that the religious scriptures could be read. Such schools operated at the village level, but it is clear that despite them, effective literacy was possessed by very few men and even fewer women. The status of literate persons, however, was of some prestige. While the Koranic school for boys is an aspect of Islamic culture in all parts of the Middle East, it is worth noting that the Christian Levantines have had a closely parallel institution. Chémali (1917-18) gives a vivid description of such a school among highland Maronites—

recitations in unison and rote memorization spurred on by liberal doses of corporal punishment.

Scripture schools continue to exist in the Arab Levant, but they are now overshadowed in all three of the Levantine countries by state-controlled secular school systems, which are intended to reach all boys and an increasing number of girls. In Lebanon, particularly, the state schools are supplemented by private schools, some of which are sponsored by foreign organizations. Lebanon is also in the lead, but no longer exclusively participant, in the development of a complete "modern" educational system through the university level. Foreign influences, chiefly French and North American, have been particularly profound in this development over the past century.

The effects of this education in developing "Western-orientations" are very sharply revealed in the village studies by Tannous and Gulick. In both Bishmizziin and Munsif, large proportions of the population have been emotionally disengaged from village farming life and impelled toward white-collar and professional careers in the city. These two cases are probably rather extreme for the Arab Levant as a whole. Both villages are Greek Orthodox, members of which religion in general seem to be more inclined away from traditional modes of life than the Maronites and the Muslims, and both are in the Lebanese littoral, which was maximally exposed to foreign-sponsored missionary education in the nineteenth century.

Though probably extreme, they are not, however, by any means unique in kind. Recent studies by means of sampling surveys in the Biqa', among rather traditionally-oriented Muslim farmers, indicate a strong positive interest in more and better education for the children, including girls, together with the prevalent attitude that a person can best make his living in the city (Armstrong 1959: 174-75). Preference for the city is nothing new, but the coupling of it with the recognition that modern education is a prerequisite to urban success is new. Again, comparable material from Jordan and Syria is lacking, and the Lebanese material is spotty. Also lacking are studies which adequately plumb the psychological processes which accompany the new type of education. Is Daniel Lerner's contention (1958) that the "moderns" in the Arab Levant are more "empathic" and psychically mobile than the "traditionals" a profound insight, or is the behavior on which the contention is based simply an artifact of their being exposed to the modern mass media of communication? If it is only the latter, it is nevertheless a significant observation, since it is primarily due to modern education that these people have become so exposed.

C. *Personality Structure*

The personality structure of the adult is the product of enculturation, formal and informal, and, to an undetermined extent, of on-going experiences. The elucidation of the subject is now notorious for its susceptibilities to various types of a posteriori reasoning and to certain ambiguities in the psychoanalytic approach to behavior. Chief among the latter, perhaps, is that given such concepts as projection, displacement, repression, and reaction formation, behavioral observations can be attributed to *opposite*, alternative origins. Another difficulty is that since psychoanalytic techniques were originated for the purpose of curing demonstrable cases of emotional disturbance in particular cultural contexts, their application to general personality analysis usually results in depictions which sound like clinical cases. Every study which this writer has read which employs psychodiagnostic tests conveys the strong impression that their subjects were at least neurotic. Perhaps the answer must be that in all cultures people have problems, and in no culture are they entirely resolved, with various types of emotional excess or rigidity revealed by the studies being consequences of this. Nevertheless, it remains to be shown how one draws the line between such a conclusion and one which, in effect, is that some cultures as wholes are systems of maladjustment. This problem has recently led a number of anthropologists to reject the psychoanalytic approach to culture that had previously been in considerable vogue. In the present writer's view, this is an overreaction. In their present state of methodology, psychoanalytic studies should not be taken as being conclusive, but neither should they be rejected simply because they seem to claim to be conclusive. Instead, they bring forth certain types of evidence which may be of profound importance and are, in any case, highly suggestive for refined thinking and further research.

This preamble seems to be necessary in view of the fact that the single culture-in-personality study which has been made in the Arab Levant (Williams 1958) yields some rather startling conclusions which, in this writer's opinion, should not be rejected but should be accepted with the cautions indicated.

Some of Williams' findings have already been mentioned. His adult personality profile, which is based on Rorschach tests and life histories, is as follows: The projections are on the whole "unproductive" and "barren" (Williams 1958: 45). The large amount of animal movement responses stress the senses of threat, flight, and burdens (p. 56). In general, there is a sense of inadequacy for tasks and an indication of inability to react freely and spontaneously when confronted with the unfamiliar (p. 63). Let us interject here that this depiction fits perfectly with Lerner's image of the "constricted traditional" person (Lerner 1958: 148-51), but that it is difficult to see it as being representative of those many Lebanese who have made successful adaptations after emigration—perhaps a selective factor at work. Williams recognizes that these characteristics may in part have been induced by the test situation itself (pp. 61-62), but nevertheless he reaches these general conclusions: (1) His subjects in general seemed to be overwhelmed by a harsh, cold, unrelenting, ungiving world, a world in which they feel helpless and dwarfed. This is dealt with in concrete terms but cannot be manipulated. There is a strong sense of inadequacy and worthlessness, especially among the women. (Prothro [1961: 69] finds that mothers typically bestow less warmth of affection on their daughters than on their sons.) The men attempt a facade of bravado and assertions of mastery. (2) Emotionally, the individual is extremely isolated from others—despite physical closeness. There is no conviction that others can really be relied and depended upon. The life histories reveal a number of cases, incidentally, of outright desertions within the nuclear family. [Interjection: if this depiction is generalizable, what implications does it have for the interpretative problems which we raised earlier in regard to the structures and structural motivations in kin groups? It *could* be seen as providing a key to the whole matter of contrasts between verbalized ideals and behavioral realities which have been reviewed.] (3) There is a general need to be dependent, passive, and taken care of, a longing for some omnipotent figure, or magical solution, which will release the individual from his burdens. Frustration of this need leads to generalized resentment and mistrust, which can sometimes lead to impulsive, aggressive outbursts (Williams 1958: 69-72). This personality profile is seen by Williams as being a product of the enculturation processes in Hadchite, plus the location of the village in an isolated, rather severe, environment.

We cannot conclude that the personality profiles of Hadchite represent *the* personality structure of the Arab Levant, for we do not have other evidence of the same type, and one suspects that there is probably more than one recurrent basic personality type in the area. Williams himself, be it said, makes no generalizations beyond the confines of his village. Nor, on the other hand, can we dismiss Williams' findings on the grounds that they are derived from aberrant sources. This study represents one probe into a very subtle subject in a complex culture area. In the opinion of this writer, Williams' findings suggest wider behavioral connections, both in Hadchite and elsewhere. Only on the basis of further research in personality and in social organization in the Arab Levant can more definite conclusions be reached.

Williams' description of personality in Hadchite is a far cry from the long current pejorative stereotype of the "Levantine personality." It might be argued that this reflects village-urban differences, and that the "Levantine"—depicted as being clever, manipulative, amoral, and utterly opportunistic—is more typical of the city. The "Levantine personality" has been identified only in humanistic terms (see Hourani 1946: 70-71, passim), and its traits have actually never been rigorously analyzed. Gulick, however, has suggested in a very general way that if the urban stereotypic "Levantine" does exist, it probably at least needs to be differentiated from another urban type of personality, that which is adept at interaction with persons representing a great variety of religious groups and nationalities but is itself nevertheless anchored in kinship, local, religious, and other norms (Gulick 1955: 172).

Before closing this subject, we should draw attention to a social psychological study among Lebanese which was conducted by means of questionnaires—under circumstances which are not made very clear—by Paul Grieger (1955). Despite the use of questionnaires, Grieger's account has a generality of tone which makes his findings difficult to apply specifically. Nevertheless, his main conclusions are worthy of note. He says that the Lebanese personality is, first, notable for its primary emotionality. This is revealed in strong, spontaneous expressions and quick reactions; sudden fluctuations from depression to exaltation; great verbal demonstrativeness; and difficulty in maintaining objectivity in thought and action. Second, the personality is said to be extroverted, turned toward others rather than the self. Social life is both a need and a pleasure. However, this personality is not well adapted to participation in organized group activities, partly because of its unwillingness to be subjected to authority. Grieger concludes: "Le libanais n'éprouve aucun interet à la vie collective de son groupe" (1955: 286).

If one accepts these findings at their face value, one is faced with difficulties. In some respects Grieger appears to agree with Williams, but in others he does not. In his characterization of social orientations, however, he seems to be suggesting traits which may fit with the group behavior phenomena which we discussed earlier. It is also difficult to relate Prothro and Melikian's finding (1953: 362) of high authoritarian reactions to the reported inability of Arab Levantines to organize efficiently and to their unwillingness to submit to authority figures; but, on the other hand, their finding possibly can be related to Williams' finding of a need for magical solutions by omnipotent figures. At the present time, Prothro (personal communication, July 2, 1960) feels that the Lebanese "do submit to authority, but in a defensive, expedient, respect-for-power way" which at least suggests a different form of authoritarianism from that associated with the German and Japanese cultures, for example. Despite the several discontinuities in these bodies of data, there are also some recurrent threads which future research and thinking should weave together.

Religion

It has already been pointed out that while the majority of Arab Levantines are Sunni Muslims, a variety of other religions are well represented in the area. The "ethnic diversity" of the Arab Levant is to a considerable degree a product of this religious diversity (see Rabbath 1938), for to some extent there are nonreligious correlates, such as differences in dress. It should also be noted that the urban-village-pastoral ecologies contribute to ethnic diversity in a manner which very largely crosscuts the religious issue. Despite these differences, nearly all of the inhabitants of the area are, by their own definition, Arabs, the four exceptions being (1) colonies of Jews in the larger cities, which continue to exist despite the close proximity of Israel; (2) a fairly large population of Armenians (Catholics and Orthodox), who fled from Turkey during and after World War I; (3) several groups of Circassians (Sunni Muslim), whose forebears were imported by the Ottoman government beginning in 1878 to serve as garrisons along the desert fringe (Proux 1938); and (4) the Kurdish-speaking Yazidis, west of Aleppo (Lescot 1938a).

There is no question but that religious identity serves as a very important means of social differentiation in the Arab Levant, and in Lebanon these differences are formally recognized in the structure of the government. Consciousness of social distance is clearly marked among them (see Prothro and Melikian 1952), one marker of which is prevailing religious endogamy. The Arabs are divided into the following religious groups: Sunni Muslims; Shi'ah Muslims; 'Alawites, or Nusairis (Weulersse 1938 and 1940), an offshoot of certain extreme Shi'ah views held at the time of the Fatimid Caliphate in Egypt and generally not recognized as being a Muslim sect; Maronites, originally a heterodox offshoot of the Byzantine Church, but for some recent centuries closely identified with the Roman Catholic Church; Greek Orthodox, whose patriarch resides in Damascus; Greek Catholics, representing an eighteenth-century shift of allegiance from Orthodox to Roman Catholic; and half a dozen other very small Christian sects, most of which, except for a few recently converted Protestants (largely urban, Western-oriented), are vestiges of very early Christian sects. Rondot (1947) provides a comprehensive view of these groups as they occur in Lebanon.

We shall not review the doctrinal characteristics of these religions.

Formally, the Sunni Muslim Arab Levantine majority does not, as far as we know, differ significantly from Sunni Muslims elsewhere, and to review the beliefs and practices of Sunni Islam in general would be far beyond the scope of this chapter. The various sources cited above provide considerable information on the rituals and beliefs of a number of the other sects. Of more general scope bearing on the Arab Levant, with special focus on the Christians, is Bliss (1912).

Apart from the differences and convergences (often due to historical ties) in the matter of formal doctrines, there are certain features of religious behavior in the Arab Levant which seem to recur in different sects. In some cases, these probably represent vestiges of very ancient religious practices which antedated all the present formal sects. In other cases, they possibly reflect certain cultural uniformities which are ongoing despite sectarian differences. We suggest that these recurrent elements are as follows:

1. De-emphasis of hierarchies of authoritarian religious functionaries. Even where formal hierarchies occur, as among the Christians, local priests generally perform their functions autonomously, and their social lives are not particularly separate from those of the rest of the population.

2. From the point of view of intensity of religious emotion, the most important rites of passage are those concerned with birth and death. Weddings, though given sacred sanctions, are primarily secular in tone. De-emphasis of puberty rituals (Muslim circumcisions, though certainly sexual in reference, are generally prepubertal).

3. A pervasive sense of both positive and negative supernatural power which can be identified with God and Satan, respectively, only by rationalization. The positive aspect is most clearly revealed in visitations to saints' shrines (often shared by Christians and Muslims, even when they are not the reputed tombs of Old Testament figures) in the fulfillment of vows or to put the self in contact with the sacredness of the place, chiefly in the interests of preserving or restoring health. Contact can be established indirectly by leaving articles of clothing at the shrine.

The negative aspect is represented most clearly, though not solely, by belief in the Evil Eye, a concept of generalized malevolence most closely associated with the fear of envy. Why should there be such fear of envy? Psychoanalytic answers could be put forward which would suggest a relationship between this phenomenon and certain aspects of interpersonal motivations which we reviewed earlier.

4. Personalization of these concepts of supernatural power in the form of saints, on the one hand, and of various mischievous if not malevolent goblins on the other. Of the latter, the Muslim jinn are the

classic example, and Touma (1958: 142 ff.) writing of Maronites as of the present time, mentions belief in jinnlike creatures as did Chémali at an earlier time. In fact, Touma uses the term to designate them. In the Arab Levant, saints appear to be largely mythical or scriptural figures—deceased in any case. If there is occurrence of interest in living holy men—along the lines of the North African marabout pattern—it has not impressed the writers on Arab Levantine religion. The same can be said concerning religious brotherhoods, although they have been mentioned as occurring in pre-World War I Arab Palestine. *Zikrs* are still occasionally performed at a small *tikkiyah* in Tripoli, Lebanon (for a vivid description of which, see Julian Huxley's *From an Antique Land*), but this pattern is apparently very nearly a thing of the past (Sullivan 1962: 26).

Being at most adjuncts, and more often violations, of formal religious doctrines, these phenomena are often referred to in the literature as "superstitions." This implies differentials in belief and practice among the Arab Levantines themselves. On this matter there is no reliable information whatever. From the descriptions at hand, the anthropologist is, frankly, inclined to suspect that most Arab Levantines who are internally committed to religious beliefs are more intensely committed emotionally to the beliefs and the hundreds of rituals subsumable under "superstitions," above, than they are to formalized theological doctrines. Externally, however, virtually all Arab Levantines are deeply committed to their religious identities. Tannous (1944b: 539 ff.), writing generally, seems to stress the emotional primacies of socioreligious identity and of "folk rituals" over commitment to formal doctrines. There are some very slight suggestions that among some Western-oriented Arab Levantines there may be some agnostic tendencies, or at least tendencies toward less emotional dependence on various ritual practices (Gulick 1955: 93).

The Arts

It is virtually impossible to differentiate the major indigenous art forms of the Arab Levant from those associated with the Islamic tradition generally. In general, the Christian Arabs of the Levant seem to participate in the same tradition except in regard to religious expressions, such as pictures of saints, apostles, the holy family, etc., which are generally rendered in a style derived from the Byzantine and, to some extent among the Maronites, in the Italian Catholic style.

The graphic arts are limited chiefly to complex floral and geometric designs in wood, metal, ceramics, textiles, and stone. Calligraphic devices are notably employed in these designs. Such materials are made by people who in the West would be called craftsmen rather than professional artists. Their products are largely ornamental, and the majority of Arab Levantines probably possess few if any such items. For example, although backgammon is played constantly in homes and in coffee houses, the writer has never seen it played on other than plain wooden boards, in spite of the fact that elaborately inlaid wooden ones are readily available.

The greatest amount of artistic participation and appreciation is in oral and musical expression. While there are professional ensembles of indigenous instrument players and singers, the ability to play, sing, dance, and recite poetry is widespread. At a Greek Orthodox wedding which the writer once attended, artistic expressions of all these types were provided, impromptu, by the villagers themselves—many of whom were quite Western-oriented in other respects. It is well known that the Arabs themselves consider poetry to be the zenith of their artistic expression. The Arab Levantines are no exception, and the emotional commitment to Arabic poetry, traditional and modern, continues to be important.

Efforts to introduce European fine arts (musical and graphic) into the Arab Levant have been made—Beirut has a symphony orchestra and a conservatory, for example. But these efforts have been largely limited to Lebanon, and even there their audiences seem to be highly restricted, consisting only of extremely Western-oriented people, some of whom, at least, seem to have become dissociated from Arab Levantine culture. The writing of novels and stories which are European in structure has not developed to the extent that it has in India.

Diffusions of more widespread appeal are Spanish and Latin American dance tunes and rhythms and the cinema, which includes not only European and North American films but also the products of the Egyptian movie industry.

For further discussions of this whole subject the reader is referred to the section on the arts, literature, music, and the theater and cinema in Patai 1956 (*Lebanon 2*: 324-61; *Syria 2*: 447-85; *Jordan*: 360-91). These presentations, which were written severally by Jacob Landau, Farid Aouad, Majed Elass, Toufic Succar, Fahim Qubain, and Anis Makdisi, include descriptions of the various types of indigenous artistic modes and, in perhaps disproportionate detail, descriptions of recent artistic innovations.

Language

Arabic is the native and first language of the vast majority of the Arab Levantines, and while there are some subregional dialectic differences, they are well within the range of mutual intelligibility. As in other Arabic-speaking areas, there is also a distinction between various colloquial dialects, on the one hand, and a modified classical Arabic on the other. This contrast has, if anything, been heightened in recent decades by the great increase of exposure to the classical form by means of the radio and the press.

Despite its primacy, Arabic is not, however, the only language which is spoken in the area. The various other linguistic usages are as follows:

1. In northern Syria, a number of people—including those belonging to the Yazidi sect—speak Kurdish, and others speak Turkish.

2. In Ma'lula and its neighboring villages (Reich 1937) on the eastern slopes of the Anti-Lebanons in Syria, there is vestigial vernacular use of Aramaic, the Semitic language that was generally replaced by Arabic after the Muslim conquest. There is some indication that Aramaic survived as the vernacular language in other areas of the Anti-Lebanons and Mount Lebanon until relatively recent times. It is the liturgical language of the Maronite religion.

3. Armenian continues to be spoken as the first language among some of the Armenian refugee population, but most of the Armenians are also fluent in Arabic, and some of the older ones are fluent in Turkish as well.

4. French is widely used as a secondary language in Lebanon—especially among the Maronites—and to some extent in Syria. This is a legacy of the French Mandate, which appears to continue in force. The Lebanese government uses French, as well as Arabic, for official purposes, and it is taught in the secondary schools. It should be noted that Selim Abou has recently made an effort to refute the idea that French is a "secondary" language in Lebanon, claiming instead that it is fully synthesized with Arabic among many Lebanese (Abou 1962: chap. 6, passim).

5. In Jordan, English has approximately the same status that French has in Lebanon. English is also widely understood in Lebanon and to a lesser degree in Syria. This seems to be a result of the presence of returned emigrants to English-speaking countries and of the various North American-sponsored educational institutions. English is the language of instruction at the American University of Beirut, an institution which has played an important part in the development of the Western-oriented segment of the Arab-Levantine population.

The polyglot nature of the Arab Levant in general, and of many Arab Levantines individually, is a product of historic events, which in turn reflect the aspect of the area that is open to cosmopolitan influences. However, the area's linguistic diversity does not appear to have the same divisive effect which its religious diversity has. One has the impression that for the Levantine whose first language is Arabic (i.e. for most Arab Levantines) fluency in other languages is largely of instrumental significance. (Abou says that this is a peculiarly Anglo-Saxon impression.) In any case, the speaking of Arabic has far greater than merely instrumental significance. The possession of the language is a highly charged emotional symbol, both of ethnolinguistic identity and of esthetic involvement. The great verbality of Arab Levantine culture is one generalization that has been made which need not be hedged with provisions. Various aspects of it have been touched upon in this chapter, and we need perhaps only add that linguistic expression is accompanied by a system of gestures which is highly elaborated (see Brewer 1951). Their awareness of their common linguistic tradition and their intense involvement in their language is a trait system which contributes materially to the fact that the Arab Levantines, despite their many differences, inhabit a culture area whose reality as such is quite objective, rather than being largely arbitrarily defined.

ADDENDUM: 1963-67

Substantial progress in the anthropology of the Arab Levant was made between 1963 and 1967. This was not only additive, as evidenced in the 1963-67 bibliography, but in addition a critical, analytic element has entered into the picture which augurs well for the future. Anthropologists specializing in the area are beginning to write explicitly in terms of each other's work, and they no longer so exclusively indulge in what has amounted to idiosyncratic monologues. A large proportion of the publications noted below appeared as parts of collective enterprises: a volume of original papers on the Middle East as a whole, two symposia on the Circum-Mediterranean area, a symposium on Middle Eastern urbanism, a symposium on Lebanese politics, and a festschrift volume for a prominent anthropologist not himself a Middle Eastern specialist. The anthropology of the Arab Levant appears to be beginning to make a contribution to wider contexts of human behavior, such as urbanization, political modernization, and the changing roles of women in the traditional, agrarian cultures of Asia and the Mediterranean. It can be hoped that there will, in turn, be an increasing feedback from such wider concerns onto studies of the area itself. The Arab Levant (along with the rest of the Middle East) is also beginning to assume a recognizable position in the professional cognitive mass of anthropology generally, and this may lead to an increase in the amount and sophistication of anthropological field work done in the area.

More anthropological research has been done recently in the Arab Levant than is indicated by this bibliography. Intensive work has been done, for example, on the Bedouin of the Negev in Israel. There is also a considerable backlog of unpublished village and other studies.

Several themes or topics of interest are shared by different authors in the works listed below. *Social class*, and various changing and stable aspects of it, is given systematic consideration in Aswad (1967), Cohen (1965), Gulick (1967), Peters (1963), and Rosenfeld (1964). It is a subject which has in the past all too often been written off by parroting the stereotype that Islam is equalitarian. *Decision making*, particularly but not exclusively in connection with the resolution of conflicts or crises, is dealt with in detail and with considerable sophistication in Antoun (1967), Ayoub (1965, 1966), Cohen (1965), and Nader (1965). Connected with this theme is the observation, remarked upon by several, that the extended kinship structure of the Arabs continues to be viable. Its segmentary structure gives it flexibility in adapting itself to changes, which can be viewed as a positive aspect of the same structure which also lends itself to instability.

Women, long the subject of massively stereotyped thinking, are given considerable attention in Aswad (1967), Gulick (1967), Khalaf (1965), and Sweet (1967). *Urban life*, and current urbanization phenomena, are the common subject of Gulick (1965b, 1967), Nader (1965), and the four papers in Morroe Berger's 1963 volume, *The New Metropolis in the Arab World* (Chakar, Chehade, Kanaan, and Riachi).

BIBLIOGRAPHY

Abū, Salīm
1962   *Le bilinguisme arabe-français au Liban*, Paris, Presses Universitaires de France.

Subtitled "Essai d'anthropologie culturelle," much of this book is concerned with Lebanese literature and with propounding the thesis that the true Lebanese culture is a synthesis of French and Arab patterns. In the course of his book, Abū shows some familiarity with anthropological and sociological publications on Lebanon, and his observations of religious and linguistic behavior in Lebanese cities and villages are of considerable interest and value.

Antoun, Richard T.
1965   "Conservatism and change in the village community: a Jordanian case study," *Human Organization 24*: 4-10.

Based on field work in an East Bank Jordanian village in 1959-60, this paper presents specific life history materials, with emphasis on relationships outside of the village.

1967   "Social organization and the life cycle in an Arab village," *Ethnology 6*: 294-308.

Based on the same field work as Antoun 1965, this paper is concerned with the structural ramifications of the arrangements involved in a single case of marriage.

Armstrong, Lincoln
1959   "Opinions on education in rural Lebanon," *Rural Sociology 24*: 162-75.

Reports certain results of a random sample, socioeconomic survey which was conducted in the southern part of the Biqaʻ in 1954. Findings tend to support other conclusions regarding education in Lebanon. The precise quantification is welcome, but since the reliability of Lebanese responses to questionnaires is not as yet understood, all findings based on this method should be regarded with caution.

Armstrong, Lincoln, and G. K. Hirabayashi
1956   "Social differentiation in selected Lebanese villages," *American Sociological Review 21*: 425-34.

Based on survey research in the Biqaʻ in 1954, this article provides some concrete information on the occupational differentiation patterns in a sample of essentially non-Western-ized villages. The findings serve as a modification of the traditional two-class image. The author's interests, however, seem to be as much in their methods as in the cultural situation they analyze.

Ashkenazi, Touvia
1938 *Tribus semi-nomades de la Palestine du Nord*, Paris, Librairie Orientaliste Paul Geuthner.

Essentially an ethnographic survey. Carefully lists, enumerates and locates the approximately 80 groups in the area as of 1937.

Aswad, Barbara C.
1967 "Key and peripheral roles of noble women in a Middle Eastern plains village," *Anthropological Quarterly 40*: 139-52.

This paper is based on field work done in 1964-65 in an Arabic-speaking village in the Hatay province of Turkey, formerly the Alexandretta province of northwestern Syria. Of central concern is the documentation of considerable de facto control of property by women. Polygyny, still a sign of high status, is a factor in this, since the property of a wife in a polygynous marriage passes only to her own children.

Ayoub, Millicent Robinson
1957 *Endogamous marriage in a Middle Eastern village*, unpublished doctoral dissertation, Cambridge, Radcliffe College.

Based on field work in 1953-54 in a predominantly Druze village in central Mount Lebanon. Field work was conducted in the company of her husband, Victor F. Ayoub. A sophisticated and very thorough study, well documented, which, in addition to describing the kinship organization of the village, explores critically the usages of kinship terminology, the genetic effects of endogamy, and, to some extent, child-training practices. A major contribution.

1959 "Parallel cousin marriage and endogamy: a study in socio-metry," *Southwestern Journal of Anthropology 15*: 266-75.

Based on material presented at greater length in Mrs. Ayoub's doctoral dissertation, this article makes the point that patri-lateral parallel cousin marriage is but one instance of a generalized preference for kin-group endogamy.

Ayoub, Victor Ferris
1955 *Political structure of a Middle East community; a Druze village in Mount Lebanon*, unpublished doctoral dissertation, Cambridge, Harvard University.

The author is a native of the United States, but is of Lebanese, though not Druze, parentage. Field work was conducted in 1953-54 in the company of his wife, Millicent R. Ayoub. The political structure of the village is analyzed not in terms of political parties but in terms of the social structure of the exercise of power, authority, and influence—these being conceptually distinguished from each other. Though concentrating on one village, the author relates his villagers to wider contexts in Lebanese society. This is the most extensive treatment of the subject in the Arab Levantine literature. The author applies the same concept of situationally-cued loyalties (derived from Evans-Pritchard) that Gulick employs in his 1955 monograph. However, Ayoub's application, while less comprehensive than Gulick's, is less schematic and more specific.

1965   "Conflict resolution and social reorganization in a Lebanese village," *Human Organization 24*: 11-17.

Three cases of conflict resolution, using intravillage *waasṭa* procedures and extravillage courts, are reviewed. *Waasṭa* is placed in the context of the segmentary kinship structure of the village, a Druze community in the Matn district of Lebanon, which the author studied in 1953-54 and again in 1961.

1966   "Resolution of conflict in a Lebanese village," in *Politics in Lebanon*, Leonard Binder, ed., New York, John Wiley and Sons: 107-26.

This covers very much the same material as Ayoub's 1965 paper, but in more general terms. It is less successful than the earlier paper in delineating the complex network of ties between the village and the national social system, but its discussion of the philosophical bases of the *waasṭa* system is very lucid.

Baldensperger, Philip J.

1894   "Birth, marriage and death among the fellahin of Palestine," *Palestine Exploration Fund Quarterly Statement 1894*: 127-44.

Written in the form of answers to 29 questions, completely divorced from cultural contexts. However, since itemized, might be useful for comparative purposes in contemporary studies.

Bazantay, Pierre

1936   *Les états du Levant sous mandat français. Enquête sur l'artisanat à Antioche*, Beirut, Imprimerie Catholique.

Primarily concerned with the technical processes of various crafts (weaving, woodworking, etc.). Also conveys some feeling of the living conditions of specialists in a small city. Well illustrated with photographs.

Bliss, Frederick J.
1912   *The religions of modern Syria and Palestine*, New York, Charles Scribner's Sons.

A useful reference for the histories and formal theological and ritual systems of the major religions in the area. Particularly important for its attention to the Christian sects.

Boucheman, Albert de
1934a "Note sur la rivalité de deux tribus moutonnières de Syrie: les 'Mwali' et les 'Hadidyn,' " *Revue des Études Islamiques 8*: 11-58.

Detailed discussion of the social organization of the Hadidiin and the Mwali—those who are in contact with northern Syrian villagers—and their patterns of leadership as revealed in conflicts.

1934b "La sédentarisation des nomades du desert de Syrie," *L'Asie Française 34*: 140-43.

Though very brief, provides a succinct picture of the various stages of transition.

1937   "Une petite cité caravanière: Suhné," *Institut Français de Damas, Documents d'Études Orientales 6*, Paris.

A first-rate community study, with detailed ethnography, of a town in the Syrian desert whose inhabitants have economic ties with the Arab Levant. Eleven photographic plates, including an aerial photograph with an overlay showing the quarters.

Bouron, Narcisse
1930   *Les Druzes*, Paris, Berger-Levrault.

A basic source on Druze history and religion. It also includes factual material on the towns, villages, and kin groups in the Jebel Druze in 1927.

Brewer, W. D.
1951   "Patterns of gesture among the Levantine Arabs," *American Anthropologist 53*: 232-37.

Based on observations in Beirut in the late 1940s and work with a Syrian informant in the United States in 1949. A valuable probe into an obviously important but neglected aspect of Arab Levantine behavior.

Canaan, Tawfik
1932-33 "The Palestinian Arab house: its architecture and folklore," *Palestine Oriental Society Journal 12*: 223-47; *13*: 1-93.

Very thorough—terminology of parts, details of construction, building tools, and rituals performed at various stages of construction. House types and floor plans. Arabic-English glossary. Relevance not entirely limited to Arab Palestine.

Chadwick, Frances
1956   "The story of Istabl," *Lands East: The Near and Middle East Magazine* (September): 9-16. Washington, D.C., Middle East Institute.

Though brief and written in "popular" style, this is a useful account of role and values conflicts resulting from a proposed cultural innovation. Istabl is one of the several southern Biqa' villages which were surveyed in 1954.

Chakar, Alexius
1963   "Damascus," in *The New Metropolis in the Arab World*, Morroe Berger, ed., New Delhi, Allied Publishers: 64-76.

A city planner's summary of the problems of Damascus, this paper includes a table presenting the results of a questionnaire on nuisances administered to 200 families, itself something quite unique.

Chéhab, Maurice
1942-43   "Le costume au Liban," Beirut, Musée National Libanais, *Bulletin du Musée de Beyrouth* 6: 47-79.

Illustrated from old plates and engravings. Essentially reviews the clothing styles of the late Ottoman period. Useful for comparative purposes.

Chéhabe-ed-Din, Saïd
1960   *Geographie humaine de Beyrouth*, Beirut, Imprimerie Calfax.

Embellished with photographs, unfortunately often not well reproduced, this book is a good supplement to Churchill's study (1954) of Beirut, since it includes additional economic, architectural, and institutional details. It is not, however, an "urban ecological" study in the sociological sense of the term.

Chehade, Nachat
1963   "Aleppo," in *The New Metropolis in the Arab World*, Morroe Berger, ed., New Delhi, Allied Publishers: 77-102.

Contains a considerable amount of descriptive material on the various parts of Aleppo, the ethnic composition of its population, and the procedures (wise and otherwise) being taken to transform the Old City.

Chelhod, Joseph
1967   "Problèmes d'ethnologie jordanienne: nomadisme et séden-

tarisation," *Objets et mondes: La Revue du Musée de l'Homme 7*: 85-102.

The author did three months of field work in Jordan in 1966, and this paper, the result, seems to be essentially the report of a sentimental journey among the "noble Bedouin." However, there are some up-to-date statistics and some excellent photographs.

Chémali, Béchara
1909   "Moeurs et usages au Liban," *Anthropos 4*: 37-53.

Deals largely with Maronite funerals. Like his other papers, includes detailed rendering of songs. The author, a priest, was convinced that the customs he described were being undermined by social change, especially emigration.

1910   "Naissance et premier age au Liban," *Anthropos 5*: 734-47, 1072-86.

Maronite beliefs concerning sterility and conception; birth techniques; cradling, weaning; protective magic (frankly labeled as superstitions); religious indoctrination, and play. Emphasis on translated songs. Photographs. Useful for comparison with Granqvist.

1915-16 "Mariage et noce au Liban," *Anthropos 10-11*: 913-41.

Considerable detail on Maronite weddings. Useful for comparison with Granqvist's Palestinian Muslim material. An important ethnographic report. Photographs.

1917-18 "Moeurs et usages au Liban: l'éducation," *Anthropos 12-13*: 625-40.

Concerned largely with the religious village schools of the Maronites. Photographs provide useful information on the costumes of early twentieth century—documenting considerable subsequent change.

Churchill, Charles W.
1954   *The city of Beirut; a socio-economic survey*, Dar El-Kitab, Lebanon, Economic Research Institute of the American University of Beirut.

The report of a sample survey of Beirut which was conducted in 1952-53. Consists largely of statistical tables on household composition, amount of mobility, and various financial conditions. Though the data are unique and therefore very valuable, the work is disappointing in that there is no interpretative discussion.

1959   "Village life in the Central Beqa' Valley of Lebanon," *Middle East Economic Papers, 1959, 1-48*, Beirut, Economic Research Institute, American University of Beirut.

Based on census surveys in 1955-56 in thirteen villages in the central Biqa', complementing the 1954 survey of villages in the southern end of the valley. Two of the villages were Christian, while the rest were Muslim, and the author stresses that similarities between the two seem to be greater than differences. A very useful study, which includes brief vignettes of each village and quantitative material on age, marital status, mobility, household size, education, etc.

Cohen, Abner
1965   *Arab border-villages in Israel: a study of continuity and change in social organization.* Manchester, Manchester University Press. 194 pp.

This is a major monograph, replete with a laudatory Foreword by Max Gluckman. It is a composite study of several villages in the border zone of Israel and Jordan between Haifa and Tel-Aviv. The fifteen months of field work were done in 1958-59. The specific, factual details on social structure, occupations, etc., are very valuable, and the author's main conclusion is of considerable interest. This is that since the war of 1948, the patrilineage structure of these villages has become increasingly strong, owing to the fact that it has proved to be functionally important in political life. Previously, during the Mandate period, the lineages were weakened because of internal social class differentiation.

Copeland, Paul W.
1955   " 'Beehive' villages of North Syria," *Antiquity 29*: 21-24.

Extremely brief but detailed description of the construction of the domed houses that are unique to this region of the Arab Levant.

Couroyer, B.
1951   "Histoire d'une tribu semi-nomade de Palestine," *Revue Biblique 58*: 75-91.

A largely historical and genealogical study of the Ta'amirah, who were becoming sedentarized in the region of Bethlehem in 1948. Can be read instructively in relation to Granqvist's study of the village of Artas, whose inhabitants were in contact with the Ta'amirah.

Crist, Raymond E.
1954   "The mountain village of Dahr, Lebanon," *Smithsonian Institution, Annual Report for 1953*: 407-23.

A brief account of observations, largely from the geographical and ecological points of view, made in 1951 and 1952. Dahr is a small Sunni village northeast of Tripoli. Photographs.

Crowfoot, Grace M.
1941   "The vertical loom in Palestine and Syria," *Palestine Explora-*
tion Fund Quarterly for October (London): 141-51.
Technical details on what was very widely a home craft.

Curtiss, Samuel I.
1902   *Primitive Semitic religion today*, Chicago, Fleming H. Revell.
Based on observations in Syria, Palestine, and Sinai in
1898-1901, this book, though very dated, is a useful reference for certain ritual practices which tend to be common to
Christian and Muslim Arab Levantines.

Daghestani, Kazem El
1932   *Étude sociologique sur la famille musulmane contemporaine*
en Syrie, Paris, Ernest Leroux.
This monograph is an invaluable source on the subject of
kinship and marriage, because of its comprehensiveness. It
reviews kinship and marriage patterns among Syrian nomads,
villagers, and city-dwellers, as well as among special groups
such as the 'Alawites and Circassians. However, the author's
statements are often highly generalized and, one often suspects, rather impressionistic. As mentioned in the text of this
chapter, it is never made clear whether or not the various
urban patterns reflect Western influences.

1953   "The evolution of the Moslem family in the Middle Eastern
countries," *International Social Science Bulletin* 5: 681-91.
In general stresses the "Westernization" of the family, but in
highly generalized, unquantified fashion.

Dalman, Gustaf Hermann
1928-42   *Arbeit und Sitte in Palästina*, 7 vols. Gütersloh, C. Bertels-
mann.
The most monumental of the works in the German-Biblical
tradition. Environment, ecological adaptations, crafts and
home industries, food, cooking, clothes, animal husbandry,
agriculture—all treated in meticulous detail. Each volume is
illustrated with photographs. Contains references to a number
of other German studies of the early twentieth century
which are not included in this bibliography. Material is, unfortunately, dated, since it was gathered in the early 1900s.

Davies, Rodger P.
1949   "Syrian Arabic kinship terms," *Southwestern Journal of*
Anthropology 5: 244-52.
Two complete paradigms, supplied by a Palestinian Christian
and a Syrian Muslim. Some functional discussion.

Dodd, Stuart Carter
1934 *A controlled experiment on rural hygiene in Syria*, Beirut, American Press.

This work deals largely with the methodological problems of constructing, administering, and scaling a questionnaire of 270 items on hygiene and illness among 'Alawite villagers west of Homs. There is some ethnographic material. The scale could prove useful as a checklist of health matters in Middle Eastern villages.

Dodge, Bayard
1940 "The Settlement of the Assyrians on the Khabbur," *Royal Central Asian Society Journal 27*: 301-20.

Though peripheral to the Arab Levant, its discussion of the relationship of kin groups to settlements is pertinent to the treatment of this subject in this chapter.

Drower, Ethel S.
1956 *Water into wine*, London, Murray.

Concerns what the author considers to be certain common themes in the sacramental use of water, wine, and bread among several of the religions of the Arab Levant and adjacent areas. Photographs.

Dubertret, Louis, and Jacques Weulersse
1940 *Manuel de géographie de Syrie, Liban et Proche Orient, vol. 1*, Beirut, Imprimerie Catholique.

Dufourg, J.-P.
1951 "La maison rurale au Djebel Druze," *Revue de Géographie de Lyon 26*: 411-21.

Excellent photographic illustrations of constructions. Emphasizes influence of the natural environment.

1959 "Notes et réflexions sur l'agriculture jordanienne," *Revue de Géographie de Lyon 34*: 255-70.

Notable for its use of aerial photographs.

Epstein, Eliahu
1938 "The Beduin of Transjordan: their social and economic problems," *Royal Central Asian Society Journal 25*: 228-36.

Concerned with the economic straits of the Beni Sakhr and the course of their partial sedentarization since the beginning of the century.

1942 "The Druzes of Palestine," *Royal Central Asian Society Journal 29*: 52-63.

Deals with the approximately 11,000 Druzes living in Palestine at that time (as opposed to the 115,000 in Lebanon and

Syria), many of whom continue to live in Israel. They are stated to lack the chiefly dynasties (predominant lineages) of the Lebanese and Syrian Druzes, and have been praised for their successful assimilation in a hostile world.

Ewing, Joseph Franklin, S.J.
1950 "Hyperbrachycephaly as influenced by cultural conditioning," *Harvard University, Peabody Museum of American Archaeology and Ethnology, Papers 23*, no. 2, Cambridge, Mass.

Though primarily a study in physical anthropology, this work contains useful material on child-rearing practices and marriage among highland-dwelling Maronites in Lebanon. The author did his field work shortly after World War II.

Féghali, Michel
1925 "La famille catholique au Liban," *Revue d'Ethnographie 6*: 291-308.

Féghali was a Maronite priest. His descriptions of rituals are not so detailed as Chémali's. The article seems largely to be a case of special pleading to show how religious the Maronite family is.

Ferguson, Charles A.
1955 "Syrian Arabic studies," *Middle East Journal 9*: 187-94.

Despite its title, this is a very concise and expert survey and commentary on linguistic studies which have been made in the Arab Levant generally.

Fetter, George C.
1961 "Attitudes toward selected aspects of rural life and technological change among central Beka'a farmers," *American University of Beirut, Faculty of Agricultural Sciences, Publication 13.*

Report of survey research conducted in 1960 among 406 farmers in one mixed Christian-Muslim, 3 Christian, and 7 Sunni Muslim villages in the Biqa' valley, Lebanon. Base data on income, land tenure, education, length of residence in the village. Findings tend to support generally recognized impressions that farmers do not readily undertake cooperative ventures, are interested in literary rather than technological education for their children, and do not respond especially enthusiastically to many of the forms of aid offered by the AUB Farm. The specificity of the data is an important contribution.

Fevret, Maurice
1950 "Un village du Liban, El Mitaïne," *Revue de Géographie de Lyon 25*: 267-87.

Chiefly considers the ecological problems of residents of this village in central Mount Lebanon consequent upon the demise of the silk industry. Also some details on village social organization.

Fisher, William B.
1958 *The Middle East; a physical, social and regional geography*, 2d ed. London and New York; Methuen, Dutton.

Perhaps the standard accessible work on the subject. Roughly one third of the book is devoted to the Arab Levant.

Frayha, Anīs
1957 *Hadaarat fi tariiq az-Zawaal [A culture on the way to ruin]*, Beirut, American University of Beirut (in Arabic).

A frankly nostalgic description of village life in Mount Lebanon prior to industrial or urban influences. Line drawings supplement detailed descriptions of technological processes, festivals, children's games, etc. Bibliography of books and articles in Arabic and various European languages. The book itself fits in with the currently popular folkloristic interests among urbanized Lebanese people.

Fuller, Anne H.
1961 *Buarij: portrait of a Lebanese Muslim village*, Cambridge, Harvard University Press.

Based on field work done in 1937-38. One of the first Arab Levantine studies to be done by an anthropologically-trained North American. The only available study of a village on the eastern slopes of Mount Lebanon. A vivid, impressionistic account, ranging over the whole gamut of village life. Lack of quantitative material is made up for by insightful generalizations.

Gorton, William W., Miles Prescott, and Gabriel Najjar
1953 *Village survey: Kasmie rural improvement project*, Beirut, Office of Statistical Surveys, Lebanese Ministry of National Economy.

Conducted in 1952, this survey provides quantitative information on population, size of household, landholdings and land use, etc., in eight villages in the southern Lebanese littoral. Photographs.

Granott, Abraham
1952 *The land system in Palestine: history and structure*, London, Eyre and Spottiswoode.

While considerable emphasis is placed on the history and conditions of Jewish settlement, there is also substantive material on the land tenure system of the Palestinian Arabs, which are shown to be clearly similar to those in the rest of the Arab Levant except, possibly, in regard to the 16 per cent of villages that had *khirbahs*, or branches, in 1938. (Originally published in Hebrew in 1948.)

Granqvist, Hilma
1931-35 *Marriage conditions in a Palestinian village*, 2 vols. Helsingfors, Akademische Buchhandlung.

Based on three years of field work between 1925 and 1931 in the Muslim village of Artas, in what is now western Jordan. The author was particularly interested in the lives of the women and children, to which she had maximum access. Volume 1 is concerned with the history, kinship structure, and general marriage patterns in the village. Detailed, quantified material, embellished with numerous verbatim quotations from informants. Volume 2 is concerned largely with details of betrothals and weddings. An ethnographic study of major importance.

1947 *Birth and childhood among the Arabs: studies in a Muhammadan village in Palestine*, Helsingfors, Söderström.

A continuation of the author's presentation of her Artas material, this volume is concerned with beliefs and practices concerning conception, birth, and very early infancy. The volume has a rather strong Biblical folklore quality.

1950 *Child problems among the Arabs: studies in a Muhammadan village in Palestine*, Helsingfors, Söderström.

Concerned with naming patterns, infant mortality, and the role of the small child in a patrilineal society. References are heavily Biblical. No analysis of a functional or psychoanalytic type.

1965 *Muslim death and burial: Arab customs and traditions studied in a village in Jordan*, Helsingfors, Central Tryckeriet.

The fourth installment in the author's series of volumes, begun in 1931, on the village of Artas in the West Bank sector of Jordan.

Grieger, Paul
1955 "Essai d'une analyse caractérologique des peuples: cas de l'éthnotype libanais," *Revue de Psychologie des Peuples 10*: 269-87.

Findings based on questionnaires, but it is not made clear to what Lebanese they were administered, when, or under what circumstances. To some extent the findings support various older observations (e.g. high degree of emotionality), and in some respects give support to other more recent psychological and social structural studies in Lebanon.

Gulick, John

1953   "The Lebanese village: an introduction," *American Anthropologist 55*: 367-72.

Intended as a "brief communication," this article explores the point that the Lebanese village is neither a deme nor a "clan community," on Murdock's definition of these terms, despite some evidence which might suggest the contrary.

1954   "Conservatism and change in a Lebanese village," *Middle East Journal 8*: 295-307.

This is essentially a precis of the author's monograph published in 1955, but it omits the latter's theoretical constructs.

1955   "Social structure and culture change in a Lebanese village," *Viking Fund Publications in Anthropology 21*.

Based on seven months of field work in 1952 in a Greek Orthodox village in the northern Lebanese littoral. The monograph is a somewhat revised version of the author's doctoral dissertation, which was submitted to Harvard University in 1953. In addition to observations on standard ethnographic subjects, the social organization of the village is examined in considerable detail and set in a wider, schematistructural context. In these terms, stable and changing aspects of the social organization are analyzed as they are related to the strong Westernized urban influences that are present among the villagers. Photographs.

1963   "Images of an Arab city," *Journal of the American Institute of Planners 29*: 179-98.

An outgrowth of field research conducted by the author in the city of Tripoli, Lebanon, in 1961-62, this paper discusses the results of the application of some ideas of the city planner, Kevin Lynch, on how the residents of a city perceive their manmade environment. A sample of middle-class Tripolitans were found to perceive sections of the city rather than individual landmarks, and this is interpreted as being consistent with various Arab values. Included in the paper are 17 photographs taken in Tripoli, two scale street maps, and two maps drawn by Tripolitans.

1965a "Old values and new institutions in a Lebanese Arab city," *Human Organization 24*: 49-52.

Originally a paper read at the VIIth International Congress of Anthropological and Ethnological Sciences, Moscow,

U.S.S.R., in 1964, this paper is a precis of issues dealt with at greater length in the author's book on Tripoli, Lebanon (Gulick 1967).

1965b "The religious structure of Lebanese culture," *Internationales Jahrbuch für Religionssoziologie 1*: 151-87.

An analysis of Lebanese "confessionalism" in terms of the sociocultural differences and similarities among the sects into which the population of Lebanon is divided. Draws partly upon field work done in Lebanon in 1961-62 and partly upon recent behavioral science publications on Lebanon, plus Lebanese magazines and newspapers.

1967 *Tripoli, a modern Arab city*, Cambridge, Harvard University Press.

This book is based on field work done in Tripoli, Lebanon, in 1961-62. Its contents range from purposely vivid descriptions of daily life in the city to philosophical discussions of the structure and conflicts of life in Tripoli in relation to twentieth-century urbanization in general. In between are chapters on the historical development of Tripoli; its political, economic, and sectarian institutions; and its kinship structure, interwoven with social class considerations. A major effort is made to present Tripoli as a case of modern urban development and change, which does not, for various reasons, fit the many facile generalizations on the subject that were current among social scientists in the 1960s.

1969 "Village and city: cultural continuities in twentieth century Middle Eastern cultures," in *Middle Eastern Cities: Ancient, Islamic, and Contemporary Middle Eastern Urbanism: A Symposium*, Ira Lapidus, ed., Berkeley and Los Angeles, University of California Press: 122-58.

Gulick, John, ed.
1965 *Dimensions of Cultural Change in the Middle East*, Special issue (Spring, vol. 24, no. 1) of *Human Organization*.

A collection of fifteen original articles on the Middle East, eight of which are devoted to materials from Lebanon and Jordan. A three-page Introduction by the editor relates the different papers to each other and to certain wider issues.

Hamidé, Abdul-Rahman
1959 *La Région d'Alep; étude de géographie rurale*, Paris, Université de Paris, Faculté des Lettres.

Hirabayashi, G. K., and May Ishaq
1958 "Social change in Jordan: a quantitative approach in a non-census area," *American Journal of Sociology 64*: 36-40.

A report on an opinion survey among women in 'Amman in 1955, probing such subjects as education, occupation, marriage age and mate selection, extent of veiling, and social participation. The younger women turn out to show marked changes in the direction of "Western" patterns. There were only 2 per cent of refusals. As in his other publications on the Arab Levant, the senior author strikes the anthropological reader as being overconcerned about justifying the use of quantitative methods as opposed to case studies and participant observation, and not enough concerned about whether the responses to survey questions are reliable.

Horton, Alan W.
1961   *A Syrian village in its changing environment*, unpublished doctoral dissertation, Cambridge, Harvard University.

The annotator has not read this work carefully, but has seen it. The data were obtained by field work done under the direction of William D. Schorger in 1954.

Hourani, Albert H.
1946   *Syria and Lebanon, a political essay*, New York, Oxford University Press.

Useful as general descriptive reference, with historical and political emphasis. Some perceptive insights.

1947   *Minorities in the Arab world*, London and New York, Oxford University Press.

Particular emphasis on various religious groups in the Arab Levant.

Jarvis, Claude S.
1936   "The desert Bedouin and his future," *Royal Central Asian Society Journal 23*: 585-93.

Concerned with the values conflicts that impede sedentarization.

Jaussen, Antonin Joseph
1927   *Coutumes palestiniennes. 1. Naplouse et son district*, Paris, Librairie Orientaliste Paul Geuthner.

Based on observations in the early 1920s, this description of the city of Nablus, in western Jordan, is essentially an ethnography placed in an urban setting. On the whole, the patterns of ritual behavior and social organization of the Nablusi people sound very similar to those reported from village Palestine. Unique in its details of urban behavior, which does not in itself sound particularly "urban" as opposed to "peasant." Photographs.

1948   *Coutumes des Arabes au pays de Moab*, Paris, Adrien-Maison-neuve.

Data gathered in 1902 and 1905 in what is now eastern Jordan. A very solid ethnography of then nomadic people. Their attitudes toward sedentarization are discussed.

Jordan, Hashemite Kingdom of
1953   *1952 census of housing*, Amman, Greek Convent Press.

Jouin, Jeanne
1934   "Le costume féminin dans l'Islam syro-palestinien," *Revue des Études Islamiques 8*: 481-505.

Well illustrated with photographs. Particularly useful because it illustrates ethnic variations.

Kanaan, Niazi Ragheb
1963   "Amman," in *The New Metropolis in the Arab World*, Morroe Berger, ed., New Delhi, Allied Publishers: 129-41.

Less informative than some of the other papers in the same volume, this one is concerned mostly with outlining the municipal services problems of Amman.

Keen, Bernard A.
1946   *The agricultural development of the Middle East*, London, H. M. Stationery Office.

A basic source, which puts the Arab Levant into the larger context of the Middle East.

Kfoury, Josette
1959   "Liban, pays de tourisme," *Revue de Géographie de Lyon 34*: 271-84.

Factual account, including map of major tourist areas. Briefly considers the human consequences of tourism, an important factor in the Lebanese economy.

Khairallah, Ibrahim A.
1941   "The law of inheritance in the Republic of Syria and Lebanon," *American University of Beirut, Publications, Social Science Series 15*, Beirut, printed at the American Press.

Though slightly dated, this is nevertheless a very detailed treatise, by an author trained in the law, on legal norms relating to aspects of kinship organization and private and religious property. It is also relevant to the relationships between shari'a and civil law in a modernizing culture.

Khalaf, Samir G.
1965   *Prostitution in a changing society; a sociological survey of legal prostitution in Beirut*, Beirut, Khayats.

This book is the result of a survey done at the request of the City of Beirut, which was planning the demolition of the red light district. Of the 207 licensed prostitutes in the district, 130 consented to be interviewed. There are numerous tables providing information on family background, attitudes toward their work, how they became prostitutes, etc. The interview schedule, in the original Arabic with an English translation, is an appendix to the book. More cross-tabulations would have been welcome, and the author seems continually to waver between an American social work approach and an "objective" sociological approach, which perhaps he does not really feel. Nevertheless, the study is unique and contains some very interesting information.

Khuri, Fuad I.
1967   "A comparative study of migration patterns in two Lebanese villages," *Human Organization 26*: 206-13.

Comparing a Shi'a village in southern Lebanon and a Christian village in northern Lebanon, this valuable paper provides specific, new information on patterns of emigration to foreign countries, settlement of villagers in the city (primarily Beirut), and selective return migration to the villages. Differences associated with social class are of particular interest, including the observation that working class migrants tend to cluster together in the city; whereas middle class ones tend not to.

Kislyakov, N. A., and A. I. Pershits, eds.
1957   *Narody Perednei Azii [Peoples of Anterior Asia]*, vol. 3 of *Narody Mira [Peoples of the World]*, S. P. Tolstov, general editor, Moskva, Akademiia Nauk, SSSR (in Russian).

The Arab Levant is covered in three chapters ("Jordanian Arabs," 8 pp.; "Syrian Arabs," 30 pp.; "Lebanese Arabs," 18 pp.). The annotator does not read Russian, but has conferred about this volume with those who do and has had a few sample passages translated. On this basis, it is his crude impression that the interests of the authors are very largely in the area of political and economic matters and change toward industrialism. For anthropologically relevant material they rely entirely on "Western" sources, all of which are noted elsewhere in this bibliography. Of Russian anthropological field work in the Arab Levant there appears to have been none whatsoever. The population density map facing p. 382 is unique in detail, and it would be interesting to know on what basis it was compiled.

Klat, Paul J.
   1957   "Musha holdings and land fragmentation in Syria," *Middle East Economic Papers, 1957*: 12-23, Beirut, American University of Beirut, Economic Research Institute.

   Traces the origin of *musha'* in a strong communal spirit to its present decadent status in excessive land fragmentation.

   1958   "The origins of land ownership in Syria," *Middle East Economic Papers, 1958*: 51-66, Beirut, American University of Beirut, Economic Research Institute.

   A useful, historically oriented, but also up-to-date study of the subject.

Latron, André
   1936   "La vie rurale en Syrie et au Liban," Damascus, *Institut Français de Damas, Mémoire 3.*

   In some contrast to Thoumin (1936), Latron's attention is concentrated, though not exclusively, on northern Syria in addition to Lebanon. In contrast to both Weulersse and Thoumin, Latron is particularly interested in the legal technicalities of Arab Levantine land tenure and agricultural contracts. The work also includes systematic review of the various units of measure and financial arrangements. This is perhaps the primary source on the subject of the fragmentation of landholdings.

Lerner, Daniel
   1958   *The passing of traditional society: modernizing the Middle East*, Glencoe, Illinois, Free Press.

   About half of this book deals with the Arab Levantine countries and the questionnaires concerning exposure to the mass media of communication and participant attitudes concerning public affairs that were administered there. Elaborate statistical analyses ignore the problem of the reliability of answers to questionnaires among people who are not accustomed to them. The author seems most interested in the new "communications elite" in the area—a social class concept—and is not conversant with anthropological findings concerning culture change.

Lescot, Roger
   1938a   "Enquete sur les Yezidis de Syrie et du Djebel Sindjār," Damascus, *Institut Français de Damas, Mémoire 5.*

   Concerned mostly with the history and nature of the Yazidi religion and the main concentration of the Yazidis in Iraq. Part II, however, describes the Yazidi settlements between Aleppo and Antioch. Discussion of "tribal" groups and their division into villages. Photographs of houses and various activities.

1938b "Les Yézidis," *La France Méditerranéenne et Africaine 1, no. 3*: 55-87.

A precis of Lescot 1938a.

Lewis, Norman
1952 "The Isma'ilis of Syria today," *Royal Central Asian Society Journal 39*: 69-77.

Chiefly concerned with the Isma'ilis' migrations from Jabal Ansariyah into the plains.

1953 "Lebanon—the mountain and its terraces," *Geographical Review 43*: 1-14.

Lucid discussion, with diagrams of the techniques of terrace-building in Lebanon.

1955 "The frontier settlement in Syria 1800-1950," *International Affairs 31*: 48-60.

Concise, detailed, and authoritative review of one of the most important demographic trends in the Arab Levant.

Lutfiyya, Abdulla M.
1966 *Baytīn: a Jordanian village*, Paris, Mouton.

Baytīn is a Muslim village on or very near the Biblical site of Bethel, in the West Bank sector of Jordan. Lutfiyya was born and spent the first twenty years of his life there, returning in 1960 for a three-month study. His chapters on community structure, Islam and village culture, popular religion and rituals, and making a living contain new and valuable material. His closing chapter, however, which simplistically fits Baytīn into the folk end of Redfield's outmoded polar model, is unrewarding and leaves one with the uncomfortable feeling that the author may be stereotyping his own village. Furthermore, the chapter on marriage customs seems like a composite, idealized exposition. It also contains the statement (pp. 140-41) that on the wedding night, the groom "almost always" must resort to force (using a whip) to get his bride to have intercourse. Is this truly typical and, if so, how widespread is the occurrence of such behavior? Its implications for the relationships between Arab men and women are obvious. Perhaps the increasingly vocal women students of Arab Levantine culture may have something to say on the subject.

Mahhouk, Adnan
1956 "Recent agricultural development and Bedouin settlement in Syria," *Middle East Journal 10*: 167-76.

Documents the continuation of agricultural settlement since 1948. Recognizes that sedentarization calls for more than merely ecological adaptation.

Melikian, Levon H., and Lutfy N. Diab
1959   "Group affiliations of university students in the Arab Middle East," *Journal of Social Psychology 49*: 145-59.

Based on questionnaires administered to 138 American University of Beirut students in 1957 and to 69 more in 1958. Seventy-five per cent of the subjects were from the Arab Levant. In the fact of culture change, it was found that the family continues to be visualized as the primary security group, but that rank ordering of other group affiliations varies to some degree depending on the sex and religious and political orientations of the subjects.

Mesnil du Buisson, R.
1932   "Instruments agricoles de Syrie," *L'Ethnographie 25*: 107-15.

Though brief, gives very detailed information, including illustrations, on the subject. Arabic nomenclature included. Equipment is presented, as far as possible, in the order in which it is used during the agricultural year. Data were collected in the Homs-Hama area in 1930.

Mills, Arthur E.
1959   *Private enterprise in Lebanon*, Beirut, American University of Beirut.

Ostensibly a monograph on economics, this book is actually strongly oriented toward the anthropological point of view. Its central theme is the discontinuity between the needs of new manufacturing concerns in Lebanon and the continuing traditional values regarding family loyalty, non-kin cooperation, the ethos of labor, and others. An indispensable reference for anyone concerned with the sociocultural concomitants of industrialization.

Murphy, Robert F., and Leonard Kasdan
1959   "The structure of parallel cousin marriage," *American Anthropologist 61*: 17-29.

Based on library research. Discusses reports of the form of marriage among the Bedouin and in the Arab Levant and functionally relates it to the segmentary character of Arab kin groups. Since parallel-cousin marriage is actually of minor occurrence, one could raise objections to the authors' specific reasoning. However, their final conclusion is a valuable one to take into consideration in planning future field work in the Arab Levant: "We would suggest that we re-evaluate some of our notions that equate cohesion, or solidarity, and integration, or structural equilibrium, and that we analyze in greater detail the typological differences between societies based on true corporate lineages and the one under discussion in this paper."

Musil, Alois
1907-08   *Arabia Petraea*, 3 vols. Wien, A. Höllander (in German).

The first two volumes are largely accounts of the topography and surface archeological features of what is now eastern Jordan. Volume 3 is an ethnography of the camel nomads of the area. The southeastern periphery of the Arab Levant at the beginning of the twentieth century is well documented.

Nader, Laura
1965   "Communication between village and city in the modern Middle East," *Human Organization 24*: 18-24.

Based partly on field work done in a Shi'a Muslim village in the southern part of the Biqa' Valley of Lebanon, but drawing widely on other materials also, this paper is concerned with conflict resolution by intravillage and extravillage means. The latter depend upon city-dwelling politicians, who are nevertheless thoroughly conversant with village life.

Oppenheim, Max von
1939-68   *Die Beduinen*, 4 vols. in 5, Leipzig and Wiesbaden, Otto Harrassowitz.

Perhaps the most comprehensive work on the locations, genealogies, and interconnections of the Arab Bedouin. Otherwise, the ethnographic descriptions are only brief. Volume 2 is perhaps the most pertinent to the pastoral peoples in contact with the Arab Levant, although parts of Volume 1 are also pertinent. Data collected in the early part of the twentieth century.

Palestine, Government of
1945-46   "Survey of social and economic conditions in Arab villages" (published in six installments from July 1945 to October 1946, in the *General Monthly Bulletin of Current Statistics*, Jerusalem).

A survey of five villages. Invaluable, though obsolete, in situ, material on land tenure, family size, village population, amount of education, marriage and kinship, etc.

Patai, Raphael
1947   "On culture contact and its working in modern Palestine," *Memoirs of the American Anthropological Association 67*.

Stresses the social distance between the Jews and Arabs in the Mandate of Palestine, which tended to limit the extent of cultural assimilation between them despite the intensive contacts. Presented in a strong Malinowskian frame of culture-change concepts.

1949   "Musha'a tenure and cooperation in Palestine," *American Anthropologist n.s. 51*: 436-45.

Makes the point that despite the superficial resemblance of *musha'a* to a cooperative enterprise, modern cooperatives have not succeeded well among the Arabs of Palestine because of the limitations of cooperative attitudes among them. Of more than historical interest, since this phenomenon has been observed elsewhere in the Arab Levant.

1957   *Jordan, Lebanon and Syria: an annotated bibliography*, New Haven, HRAF Press.

Though one of several Middle East bibliographies, this is the only extensive one (1605 items) which concentrates exclusively on the Arab Levant. A number of works on Arab Palestine are subsumed under Jordan. Compiled by an anthropologist, its coverage of the anthropologically relevant literature is particularly thorough.

Patai, Raphael, ed.
1956a   *The Republic of Lebanon*, 2 vols. New Haven, Human Relations Area Files.
1956b   *The Republic of Syria*, 2 vols. New Haven, Human Relations Area Files.
1956c   *The Hashemite Kingdom of Jordan*, New Haven, Human Relations Area Files.

These three works were produced together under the same format and organization. They were written by the same group of contributors, who, besides the editor, included Farid Aouad, M. M. Bravmann, Kingsley Davis, Robert W. Ehrich, John Gulick, Philip K. Hitti, J. C. Hurewitz, Charles Issawi, Jacob Landau, Anis K. Makdisi, Simon D. Messing, Don Peretz, Moshe Perlmann, Fahim Qubain, and Toufic Succar. Part of the long series of monographs produced under subcontracts between the Human Relations Area Files and various universities, these three volumes are unusual in having been edited and partly written by an anthropologist, and partly written by two other anthropologists, Ehrich and Gulick. Widely criticized on various counts, they nevertheless provide the most comprehensive and compact coverage in the literature of the national cultures, trait complex by trait complex, of the component Arab Levantine states.

The Jordan subcontractor's monograph has served as the basis of no less than three subsequent books on Jordan. The first, *Jordan* (Raphael Patai, ed., New Haven, HRAF, 1957), was one of the HRAF Country Survey Series and was essentially a revised edition of the subcontractor's monograph. The second, *The Hashemite Kingdom of Jordan* by Raphael Patai, Princeton University Press, 1958, presented a selection of the topics covered in the subcontractor's monograph. The third, *Jordan*, New Haven, 1958, George L. Harris, ed., one of the HRAF Survey of World Cultures series, though stylistically better than the original monograph, omits many details of anthropological relevance. It was prepared by a staff far less expert on the Arab Levant than was the original group of contributors.

Peters, Emrys L.
  1956   "A Muslim passion play: key to a Lebanese village," *Atlantic Monthly 198*: 176-80.

          Based on field work in 1952, this is a brief description by a British social anthropologist of the social organization of a southern Lebanese Shi'a village and of the ways in which the participation in the annual Husayn miracle play reflect social differentials and tensions in the village.

  1963   "Aspects of rank and status among Muslims in a Lebanese village," in *Mediterranean Countrymen*, Julian Pitt-Rivers, ed., Paris, Mouton: 159-200.

          Essentially a short monograph, this is a meticulous study of a Shi'a village in southern Lebanon. This field work was done in 1952-53 and 1956. Well illustrated with maps, genealogies, and diagrams, the focus of the study is on the hereditary power structure of the "Learned Families" of the village and the way in which their power is revalidated in the annual Husayn Miracle Play.

Phillips, Paul G.
  1954   *The Hashemite Kingdom of Jordan: prolegomena to a technical assistance program*, Chicago, University of Chicago, Department of Geography, Research Paper 34.

          Despite the specialized orientation suggested by its title, this is a firstrate study in human geography. To some degree, it does for Jordan what Weulersse, Latron, and Thoumin did for Syria and Lebanon. Considerable attention is paid to the history and even the archeology of Jordan. Meticulous detail, including maps, of land use patterns, settlement patterns, crops, distribution of population, and the relationships between pastoralism and agriculture.

Potter, Dalton
   1955   "The bazaar merchant," in *Social Forces in the Middle East*, Sydney Nettleton Fisher, ed., Ithaca, Cornell University Press: 99-115.

   Based on first-hand studies of *suqs* (bazaars) in the Arab Levant, which the author, a sociologist, made about 1950. Brief descriptions of *suqs* and of various types of merchants. Stresses the part the *suq* plays in diffusion and acculturation.

Prins, A. H. J.
   1965   "The modified Syrian schooner: problem formulation in maritime change," *Human Organization* 24: 34-42.

   A technical consideration of the schooners which continue to ply their trade in the eastern Mediterranean, despite severe competition, but because of the adaptations which have been made in their rig and fittings. This is a rare article on a very much neglected subject, which the author, who has also studied the dhow trade in the Indian Ocean, clearly loves.

Prothro, Edwin Terry
   1954a   "Lebanese stereotypes of America as revealed by the sentence completion technique," *Journal of Social Psychology* 40: 39-42.

   Test administered to 104 Lebanese schoolgirls, compared with a similar test administered to European schoolgirls. Open-end responses about America reflect Lebanese girls' concern about their own sex and educational statuses.

   1954b   "Studies in stereotypes: IV. Lebanese business men," *Journal of Social Psychology* 40: 275-80.

   Results of this study confirm the fact that 90 Beirut business men expressed stereotypic attitudes toward various national groups which are similar to those expressed by Lebanese university students.

   1961   *Child rearing in the Lebanon*, Cambridge, Harvard University Press.

   The author was the designer and director of the research that was conducted in 1958-59 among 468 Lebanese mothers and the five-year-old children of 397 of them. The interviewers were Lebanese women with social science training. In his analysis, the author incorporates not only cross-cultural psychological materials but also relevant findings from anthropological, economic, historical, and sociological studies in Lebanon and other parts of the Middle East. An original contribution of major proportions, which includes syntheses of already available studies.

Prothro, Edwin Terry, and Levon H. Melikian
1952 "Social distance and social change in the Near East," *Sociology and Social Research 37*: 3-11.

Report of a questionnaire administered to 130 students at the American University of Beirut, most of whom were natives of the Arab Levant. The results, based on the Bogardus Social Distance Scale, showed that social distances are more strongly felt than in the United States, that national identities are more strongly felt than religious ones (the reverse of what was revealed in a similar test administered 10 years previously), and that nationalistic feelings are more strongly felt among Muslims than Christians.

1953a "The California Public Opinion Scale in an authoritarian culture," *Public Opinion Quarterly 17*: 352-62.

Results of testing among students at the American University of Beirut, most of whom were natives of the Arab Levant, indicate that the subjects score higher in the F-scale of authoritarianism than do equivalent North American populations and that Muslims score somewhat higher than Christians. These results are related to the supposed authoritarian nature of Near Eastern culture, beginning with the family.

1953b "Generalized ethnic attitudes in the Arab Near East," *Sociology and Social Research 37*: 375-79.

Report of a questionnaire administered to two groups of Near Eastern students, mostly natives of the Arab Levant. The results indicate that though there are strong ethnic attitudes in this population, ethnocentrism (associated with the "authoritarian personality") is not a generalized personality trait.

Proux, Mademoiselle
1938 "Les Tscherkesses," *La France Méditerranéenne et Africaine 1, no. 4*: 43-87.

The primary source on the brief history of Circassian settlement in Syria. Includes a map showing their principal locations and a discussion of their social organization and adaptations to Arab Levantine culture.

Rabbath, Edmond
1938 "Esquisse sur les populations syriennes," *Revue International de Sociologie* (Paris) *46*: 443-525.

Despite its considerable length, this study has an impressionistic quality. However, its coverage is unusually comprehensive, including religious groups, social classes and tribal groups. Tables on pp. 448-49 enumerate the Christians and Muslims in Lebanon and Syria in 1933.

Raphael, Pierre
1931 "Delebta: Nabdha Tarikhiyyah (Monographie d'un village libanais)," *Al-Machriq 31*: 100-07 ff., in several installments, Beirut (in Arabic).

A study by a Maronite priest, which stresses the history of a village in the neighborhood of Juniah. Major emphasis is placed on the prominent Maronites—many of them ecclesiastical figures—who were born and raised in the village. Little of anthropological interest, although it might be analyzed thematically in terms of the author's selective preferences. Does contain an interesting description of how Maronites gradually took over the site from its previous Shi'a inhabitants between about 1500 and 1700.

Reich, Sigismund
1937 "Études sur les villages araméens de l'Anti-Liban," Damascus, *Institut Français de Damas, Documents d'Études Orientales 7*.

This study concentrates on the usage of the Aramaic language in three villages on the eastern slope of the Anti-Lebanon massif, particularly in the village of Ma'lula. Though the emphasis is primarily linguistic, some idea of the social organization of Ma'lula in particular is conveyed. Photographs.

Riachi, Georges
1963 "Beirut," in *The New Metropolis in the Arab World*, Morroe Berger, ed., New Delhi, Allied Publishers: 103-15.

This chapter contains some factual information about the growth of Beirut, but it is primarily an idealized planner's statement, which might apply to almost any city.

Rintz, Frances C.
1956 "A frame for random sampling: three villages of the Lebanon," *Report on Current Research, Spring 1956*: 27-37, Washington, D.C., Middle East Institute.

The gist of this article is that *mukhtars'* lists of village residents are very unreliable and that a survey of houses in the village should be used as the basis of enumerating households to be random-sampled. This conclusion is hardly a new revelation to anthropologists who have worked in the area.

Ritsher, Walter H.
1932 *Municipal government in the Lebanon*, Beirut, American University of Beirut, printed at the American Press.

Though a bit dated, still useful as a guide to the various formal types of village, town, and city government.

Rondot, Pierre

1936 "Les tribus montagnardes de l'Asie antérieure; quelques aspects sociaux des populations kurdes et assyriennes," Damascus, *Institut Français de Damas, Bulletin d'Études Orientales 6*: 1-50.

Dealing with Kurds and Assyrians in the High Jezirah in both Syria and Turkey, this study presents material which is peripheral to the Arab Levant. Nevertheless, it is of definite anthropological interest; note the discussion of kinship organization of towns, pp. 22-25. Photographs.

1939 "Les Kurdes de Syrie," *La France Méditerranéenne et Africaine 2, no. 1*: 81-126.

The primary source on this subject.

1947 *Les institutions politiques du Liban*, Paris, Institut d'Études de l'Orient Contemporain.

Particularly useful reference for the religious groups of Lebanon.

Rosenfeld, Henry

1958 "Processes of structural change within the Arab village extended family," *American Anthropologist 60*: 1127-39.

Based on field work in an Israeli Arab village, apparently in 1954. Considers household composition in specific terms and analyzes the structural and economic factors that, alternatively, tend to preserve or to disperse the extended family. Offers possibilities for further research in the Arab Levant.

1964 "From peasantry to wage labor and residual peasantry: the transformation of an Arab village," in *Process and Pattern in Culture*, Robert A. Manners, ed., Chicago, Aldine Publishing Co.: 211-34.

A longitudinal study of an Arab village in the lower Galilee area of Israel from 1920 to 1963, this paper's main point is that despite increasing wage labor outside the village, the villagers are not yet "proletarianized," owing to the continuing importance of lineage control of the land and related factors.

Russell, Alexander

1794 *The natural history of Aleppo*, 2d ed., 2 vols. London, C. G. and J. Robinson.

The author was the physician for the British Factory in Aleppo during the middle of the eighteenth century. Of particular anthropological interest are his observations and comments upon the people and customs of the city as he saw them.

Safi, M.
1917-18 "Mariage au nord du Liban," *Anthropos 12-13*: 134-43.

In general, Chémali covers the subject more thoroughly.

Salamé, Michel
1955 "L'élévage au Liban," *Revue de Géographie de Lyon 30*: 81-101.

In a sense, this updates Thoumin's survey of the subject published in 1936. Concentrates on the sedentary herders who practice limited transhumance. Photographs and maps.

1957 "Une tribu chiite des montagnes de Hermel (Liban): les Nacer ed-Dine," *Revue de Géographie de Lyon 32*: 115-26.

This brief paper has a considerable amount of information on a group of people, numbering about 2,500, whose early nineteenth-century forebears migrated from the Lebanese coast. They are primarily subsistence farmers, growing hashish as a cash crop.

Sauvaget, Jean
1941 *Alep: essai sur le developpement d'une grande ville syrienne, des origins au milieu du XIXe siecle*, 2 vols. Paris, Paul Geuthner.

The second volume consists entirely of photographic plates, which accompany, but are not absolutely necessary for the appreciation of the text in the first volume. Essentially a history of Aleppo, this work is not particularly useful in gaining an understanding of on-going life in Aleppo. Aleppine history is traced largely in terms of remaining architectural monuments and street patterns which, in itself, is of considerable interest.

Sayigh, Yusif A.
1957 "Lebanon: special economic problems arising from a special structure," *Middle East Economic Papers 1957*: 60-88, Beirut.

The Lebanese economy, because of the nature of Lebanese culture, is commercial rather than industrial, superficial appearances to the contrary notwithstanding.

Shim'onī, Ya'qov
1947 *'Arve Erets Yisrael*, Tel Aviv (in Hebrew).

Though dated and not entirely objective, since it deals heavily with the political organization of Arab Palestine (which is no more) from the Jewish point of view, this work nevertheless contains a large amount of data on village and kinship organization which is of at least historical interest. It also contains numerous references to the Hebrew literature on the Arabs of Palestine. (A complete translation, under the title *The Arabs of Palestine*, is in the Human Relations Area Files.)

Sullivan, Theodore
1962 "The whirling dervishes," *Middle East Forum 38, no. 2*: 23-26.

Brief and journalistic, but valuable for its account of an interview with the head of the dervishery in Tripoli, Lebanon.

Sweet, Louise E.
1960 "Tell Ṭoqaan: a Syrian village," *Anthropological Papers of the Museum of Anthropology of the University of Michigan 14.*

Based on five months of field work in 1954, directed by William D. Schorger. This is the only available study of a desert fringe village inhabited by relatively recently sedentarized nomads. Though emphasizing ecological matters, it is a thorough ethnography, very well documented, going into great detail on social organization and the various relationships of the villagers to the larger society of which they are a part. This is the published version of the author's doctoral dissertation in anthropology, which was submitted to the University of Michigan in 1957.

1967 "The women of 'Ain ad Dayr," *Anthropological Quarterly 40*: 167-83.

In 1964-65, the author studied the village of " 'Ain ad Dayr," a Druze village in the Anti-Lebanon mountains of Lebanon. Points emphasized in the paper are the role of women in mediating political difficulties, and at the same time, their continued traditional economic restrictions, owing to the relative lack of industrialization in Lebanon.

1968 "The extension of closeness: the dynamics of kin term usage in a Lebanese Druze village," *Bustan* (in German).

1969 "Child's play for the ethnographer," *Behavior Science Notes 4*: 237-45.

The same Lebanese Druze village of " 'Ain ad Dayr" is the scene of three incidents of children's play in which the ethnographer found reflected fuller contexts of village life than her own observations appreciated.

Tannous, Afif Ishaq

1939   *Trends of social and cultural change in an Arab village*, unpublished doctoral dissertation, Ithaca, Cornell University.

Based on personal experience as a native and field work in
Bishmizziin, a predominantly Greek Orthodox village in the
plain of Koura, south of Tripoli, North Lebanon. Though
never published as a single work, it has served as the basis of
several of the author's widely quoted published papers. Part I
describes the "base line" traditional culture in "folk society"
terms, from which Tannous 1944b would appear to be a
generalization. Part II deals with various factors of change
which occurred in Bishmizziin beginning in the second half
of the nineteenth century. Four published articles, Tannous
1941, 1942a, 1942b, and 1943, are derived from this part,
especially, of the dissertation. Whether considered as one or
several works, this is one of the major pioneering village
studies in the Arab Levant.

1941   "Social change in an Arab village," *American Sociological
Review 6*: 650-62.

Introductory article on cultural change in Bishmizziin, Lebanon. Deals largely with the effects of the rise and decline of
a silk-spinning factory.

1942a "Emigration, a force of social change in an Arab village,"
Rural Sociology 7: 62-74.

Closely documents the effects of this general Lebanese
phenomenon in the village of Bishmizziin. Particularly interesting are the quotations from letters illustrating the disrup-
tions in kinship ties.

1942b "Group behavior in the village community of Lebanon,"
American Journal of Sociology 48: 231-39.

Close illustrations of the "in-group" phenomenon in a Lebanese village.

1943   "Missionary education in Lebanon: a study in acculturation,"
Social Forces 21: 338-43.

A case study of the effects not only of American Protestant
missionary education in a Lebanese village but of "modern"
education in general.

1944a "Extension work among the Arab fellahin," *Applied Anthropology 3, no. iii*: 1-12.

Essentially a review of Arab peasant values and a series of
suggestions as to how most effectively these values can be
accommodated to rural development projects. Has been
rather widely reprinted and anthologized.

1944b "The Arab village community of the Middle East," *Annual Report of the Smithsonian Institution for 1944*: 524-44.

Valuable as an introductory review of traditional patterns which the author says are characteristic of villages in the Fertile Crescent generally. The village culture is presented as revolving around four basic themes: religious rituals, kin groups, devotion to the land, and village cohesion.

1949 "The village in the national life of Lebanon," *Middle East Journal 3*: 151-63.

In part a recapitulation of earlier presentations on the Lebanese village, but makes the further point that nationalistic awakening may threaten integrity of village organization—a serious threat, since the village will continue to be an important aspect of the national society.

Thoumin, Richard

1931 "Deux quartiers de Damas; le quartier chrétien de Bab Muṣalla et le quartier kurde," *Bulletin d'Études Orientales 1*: 99-135, Damascus, Institut Français de Damas.

Provides a detailed description of the Christian and Kurdish quarters of Damascus, especially the former, largely in physical and economic terms. Little on social relationships, but it is, nevertheless, useful.

1932 "La maison syrienne dans la plaine hauranaise, le bassin du Barada et sur les plateaux du Qalamūn," Damascus, *Institut Français de Damas, Documents d'Études Orientales 2*.

Thorough, authoritative study. Emphasizes house types, their distribution, details of their construction, decoration, and floor plans. Thirty-five photographic plates.

1933 "De la vie nomade à la vie sédentaire: un village Syrien: Adra," *Mélanges Géographiques offerts par ses élevés à Raoul Blanchard*: 621-41, Grenoble.

A very valuable study, which considers the relationships of nomadic and sedentary people in a Syrian desert fringe village. It is unfortunate that the French did not publish more such studies.

1934 "Notes sur l'amenagement et la distribution des eaux à Damas et dans sa ghouta," *Bulletin d'Études Orientales 4*: 1-26, Damascus, Institut Français de Damas.

Primarily concerned with technical details of the division of water in Damascus.

1936 *Géographie humaine de la Syrie centrale*, Paris, Librairie Ernest Leroux.

One of the major works produced by the group of French human geographers. Concentrating on Lebanon and southern Syria east of Lebanon, it is a primary source on such subjects as land tenure, the distribution of water, and rural-urban movements. Very richly illustrated.

Touma, Toufic
1958   *Un village de montagne au Liban (Hadeth el-Jobbé)*, Paris, Mouton.

An account evidently based on personal experiences of no pinpointed date. Hadeth el-Jobbé is in the same locale as Hadchite studies by Herbert Williams and Kepler Lewis, but Touma writes more in the tradition of Chémali, Feghali, and Safi than of contemporary social science. Nevertheless, the monograph contains concrete data—especially on ecological matters—together with some subtle insights.

Tresse, R.
1938   "L'évolution du costume des citadins syrolibanais depuis un siècle," *La Géographie 70*: 1-16, 76-82 (Paris, Société de Géographie).

1939   "L'évolution du costume des citadines en Syrie depuis le XIX siècle," *La Géographie 71*: 257-71; *72*: 29-40 (Paris, Société de Géographie).

The annotator has not seen these works. As far as he knows, however, they are the only sources in the literature on the subject.

United Nations Educational, Scientific, and Cultural Organization
1954   *Lebanon: suggestions for the Plan of Tripoli and for the surroundings of the Baalbek Acropolis*. Paris, UNESCO.

Contains the most detailed, readily available map of the "Old City" of Tripoli, which has already in fact been altered in part by the opening, according to plan, of new streets. While concentrating on the architectural monuments of the Mamluk period (about which most of the people of Tripoli care nothing) and ignoring the locations of *suqs* and residential areas in the old city, the book nevertheless has excellent photographs and is useful in other ways.

Walpole, G. F.
1948   "Land problems in Transjordan," *Royal Central Asian Society Journal 35*: 52-65.

Useful reference on the land tenure situation in which the present state of Jordan began. Considerable detail relevant to village organization and the efforts of the British Mandate to reduce the amount of musha' holdings.

Warriner, Doreen
1948 *Land and poverty in the Middle East*, New York and London, Royal Institute of International Affairs.
A basic source. Particularly detailed material from the Arab Levant. The author's perspectives are not purely economic. A new edition was published in 1957.

Weinryb, Bernard D.
1946 "The Arab village of Palestine," *Palestine Affairs 1, no. 10*: 1-4.
Essentially a selective precis of materials from the official village survey of 1945, which is, unfortunately, a less accessible source.

Weulersse, Jacques
1934 "Antioche; essai de géographie urbaine," Damascus, Institut Français de Damas, *Bulletin d'Études Orientales 4*: 27-79.
A beautifully meticulous study, including photographs, figures, and overlay maps. Emphasizes the plan of the town: *suqs*, Christian, Alawite, and Turkish quarters. An important contribution to urban studies in the area.

1938 "Les Alaouites," *La France Méditerranéenne et Africaine 1, no. 2*: 41-61.

1940 *Le pays des Alaouites*, 2 vols. Tours, Arrault.
Volume 2 consists of a magnificent collection of 104 photographic plates: natural features, technological processes, settlements, etc. While Volume 1 concentrates on the ethnography of the Alawites themselves, it covers Jabal Ansariyah in general, noting the distribution of other religions. Seasonal movements, village plans, and a plan of the quarters of the city of Latakia. A major source.

1946 *Paysans de Syrie et du Proche-Orient*, Paris, Librairie Gallimard.
Of the major works of the French human geographers, this is perhaps the most comprehensive, inasmuch as it encompasses the findings of Latron (1936) and Thoumin (1936), their volumes being similar in orientation. This is a classic and indispensable reference. Photographs by the author and many text figures.

Williams, Herbert H.
1958 "Some aspects of culture and personality in a Lebanese Maronite village," *Dissertation Abstracts 19*: 632.
Based on field work in 1949-50, which was conducted by Williams in the company of his wife and a fellow student,

Ralph Kepler Lewis, whose investigations of the village were concentrated on kinship organization and settlement patterns. Directed, initially, by Abram Kardiner of Columbia, and later by A. I. Hallowell of Pennsylvania, this is the only full-dress study of personality-in-culture in the Arab Levant. The study analyzes 58 Rorschach protocols taken from men and women, representing all sections of the village; 7 life histories (4 of women, 3 of men); and observations of child-training practices. If these findings are generalizable, they lend support to the contention of Daniel Lerner that "traditional personalities" in Lebanon are constricted.

Williams, Herbert H., and Judith R. Williams
1965   "The extended family as a vehicle of culture change," *Human Organization 24*: 59-64.

The authors studied the Sunni Muslim village of Haouch al—Harimi in the center of the Biqa' Valley of Lebanon during portions of two periods, 1949-51 and 1963-65. This paper stresses the fact that the extended family has continued to be an important functional unit in Haouch, not in spite of change, but rather as a means of facilitating various adaptations to change of its members.

Wulzinger, Karl, and Carl Watzinger
1924   *Damaskus; Die Islamische Stadt*, Berlin and Leipzig, Walter de Gruyter.

Valuable for its street plans and house plans, and notable for its excellent photographs, although these are mostly of the older "monuments." Includes 62 plates.

Yaukey, David
1961   *Fertility differences in a modernizing country; a survey of Lebanese couples*, Princeton, Princeton University Press.

Based on survey research by a team of Lebanese women, under the author's direction, in 1958-59. About 900 women were interviewed, a third of them in a Christian village and a Muslim village; the rest in Beirut. Statistical information on rural-urban, Christian-Muslim, fertility rates, related to such factors as level of education, age at marriage, contraceptive practices, etc. A valuable source, especially in regard to the issue of Christian-Muslim differences.

Zarour, Mariam
1953   "Ramallah: my home town," *Middle East Journal 7*: 430-39.

A rather nostalgic account, which nevertheless contains useful ethnographic observations.

CHAPTER *3*

Southern Mesopotamia*

ROBERT A. FERNEA

The countryside of southern Iraq, between Baghdad and Basrah, presents a predominantly flat, brown landscape with variations primarily caused by the Twin Rivers, the Tigris and Euphrates. The unirrigated, uncultivated portions of the land are sparsely covered with dun-colored grasses and low bushes and the occasional field of barley, wheat, or rice provides in its rich green a striking contrast with the surrounding land. In many areas, glistening white ground-salt crystals extend over wide areas, forming patches and traceries like half-melted snow on the brown earth. In places fields of date palms stretch along the waterways for miles, accounting for Iraq's position as the world's foremost producer of dates. Even the topographical variations are frequently a result of the rivers: mounds of earth sometimes meters high signal the presence of

*This essay on southern Iraq was written in 1959 and has not been revised since. I am unaware of any ethnological research undertaken since that time which would require basic modification of the observations made in this essay. However, several books have been published which significantly add to our fund of information about the area. Three of these are devoted to the people of the southern marshes. Two are essentially travel books: Gavin Maxwell (1957) and Wilfred Thesiger (1964) both provide well written if somewhat fragmentary descriptions of the life of the marshes, and Thesiger's book is particularly valuable for its excellent photographs. An ethnography written in German by Sigrid Westphal-Hellbusch and Heinz Westphal (1962) is based upon original research among the marsh dwellers and is a source of detailed ethnographic description.

My wife and I have both published books about the people of Daghara town and its environs, which I have briefly discussed in this essay. Elizabeth W. Fernea has written a personal account (1965) of her experiences with the women of this community, which contains much useful information about their activities and ways of life. My account (1970) is a more formal analysis of the social organization of town and tribe and the ecological and social consequences of irrigation agriculture, with particular emphasis on changing patterns of local leadership. Both books take up in more detail a number of points raised in this essay.

irrigation canals, both in use and abandoned, while the large depressions that occur are frequently empty river beds or dried-up marshes.

The fertile land of southern Iraq consists of alluvial plains created by the two rivers over thousands of years. The process of silt deposition appears to have pushed the delta of the rivers further southward, even since the geologically recent days of Babylon, and has left a large area (some 4,000 square miles during flood season) of marshland and shallow lakes in which the waters linger and merge before collecting finally as the Shatt-al-Arab, whose waters feed the Persian Gulf.[1] Today in southern Iraq, the traveler, seeing only bits and pieces of the fragmented rivers and canals, may forget that he is viewing two of the world's important rivers until he sees the great Shatt-al-Arab flow by at Basrah.

Despite the monotony of much of its landscape, southern Iraq is in many ways a land of extremes. In addition to the excesses of marshland and desert, there is great variation in the diurnal and annual temperatures: the average 3 P.M. mean monthly temperature recorded in Baghdad during the hottest month, July, from 1938 to 1960, was 43°C. Summer temperatures frequently rise as high as 45°C., yet in winter frosts are not uncommon. While the relative humidity is low in the deserts, in the marsh areas as well as in regions of intensive irrigation hot summer days can also be very damp. Although rainfall is occasionally heavy in the winter months (the highest monthly rainfall in Baghdad was 29.0 mms. in February from 1938 to 1960), there has been no trace of precipitation in August in the capital from 1938 to the present.[2] Ordinarily May, June, July, August, September, and October are without any appreciable rainfall; the other six months may bring rains which last for several days and leave the countryside an impassable sea of slippery, sticky mud over which even horses and cows cannot travel.

The flood pattern of the Twin Rivers constitutes another uncongenial extreme in southern Iraq. There is no great distance between the headwaters of the rivers and its alluvial plain (as in the case of the Nile River for instance), and thus the flood follows quickly upon the winter rains, the April peak coming too late for the winter crops and too early for the summer planting. Until 1958, when flood control installations were completed at Wadi Tharthar, the Tigris frequently flowed into the streets of Baghdad in flood season and ravaged the countryside between

[1] Because of the silting and scouring action of the rivers, the Tigris and Euphrates have repeatedly shifted course, while the Euphrates in particular breaks into a series of shifting bifurcations south of Baghdad. Herodotus, noting this characteristic, commented that of all great rivers, the Euphrates alone appears to grow smaller as it approaches the sea.

[2] Temperature reports are taken from *Statistical Abstract 1960* (Iraq 1961).

the capital and the Gulf. On the other hand, in midsummer the supply dwindles radically and severely limits cultivation, many canals providing barely enough water to satisfy human and animal thirst.

Local tradition places the Garden of Eden in southern Iraq, but in fact the great riverine oases there offer a considerably more rigorous natural environment than is found along the Nile: hotter and colder weather than is found on the Egyptian Delta, heavier rains in winter, proportionally more marshland with less cultivatable delta, and an annual flood cycle which does not complement the agricultural seasons. To these disadvantages must be added generally impervious saline subsoil of marine origin which, unlike the porous subsurfaces underlying much of the Egyptian alluvium, causes poor drainage in irrigated regions and frequently salination of the soils. At the same time, the Arabs of southern Iraq have been obliged to develop adequate exploitive technology in these rigorous environmental extremes with approximately the same material resources at hand as may be found in Egypt. These conditions undoubtedly help explain the much lower density of population in Iraq as compared with Egypt; Iraq has approximately 20 times as much agricultural land per individual agriculturalist as Egypt (Warriner 1957: 115).

The majority of Iraqis living south of Baghdad today either farm or earn their living through related activities. With the exception of Basrah, the only seaport in Iraq, all the southern towns are essentially market and district administrative centers, and any nonagricultural industry is a recent development. Yet the technology associated with cultivation is relatively simple and clearly of a kind suitable for subsistence agriculture; cash cropping is generally a recent innovation. Herding is also a means of subsistence, though its importance has declined somewhat in the last few decades. Finally, the environmental conditions peculiar to the marshlands of southern Mesopotamia have encouraged there the development of special modes of existence which are quite different from the rest of the country.

In southern Iraq, all summer and, to a lesser extent, winter cultivation is dependent on water taken from the Twin Rivers. The unpredictable winter rains frequently drown young plants or damage mature ones and in any case may not arrive at the crucial points in the agricultural season. Fortunately, the Euphrates and, to some extent, the Tigris have provided a manageable source of water accessible for irrigation purposes by tribal cultivators without the necessity of elaborately-engineered controls. This is because of the bifurcating, braided nature of these streams, which makes it possible to dam small portions of them at one time with a minimum of effort. Thus, before the institution of modern irrigation works beginning in 1916, tribal groups would make temporary dams of rolled reed matting reinforced with brush and mud, blocking a bifurcation and forcing the water over the land in floods or through prepared canals. Tribesmen, called to work by traditional leaders with attendant ceremony similar to that accompanying preparation for warfare, would establish and maintain the canal system. Access to a dependable water supply was often hotly contested, and neighboring tribes settled along the banks of the same stream were likely to fight over scarce water unless firm bonds united the two groups. So far as can be determined, canal systems rarely went beyond the lands controlled by single tribes, and there is no record of intertribal cooperation over water control, but rather plentiful evidence that water rights were frequently the cause of tribal warfare.

Compared with the effort devoted to acquiring and defending lands and water supplies, the agricultural techniques employed were (and are today) relatively simple. A straight-tipped, shallow draft plow is used to break the soil; unlike the American prairie plow, the Mesopotamian model parts the surface but does not turn over the clods.[3] The plow is pulled by a cow or horse. Little attempt is made to clear the land of voluntary growth, though the land may be burned off before plowing. Seeds are broadcast by hand without furrowing and harrowing. Not every farmer has a plow, and it is common practice to hire plowing done, even among sharecroppers. On the other hand, every adult agriculturalist owns a spade, as this is essential in irrigation work. Also universally owned are one-handed sickles, by means of which men and women harvest their crops. Crops are threshed by being trampled with a string of cows and donkeys; threshing carts are not common in the south as they are in the north of Iraq.

Except for plowing, no division of labor by sex prevents women from performing farming tasks. While men supervise the work, women and children participate in most agricultural tasks. It is the men, however, who dig and clean canals and who attend to the distribution of water within the fields. In order to insure an even distribution of water over the land, the fields are commonly divided into *hōds*, rectangular basins of land a few square yards in area, defined by low walls of earth which serve to hold a small quantity of water. Small feeder canals run between these *hōds*, and as a farmer irrigates his field he lets water into one after another of these divisions, thereby insuring that all sections of his plot

---

[3] Professor Jouette Russell has suggested that this type of plow is well suited to this land of fine soils and strong wind, where more radical disturbance of soil surface would favor dust storms—already a troublesome feature of Mesopotamian life (personal communication).

are watered in spite of variations in height from one end of the field to the other. The borders of the *hōds* may also mark property divisions between one farmer and another and are carefully restored each agricultural season. These *hōds* vary in size, depending on the limits of the holding and the irregularities in the topography of the land.

The majority of farmers in southern Iraq who still adhere to tribal standards of conduct regard vegetable cultivation as demeaning. True, many families maintain small gardens in which tomatoes, cucumbers, and some legumes may be grown for home consumption and for modest sales to vegetable peddlers in country towns, but there is considerable resistance to full-time farming of this sort in spite of a ready urban market for vegetable products. Similarly, while fruits and melons can be successfully grown in this region, such farming is still of limited commercial importance except in commercial farms near Baghdad.

Thus, the principal southern crops are barley, wheat, and rice. While wheat is a preferred crop, barley is most generally planted and is increasing in popularity due to its apparently greater tolerance for saline soils. The cultivation of rice is generally limited to the fringes of the marshlands, where large amounts of water are naturally available.[4] In some regions along the Euphrates (such as in Shamiya province) large and small landholdings are planted in rice by local sharecroppers and owners, but the harvesting is done by special groups of men, women, and children from the marsh regions of the Tigris. They move from place to place, harvesting the rice in return for a small share of the crop. This occupationally specialized group is held in low esteem, and the work is considered to be both arduous and demeaning.

As an alternative to sedentary agriculture, sheepherding is still important in southern Iraq. While the relative number of persons dependent on this form of subsistence has undoubtedly declined since the turn of the century, sheepherding is both a full-time occupation for some men and an alternative to cultivation for others. Sheepherders spend part of the year in the valley, grazing their flocks on harvested or fallow lands. Traditional relationships give certain shepherds, and camel-owning Bedouin as well, the right to graze on certain lands at mutually agreeable rates of compensation. As the warmer weather and spring rains bring the desert into bloom, there is a general exodus of animals who will feed on the temporary cover of grass only to return to the fertile valley as the summer sun terminates plant growth.

[4] Rice growing is thus predominantly found in the region between Amara and Basrah along the Tigris and in the area around Nasiriya on the Euphrates. The marshlands near Shamiya and Abu Sukhair in the Middle Euphrates region are also a center of rice cultivation.

The social relationships among the sheepherders vary. In some cases, groups of herders and their families constitute shallow patrilineages: brothers and cousins with perhaps a more distant relative or two as part of the group. In one case, where the shaykh of a small tribe and his brothers and uncles had succeeded in registering all the tribal lands in their names, most of the tribesmen, rather than work as sharecroppers, chose to herd, leaving the land to be tilled by men unrelated to the shaykh. However, these shepherds maintained their tribal ties and regularly assembled at the guesthouse of the sedentary shaykh not only for religious festivals (particularly Muharram) but also to settle intratribal disputes.

Perhaps the most common pattern of sheepherding is for one man to collect the sheep of several relatives and friends and, in the company of a few other fellow tribesmen, take the tribal animals out on the desert, availing themselves of the spring pasturage. Thus many farm families have a few sheep which each year go out beyond the cultivated valley for grazing, though their owner may himself remain at home.

In addition to these shepherds, who travel with their flocks by foot, there are nomadic tribes or tribal sections following a pastoral existence on donkeyback; such groups are commonly referred to as *shawiya*. They may venture further onto the desert after the rains than their pedestrian neighbors. However: "This distinction is not necessarily either tribal or regional. Though tribes may be wholly nomadic or wholly fellahin, many tribes, particularly the larger, contain subsections both of *shawiya* [and pedestrian shepherds], and of fellahin, and the two ways of life are intermingled within the various regions of the country, though the fellahin are tied to the localities where there is water for irrigation" (Mason 1944: 337).

More exclusive in nature is the practice of camel herding. The classical pattern of Bedouin camel herding nomadism is more appropriately discussed in connection with the Arabian Peninsula, but it is important to note that such tribes move in and out of the Euphrates Valley quite regularly and have longstanding relationships with some of the sedentary tribes of this region. Thus some camel-owning groups regularly camp on certain fallow lands each summer and appear at harvest times to haul crops to market with their camels in return for a small share of the grain. Such relations between nomadic and sedentary peoples are frequently cemented by marital exchanges between the leaders of the groups involved. In addition to the economic importance of such relationships, interaction between the nomads and the sedentary groups may reinforce ideals of conduct and tribal organization, in spite of the fact that among farming groups originating under nomadic conditions, these ideals are not well attuned to the circumstances of sedentary living (R. Fernea: 1960).

Life in the marsh areas of southern Iraq has been made possible through several technological developments appropriate to the resources of the area. One of these, the collection of marsh reeds and the weaving of mats for local use and commercial sale, has been described in detail by Shakir M. Salim, whose recent book, *Marsh Dwellers of the Euphrates Delta* (1962) is the only modern social anthropological monograph about the southern Iraq region. Utilizing the abundant volunteer growths of reeds, the people weave mats and fashion from them huts, guesthouses, animal shelters, and even floating islands for living space. In addition, the mats are exported through sale and barter to other regions of Iraq. However, in a sample of 120 families taken by Salim in the Ech-Chabayish region of the Euphrates Delta, a center of this industry, only 75 families practiced mat-weaving, and of these only 27 were solely dependent on this activity for their living. Cereal cultivation was the most important alternative activity. As with sheepherding and cultivation, the weaving and cultivating occupations are not mutually exclusive but are frequently complementary adjustments within the same community.

A more exclusive occupational specialization, buffalo breeding, is found among those marsh dwellers called Ma'adan. As Salim notes, the terms Marsh Arab and Ma'adan have frequently been used indiscriminately. He distinguishes between the people on the Euphrates side of the marshes (who have long had contact with and absorbed increments of population from the Bedouin), and those of the Tigris side (whose contacts have been more with Persians). It is the latter group which tends to specialize in buffalo breeding and which is referred to as Ma'adan by Salim. As among the dry land cultivators of the southern Iraqi alluvium, the Bedouin are accorded some prestige among the Euphrates marsh dwellers. Among the latter (both cultivators and weavers), the buffalo breeders by contrast constitute a despised occupational group. Families of Ma'adan, who may own as many as ten buffalo, sell their dairy products to mobile canoe-shopkeepers for transport to Basrah and buy other food supplies from the villages on the fringes of the marsh. While mat-weaving, hired labor, or cultivation may supplement the incomes of less prosperous Ma'adan, such efforts " . . . make up but a small proportion of the Ma'adan economy" (Salim 1962: 11).

The social organizations uniting and dividing the peoples of southern Iraq are so complex that it is difficult to avoid oversimplification in so brief a review as this. The complexity is in part a historical fact and in part a result of the rapid changes that have been taking place in this country since the turn of the century.

The historic complexity of this region of primarily sedentary tribal groups has multiple origins. The marshland, dryland environmental variations in the region that we have mentioned have necessitated different technological adaptations and controlled to some extent the patterns of settlement. In addition, the lower Tigris and Euphrates valleys have been subject to two quite different centers of cultural and social influence, through contact and immigration from Persia on the east and from the Bedouins on the west (Salim 1962: 8). There have been no detailed comparisons between the tribal groups of these two valleys, but the most superficial familiarity reveals differences in folk tales and dialect, for example, which suggest the possible outcome of more complete studies.[5] No recent social studies of Tigris groups are available. Surely one of the outstanding tasks for future anthropologists in Iraq will consist of systematic comparisons between the two valleys and of understanding these two regions in the context of the larger cultural areas of Southwest Asia.

Contemporary complexities also militate against generalizations, particularly about the nature of tribal social structure. A variety of economic and political conditions have unequally affected subregions of southern Iraq, the most important of which have been land tenure and the nature of land registration. Both Turkish and, later, British policy resulted in the widespread, though not universal, registration of tribal lands in the name of the incumbent shaykh. Where this has happened, tribesmen have frequently left their ancestral lands or have been reduced to the status of sharecroppers, while the shaykhs, in the more extreme cases, have become absentee landlords, residing in the city. In general, tribal organization in these situations has been reduced to a collection of named groupings with little or no contemporary function or corporate existence. On the other hand, where land registration procedure allowed individual tribal families to retain ownership of a certain amount of land, some of the social and economic features of tribal life have been retained until the present. Again, this is a problem requiring more systematic studies, but it may be suggested that such research would probably show that the more widely the land has been distributed among

---

[5]The following comments are based on my own work as well as that of Dr. Salim. It would be erroneous, however, to suppose that these generalizations necessarily apply to the Tigris Valley, as Salim's work as well as my own was done among marsh and dryland tribes, respectively, of the Euphrates region.

tribesmen, the more likely it is that there is some form of tribal organization of contemporary social significance.[6]
The varying conditions of land tenure, settlement pattern, and political development have produced a bewildering variety in contemporary expressions of tribal organization. Within a radius of a few miles the names for tribal subdivisions may differ, and organizational features found in one area may not exist in tribal groups a short distance away. Similarly, the degree to which tribal organization is an important feature in the lives of contemporary rural Iraqis also varies considerably. While most of the rural citizens of southern Iraq were born members of a tribe, the importance of this membership to the individual and the subsequent viability of tribal life is by no means uniform. The imposition of administrative and judicial systems from Baghdad and the pacification of the countryside have robbed the tribal organization of most of its historic purpose and strengthened the disintegrative processes set in motion through the registration of tribal lands in the names of a favored few. That some aspects of the social life of men in most of southern Iraq remain tribally organized is probably due in large part to the facts that nothing has yet replaced kin relationships as the principal mode of social intercourse in this region, and that the tribal system is, in many ways, an expression and extension of kinship.

The tribesman is born into a named agnatic lineage, usually four or five generations in depth, within which all men trace descent to a common ancestor and can specify their collateral relationships. The preference for patri-parallel cousin marriages means that the maternal line is frequently identical with the paternal. This lineage group traditionally shared responsibility in feuds and warfare, restricted and controlled marriage choice, and jointly occupied a single area of land. The right to demand and receive assistance within this group has served to restrict economic differentiation within the lineage. Nor is a single man generally recognized as having higher political status, for authority ideally rests

[6]However, in some areas (as near Rumaytha, on the Hilla branch of the Euphrates below Diwaniya), where the landholdings have been widely distributed among tribesmen and subject to fragmentation through inheritance, many of the shaykhs have holdings no larger than average, yet little remains of a functioning tribal system. In such cases, the traditional leaders lack economic means to maintain the guesthouses, where tribesmen traditionally gather, and have lost the political and social standing in Iraqi society-at-large which might make them valuable intermediaries for the ordinary tribesman in dealings with the administration. Thus either extreme—radical equality of land distribution or radical concentration of land in the hands of the shaykh—may be inimicable to the contemporary political functions of a tribal system (see below).

equally among the older men of the group. The sense of solidarity within this group is customarily very strong. All the men of ego's father's generation are customarily addressed as "my father's brother" (*'ammi*), except when mother's actual brother and ego's age-mates are described as "brothers" or "cousins."

The lineage "nests" within a second, larger unit of association, composed of two or more lineage groupings believed to be related by descent from a common ancestor or by adoption.[7] Traditionally, the men within this grouping consider each other kinsmen and display complete solidarity in the case of disputes with other groupings of similar size and composition within the tribe. At the same time, the primary lineages may be at odds over many issues, even to the point of bloodshed. The adult males of the secondary lineage not directly involved in the dispute act to reconcile the antagonists under the leadership of the *sirkal*.[8] The primary lineages within the secondary grouping commonly occupy adjacent territories, so that they frequently share territorial interests as well as kinship ties.

While, except for the institution of adoption, the secondary lineages are structurally merely more inclusive units of agnatic kinsmen, Salim refers to such groups as clans (Salim 1962: 43ff.).[9] Where such groups are found today, they may practice certain forms of mutual aid and usually are a territorial as well as a social unit. These groups frequently have certain flags, which are considered common property, and in some cases one or more guesthouses, the support of which may be shared by some if not all of the kinsmen within this group. Furthermore, an offense against a member of these secondary lineages or clan groups by someone from other similar segments within the same tribe is considered to be an offense to the entire membership.

[7] Adoption is a common method by which tribal groups have historically regrouped themselves. It involves the swearing of allegiance before witnesses as groups of tribesmen leave their ancestral tribal associations in preference for a more powerful and numerically superior grouping.

[8] This title refers to the leader of secondary lineages (clans). However, tribal informants report that this title was introduced during the Ottoman period by Turkish administrators who wished to have someone with whom they could deal at a lower level of tribal organization than that represented by shaykhs. In the Middle Euphrates area, this "office" was of little importance in tribal affairs; Salim reports a contrary situation among the Beni Isad (1962: 34-37).

[9] The use of the word "clan" by Salim (and others) in speaking of these secondary lineages is somewhat exceptional if one's introduction to the term has been through studies of American Indian societies. Many features commonly associated with such organizations in the latter instances (e.g. totemism and exogamy) are not present.

A third unit of organization common among the Arabs of southern Iraq unites several secondary lineages or clans under the leadership of a shaykh. The unit is usually referred to as a tribe in English and *ashīra* in Arabic. Composed of secondary lineages or clans presumed to have been founded by descendants (frequently sons) of the ancestor from whom the name of the tribe is generally derived, the tribe was traditionally the chief military and political organization in southern Iraq. Here again, however, voluntary and forced alliances between tribes sometimes produced confederations (such as the famous Muntafiq "tribe") with a paramount shaykh. Members of such groups stood together in disputes with government authorities or other tribes and frequently controlled large areas of land.

As a military and political unit, the tribe or confederation of tribes is of little importance today. In some regions, the shaykhdoms have been deliberately abolished by the central government and in other places (principally in the Kut and Amara regions on the Tigris River) so-called shaykhs have been made the de facto agents of the government. They are recognized both as owners of large tracts of land (once controlled by individual tribal segments or tribesmen) and as the authorities responsible for maintaining law and order among their now sharecropping tribal subjects.[10] In the Middle Euphrates region, where many individual tribesmen have succeeded in having small amounts of land registered in their names, traditional organization persists to some degree. However, even here, the absence of military and political functions has robbed this unit of social organization of its raison d'etre. The shaykh, if there be such, frequently acts as a focus for certain ceremonial activities as when, during certain religious festivals, tribesmen gather at his guesthouse and contribute food for communitywide feasts. A contemporary shaykh may also rally enough support to field a labor force for the cleaning of certain irrigation canals (often a source of water for more than his own lands) or for the building of a new guesthouse. If he enjoys sufficient prestige, he may also take a hand in the settlement of disputes between members of two or more secondary lineages, and thus the tribe may continue to constitute a jural community in matters where traditional

---

[10]While the policy of the Kassem government after the 1958 revolution in Iraq included agrarian reform programs for the redistribution of such landholdings, together with abolition of government recognition and support for tribal shaykhs, unofficial reports indicate that the postrevolutionary government on more than one occasion called on these men for assistance: in one instance some southern Iraqi shaykhs were asked to advance seeds to their exsharecroppers and help stem the rising tide of migration into Baghdad. However, my remarks refer to the situation prior to the 1958 revolution unless otherwise indicated.

law is preferred to, or supplements, the national legal system. Yet all of this depends in large degree on the character of the individual shaykh—whether he chooses to reside among his tribesmen or in the city; to spend some of his own money on maintaining his guesthouse or leave it unattended; or whether his position with respect to administrators and politicians is such as to make him a valuable "contact" for tribesmen in securing jobs or justice from the government. If, as seems to be the case, both the tribe and the shaykhship depend upon the persistent need for mutual cooperation and central direction in military action against outside forces, their continued existence under present conditions seems to be in doubt.

Students of classical Arab social organization will recognize the segmental, kinship-oriented character of the tribal structure we have briefly outlined. The "nesting" of primary within secondary segments, and the latter within still larger sections, places the individual tribesman in the center of a concentrically arranged social system composed of ever more distant kinsmen, related by birth or "adoption." This much the sedentary tribesmen of the southern Euphrates share with their nomadic neighbors. However, the circumstances of life in southern Iraq are obviously quite different from those in the Arabian and Syrian deserts. The classical Arabian or Syrian system developed under ecological conditions which encouraged tribesmen to travel and live as small groups of agnatic kinsmen, often separated by miles of desert from more distant kinsmen. Resources severely limited the periods of time during which whole tribes or large segments of tribes could camp together, but within the territories reserved to specific tribes or confederations small groups of tribesmen were comparatively free to associate or separate as they wished.

The sedentary tribes of southern Iraq are, however, frozen to a limited territory; the "nesting" model of a segmentary system is actually expressed in occupation patterns: primary lineages live within and cultivate an area of land next to other primary lineages, which are part of the same secondary lineage. The latter are also contiguous groupings, whose lands together comprise the area occupied by the tribe; several tribes, which together constitute a confederation, may also be neighbors. (There are exceptions to this pattern, of course, and in many cases landless tribesmen are widely scattered about, working as sharecroppers.) Lineages cannot split and physically separate when quarrels divide groups of· kinsmen, for whoever moves away loses his land. Nor can the demographic problems which arise from microscopic variations in birthrate among sections of a tribe be easily resolved without an authority to redistribute landholdings. Threats of occupation from neighboring tribes and from desert nomads tempted by the riverine countryside put a premium on maintaining the tribe at the greatest strength possible and on close cooperation between tribal segments. And, in many cases, invading nomadic tribes have settled in the river valleys and adopted weaker segments of sedentary groups who were unable to defend themselves and who preferred affiliation to oblivion.

Whether for these or other reasons, the segmentally-structured tribal organizations of southern Iraq have characteristically exhibited tendencies toward political centralization. These tendencies have been expressed in several ways. One is the development of tribal codes embracing the largest recognized units of affiliation, according to which rates of compensation and punishment for established offenses are applied in individual cases by tribal leaders. These codes, of which some have been in written form for many years, have formed a growing body of law, as new precedents have been established to fit new circumstances. They deserve close comparative study before they are forgotten as they are replaced by civil codes.

The most important feature of this centralization relates to changes in the manner of selection of the sedentary shaykh and the rights and duties associated with that position. As both Salim and I have noted, the values of the sedentary Iraqi tribes have, to a large degree, remained those of a nomadic, warrior society (Salim 1962: 141-43; R. Fernea 1960: 74-75). Thus it is not surprising that even today, statements from tribesmen as to the qualities of a proper shaykh stress bravery in battle and generosity of hospitality before all else, and emphasize the possibility of any well-born man achieving such a position. In fact, however, lists of successive shaykhs suggest that primogeniture is extremely important in the selection of a shaykh in many parts of southern Iraq. Salim states that in this area feudal shaykhdoms had existed for a period of seven centuries prior to 1893. He emphasizes that the need for constant military action strengthened the hand of these chiefdoms, and that the price of dissension within the tribe was defeat from outside forces. In this situation, according to Salim, the "executive power of the shaykh was administered by the Mukhtar or clan heads, by members of the ruling clan, especially the shaykh's own sons and brothers, and by his slaves. The clan heads had no power of their own. They were instruments of the shaykh" (Salim 1962: 28). During this period, the successful southern Mesopotamian shaykh controlled the use and disposition of land occupied by his people, was the final judge in all disputes, and was the commander of all armed forces. Frequently such men also directed limited public works in their territory, such as dam construction and the digging of canals, but local tradition does not honor them for this work so much as it does for their military abilities.

Thus, the institution of the shaykhdom, with its centralization of power and administrative bureaucracy, seems to have come about during conditions of sporadic hostility in which segmentally-structured tribal organizations jointly occupied a single territory and were obliged to defend it against the attacks of antagonists, including both sedentary neighbors and nomadic raiders from the deserts. During lengthy Ottoman administration (1534-1918), the local authority of tribal leaders was never successfully challenged for long periods of time by the central government. In fact, it might be suggested that Turkish policy strengthened the hands of tribal leaders by frequently presenting occasions requiring concerted action among large tribal groups and encouraging centralization of leadership among the tribes for military purposes. (See Longrigg [1925] for a detailed discussion of Turkish policy with respect to the tribes of Mesopotamia.) With the effective pacification of the countryside by the British after World War I, strongly centralized tribal government all but disappeared except where deliberately maintained by the British administration in Baghdad. As Salim (1962) so well describes in the case of the Beni Isad, it was at this time that most tribes ceased to act as cohesive political and military units. Whether or not, as Salim and others suggest, the tribesmen of Iraq welcomed the opportunity to throw off the yoke of an unloved autocracy, the end of armed conflict certainly meant the loss of the primary field of activity in which leaders could express their personal charisma and gain social validation of their authority.

The dissolution of the shaykhdoms was widely accompanied by a breaking up of many larger tribes and confederations of tribes into smaller units, for the suppression of outside forces favored processes of fission rather than fusion. It is probably from this period, after the turn of the century, that many of the present apparent "inconsistencies" in tribal organization date. Thus, for instance, Salim notes there is "confusion" among the Beni Isad tribesmen today between the terms for tribe and for clan, with many referring to their clan as a tribe and subdividing it into clans (Salim 1962: 41). The same tendency can be observed among the El Shabana, though it is not entirely clear whether the situation stems from confusion or from the predictable outcome of the contemporary circumstances. There is considerable lack of regularity in the terms given to various segments of tribal organization from place to place. For instance, in comparing the Beni Isad with the El Shabana, the terms for the tribal segments (from most to least inclusive) are as follows:

Beni Isad	El Shabana
ashīra	*ashīra*
hamula	*shubba'*
fukhid (or *lahama kishba*)	*fukhid*
khowwan	*hamula*

A series of carefully comparative studies of tribal organizations which have been subject to a variety of environmental conditions might help determine how these variations have come about. Do such nominal differences signify structural changes, or are they merely accidents or "confusions" of naming?[11]

The Beni Isad and El Shabana also exhibit variation in terms of social stratification and political organization, suggesting another area in which controlled comparisons of several tribal organizations might fruitfully be undertaken. Salim identifies five hierarchically organized classes among the Beni Isad: the Is-sada (decendants of the prophet); the once-ruling clan; the heads of other clans and lineages and ordinary tribesmen; the slaves; and lastly the Subba (Mandeans). Membership in these traditional classes is determined by birth, and the members of each are expected to marry endogamously (Salim 1962: 43-54). The Is-sada are also honored among the El Shabana, but have no special political position, though they are often called upon to act as mediators in the settlement of hostilities between tribal groups.

The El Shabana do not, however, have a traditional ruling clan. In fact, these tribesmen insisted that the shaykh could and had actually come from any section of the tribe. It seems to have been the British administration, after World War I, that favored primogeniture as a means of filling tribal office to untidy, peace-breaking struggles for power within the tribe. Thus pacification, coupled with the registration in the name of the shaykh of land previously regarded as belonging to the tribe, have fostered the development of a politically and economically superior clan among the El Shabana, a situation which does not seem to enjoy cultural validation even today, however.

---

[11] More research must be done before these terminological differences will be understood. For instance, the term *shubba'* refers to an area of land as well as a social division and may have been applied to the social grouping that results when members of a *fukhid* socially divide and adopt individual names but are unable to physically separate due to an absence of unoccupied lands. It is not understood why the term *hamula* refers to a more inclusive group than the *fukhid* among the Beni Isad, while the reverse is true among the El Shabana, however.

The reasons why political authority should be rooted in a traditional hierarchy in one case and should shift among segmentally equal groupings in another may well be related to the much longer history of sedentary life among the Beni Isad (several centuries as compared to 80-100 years), plus the persistent contacts which the El Shabana enjoy with their Bedouin neighbors, whose political organization more closely resembles their own. An examination of several tribes in southern Iraq would probably reveal a positive association between length of sedentarization and the development of clan hierarchies associated with centralized political authority.

Contemporary southern Iraq is not, of course, occupied solely by tribesmen carrying on the activities we have thus far discussed. Only the smaller hamlets scattered throughout the cultivated area are populated by tribesmen alone. Most villages and every town have their own tradesmen and government employees attending to the economic and administrative needs of the surrounding population. These groups, referred to locally as the *ahl es-suq* (people of the market) and *muwadhafiin* (employees), constitute an essential element in the fabric of daily life. Little systematic attention has been paid to the organization of these groups and their relationships with the larger tribal population, and we can only provide some general observations about them, indicating possible areas of further research.

In Daghghara,[12] the village nearest the hamlets of the El Shabana, the lines that have traditionally been drawn between the people of the market and the tribesmen are still quite distinct. Ordinarily, intermarriage between the two groups does not take place, nor do members of one group engage in the occupation of the other. In fact, the tribesman scornfully regards the occupations of the marketplace as unfitting for a man of distinguished lineage. Tribesmen of good standing do not frequent the marketplace more than absolutely necessary. Even passing time in the coffeeshops that dot the bazaars is considered unfitting behavior. While some shopkeepers have better reputations than others among the tribesmen for fair dealing, tribesmen make the general distinction that the people of the market are concerned primarily with money, while the tribesmen are primarily concerned with honor.

At the same time, only the richest of the tribesmen are ever out of debt to one or more shopkeepers. In most cases, the day-to-day purchases are recorded at prices slightly above cash value, and the farmer's crop, which he brings to his merchant, is estimated at slightly less than

---

[12]Located on the Daghghara Canal in the Liwa (province) of Diwaniya.

it might be worth were the farmer free to choose his own time and place for disposing of it. These discrepancies are deplored by the tribesman, who considers them as a kind of usury. On the other hand, as the soil in many areas progressively deteriorates through salination, and the size of the farmer's crop diminishes, merchants worry that many debts will never be fully repaid. The merchant is thus likely to complain that he is constantly being taken advantage of and to call the tribesmen lazy and unenterprising.

The government employees who administer, teach, and police southern Iraq are often outsiders with respect to both the people of the market and the tribesmen. In an area where nationalism is still a relatively new phenomenon, and where the central government until the recent past was locally represented only by the tax collector and his police or soldiers, the origins of the suspicion and distrust which frequently characterize the relations between the *muwadhafiin* and the local population are not difficult to understand. Only recently have villages begun to be administrated by country-bred employees. Many Baghdadis, sent out from their city offices to work in the provinces, regard themselves as exiles in a savage land. In addition, the administrators from Baghdad are frequently Sunni Muslims, while the southern population is almost entirely Shi'a, thus further aggravating the situation, especially when local governors and district officials are obliged to police and control religious demonstrations. Until recently, when a uniform code of justice replaced a special tribal code in rural areas, administrators with city backgrounds were obliged to rely heavily upon tribal leaders for the interpretation of local custom and the unraveling of historic relationships between tribal groups, a fact which many *muwadhafiin* resented.

Although in Daghghara the employees and the people of the marketplace are, as groups, better off economically than the tribesmen, there is no question but that the members of each of these sections of the population consider themselves superior to the other. Granting the obvious functional interdependencies, each group nevertheless has its own leadership, standards of conduct, and realm of activity. In 1959, however, there were signs of change in the relations between these groups. The wealthier tribesmen were known to have investments in certain market enterprises and to take an active, if inconspicuous, interest in their success. Several of the administrators were educated men who had come originally from neighboring tribes, and a few were from tribes of the area itself. Most tribesmen appeared to spend far more time in the less formal atmosphere of the market coffeeshops than in the traditional tribal guesthouses and, if intermarriage between the groups was rare, it certainly was not unheard of. In comparison, Salim (1962), in his description of Ech-Chabayish, presents a radically different view of these relationships under rather different economic circumstances.

In Ech-Chabayish, before World War I none of the Beni Isad tribesmen participated in market activities, which were exclusively the province of a few Persian merchants. During and after the War, a few local people began to venture into business, but, Salim notes, these were of the lowest social status within the tribe. As the demand for marsh-reed mats grew throughout Iraq, and trade in this item became more profitable, the local economy gradually switched from a subsistence to a cash basis, and opportunities to engage in wholesale and retail commerce multiplied. While mat-making is considered an acceptable occupation, trading in mats and other forms of commerce are traditionally as unfitting for men of honor among the Beni Isad as among the El Shabana in Daghghara. Nevertheless, the rapid local economic growth has led many tribesmen into marketing activities, and now many tribesmen of respectable family are active businessmen.

From this situation have emerged "two opposed sets of values, the mercantile and the tribal in the same society" (Salim 1962: 143). The market group includes tribesmen, many of whom care about their tribal standing; they are also businessmen who want to make money.

> The businessmen have, by the very nature of their work, to give up guest houses, which involve a loss of money and time. They tend to think and act individually, to put business matters above tribal ideas. Indeed, many of the businessmen at Ech-Chabayish have confirmed the tribesmen in their belief that business is incompatible with tribal loyalty [Salim 1962: 142].

Yet, says Salim:

> ... though members of the market group pay more attention to business obligations, they do not totally neglect tribal obligations; for it is in their interest to comply with these as far as they can. ... The people of the market do not yet show any tendency to act as a distinct group, nor do they show any inclination to intermarry; they follow the customary principles of tribal marriage. ... The market people have not yet adopted wholesale a set of new values incompatible with tribal life. They are tempted by the exigencies of business to abandon certain tribal values, while still desiring to maintain their prestige in the eyes of their fellow tribesmen. Sufficient time has not yet elapsed to separate them into a distinct group, but with the increase of trade, extension of business in the village, and with more tribesmen breaking the barriers of the traditional economic pattern, this class may well come

to form, in the near future, a social unit different from the old tribal one, not only in economic pursuits, but in all its ideals and values [Salim 1962: 143].

It would appear that Salim anticipates the development of a new "people of the market" in Ech-Chabayish, while for Daghghara I have suggested, to the contrary, that the distinction between tribesmen and people of the market may be waning, judging at least from the discrepancies that are currently developing between tradition and practice. Is the presence of incompatible sets of values within the same community, as in Ech-Chabayish, a precondition to the development of the vertical divisions that exist in Daghghara? Why, in Daghghara, where there has been a decline in economic activity, should there be signs of lessening distinction between tribal and market peoples whereas in Ech-Chabayish, under comparatively favorable economic conditions, the opposite is true? Is it possible that, in the case of Ech-Chabayish, the traditionalist tribesmen may come to accommodate themselves to an economically determined status system, in effect avoiding an ultimate split between tribe and market? Clearly, the south of Iraq presents excellent opportunities for comparative studies of small-scale socioeconomic processes, studies which, among other things, might shed light on the development of the supposedly typical "mosaic" or "kelim" social structure of the Middle East.

In so short a statement as this, it is not possible to provide a detailed discussion of Shi'ism, the Islamic sect which predominates in southern Iraq. Ignoring most of the history and formal theology of Shi'ism, most adequately described elsewhere in references, I can only touch upon a few of the regional manifestations of this religious system, particularly as it affects other aspects of the social and cultural life of this country (see, e.g., Donaldson 1933).

Commitment to the Sunni or Shi'a sect of Islam divides the northern from the southern half of Iraq roughly at Baghdad. Within the capital itself, certain districts are traditionally occupied by Shi'a, others by Sunni; the tomb of Il-Kadhum, an important shrine for Shi'a pilgrimage, is the center of a large Baghdad Shi'a residential area. In the cities of Najaf and Karbala, about 60 miles south of Baghdad, lie the tombs of the imams Ali, Husayn, and Abbas, whose struggles for the leadership of the Muslim world after the death of the Prophet led to their martyrdom. This in turn eventually created the permanent schism between their followers (Shi'a) and the partisans of the Umayyid caliphates (Sunni). Pilgrimage to the holy cities of Najaf and Karbala is a duty for all pious Shi'a, and burial in the ground around Najaf is regarded as a means of insuring residence in Paradise. The holy cities annually attract tens of thousands of Shi'a pilgrims, not only the Arabs of southern Iraq but also Persians, Pakistanis, Arabs from the southern Arabian Peninsula and the Persian Gulf, and members of Shi'a minorities from practically all sections of the Muslim world. Many of the pilgrims use modern means of transportation, which limits their contact with southern tribesmen and villagers, but others travel long distances by animal and on foot, exercising the stranger's traditional right to tribal hospitality. As a result of these (as well as other) contacts, the culture of Mesopotamia reflects a variety of alien influences. The local dialect of Arabic, for example, contains many Farsi morphemes,[13] and the legends and folk tales reveal origins in Persia, the Persian Gulf area, and beyond.

However, it is the people of southern Iraq who are most easily able to make the pilgrimages to the holy cities. Many make this trip at least once a year, preferably during the ceremonies held in Karbala 40 days after the anniversary of the death of the martyr Husayn. In the towns and villages, processions and ceremonies are held during the month of Muharram, especially on the tenth day of Muharram, also called Ashur, the anniversary of Husayn's death. Ashur is marked by the ceremonies of ritual mourning (*matam*), in which groups of men (*taaziya*) dressed in trousers and open-backed black shirts march through the streets, beating themselves with short lengths of chain or striking their foreheads with swords. This self-inflicted, ritualized punishment is performed not so much in a spirit of personal mortification as to demonstrate a group expression of despair and mourning over the martyrdom. Participation in such events is highly formalized: *taaziya* groups are organized in villages and towns all over Iraq. Each such group may contain anywhere from 5 to 20 or more men. Membership may be voluntary adult choice, or a child may grow up belonging to a group as a result of a religious vow made by his mother. It is not uncommon for women who are unable to conceive or who have borne only daughters to pledge, as a condition of his birth, the services of the hoped-for son to a local *taaziya* group. Young children walk in procession with such groups, though self-flagellation does not commonly begin until after puberty.

Contributions are solicited among villagers and townsmen to help pay the cost of transporting the *taaziya* groups from villages in all parts of southern Iraq to Karbala for the ceremonies. It is a matter of some local pride to be represented by a group that performs well, and feelings run

[13] Such as the suffix "*chi*," which indicates the doer of the action. An *arabanchi* is a man who drives a carriage or *arabiya*, a *gahawchi* is a man who makes the coffee or *gahwa*. Indian words (like *cherpava*—bed) are found, and words of Turkish origin are also common in the dialect.

high on such occasions. It is not unusual for scuffles and even more serious fights to break out between rival *taaziya* groups from differing villages or tribal groups, incidents which may reflect a longstanding history of hostile tribal relations.

In addition to the *matam*, religious readings (*iq-qry*) are held throughout the months of Ramadan and Muharram. The *qry* may be held in the tribal guesthouse, in the marketplace, or in a private home (the latter is always the place for *qrys* held by women). Participants listen to the recitation of a leader, preferably a *mu'min*, a man who has had some training at the religious schools in Najaf, or a *mullah*, a man or woman who has trained with an older person specialized in this activity. The *qrys* are also occasions which require the participants to give formal expression of grief at appropriate moments in the narration. The women characteristically are more expressive in their participation than the men, for they beat their breasts, weep, and move together in a circle, chanting. It is considered the duty of the shaykhs or clan elders, as well as of the older and well-to-do merchants, to sponsor *qrys*. The shaykh of the El Shabana would customarily engage the services of a gifted *mu'min* for the entire period of Ramadan, feeding and sheltering him for the duration of the readings and paying for his labor with an appropriate amount of grain.

Another important public manifestation of Shi'a religious life is found in the morality plays. These may be given on the anniversaries of the deaths of any of the first twelve imams of the Shi'a sect,[14] but the most widely celebrated ordinarily involves the participation of both market and tribal people in a depiction of the events of Husayn's martyrdom. Costumed men on horseback represent the forces of Husayn and those of Mu'awiya, who opposed him. A realistic battle scene is recreated for the people of the village, who crowd the streets for the annual spectacle. Emrys Peters has given us a good account of such a play in a Lebanese Shi'a community (Peters 1956), and descriptions of these plays are available in literature about Persia and the Indian subcontinent, but studies for the Shi'a community of southern Iraq do not seem to be available.

The Nuri es-Said government tended to discourage these public displays, apparently because they strengthened Shi'a feelings of opposition to the rest of Sunni Iraq, and also because they often became occasions for outbreaks of violence among the participants and observers. In 1957, the central Baghdad administration asked the shaykhs of the Daghghara region to pledge several thousand pounds which would be forfeited in

[14]On February 14, 1958, I witnessed in Daghghara a play commemorating events in the life of Imam Moussa ibn Jaffar.

case the peace was breached; the play was not held. The details of how these morality plays are locally organized are not completely known, though my own unverified impression is that in the central Euphrates area, the "people of the market" are the most active group in both the plays and the *matam* ceremonies. However, the relationship between these religious activities and the features of social organization described above is not fully understood and needs future study.

It is perhaps not surprising to find that the most dramatic features of Shi'a ceremonialism are those that emphasize grievances against Sunni orthodoxy. According to Donaldson (1933) and others, the Shi'a believe that Imam Husayn and his family died in order to save their followers from the sinful existence being imposed on them by the Umayyid rulers, who, by treachery and violence, had deprived Ali and his descendants of their roles as leaders of the entire Muslim community. This doctrine of redemption through death has led Lewis (1940), Donaldson (1933), and others to see parallels between Shi'a and Christian theology. My own research did not include a systematic study of Shi'a practices, but I was reminded by them of the emotional quality found in Christian fundamentalism. Certainly Shi'a rituals provide the one legitimate opportunity for public display of emotions in which the entire community is joined together, regardless of the traditional divisions along tribal and occupational lines.

In addition to providing a brief descriptive account of southern Iraqi life, I have tried to indicate something of the range of problems awaiting analysis. In contrast with many other regions of the Middle East, where, within comparatively large areas, one village is essentially like the next, southern Iraq offers macroscopic comparisons between neighboring villages and tribes which provide contrasts in limited aspects of social and cultural life against a background of general historically derived similarity. The contrasts appear related to variations in ecological circumstances, length of sedentary existence, government policies (particularly with respect to land registration), and contact with "alien" groups, as well as differentials in economic opportunity. It is thus an area well suited to methods of controlled comparison involving synchronic analyses of social change. It is also one of the comparatively few areas in the modern world where the dynamics of change are not embedded exclusively in the dialectic between "Western" and "non-Western" culture-contact.

REFERENCES CITED

Donaldson, Dwight M.
1933   *The Shi'ite religion; a history of Islam in Persia and Irak*, London, Luzac.

Fernea, Robert A.
1960   "Cultural similarities and sociological differences between the nomadic and settled Arabs of Iraq," *Actes du VI Congrès International des Sciences Anthropologiques et Ethnologiques* (Paris), *2:* 71-75.
1970   *Shaykh and effendi*, Cambridge, Harvard University Press.

Iraq, Ministry of Economics, Central Bureau of Statistics
1961   *Statistical abstract 1960*, Baghdad, Zahra' Press.

Lewis, Bernard
1940   *The origins of Ismāʿīlism*, Cambridge, W. Heffer & Sons.

Longrigg, Stephen H.
1925   *Four centuries of modern Iraq*, Oxford, Clarendon Press.

Mason, Kenneth, et al.
1944   "Shepherding tribes of Syria and Mesopotamia," in *Iraq and the Persian Gulf, Geographical Handbook Series*, B.R. 524, Great Britain, Naval Intelligence Division, London, H.M.S. Office.

Maxwell, Gavin
1957   *People of the reeds*, New York, Harper.

Peters, Emrys
1956   "A Muslim passion play; key to a Lebanese village," *Atlantic Monthly 198, 4:* 176-80.

MESOPOTAMIA:
AN ANNOTATED BIBLIOGRAPHY
(compiled by Louise E. Sweet)

As Fernea's chapter on southern Mesopotamia indicates, the truly anthropological literature on Iraq scarcely exists or does justice to the ethnographic richness of the country. The most significant and helpful titles are listed here. Their bibliographies will serve as additional resources but these are, in the main, administrative documents and political histories.

Arfa, Hassan
   1966   *The Kurds: an historical and political study*, New York, Oxford University Press.

        The author was Chief of Staff of the Iranian Army (1944-46) and Iranian Ambassador to Turkey (1958-61). "He fought the Kurds for many years in the frontier districts of Iran, but kept friendly relations with most of the Kurdish Chiefs (note on book jacket)."

Barth, Fredrik
   1953   "Principles of social organization in Southern Kurdistan," *Universitetets Etnografiske Museum Bulletin No. 7*, Oslo, Brødrene Jørgensen Boktr.

        An analysis of Iraqi Kurdish Society in the vicinity of Kirkuk and Sulymaniyeh, considerably to the west of Leach's 1940 study.

   1954   "Father's brother's daughter marriage in Kurdistan," *Southwestern Journal of Anthropology 10:* 164-71.

        Barth explains functionally (reliable political alliance) this form of marriage, which shows a relatively high frequency among the "tribal" and patrilineal Kurds in his area of study, as it does among comparable Arab groups.

Bois, P. Thomas
   1965   *Connaissance des Kurdes*, Beirut, Khayats.

        A French Dominican priest's synthesizing account, with attention to social organization, marriage, and folklore of the Kurds. An informal account by a scholar of Kurdish language, literature, and history. Bibliography.

Dickson, H. R. P.

1949 *The Arab of the desert: a glimpse into Badawin life in Kuwait and Sau'di Arabia*, London, Allen and Unwin.

Another of the reminiscence volumes of a British officer and political resident from the first half of this century: a unique hodgepodge of variably useful and accurate information. Chapter 15 deals specifically with the Muntafiq shepherd tribes of southern Iraq, some of whose sections traditionally grazed their flocks in Kuwait.

1956 *Kuwait and her neighbors*, London, Allen and Unwin.

Like *The Arab of the Desert*, but with the author's version of Kuwait recent history, also. Valuable data and genealogical materials embedded in chitchat. Chapters 7-9 deal specifically with Dickson's experiences as a British political officer in southern Iraq and provide information on the cultural diversity and tribes in and about the marshes.

Drower, Lady Ethel S. (E. S. Stevens)

1923 *By Tigris and Euphrates*, London, Hurst & Blackett.

One of many books by a scholarly Englishwoman, wife of a member of the British staff stationed there during the First World War and after. Her intent is to present the "infinite variety and complexity" of Iraq at that time. It is one of the few appreciative descriptive surveys of cities, sacred and secular, such "cult" groups or events as the little known Yazidis, the Shi'a "passion play" of Muharram, and the various minority groups and specialists of the southern marshes. Folkloristic.

1937 *The Mandaeans of Iraq and Iran*, Oxford, Clarendon Press.

A scholarly, historical, but not anthropological discussion of the customs and rituals of the dwindling Mandean community.

1949 "Arabs of the Hor al Hawiza," Chapter 5 in Henry Field, ed., *The Anthropology of Iraq, the Lower Euphrates-Tigris Region*, Part 1, *Field Museum of Natural History Anthropological Series, Vol. 30, no. 2*, Chicago.

The only accurate, ethnologically useful part of the whole volume in which this brief section appears. The villagers of the marshes of southern Iraq are depicted in detail by an acute observer of costume, reed dwelling, household activities.

Fernea, Elizabeth Warnock

1965 *Guests of the Sheikh*, Garden City, N.Y., Doubleday. (Reprinted by Anchor Books, 1969.)

An anthropologist's wife gives a personal account of her life in a village in southern Iraq.

Fernea, Robert A.
1960   "Cultural similarities and sociological differences between the nomadic and settled Arabs of Iraq," *Actes du VI Congrès International des Sciences Anthropologiques et Ethnologiques* (Paris), *2:* 71-75.

"Fulanain" (S. E. and M. G. Hedgcock)
1928   *The Marsh Arab: Haji Rikkan*, Philadelphia, J. B. Lippincott.

An educated, if semifictional, account of the Al Bu Muhammad and Bani Lam tribes of the southern marshes during the British Mandate period. Good on commerce.

Great Britain, Naval Intelligence Division
1916-17   *Handbook of Mesopotamia*, 4 vols. London, H.M.S. Office.
1944   *Iraq and the Persian Gulf, Geographical Handbook Series*, B.R. 524, London, H.M.S. Office.

Produced for official use during the 1939-45 war, it does not have the quality in detailed information of the earlier *Handbook* series (1916-17). Excellent maps.

Hansen, Henny Harald
1961   "The Kurdish woman's life: Field Research in a Muslim Society Iraq," *Nationalmuseets Skrifter, Etnografisk Raekke* 7, Copenhagen.

A study of women's cultural patterns made in 1957 among sedentary Kurds of the mountainous Sulaimani district.

Harris, George L., et al.
1958   *Iraq: its people, its society, its culture*, New Haven, HRAF Press.

One of the HRAF Survey of World Cultures Series. Presents a synthesis of varied data within a format which emphasizes the national structure and the state of its integration from a Western point of view. Ethnographic material and a useful bibliography.

Leach, E. R.
1940   "Social and Economic Organisation of the Rowanduz Kurds," *London School of Economics, Monographs on Social Anthropology, No. 3*, London, Percy, Lund, Humphries.

Brief but useful notes from a five-week field survey; one of the few particular ethnographic studies available on a Kurdish community in the mountains of northern Iraq, close to the border of Iran.

Longrigg, Stephen Hemsley
1953   *Iraq, 1900-1950: a political, social, and economic history*, London, Oxford University Press (for the Royal Institute of International Affairs).
       Chiefly a political history from the enlightened British official's point of view. Very useful bibliography.

Salim, Shakir M.
1962   "Marsh dwellers of the Euphrates Delta," *London School of Economics, Monographs on Social Anthropology, No. 23*, London, University of London, Athlone Press.
       One of the rare anthropological studies from Iraq of Arabs of desert origin who have settled in the marginal marsh areas as cultivators and mat-makers.

Thesiger, Wilfred
1964   *The Marsh Arabs*, London, Longmans, Green.
       Magnificient photographs and an informative, romantic text by a British adventurer thoroughly experienced in Arabian and other societies. Records visits between 1951 and 1958.

Warriner, Doreen
1957   *Land reform and development in the Middle East: a study of Egypt, Syria, and Iraq*, New York, Oxford University Press (for the Royal Institute of International Affairs).
       A biased economist's critique of agricultural practices and reform programs in three Middle Eastern countries.

Westphal-Hellbusch, Sigrid, and Heinz Westphal
1962   *Die Ma'dan: Kultur und Geschichte der Marschenbewohner in Süd-Iraq*, Berlin: Duncker und Humblot.
       Based on field work done in 1955-56, probably the only professional ethnological study of the Ma'dan of the southern marshes. Excellent photographs and maps.

CHAPTER *4*

The Arabian Peninsula*

LOUISE E. SWEET

I. *Introduction*

A. *Cultural Uniformity and Variability*

The Arabian Peninsula lies as a great land mass with considerable physiographic unity between Africa, India, and Western Asia. By and large, the conventional historical concept of Arabia is also one of considerable cultural uniformity, at least over the last thousand years. For more recent centuries, this concept of cultural uniformity is reinforced by the predominance of Islam throughout the ideological systems found in this area, together with the general linguistic unity under Arabic. In many traits of culture—such as patrilineal and segmentary principles of social organization—and in the geographical recurrence of nomadic pastoralism, oasis or mountain intensive agriculture, and maritime fishing and navigation as complexes in themselves, widespread similarity of content is revealed. The Arabian Peninsula thus seems to stand as an area of greater cultural homogeneity than other areas of comparable size—India, for example.

This apparent cultural unity of the Peninsula is one chiefly of content, a unity of similar traits or complexes in the ethnographic sense,

*Some revision of this text, originally written in 1961, brings it up to date (1967). The bibliography has been revised, also. But in spite of some interesting political changes in the Arabian Peninsula, the ethnology of this area remains in a far more primitive state than the state of its inhabitants, and information that is stored in various archives remains inaccessible to scholars. The indebtedness of the conceptual framework used here to B. J. Meggers' "Environmental Limitation on the Evolution of Culture" (*American Anthropologist 56* [1954]: 801-24) is clear, and is hereby gratefully acknowledged.

which recur under similar conditions. Most of the traits or complexes that establish the over-all uniformity of this area are very ancient, and little is known of their history in the Arabian Peninsula. Examples are: cultivation of the date palm, of the various Old World grains (wheat, barley, sorghum), of a number of other fruits and vegetables, of tobacco, and of perhaps a few other industrial crops; husbanding of the Old World domesticated animals; employment of such intensive irrigation techniques as *qanats* (subterranean canals), terracing of slopes for cultivation; water storage and conservation techniques—and so on through a long list of the achievements of ancient civilizations. Of all of these, and of all the many more that might be listed, only a few may be claimed to originate in the Arabian Peninsula: Islam, the black tent of the pastoralists, the single humped camel (Mikesell 1955), and perhaps the multistoried architecture of Yemen and the Hadhramaut. For the present, at least, all other traits are regarded as having been introduced from external areas of origin. It is implicit in the scanty archeological work to date and in the conclusions drawn by investigations of physical anthropologists (Keith and Krogman 1932) that the Peninsula has been a passageway or in some locales a refuge area of societies and cultures, a location of secondary developments, but never a primary center of cultural inventions. Even the camel, possibly the only indigenous cultigen of the Peninsula, is thought to have been domesticated secondarily in application of the techniques of handling cattle (Coon 1943: 211). This statement concerning the secondary status of the Peninsular cultures may be questioned in its accuracy: archeological, ethnohistorical, and ethnographic work in Arabia have scarcely begun, and erroneous concepts will survive as long as the fund of knowledge to date is so small, unreliable, and inaccessible to anthropological study.

B. *Factors of Variability*

While from one point of view there is considerable cultural unity over the Arabian Peninsula, based upon the prevalence of a number of core culture traits, enough information exists to show that preindustrial sociocultural systems in the Peninsula show variability within several dimensions.

The total culture content pattern of Arabia may be represented for the moment by the major subsistence patterns dependent on local resources—camel, cattle, and sheep and goat pastoralisms, oasis cultivation, mountain cultivation, and fishing. Habitat or geographical factors clearly have much to do with the distribution of these patterns in Arabia and account, for example, for the greater variability of the southern rim as compared to Arabia north of the Rub' al Khali Desert. Such factors may also account for the persistence in the south of such localized patterns as the cattle pastoralism of Dhufar or of such widespread traits as the South Arab man's kilt, both of apparent great antiquity.

A second variability of culture in the Peninsula is in terms of proximity or contact with differing external areas. Thus in the southern rim of the Peninsula are found distinctive traits which ally it closely to India and Africa: millet cultivation, domed thatched houses on the Yemen Tihama, magical curing rituals. The west coast of the Persian Gulf reflects its proximity to Iran and India and its contacts with Africa, not to mention minor details derived from sixteenth-century Portuguese and later British-derived culture; Central and North Arabia reflect the closer contacts of these areas with the Levant and, perhaps, Egypt. As an aspect of diffusion, isolation or cessation from contact accounts for variation also. The Qarah people of Dhufar and the little-known Shihuh of the Ras Musandam Peninsula of Oman appear to have stabilized unique patterns through relative security from penetration.

In the Arabian Peninsula, more than in any other area of the world, perhaps, isolation is rather clearly a function of temporal changes in the routes, intensity, and technical level of contact and communication between the centers of complex civilizations lying outside the boundaries of Arabia but of necessity passing over it. Coupled with this factor have been the changes in demand for Arabian products in external markets—horses, desert economy products (clarified butter, hides, camels), dates, pearls, and aromatic tree resins. Little is known in detail of the function of horses and desert products as the economic bases of polities in Arabia, and little use has been made for ethnological purposes of the information on dates, pearls, and resins. The decline of pearling in the Persian Gulf and the loss of date markets in America in the nineteenth century by Muscat-Oman have been noted by various writers, but have not been exploited in cultural studies. Western changes in ship construction and naval armament have also deeply affected Arabian maritime patterns since the early nineteenth century.

A third factor in variability among Arabian systems is that of economic productivity and its consequence for population density, social complexity, and cohesion or unification. Thus, while Arabian habitats exploitable only by pastoral economies differ from those exploited by cultivation or fishing, the pastoral habitats vary among themselves in the abundance of water and pasturage, with consequences for the size, cultural elaboration, and power of pastoral social units. For example, the meagerness of pastoral development in the Wadi Hadhramaut, and its consequent subordinate and integrated status relative to the agriculturally-based villages and towns, stands in surprising contrast to the power of the camel tribes of the North Arabian steppes relative to the oasis and to the fringe settlement of the desert. Again, the agricultural productivity of the Yemen highlands and the consequent continuity of the Yemen's sociopolitical structure at the level of a theocratic kingdom over, probably, 3,000 years, contrasts with the tribal chiefdoms of pastoral tribes and with the possible band level of development among the Salubba hunters and guides of the northern steppes, who live in symbiotic relations with the camel pastoralists. This variability in social structural complexity in Arabia has been appreciated to some extent in the extensive historical and geographical literature on the region, a literature that extends into classical antiquity but has not yet been exploited by anthropology. Under the protective cover of Islam and the traditional subsistence trichotomy of pastoral tribesmen, cultivating peasants, and urban craftsmen, variety or diversity in structure has been obscured.

The factors of variability noted here have been only crudely sketched out. Their interplay in any particular locus of attention will be complex and determinable only by the precise studies for which scientists have called for many decades now (Coon 1943, Patai 1947-48, Schorger 1958). While a substantial, if unintegrated, amount of information in terms of culture traits is available in the vast literature on the Arabian Peninsula, little of this has been mapped, even in the superficial approach of distribution (Patai 1952). And rarest of all, still, are structural studies of institutions, communities, tribes, or states. Only recently have a few emerged. The impression given by reading travelers' or historians' accounts is, to submit one example, that the structures of Arab commercial enterprises are well known; but this is perhaps because commerce is familiar—the details of organization and operation are more frequently assumed than described. Villiers' accounts of maritime trade and voyages are the most detailed available (Villiers 1940, 1948).

C. Geographical and Ecological Features

Of the three factors of variability discussed above, adaptation to habitat is both fundamental to survival and productive of uniqueness of pattern. The following discussion of Arabian cultures will revolve chiefly around this variable; it is relatively well known and documented for the whole Peninsula. After an initial attempt at an over-all classification of habitats and their cultural adaptations, five subareas will be summarized briefly.

The size of the Arabian Peninsula is comparable to India, but geographically and culturally it is far more uniform, and the size of its population is relatively minute—at most 10 millions as compared to the 400 millions of India (Bullard 1958: 73). Included within the concept of the

Peninsular culture sphere are the Red Sea islands of Farasan, Kamaran, and others; the Arabian Ocean islands of Socotra, Kuria Muria, and Masira; and the Persian Gulf islands of Bahrain and other smaller islets. On the western, southern, and on half of the eastern sides of the Peninsula lie seas or gulfs: the Red Sea, the Arabian Ocean, and the Persian and Arabian gulfs. The northern and northeastern boundaries are landbound and less determinable. Politically they are now established by the boundaries of Iraq and Jordan, but by more general cultural criteria they extend well across these boundaries to the limits of desert pastoralism and the beginning of Levant or Mesopotamian cultivation economies. Recognition may be also given to the fact that at one time Zanzibar and portions of East Africa were politically within the control of Muscat-Oman, as well as portions of the Persian side of the Gulf (e.g. Gwadur and Lingah). In fact, as far inland as Shiraz in Iran, one encounters traces, such as the costumes of "tribal" women, which predominate in the Arab settlements of the Gulf. Neither geographical nor current political boundaries are satisfactory or wholly accurate. Moreover, the economic dependence of societies within the Peninsula, such as those of the Wadi Hadhramaut, upon such distant places as commercial towns and networks in Southeast Asia, is one of the facts that make a description of traditional Arabian cultures in terms of Peninsular features alone a distortion. As a system, the network of Arab trade reaches far beyond Arabia, as do the major institutions of Islam and the Meccan pilgrimage. The three bodies of water surrounding Arabia have, as Coon has noted, served as highways of communication rather than as barriers, together with desert pastoralism and oasis cultivation. The roles of Arab commerce and marine economy and technology are fundamental aspects of the Peninsular cultures; and duality of such apparently mutually exclusive occupations within one social unit or one man's experience is not unusual.

Within the Peninsula a number of geographical features are outstanding in their relationship to culture. These are generally well known, and fair descriptions are widely available for much of Arabia (Fisher 1958, Twitchell 1958). The whole Peninsula lies within subtropical and tropical climate zones. Extensive aridity characterizes nearly the whole, with an annual rainfall of under ten inches everywhere except for a few locations such as Yemen, the Hadhramaut, Dhufar, and perhaps the highlands of Muscat-Oman. The types of water supply and their location and distribution are the primary factors that determine subsistence pattern distributions. There is only one perennial river: the Wadi Hajir in the East Aden Protectorate, but there are a number of seasonal streams flowing for a few weeks or months out of their highland sources of supply in the southwest (Yemen, Aden Protectorate). There are also many spate streams, producing storm torrents and floods, which are more widely distributed. Springs and artesian aquifers occur in the mountains of the southwest and southeast and in the eastern lowlands—Al Hasa, Bahrain, and the Trucial states. In a few places such as the island of Kharj and the East Aden Protectorate water pits of the cenote type occur. Finally, the great wadi systems of Arabia, the dry beds of extinct rivers, cover relatively shallow water tables, which man has tapped with a variety of wells. By and large, the chains of oases follow the great wadis of Sirhan, Dawasir, and others.

Cycles of drought over the years characterize the Peninsula, but the length of these is not known. It would seem to be an important habitat feature to investigate as a factor to which the ancient technological and economic patterns may well be specifically adapted. There is some suggestion for a ten-year cycle from the Kuwait area, and of a 20- to 30-year cycle in Muscat-Oman (Harrison 1940: 215-28). Philby sets down the recollection of periodic droughts at wide intervals for the Khurma area, east of Mecca at the head of Wadi Ranya (Philby 1952: 89). The ruins or the known histories of abandoned or reduced oasis communities seem clearly related to these cycles.

Variation in the geographical distribution of rainfall within any one year is also significant, apparently recognized as influential in pastoral economy, but it has not been systematically investigated in its relation to inherent cultural adaptations (but see Sweet 1965a, 1965b).

These very briefly noted features of water supply in Arabia may convey some notion of the apparent uniqueness of the Peninsula in this respect. Whether the elaborate and diverse means found in Arabia of securing, trapping, and conserving water originated there or were "diffused" successfully from ecologically similar neighboring areas, the water control technology of the Peninsula is one of its striking cultural features. *Qanats*, dams, reservoirs, deep and shallow wells, aqueducts, and run-off traps are merely some of the devices employed. The scale of these is little known, as are the systems of management. It can be observed, however, that no water-control bureaucracy is as yet apparent, even for the Yemen.

Together with the peculiarities of its water supply, Arabia's topographical features are distinctive and important. In brief, there is a basic contrast between flat or relatively flat terrains and dissected and rugged highland areas. Along the western coast, on the Red Sea, and from north to south rise the series of ranges that culminate, in the south in the Asir and Yemen highlands. Here peaks reach 14,000 feet, and the plateau lies at 8,000 to 9,000 feet. This knotted-mountainous area is marked by high long scarps, usually facing the seacoast, and by innumerable gorges and valleys cutting them and draining to the west or south or, more gently, eastward. Highlands continue, diminishing, along the southern coast of Arabia to the east, and are of a different formation in the Hadhramaut—flat-topped, limestone tablelands; these level off eastward beyond the Dhufar area. The Muscat-Oman Peninsula is again a rugged highland area centrally, with gorges and valleys draining either to the seaward or the interior. This highland rim of the Arabian Peninsula, dominating the west and south and southeast, is contrasted with the interior, where the terrain, whether desert or steppe, is far less rugged and ultimately flattens out onto the low salt mud flats along the Persian Gulf.

The western and southern ranges trap the monsoon rains and are at once the most densely populated and most economically productive areas of Arabia. The interior of Arabia is at once more sparsely and intermittently occupied by man, and settlement is permanent only along the oasis chains, which follow the wadi systems. Areas of volcanic debris, salt swamp, and waterless desert or rocky ridges are extensive and widely distributed.

Little information is available on the soils of Arabia; they are lacking in organic components but are very fertile wherever maintenance techniques are applied. Besides well-developed irrigation technology, rotation and fertilizing are practiced. The destructive factor of salination is recognized in some quarters, but perhaps not by the indigenous culture explicitly.

Vegetation or fauna below 5,000 feet of elevation is small, sparse, and xerophytic, except in the Yemen and in oases. Scott (1942) has noted the similarities in these respects of the southwestern corner of Arabia to the neighboring African lands. Wolves, gazelle, ostrich, oryx are among the more famous wild animals, but they are rapidly becoming almost, if not entirely, extinct. The *dom* palm in the southwest, the ubiquitous *sidr* tree with its edible berry, and the frankincense tree of Dhufar are among the culturally important wild plants. Insects such as malaria-bearing mosquitoes, locusts, and bees have special cultural or demographic significance, as do snakes and lizards.

While the mountains and the deserts and steppes of North Arabia have attracted considerable attention, exploration, and description, the marine coasts and their resources have been somewhat less noticed and integrated into the cultural concept of the Arabian Peninsula. And yet it is possibly this aspect of Arabia that has been more important than the others. The coastline is extended, but topographical features associated with it have limited its exploitation or, more significantly, its approach by deep-draft vessels. The frequent absence of fresh water near the coast, the presence of reefs and shallows, the few sheltered harbors, and the frequency of precipitous sea cliffs or salt swamp have provided some barriers to indigenous use, but have been more frequently barriers to external approach by foreign systems. Nevertheless, the coasts of Arabia are abundant in marine resources—fish for food or animal fodder; turtle oil and shell; coral, pearls, shells, and fish oil, and other specialities like sharks' fins. These suggest, as does the frankincense tree and the Arabian horse, that secondary products rather than subsistence staples have characterized the economic usefulness of Arabia for other economies of the preindustrial past.

Besides those mentioned, the range of natural resources of the Peninsula is either little known or meager in kind and in quantity. Salt and limestone (as stone or as lime) are internally and widely distributed; valuable ores are not known much beyond the legendary stage of report, with the exception of gold in the Hejaz area. The most important recent discovery has been that of petroleum, a fuel significant only to the external industrial societies which, at present, are still essentially in control of its technology and economics of exploitation, distribution, and use. As yet it has not, apparently, fundamentally altered the cultural systems of the Peninsula. The primary reason for this may well be that the subsidies and compensation paid in money to ruling elites is a very sophisticated barrier to any radical proliferation of industrial skills and organization into the indigenous societies.

II. *Four Cultural-Ecological Habitats*

The sharply marked geographic features of the Arabian Peninsula, the contrasts between desolate and sterile tracts—areas with thinly distributed water and soil resources necessary to produce food or with low potential to do so—and areas with greater potential make it possible to set out four categories of habitat in the Peninsula. They are distinctive in the kind of cultural adaptations made to them or are important to those adaptations. They emphasize the very strong patterning of cultural systems in Arabia in terms of specialized subsistence and exporting economic activities. These diverse activities may be closely associated with each other geographically, but they are not always united in single diversified but politically unified economic systems. In some areas, they clearly compete for dominance (Sweet 1965b). Why this is so remains a basic problem in Arabian ethnology.

The following delineation of four "habitats" attends primarily to exploitative use of the earth's resources, but it is not possible to adhere rigidly to this criterion. The sociocultural importance of uninhabitable lands and the extensive development of trade and communication systems make a taxonomy of habitats based on subsistence ecology alone inadequate for handling the Arabian Peninsula data. Discussion of the level of development of cultural systems in the Peninsula, or a typology of such systems, has gone so little beyond the old tribal pastoral vis-à-vis state agricultural societies that, in fact, this present attempt is in the nature of an experimental synthesis of the available data.

Habitat Type I: The uninhabitable areas. These areas are not inhabited by any groups nor exploited through any subsistence pattern at any time or for any part of the year (or only at rare intervals under unusual conditions of receiving some rainfall). They may be crossed or skirted by occasional travelers and caravans. Lack of water, totally barren rock surface or precipitousness, sterile saline soils, or quicksand swamp characterize such desolate localities. The Rub' al Khali Desert of the south, parts of the Madian coast and uplands of the northern Hejaz, the sporadically distributed lava fields from north to south on the western side of the Peninsula, and the salt and mud flats and waterless coasts on the east and southeast are conspicuous examples. Much of the Peninsula may thus be "useless," and smaller, similar areas are probably to be found in virtually every locality. They set effective barriers to integration of habitable areas at scales that range from regional to very local. There may, however, be some cultural adaptations or exploitations which are not insignificant. Some barren rock surfaces are found in areas of rainfall—in the Yemen and the East Aden highlands and on the flat limestone surfaces of the southern Hadhramaut; here the rainfall that falls on these surfaces is trapped and either stored in cisterns or led to field terraces. In the East Aden highlands, an estimate has been made of the amount of bare rock that is required to provide adequate run-off for cultivation (B. J. Hartley 1944). Folklore and legends surround some areas, such as the Rub' al Khali Desert, but they have not been seriously collected.

The most conspicuous adaptation, however, is the long-distance overland camel caravan, which can skirt or cross these areas, as well as less desolate ones, on the basis of the capacities of the camel to tolerate heat and lack of water or moist forage and to bear loads of up to 400 pounds. Caravan organization itself varies, and a synthesis of the data would be useful. In North Arabia, for example, commercial caravans have their organization initiated among city merchants, and the transport animals are provided at urban termini; they cross territories of dominant camel pastoral tribes, and the crossing is secured by various modes of escort and payment. In the south, below the southern desert,

and in the regions once actively engaged in ancient transfreighting of incense and other goods brought from India, caravan transport is more
variable in organization. The tribal camel breeders themselves, in contrast to those of North Arabia, also control the caravan organization and
provide transport across their own territories; animals must be changed
at each tribal boundary, and customs and other duties must be paid.
Such polities may not, in fact, be accurately designated as tribal, for the
caravaneers are frequently subordinate to politically elite families situated in the towns which command each such territory, variously designated sultanate or emirate in South Arabia during the period of British
control. There is no question, however, that the roles of the commercial
or pilgrimage caravans are major features of the nature of political and
economic organization of Arabian societies, but this has not been fully
described or analyzed for recent times in Arabia.

   Habitat Type II: Areas exploited by pastoral and hunting economies.
These areas are probably more extensive than any other habitable area
in the Arabian Peninsula, and it seems evident that a considerable variety of socioeconomic organizations is to be found in this category, in
correlation with the variety of habitats and types of animals herded, and
in consequence of varying relations with neighboring or encapsulated
agricultural societies.

   This category of habitat is characterized by the possession of the req-
uisites in water and plant food to support the forms of animal life that
support man. Such areas vary in quality and quantity, as the works of
such travelers and geographers as Musil, Philby, Thomas, and others at-
test. Only one source, however, provides a vegetation map sketch suggesting the distribution of plants favored for pasturage of different
animals in the Kuwait area (V. Dickson 1955: map 4).

   The kinds of environments which pastoralists occupy include steppe
and desert of the interior, from the Syrian Desert to the northern edge
of the Rub' al Khali Desert, as well as around the edges of this southern
desert. Such coastal deserts as the Asir and the Yemen Tihama are also
pastoral habitats. In these environments, pastoralism exploits arid regions
by providing seasonal pasturages and permanent watering points in the
dry season to which the herds and people must retire during the dry
summers. In the highland and rugged regions of the Oman and the west
there appear to be localities where topography and lack of suitable soil
make cultivation impossible, but which can be exploited by sheep and
goat raisers. So little is known of the central portion of the southern
rim of Arabia that the patterns are not clear. The cattle pastoralists of
the Jabal Qarah, back of Dhufar, are a unique group here, and the economic status of the Mahra peoples neighboring them is even less known.

The animals upon which pastoral economies depend in Arabia are sheep, goats, camels, and cattle. Each species has different requirements, adaptations, and capacities. Horsebreeding exists as an adjunct of pastoralism in northeastern Arabia and perhaps also among the 'Ujman of the east-central portion. While the lore of the Arabian horse and its military and sociological significance in Arabian Bedouin society has been the focus of many studies, its economic significance has received less treatment. It appears to have been an important export item from the Persian Gulf ports to India, perhaps from antiquity; breeding has been practiced also in the Yemen and Muscat-Oman, as well as among northern pastoralists.

Husbandry of all these animals is mixed with agriculture in many areas, but should be distinguished in these cases from purely pastoral economies. A precise catalogue of distinctions has not been made for the whole Peninsula and is relatively well known only for the North Arabian steppe and desert and the Kuwait area (Bacon 1954; Boucheman 1934a, 1934b: 19; H. R. P. Dickson 1949; Montagne 1932, 1947; Musil 1926, 1927a, 1927b, 1928a, 1928b, 1928c; Patai 1951; Sweet 1965a, 1965b).

Hunting and gathering activities comprise an aspect of many otherwise pastoral economies, one which has not been emphasized, however. Yet it is clear from Musil's accounts that both constitute an important part of subsistence for many pastoralists; the lizard, gazelle, rabbit, and locust, the *semḥ* seed, and various fungi are well-known resources, but require further study. Hunters per se exist in only one named group, the Salubba peoples of North Arabia, who live among the pastoralists. Hunters are mentioned as such, but not named nor further described, and are located on the northern edge of the Rub' al Khali (Fisher 1958: 446).

Habitat Type III: Areas where fishing is the basic or predominant subsistence pattern. The coasts of the Red Sea, the Arabian Sea, and the Oman and Persian gulfs are all abundant in marine life and support fishing economies. The nature of these coasts and the lack of large timber has limited accessibility and development in certain directions. Because of reefs, waterless stretches of littoral in the Red Sea and elsewhere, the scarcity of sheltered harbors on the Arabian Sea coast and the monsoon wind system prevailing there, and the shallow coasts and mud flats on the Persian Gulf coast, local marine technology in all its local exploitative activities depends upon small, shallow draft craft and handmade and operated equipment.

The extent to which fishing is a year-round activity is not clear, and probably varies subregionally. In the Muscat area it is reported (Harrison

1940) that winter is the fishing season and that summer is spent in date harvesting. In the Persian Gulf area, seasonal variation follows the appearance of various species pursued. "Nomadisln" of fishing peoples has also been noted from Muscat to the Red Sea. Further consideration of possible dual subsistence and economic patterns may be given in the subregional descriptions. The varieties of marine life taken are numerous: for the Persian Gulf area well over 300 species have been listed. Special patterns of usage, with development of interior and external export systems, are found, such as the use of sardines as fodder, taking of sharks for export to China, and drying of fish for various foreign markets, either as food or fertilizer.

Two patterns of fishing technology seem clear. One, employing tidal traps and weirs, hand nets, inflated skin floats or palm frond craft, suggests adaptation to fishing without the use of plank boats or dugouts in the shallow coastal areas. Since apart from palm there is little or no timber in Arabia suitable for constructing planked craft, these techniques seem to imply the more ancient pattern, and it has been noted that at least one sector of the South Arabian coast is occupied by fishing peoples who have no craft other than inflated skins or palmfrond floats and whose subsistence includes goatherding. The second pattern uses small wooden craft, sailed or propelled by oars or paddles, and probably is a later development, accompanying the indigenous development of marine technology for coasting and long distance trading voyages. Timber for such craft was then brought from India and East Africa. Deep water drag nets and clusters of sunken traps may be associated with this or adapted to it from the older pattern.

Brief allusion may be made here to two questions of origin: shipbuilding and pearling. The background role of ancient influence and diffusion from India and Ceylon should not be overlooked in both respects. These will be treated in the subregional discussion of the Persian Gulf.

Habitat IV: Areas where cultivation is practiced. With the possible exception of the Yemen plateau in the southwestern corner of the Peninsula, a striking attribute of Arabia is the lack of extensive zones where favorable conditions for cultivation are present. The over-all pattern is one of restricted localities closely related to localized water supply and often widely separated from each other by the much more extensive pastoral or uninhabitable zones.

Two subcategories of habitats suitable for cultivation are suggested by the kinds of water supply, coupled with soil and topographical features. There are first the areas in mountain zones which receive adequate or nearly adequate rainfall; here direct fall of rain on the fields may also be supplemented by techniques of trapping run-off and by irrigation from springs or wells. Altitude, such as that of the Yemen plateau at 7,000 to 9,000 feet, has its effect on the kinds of crops distinguishing the area. In such areas (Asir, Yemen, Hadhramaut and West Aden, and the Oman) the topographical dissection also presents greater local diversity and the character of varying microhabitats in contrast to the relatively homogeneous oasis locales. In this first cultivation habitat subtype, three such further divisions are associated with the mountainous scene: the high plateau, valley slopes, and valley floors. All are exploited by intensive techniques.

The second cultivation habitat subtype comprises localities dependent primarily upon raising subsurface water supplies and are characteristically the oases of the great wadi systems of Central and North Arabia.

There is widespread evidence in ruins of irrigation systems and city or ceremonial centers, and in historical accounts, of the decline of the extent of cultivation in Arabia, particularly along the western mountain chains and the steppes adjacent to them. The extent to which present sociocultural systems may be deculturated remnants could be further explored. Cultural decline may, however, be relatively recent and associated with the expansion of European mercantilism and colonialism and the decline of the Ottoman Empire, rather than with the ancient decline of frankincense trade routes across South Arabia or the increasing climate desiccation (Bowen 1958, Caton-Thompson and Gardiner 1939).

Crops vary to a considerable extent with the two major habitat subtypes. Subsistence crops include dates, grains, fruits and vegetables in wide variety. Industrial or cash crops, such as coffee, *qat*, indigo, and cotton, are rare and are found solely in the southwest. The range and scale of productivity is not fully known. Subsistence production, without surplus, and at the undifferentiated level of simple tribal gardening economies does not seem to be known, although very low productivity is claimed for many areas. It may be that the Shihuh peoples of the Ras Musandam Peninsula, Oman, the interior Mahra, and a few marginal oasis folk may subsist at this level or near it. By and large, in oasis or highland habitat, subsistence plus surplus farming for tribute, tax, or cash seems general; cash cropping is or has been a feature of the Yemen and the large oases in eastern Arabia for many centuries. Land tenure and systems usage have not been extensively examined, but tribal control and familial or individual ownership, with tenantry, appear to be the two main systems. Aside from Vidal's study of Al Hasa (Vidal 1955), probably the only precise data remain in unpublished British Colonial Office papers for territories under British protection or administration (cf. D. Ingrams 1949: 111). It seems generally assumed that tenure and usage everywhere are continuous with the past as represented in classical Muslim categories of private (*mulk*), state (*miri*), religious endowment (*waqf*), and collective (*musha'*), or tribal.

III. *Regional Discussions*

It will be convenient, if arbitrary, to summarize the ethnographic data on the subregions of the Peninsula partly in terms of the recent political entities or, where possible, as in the case of the Persian Gulf, in terms of relatively homogeneous areas. These are: (1) Yemen (2) South Aden (3) Muscat-Oman (4) Persian Gulf (5) Central and North Arabia (Saudi Arabia).

A. *Yemen*

The former theocratic state and present republic of the Yemen occupies the highest sector of the southwestern Arabian highlands and a strip of coastal plain between latitudes 18° to 12° N., and comprises a territory about 300 miles long and 200 broad. Its population is estimated at about four and a half million, most of whom occupy the highlands as "tribal" enclaves of mountain farmers (Bullard 1958: 74). The narrow, arid coastal plain is backed by a range of foothills and a sharply rising, jagged escarpment cut by a few seasonal streams into deep valleys and gorges. The interior consists of a high plateau, 7,000-9,000 feet in altitude, surrounded by rugged mountains reaching to 14,000 feet. While the west and south are rugged and abrupt, the decline of land eastward toward the interior desert is more gradual. The southern heights of the Yemen receive more rainfall than other parts of Arabia, probably 20 inches. The major part of the Yemen occupies a habitat of Type IV (supporting cultivation); while the coastal strip, exploited by pastoralists and fishing and port town activities, may be classed as Types II and III. The pastoral and fishing economies here seem to have little significance for the highlands. Apart from the subsistence economies, nothing is known of other resources exploited in the Yemen except the use of earth and stone for pottery and construction.

Intensive terraced mountain slope and irrigated plateau agriculture of considerable diversity and productivity supports the Yemen; descriptions of the water and soil conservation technology are found in most accounts, but little is known of cultivation techniques in detail. The crop list is the most varied in Arabia and reflects the differences in altitude of cultivated areas. There seems to be some regional specialization, in consequence, but the system and range of distribution and export is unknown except for the export of coffee and *qat* leaves, concentrated in the south. The Yemen is reputed to be one of the centers of horse breeding in Arabia; mules, donkeys, and camels and cattle are also present, but nothing is known of their husbandry.

Most of the coastal Tihama of Yemen is a desert. Where the wadi outlets from the highlands run in spate flows with the seasonal rains, oasis cultivation and irrigated gardens are found. Well inland in the foothills are arable rainfed tracts. In the cultivated areas here red and white millet and sesame seed (a source of cooking oil) are the chief food crops; indigo and cotton are or were Tihama cash industrial crops. Sometimes three crops a year are possible; the first is sown after the spates of the first spring rains.

Transitional to the highlands are the maritime hills, where little cultivation is possible except in the larger valleys. There is little suitable soil. Cultivation of millet, sesame, and maize follows the valleys and is irrigated by trapping the flood waters, which arrive after the thunderstorms from April to early summer.

The Zaraniq tribe has been noted briefly in this area (Bury 1915: 29), occupying the coastal plain as cultivators and the maritime hills with flocks. Bury distinguished the Zaraniq men from highland tribesmen by their short beards and use of turban headdresses. They wear the usual South Arabian kilt. They impressed Bury as being smaller in stature than the highland tribesmen. Living also in the Tihama are peoples of marked African appearance; Bury classifies some as being of slave status (Bury 1915: 29); while others are of the *khadam* or *hojeri* caste of menials. Conical thatched houses, their furnishings and their surrounding compounds, and items of dress such as straw hats have struck several observers as closely allied to African cultures.

The chief towns of the Tihama are Zabid (inland), and Hodeida and Mocha, both ports. At Zabid and Hodeidah, indigo dyeing was once a prominent local industry. Weaving is found at Hodeidah, Bait al Fakih, and Zabid; a little 'boatbuilding at Hodeidah; leather work and sandal making are also among the crafts of the Tihama towns mentioned by Bury (1915: 123-24). Until the rise of Aden as a free port, Mocha and later Hodeidah were the chief coastal towns of Yemen, out of which went the major exports—coffee and hides, pre-eminently. When Bury passed through Hodeidah in 1915 or shortly before, a little coffee was still exported, but the chief commerce lay in sheep and goat skins and bullock hides. His description of the trading process contributes to the material available on Arab commercial operations: the role of the broker who arranges the exchange between the buyer and seller; the mode of concealing price bargaining by employing a code of signaling with the fingers under cover of a cloth. Mention of this procedure is found for the Hadhramaut and in Gulf pearl dealing and is evidently a trait closely associated with commercial activities in the open market throughout the peripheral areas of Arabia, at least.

The Yemen highlands behind the Tihama area are approached by routes which of necessity wind up one or the other of the few great valleys draining out from the plateau and peaks surmounting it. Two major wadis, the Tiban and the Bana, drain into the Aden Protectorate; others cut through the precipitous escarpment to the Red Sea—the Arish, Mawr, and others. The Kharifi valley is described by Bury as an example of Yemeni mountain terracing; about five miles across, it is terraced for crops and dotted with stone towers and villages from the 3,000 foot crests to the bed of the valley (Bury 1915: 65). Mountain cultivation employs hand tools and utensils; width of terrace and accessibility probably limit the use of the plow; the terraces are stone-faced and follow the hill contours; soil is renewed by bringing it afresh and is fertilized from stores of animal manure. Water is stored in masonry cisterns, cement plastered, which are built along ravines to collect surface drainage. A star calendar guides the agricultural year. Rain ceremonies in time of drought are mentioned by Bury, one including sacrifice of an animal (Bury 1915: 105-06). Crops of the cooler highlands include coffee and *qat* (in restricted districts most suitable to their growth—i.e. the moister western slopes), white millet, barley, wheat, lucerne, chickpeas, grapes, peaches, and other fruits and garden produce. Crops of the lower hill regions, such as at Ta'izz, include the millets, maize, wheat, dates, and other fruits (mango, banana, tamarind, citrus) of subtropical categories.

The tribes of the highlands and plateau number some 25 or more named groups. A few of these are further grouped under names that suggest alliances or confederations or cultural distinctiveness of some sort: Ahl-al-Mashrik (People of the East) includes the tribesmen of Najran (now in Saudi Arabia), Jauf, and vicinity who are Sunni Muslims (Bury 1915: 32) and who may now be included within Saudi Arabian hegemony.

The peoples of the highlands appear to be taller than those of the lowlands or of districts of South Arabia east of the Hadhramaut, who, particularly the Mahra, Qarah, and related groups, are all reported as being "diminutive." Urban dwellers and village tribesmen are distinctive in dress, and urban classes are further so differentiated by class or caste.

Coon's (1943) summary and the accounts of travelers in the Yemen indicate that the economy of the country is organized within tribal districts over which is imposed the structure of the state's tax collecting, judicial, and garrisoning apparatus. Most of the population thus live in villages near their arable lands; towns and small cities, clearly more heterogeneous in structure, are the loci of state officials, trade route stops with caravanserai accommodations, and permanent bazaars, with their traditional crafts and specialists, mosques, and schools. Periodic open market sites are also indicated in some accounts, but little is known of the system. Names of large villages or such sites indicate cycling weekly markets.

The social composition and structure of the whole of the Yemen are not easy to summarize. Since major elements recur, however, in the other Arabian systems, and since the Yemen kingdom seems to have preserved until recently the longest history of integration of any state in the Peninsula, it may be taken hypothetically as the most complex pattern that can persist in Arabia (given the habitat conditions and preindustrial technology locally employed, as well as the fluctuations of external market and resource conditions which may affect the Peninsular states or other societies).

The most fundamental division of the society appears to be that between tribesmen and the ruling dynasty and its state apparatus. This seems to correspond rather closely to the diversity of settlement, as between town and village, urban and rural populations. The state structure is dominated by the office of the imam, whose control is said to be personal and autocratic. The present family dynasty, Ar Rassi, has held the office since about 1170 (Scott 1942: 224-25). The role of the imam is equated by Coon (1943) to that of the "priestly kings" of the ancient South Arabian kingdoms; the imam is at once the civil and religious leader of the society. Since virtually all contacts made by Westerners with the Yemen have been negotiated through the state, this outward aspect of the Yemen kingdom is perhaps the best known. The administration includes the small dual ministerial apparatus; each minister has a council of "notables" as advisors; provincial governors, judges, tax collectors, and the standing army which garrisons and polices the country complete the outline. The economic basis of power of the state is not clear; it appears to lie in taxes upon the agricultural and husbandry production, upon customs and markets, and upon the nontribal subjects of the Imam—the merchants, shopkeepers, artisans, and such ethnic groups as the former sizable enclave of Jews. A number of towns in the Yemen retain from medieval times a reputation as centers of learning and of Muslim schools, but aside from the ritual leadership of the Imam, little is known of the present status of Zaidi Muslim educational institutions.

Class divisions and ethnic segments of Yemen society are again best considered separately in urban and rural contexts, although this may well be an unwarranted division. Only the general outlines are known.

One class, that of the *sayyids*, does appear to be widely distributed throughout the Yemen. As elsewhere in South Arabia, they constitute a sacrosanct class or "ecclesiastical" aristocracy. In the Yemen, their economic role is not clear. Outside of the capital, San'a, they appear to fill the roles of provincial and tribal district *qadhis*, or judges. They are socially united as a class by the ideology of a shared genealogy, which distinguishes all members as descendants of the Prophet through Hasan (Coon 1943: 197). In the towns, the merchant class and the artisans and other laborers are little known in terms of occupational or entrepreneurial organization, hierarchical distinctions, insignia, etc., with the exception of the Jews, who by 1947 had almost all emigrated to Israel. The quarters, houses, dress, crafts, and functions in the Yemen economy of the Jews are fairly well delineated in the various travelers' accounts and in studies made since their arrival in Israel. In the Yemen, they seem to have functioned chiefly as town craftsmen, particularly in metals, and in winemaking, and to have been prohibited from owning arable land as customary to the structure of traditional Islamic society. They were not, on the other hand, conscripted into military service or persecuted.

Whether or not there was or is a slave *class* in the urban Yemen is not clear; in any event it is insignificant and domestic if it exists, in contrast to the role of slaves in such other parts of the Peninsula as Muscat-Oman, and is said to be contrary to the tenets of Zaidi Islam.

The bulk of the population of the Yemen, like that of the Aden Protectorate and probably the rest of Arabia, are the people of the cultivating tribes, of the highlands, terraced valleys, and plateaus. The tribes are localized, controlling the territories of their districts which constitute the provinces of the state, and segments of the tribes are further localized in lineage villages attached to their lands. If Coon's brief sketch is accurate (Coon 1943: 197-98), the structure of the Yemeni tribe is probably one of ranked patrilineal segments and lineages; the offices of paramount chief and lesser segment (or clan) chiefs are held by chiefly families, and the successor to a deceased chief is elected from that family by the "notables" of the tribe. Confirmation by the Imam of the paramount chief of a tribe is required, and this man is the representative and tax collector of the provincial governor, an appointee of the Imam. In view of the more detailed information on Aden tribes, much more could be known of Yemen highland tribal structure and organization.

In the southern Yemen and the Tihama coastal strip are found a class of landless laborers whose status is the lowest in the Yemen. Called the *khadam* or *hojeri* (*hujara* or *hujri*, elsewhere), their function is to perform menial labor and army service. Little is known of them in the

Yemen; but they may be the northern margin of wandering groups of similar type found in the Aden Protectorate; and, in fact, they may be comparable to similar servile castes elsewhere in oasis or urban settlements, where the division of labor is fairly complex. A number of speculations and legends surround the question of their origin and descent: an aboriginal ethnic strain, Abyssinian descendants, migrants from Africa (cf. Coon 1943: 199).

Travelers have recorded in some detail traits of dress, jewelry, weapons, architecture, city plans, the appearance of the bazaars of the towns, cultivation, and the roads of the Yemen—such traits as can be set down from passing observation. A few observations on domestic scenes and life, equally superficial, are also available (e.g. Fayein 1957, Harris 1895). All of these could be deepened, but the chief gaps seem to lie in details of structural operation, whether of tribe, community type, or state, and in the explanation of the economy as an important factor in the self-sufficiency of the Yemen, although its ancient and medieval export and transit business seem almost to have disappeared.

Since the early 1960s, the Yemen has undergone a partially successful political revolution. The old Ar Rassi dynasty has been deposed, and a military "republican" government has succeeded in holding control of the capital, the routes to the sea, and the southern part of the country, with extensive Egyptian aid for a number of years. The northern and highland tribes still support the Ar Rassi dynasty and the son of the former imam, with aid from Saudi Arabia. While various foreign aid projects have constructed important highways from the coast to inland cities, and other installations, the extent and depth of change is unknown. No modern anthropological studies of the Yemen are known.

B. *South Arabia*

From the point of view of indigenous sociocultural systems occupying distinctive habitats, the unit discussed here is an arbitrary sector of the southern rim of Arabia, until recently more or less under the control of the Colonial Office of Great Britain and defined by its colonial administration. This control had been extending and deepening since marginal incursions were begun in 1839, with the British conquest of Aden. It seems clear that structural features of the several types of polities within the Protectorate are at once an intensification of features present before the British assumed control, and a response to that control and subsidization of selected local powers, such as the sultanate of Lahej and the Qu'aiti state. The Aden Protectorate, as this area has been called, is far better known ethnographically than other parts of the Peninsula, and at least one relatively complete if confusing summary of many aspects is available in D. Ingrams (1949).

Geographically, the old Protectorate area is diverse. It extends from the point opposite Perim Island in the west eastward along the coast to Ras Dharbat Ali Point, a distance of some 700 miles. Its depth into the interior varies from the southern boundary of the Yemen, 30-120 miles deep, to the borders of the Rub' al Khali Desert, which begins to form an effective barrier 150 or more miles inland. This interior border is by no means clear politically, and the desert is perhaps the most significant one for the present purposes. The most eastern end of the Protectorate, from the Wadi Maseila to Ras Dharbat Ali is the territory of the Mahri peoples. Linguistically and historically, they are more closely allied to the peoples to the east, such as the Qarah, and will be considered with them.

Within this area, topography, drainage, and the Indian Ocean monsoon regime combine to produce a heterogeneous distribution of the four categories of habitat. From east to west, the coast is composed of arid plains broken by extensions of the central highland areas to the sea in precipitous cliffs. Aden and Mukalla are the most important harbors, and very few others are to be found, although fishing villages are numerous. The drainage of the wadi systems provides a number of oases on this coastal plain and in the Wadi Hajir, the only perennial river in Arabia. Two highland systems mark the interior. One in the west is the continuation and southern watershed of the Yemeni ranges. These ranges break down into dissected and rugged country that is little known between the Aulaqi territories and the Hadhramaut. The northern and interior part of this central area is a sand and gravel desert, marked by pastoral occupation, which extends north of the eastern highland of the Protectorate along the border of the Rub' al Khali. The eastern portion of the Protectorate is marked by the Wadi Hadhramaut, a broad valley rising in the central desert region (Ramlat Sabatain) near Yemen and cutting eastward through an elevated limestone tableland, or *jol*, for 130 miles to the point where it veers southward toward the sea and is here called the Wadi Maseila. The Hadhramaut *jol* rises some 6,000 feet on the south side of the Wadi Hadhramaut. A series of deep wadis drain into the Hadhramaut valley, especially 'Amd, Du'an, and Leisar. Others, especially the Wadi Hajir, drain southward toward the coastal plain. The *jol* north of the Wadi Hadhramaut has a similar watershed; it is only 3,500 feet high, however, and descends gradually to the desert plains bordering the Rub' al Khali. The island of Socotra is included within the Protectorate regime, and is attached to the Mahri Sultanate.

Rainfall is meager on this coast, averaging two inches annually, but in the highlands, especially in the west, it may reach 25 inches, most of it falling in storms between April and October. Water supply for wadi and coastal oasis cultivation comes, typically, in spates from the highlands, or from well sources; in the highlands, rain falls directly on the fields, but it is also trapped by run-off barriers aligned on barren rock areas. Deflector dams, channels, and reservoirs of various types are extensively developed to secure water for cultivation. One report of an intensive study of agricultural technology in the Western Protectorate highlands is available and refers primarily to the Audhali highland (B. J. Hartley 1944). D. Ingrams (1949) provides summaries of similar studies of fishing economy and cultivation in the Eastern Protectorate, or Hadhramaut area. There are no studies of pastoralist practices.

The pre-Republic indigenous social entities of the recent Aden Protectorate were numerous and variable in structure. The old administrative division between the Western and Eastern Protectorates aids in discussing them. Some of those of the western sector were at one time under more or less control from the Yemen as provinces with appointed governors, but, as in the case of the Lahej sultanate, gained independence in the mid-eighteenth century. Hamilton (1942, 1949) has distinguished two types, although these are not clearly delineated and do not account for all the units. "Tribal" organization, apparently similar to that of the Yemen tribes, forms the major structural system of each. The first may be called the remnant state and retains the stratified composition of a Yemini province, with divisions occurring at the levels of the ruling family, the nontribal subjects or classes, and the tribal population. In most cases, while agricultural production forms the economic base of such polities and includes such industrial crops as cotton and indigo, a major portion of the ruling family's income is derived from customs and transit dues, taxes upon the subjects (the few Jews, merchants, and artisans resident in the central town) and on tithe taxes (*zakat*) upon the tribesmen's agricultural production. The Lahej sultanate, Dhala, and the Haushabi territory appear to be examples of this type of organization.

The second type, the confederation, is said to consist of a ranked system of tribes. There is in each of the several confederations a central tribe to which the others are allied; the leader or chief is provided from a ranking chiefly family in this central tribe, and the office is filled by election by the whole tribe and by chiefs of the allied tribes. The office of chief is a priestly one rather than one of coercive power and includes, in the case of the Yafa' confederation, the keeping of the tribal emblems—a set of drums—a trait reminiscent of Africa. The Yafa' and Aulaqi confederations are examples of this type.

Hamilton has also stated (1942) that there is a distinctive "culture area" difference between the two types, and names the second the "Mushreqi," locating it in the broken and rugged region between the eastern border of Yemen and the Hadhramaut. While he has not extended systematically the list of traits which distinguish this area, they are said to include a diverse assemblage of customs of dress—especially the use of a body ointment of indigo and sesame oil by men, an extended ceremonial greeting ritual, the widespread role and institution of the *manaqid*, or hereditary judges, and saints' tombs maintained by the villages and guarded by a class of shaykhly families. To the guardian shaykhs are attributed occult powers, and annual fairs and pilgrimages are associated with the shrines and tombs. Both the *manaqid* and the shaykhs appear to be marginal pre-Islamic survivors whose influence in the Hadhramaut has dwindled in the face of competition from the Hadhramaut class of *sayyids*. The *manaqid* and the *sayyids* function as peacemakers and arbitrators of local disputes.

The Eastern Protectorate, primarily the Hadhramaut, comprises six subdivisions: The Qu'aiti and Kathiri "states," the Wahidi sultanates of Bal Haf and Bir Ali, the shaykhdoms of Irqa and Haura, and the Mahri sultanates of Qishn and Socotra. Only the first two have any historical record of depth, and all are in part creations of British colonial administration emphasizing certain indigenous patterns by subsidization of key incumbents of leadership statuses or roles. Of the little-known tribal organizations of the peoples in this area, the coastal town of Mukalla and those of the Wadi Hadhramaut are best known. The latter compose the remnants of ancient and medieval Muslim settlement, together with the consequences of the extension of Arab commercial enterprise into the East Indies, India, and East Africa. Little is known, indeed, of the inception of the connection between the Hadhramaut and the East Indies or India, but it seems clear that between the fifteenth and twentieth centuries and, indeed, more surely earlier, the level of social organization was maintained largely by this connection. Fortunes made in external areas supported the power of *sayyid* and merchant families in the traditional towns of the Wadi Hadhramaut. It is only from this area that a suggestion of the presence of a "water control" bureaucracy, of small scale, is to be found. Van der Meulen, when he visited Henin in 1939, met there a landholder, not of the *sayyid* class, who reflected that at one time the leading representative of the *sayyid* families was designated by the Sultan of Shibam to oversee the organization and maintenance of the practices necessary to control the dikes and distribute the spate waters of the seasonal flooding (Van der Meulen 1947: 163). However, this may refer to only a limited local area under the control or influence of a major town center.

One recent study by an anthropologist (J. Hartley 1961) casts considerable light upon the political structure and function of the Nahid tribe of the Hadhramaut, and features of this tribal culture can probably be extended to other tribes of the Hadhramaut. In brief, Hartley finds the Nahid to be settled agriculturalists practicing flood control farming, primarily of sorghum and dates; to number about 6,000 persons; and to occupy small villages strung along the water channels of the tributary wadis ('Amd, Kasr, etc.) and part of the main Wadi Hadhramaut. He notes that they occupy arable areas and sites marked by ancient and extensive flood control devices, but that they do not have a specialized water control bureaucracy; tribal custom and rights are attached to the use of water channels; little maintenance work is required, and whatever is done is performed by hired, nontribal laborers. There is no means to mobilize and control a corvée from among the major portion of the population who are tribesmen.

The distinctive feature of the Nahid is the dual chieftaincy, a structure which J. Hartley (1961) suggests may be found elsewhere in southwestern Arabia. The major role of the chieftains is judicial rather than military; the office is hereditary, in particular within subclans of one clan of the Nahid. Succession is accompanied by a ceremony which has been called election, but it might be more accurately described as confirmation of an experienced candidate by public acclamation that explicitly recognizes competency. Hartley names the patrilineal segments of the Nahid, below the tribal unit, as clan, subclan, and lineage, the last being the unit with a territorial base, the village, and with collective rights over the cultivated lands. The local lineage also constitutes the vengeance unit, and as such is the basic political unit of the tribe. The dynamics of intra- and intertribal life for the Nahid revolve around settlement of two major categories of disputes, those involving land and water rights and those involving murders and 'aib, shame or feuding. It is the role of the two chieftains to unite and control their fellow tribesmen through competition to be chosen as the judges of disputes, whether the disputes are intra- or intertribal.

Confederations of tribes are found also in the Hadhramaut, or East Aden Protectorate. These as well as other tribes are also involved in or are subordinate to the "state" systems of the Qu'aiti and Kathiri sultanates, both of which have been supported largely from funds available to the ruling families from their enterprises in India, Southeast Asia, or East Africa. Control of the major towns of the interior (Shibam Sayyun, Tarim) and the major port, Mukalla, their markets and trade, appears to be the basis of their security of position.

Throughout the Aden Protectorate people are grouped into categories determined by birth which most writers on the area have called classes, and the tendency has been to imply that this social hierarchy is found nearly everywhere. But it seems rather to be a lumping of class, caste, and ethnic group into one ethnocentrically conceived system; whereas more than one social system is, in fact, present beneath the arbitrary notions of the old colonial administration. Thus, nearly all, especially the lower classes, may be found in urban centers, whether inland or coastal, but of course may not be found in tribal rural farming and pastoral units. Members of a single class may, however, compose such communities as the fishing villages.

These classes are given by D. Ingrams (1949: 48-54) as follows:

1. "Tribal classes," including the chiefs, the tribesmen (whether farmers or pastoralists), and the Mahra peoples as a "racially" and culturally distinct group.

2. "Influential classes," including the *sayyids*, the shaykhs (both the hereditary religious "aristocracy"), and the *manaqid* or hereditary judges of the central tribes of the Protectorate. Townsmen are also included, especially those of the Hadhramaut who are descendants of the 80 migrant families from Iraq who accompanied the reputed "progenitor" of the *sayyid* class and who are mostly the leading merchants of the Hadhramaut. And finally there are the government officials who derive from the other categories of this class (*sayyid*, merchant), but whose occupation now sets them apart.

3. Subject or depressed classes include the "subjects" (*ra'ya*) who are landless agricultural laborers without tribal affiliation or rights, but who may bear arms as supporters (i.e. clients?) of a chief and who are subject to taxation; the *dha'if* (sing.) *dhafa*, or *heiq*, who are laborers, small shopkeepers, and "artisans," who do not bear arms and are not subject to blood feud rules; and the Akhdam, Hajur, and Subian, who all appear to be of African origin and to maintain African customs. Members of this last group, ethnically distinct, perform the most menial labor, and their status is clearly of low order. Itinerant minstrel groups are also found in the West Protectorate. Slaves and descendants of slaves are found widely, and their functions are primarily those of retainers, guards, and confidants to chiefs; they do not seem to have formed a labor force in this region.

4. Scattered communities of Jews are found, mostly in the West Protectorate towns, where their status and functions were similar to those of the Jews of Yemen.

5. Mercenaries (*asakir*) are found as a distinct class of former Yafa' tribesmen who have, in leaving their tribal territories to the west and becoming paid soldiers for chieftains, particularly the Qu'aiti sultan, lost

their rights as tribesmen in their home territories.

The cities of the Hadhramaut–Shibam, Sayyun, Tarim, and the port of Mukalla–being available to scholars, have to some extent been studied in particular respects. The Hadhramaut architecture, multi-storied dwellings reminiscent of the Yemen, have been described (W. H. Ingrams 1935, Van der Meulen and Wissman 1932, Van der Meulen 1947); the segregated cemeteries of Tarim and their sociological significance have been delineated, together with the hereditary guild of Tarim gravediggers (Serjeant 1949). There is also a brief description of the quarters of Tarim, their organization, and their means of calling up the members of the quarters with traditional rallying cries in time of flood or fire (Serjeant 1950). Brief descriptions of Mukalla are found in most travelers' accounts; the report by Little (1925) provides a more extended view, covering such local industries as shipbuilding, fishing, lime burning, carpet making, and matchlock rifle manufacture.

These fragmentary "urban" studies, together with journalistic travelers' observations such as Stark (1946) and Van der Meulen provide, indicate the persistence of organization of the medieval Muslim town, divided into quarters and classes, and dominating or dependent upon a more or less extended rural hinterland of tribal cultivators. The town contains also a permanent bazaar of craft and goods shops, services, mosques, and schools.

The roles of the *sayyids* and the shaykhs are known in part in the historical and sacerdotal sense, as well as the cults of saints' tombs (cf. Serjeant 1957) and the annual festivals attending them. A detailed study of prose and poetry of the Hadhramaut, with texts, has been published by Serjeant (1951). The description of literary and musical types contains a wealth of ethnographic detail, as do the texts with translations of the Comte de Landberg (1901-13). At the present time, however, only John Hartley's recent monograph (1961) on the Nahid provides a structural study into which trait data can be seen to fit as parts of a cultural system. The bewildering diversity of South Arabia can only be brought into order by more such work, by research which is more objectively oriented than that which was supported by an obsolete colonial administration.

C. *Muscat-Oman*

This sector of southern and southeastern Arabia includes the Mahra area and Socotra Island; it remains the least publicly known of all parts of Arabia, and much of the information that is available and of value dates from the late nineteenth century, with the exception of one recent historical synthesis (Landen 1967).

The population of Muscat-Oman is guessed to be about 550,000 (Bullard 1958: 143), that of the Mahra area 50,000, and Socotra 2,000 or 6,000 or 12,000, according to different sources (D. Ingrams 1949: 35). These have no other significance than to indicate that the Muscat-Oman sultanate, with a probable area of 82,000 square miles, is more densely populated than the Mahra sector.

This area which extends from the Wadi Maseila to the Ras Musandam Peninsula encompasses the southeastern corner and prong of the Arabian Peninsula and continues the pattern of a dry coast backed by hills or ranges, beyond which the slopes of the interior extend down to steppe and desert. In the west, the hills are too low to catch much rainfall except in the Dhufar province, but from Oman proper to Ras Musandam the mountains rise once more, and in the Jabal Akhdar attain a height of 9,000 feet, enough to trap adequate rainfall for intensive cultivation, which clearly produces a surplus above immediate subsistence needs of the cultivators.

This sector of Arabia is most conveniently treated in two parts, the western Mahra-Dhufar area and the Muscat-Oman proper. The Mahra-Dhufar area centers upon the Dhufar plain, with its port of Salala. Here the surrounding hills of the Jabal Qarah and the southwest monsoon interact to provide enough rain to support, with well irrigation, a varied cultivation of coconut palm, lucerne, sugarcane, plantain, wheat, millet, cotton, and indigo in the narrow, crescent-shaped plain. Dhufar is administered from Muscat as a province of the sultan, and presents a stratified social structure that, though poorly delineated, resembles similar port town and vicinity enclaves in the Aden Protectorate or Muscat-Oman. Cultivation on the plain is under the control of the tribally organized Al Kathir, some of whom also engage in fishing and trade. Thomas (1932: 8-35) indicates that the port of Salala includes, besides the sultan's administrators, a prosperous merchant group, petty shopkeepers and middlemen in the frankincense trade (who are, in fact, Somalis), and a large community of slaves or descendants of slaves whose customs and organization, as elsewhere, are considered to be of African origin. It should be noted that such African traits, whether of house type, ritual, or status of women, are chiefly confined to the lowest castes and have not necessarily diffused into the wider society. Two other low "castes," the Dha'af and the Bahara, complete the scanty information on social structure in Dhufar. The latter, like slaves, are chiefly engaged in fishing (Thomas 1932: 12).

Behind Salala and the Dhufar plain rise the Qarah hills, densely vegetated on the seaward side, but more barren on the interior slopes. From these hills southwestward and northeastward the topography, rainfall, and terrain are little known. This area is occupied by a group of tribes called collectively the Hadara, who are distinguished for their linguistic and cultural differences from other peoples of the Arabian Peninsula. In the Qarah hills, the Qarah peoples are dependent primarily upon a pastoral economy elaborated about a limited transhumant cattle pastoralism, but they also possess camels and control exploitation of the frankincense trees. Modes of handling the cattle have been likened to such other distant cattle pastoralists as the Toda of India and the Hottentots of South Africa and are considered to be survivals of unknown but great antiquity (Coon 1943: 209-10). These traits include prohibition against women milking cows and vaginal blowing techniques to stimulate the flow of milk; however, women also enjoy rights of inheritance of property in cattle, which are distinct from orthodox Muslim practices if they regularly claim their inheritance. The Qarah social structure is said to comprise patrilineal clans with one ranked as the shaykhly clan. Living among the Qarah in small groups as a subordinate caste providing menial labor are the Shahara, whose organization above the family unit is unknown. They are regarded as predecessors to the Qarah in the area (cf. Thomas 1929: 100).

The Qarah and Shahara speak one of two Semitic but non-Arabic languages, which they share with two other tribes in the area, the Barahama and Bait ash Shaykh. The second is spoken in local variants by the Harasis, who are "clients," i.e. subordinate to the Janabah to the northeast, the 'Afar, the Bautahara shark fishers of low caste, and the Mahra—the most numerous tribe, who occupy the territory north of the Jabal Qarah and west to the Wadi Maseila—and their "clients," the Bil Haf.

The Mahra seem to be one of the least known peoples in Arabia. Their territory west of Dhufar has been crossed by few Westerners who have published their observations; it appears to be rugged, dissected by a drainage system of wadis which provides enough water for scattered villages and cultivation (cf. Thesiger 1959: 165-86) at a subsistence level.

North of the Mahra territory the terrain leads out into the southern desert and is occupied by pastoral tribes, the Manahil, Bait Imami, Bait Kathiri, and Rawashid.

The extreme habitat conditions for camel pastoralism are to be found in this southeastern borderland of the Rub' al Khali, occupied by these tribes, and particularly in the range of the Rawashid. Here the heat, the glare of the sun, and the aridity in summer are at their most intense, and camels require watering every two days. The radius of movement away from the wells is thus more restricted than for any other camel pastoral groups in Arabia so far as is known at present (cf. Thomas 1932: 200-01). Herds are smaller, and, except in time of raid threats, nomadizing in single family units is usual. Camel breeding appears here to be virtually a subsistence economy, with only a sporadic exchange in coastal markets of camels for hardware or weapons. Household equipment is meager; and the South Arabian pastoralists are distinguished for the absence of the black tent, for a small camel saddle that fits behind rather than on the hump, and similar practices that distinguish them from the pastoral peoples of North and Central Arabia.

The Mahra-Dhufar subregion is thus largely locally autonomous, by tribal areas, so far as is known, with the immediate vicinity of Dhufar presenting the only suggestion of interregional dependence and tenuous state control from Muscat. Salala is the port of export for frankincense, the latter controlled by the Qarah of the hills. The economics of fishing, cultivation, and mountain cattle herding provide a further interdependence. In summer the monsoon makes the sea too rough for maritime activities, and there is an exodus to the hills from the plain, presumably to tap the frankincense trees. At some time during this season when the light rains fall, some cattle herding Qarah come to the plain for grazing. During the winter dry season, when forage for animals is short, fish (sardines) are transported to the hills for cattle fodder. Cutting off the supply of fish to the hills in the dry season is said to be a measure taken by the Muscat governor when he feels it necessary to bring the Qarah under control (cf. Thomas 1932: 8-9, 13). But beyond this local economic network, the Mahra and the pastoralists deeper in the interior appear to have little regular intercourse with the Dhufar coastal market and cultivating settlements.

Muscat-Oman is little known in any detailed ethnological sense beyond geographical features and distributions of tribes and settlements. The most substantial data are historical and political, and much that are available are out of date or journalistic. Apart from the outlying Dhufar province and the Trucial Oman, the territory comprises the rectangular projection of the southeastern portion of the Peninsula. With the Ras Musandam Peninsula marking the northeastern corner, the major geographical feature of Muscat-Oman is the central range of jagged mountains which run from Ras Musandam in an arc curving inland and then returning to the southeastern corner at Ras al Hadd. Jabal Akhdar, the highest peak, rises to 9,000 feet just south of the center, and the altitude of the whole range is enough to trap rain in the amount of perhaps 20 inches a year. Valleys dissect the range deeply, running inland toward the desert or toward the sea, with a number of passes crossing the watershed and connecting interior and seaward slopes. The valleys or wadis are inhabited by both pastoral and agricultural settlements, according to the nature of the water supply from springs and seasonal spates, and according to the supply of soil.

The Muscat-Oman divides into seven or eight subdistricts, which reflect ecological as well as ethnic and cultural differences. The whole area is nominally dominated from Muscat, the major port located on the Gulf of Oman coast at about the latitude of the Jabal Akhdar. Periods of most cohesive integration as a state appear to correlate with periods of response to external threat (e.g. the eighteenth-century invasion from Persia), or to the prosperity of the ruling dynasty, with its consequent ability to support with force its claims to tribute and tax. The indigenous political structure and dynamics are by no means clear, for the present dynasty seems to have been supported largely by British advice and military strength since at least the last quarter of the nineteenth century. Previous to this, or concurrent with the nominal state structure, the area seems to be divided into a diversity of autonomous districts, all of "tribal" structure in the Arabian sense, with a loose sense of unity under an "elected" imam and a tradition of Ibadhite Muslim sectarianism. A second political trait indigenous to the area is the factional division into Hinawi and Ghafiri factions, which are said to have reflected, after the First World War, Ibadhi and Wahhabi sectarian preferences, respectively (Eccles 1927). In any event, the nature of the indigenous sultanate structure appears to consist of a ruling family able to hold its position largely by force and control of the ports and markets (its sphere of influence sometimes being reduced to the port of Muscat alone), and through ownership of productive date gardens and trading ships. At height of power, the various subdistricts of Muscat-Oman are "ruled" by *walis*, or governors, confirmed or appointed by the sultan. A survey of the districts of Muscat-Oman will indicate, perhaps, factors contributing to the absence of a strong state structure.

The Ras Musandam Peninsula is isolated politically from the rest of Muscat-Oman by the continuation of Sharja territory in the Trucial Oman across the Peninsula to the south from the Persian Gulf. The Ras Musandam Peninsula is rugged and rocky, with precipice-walled coves. The interior is unknown except for the fact that it is inhabited by the Shihuh people, who are not known to acknowledge any outside authority, apart from a cursory alliance with Muscat and their acceptance of a *wali* from the sultanate as protection against further penetration. Thomas (1932) provides a map of Shihuh land which shows three territorial divisions, Kumsara, Bani Hadiyah, and Bani Shatair, and indicates that they are not linguistically homogeneous, nor is their language known certainly to be Arabic. Within their territory they are said to be subsistence-level, small cattle and goat herders and plot cultivators of wheat and barley. They dwell in caves or pithouses. As in many South

Arabian societies, the men leave home to work as fishermen, pearl divers, or at date harvesting in the Gulf area in season; but the women never leave Shihuh territory (Thomas 1931: 214-38).

South of the intervening strip of Sharja territory, the central range of the Oman curves away from the coast, leaving a coastal plain some 200 miles long from Liwa to Sib and up to 20 miles wide. This is the Batinah coast, a nearly continuous line of date cultivation dependent upon irrigation from wells. With the exception of the Oman district, it is or was one of the most densely populated and productive areas of the sultanate, and seems to have been usually the most closely allied to the ruling dynasty at Muscat. Harrison has suggested that with the forcible prohibition of the slave trade in the nineteenth century, the loss of the American date market in the early twentieth century, and the migration of Arab landholders and merchants to Zanzibar, socioeconomic patterns have changed fundamentally on the Batinah coast. The large date plantations of the nineteenth century, operated by slave and animal labor, gave way to small tenant gardening by migrant Baluch peoples from the Makran coast and resulted in reduced production (Harrison 1940: 129, 162-77).

Inland and over the central ranges from the Batinah coast is the Dhahirah district, an arid and stony plain, with scattered oasis cultivation and settlement. The wadis leading into the mountains from either side are tribally claimed and settled, as well as the plains. South of the Dhahirah plain and running back into the heart of the hilly district west and southwest of Muscat are Sharqiyah and Oman districts. The major bisecting valley is the Wadi Sama'il, densely cultivated and settled and rivaling the Batinah coast in productivity. This interior province has also provided the most active resistance to sultanate control from Muscat, under the leadership of the Imam of Oman. South of these districts and approaching the sea southeast of Muscat town and beyond the Ja'alan district, is a hill mass which is more sparsely settled. Between these areas and the Rub' al Khali is a pastoral zone occupied by the Nu'aim, Duru, Wahibah, and other predominately pastoral tribes.

Cultivation in the mountain valleys depends primarily on tapping springs and conducting water by underground tunnels, or *qanats*, to the gardens that stretch for miles along the valley sides. Tribal villages and small towns characterize the settlement pattern, with the largest, such as Rostock and Nezwa, numbering 4,000-5,000 in population. Harrison estimates a total of some 200-300 of such small mountain valley oases spaced at intervals of 15 to 25 miles from each other. The socioeconomic structure is not at all clear, since on the one hand tribal structure is described by Miles for the whole area, while freehold and tenant cultivation are described by Harrison (Miles 1881: 29-44; Harrison 1940: 216-18).

Date palm cultivation predominates in the Muscat-Oman and is the only *apparent* export crop; lucerne as a fodder crop, vegetables, and fruits are consumed locally or distributed interregionally, with a good deal going to the barren coastal ports of the Trucial Oman. Tenant cultivators in the mountain oases customarily receive one spray from each tree or, alternatively, one eighth of the crop, with the privilege of raising other crops of their own among the palms.

Goats, rather than sheep, are the chief source of butter and meat. Camels, cattle, horses, and donkeys are also common animals, but apart from the fame of the Oman riding camels, little is known of their husbandry in this area. Chickens are also to be found, but here, as in other parts of South Arabia, various taboos or usages are attached to them which are not Muslim. Men, for example, will not handle live fowls.

Along the coast, fishing is a predominant economic activity; boats are leased by the crews from their owners for a one-fifth share of the catch. Three markets are supplied: the local market, the inland market for salted or partly cooked fish, and an export market for dried and salted fish. Trading and long distance voyaging, and the concomitant boatbuilding industry, are also characteristic of Muscat-Oman, but there are no details available concerning these activities. Miles has noted that "tribesmen" of the interior towns owned ships and engaged in trading voyages, and Harrison has delineated the exodus of Arab merchants and owners of date plantations to Zanzibar early in this century.

While the only available material on the tribes of Muscat-Oman dates from the nineteenth century, it may be briefly summarized with the hope that it may be corrected by future work. Miles lists 135 tribes, with populations that vary from less than a hundred to 60,000. They appear to occupy or predominate in districts or territories. Miles recognizes two levels of subdivision, the *"fakhooth"* (*fakhdh*), each of which is further subdivided into *bayts*, or houses. These are clearly the clan and its component lineage segments of other Arabian tribes. Only a few of the tribes have or recognize a paramount shaykh, called a *"temeemeh"* by Miles, who says that such chiefs have despotic powers. For most tribes, the effective unit is the *"fakhooth"* (or clan, to follow J. Hartley). Chieftainship is usually hereditary, according to Miles, and succession is by the eldest capable male of the family. It would probably be more precise to say that the chieftainship, as elsewhere, is hereditary in a particular lineage, but the successor is chosen by the males of the lineage; there is no strict rule of succession. Miles reports leagues or confederations of the largest tribes. The smaller ones stand in subordinate or client relations to the larger, but maintain sociological distinction by the genealogical fiction. The tribally organized groups comprise the major proportion of the population and predominate in the interior. But about one fourth of the population, found chiefly in the coastal towns and on the Batinah coast, are African slaves and their descendants, Indian merchants and shopkeepers, Persians, and Baluchis. Many Baluchis are of slave descent, but two tribes in the interior are of recognized status comparable with that of the Arab tribes. In the coastal settlements, all of these ethnic groups maintain residential distinction from the Arab population, live in their own quarters, and are generally of lower status than the Muslim Arabs (Jayakar 1900). Two other groups are mentioned by Miles, the Biyasara and the gypsies, or Zatut. The Biyasara are reported by Thomas to be "half-castes"; the men must marry within their own group, but Arabs may take wives from among them (Thomas 1931: 152). The Zatut or gypsies are the lowest caste, lower than the slaves; they may not settle permanently in any place. Along with the Baluchis and the Biyasara, they follow the outcaste occupations of barbers, bloodletters, bazaar auctioneers, and workers in iron. In Oman they have an important ceremonial function as circumcisers, with the Zatut men performing the operations for boys and the Zatut women performing the clitoridectomy for girls (Thomas 1931: 151-52).

In Jayakar's report (1900) of the 1893 cholera plague and in Harrison (1924, 1940) descriptions of a considerable amount of Oman folk medicine may be found.

D. *The Persian Gulf*

Since the first quarter of the nineteenth century, when Great Britain moved in force to check the growing power of the maritime Arabs of the Persian Gulf, the political status of a group of small states or chiefdoms dispersed along the Arab side of the Gulf has not changed significantly, and any potential for unification in larger political units than were held at that time has not been expressed. All of the ten entities were until the past few years mediated shaykhdoms under the protection of or in close treaty relations with Great Britain.

Kuwait is a mainland shaykhdom at the northwestern corner of the Gulf, occupying a territory of about 6,000 square miles whose boundaries were established following the First World War. Its population at present is 206,000, swollen from a "normal" pre-oil population of at most 100,000. The development of oil in Kuwait has grafted to its indigenous system the complexities of partial incorporation into the network of industrial economies. Political independence from British control and some internal state structural changes were achieved in 1961.

Bahrain is an island emirate in the central part of the Gulf, close to the Arabian mainland, occupying islands of about 220 square miles in area and having a population in 1955 of about 120,000. Bahrain also has participated in the oil development, and expects to become politically independent in the near future. In spite of its very small size, Bahrain has held more political and economic significance over history than probably any of the other small Arab polities of the Gulf. A center of pearling and the pearl market from antiquity, and a port of export for Arabia probably account for this, as well as its local resources in fresh water, cultivable soil, and other products.

Qatar comprises a barren peninsula of 8,000 square miles, with a population of 25,000 people who are largely concentrated in the vicinity of Doha, on the east coast. Oil development here has also had its effect.

The Trucial Oman shaykhdoms, with their estimated populations, are Abu Dhabi (2,000), Dubai (40,000), Umm al Gawain (3,000), Ajman (2,000), Sharjah (3,000), Ras al Khayma (15,000), and Fujaira (3,000). They occupy territories with undelineated boundaries along the coast from the Qatar Peninsula to Ras Musandam Peninsula, in the order given, with the exception of Fujaira, a recently recognized shaykhdom on the Gulf of Oman side of the Peninsula.

The political structure of the shaykhdoms or emirates, so far as it is known, varies slightly from place to place. A century and a half of British subsidization of the chiefs or shaykhs and of dealing with the populace through them has probably contributed to the development of political power of the chiefs and their lineages over their fellow or allied tribesmen. In each of the shaykhdoms except, perhaps, Bahrain, the original role of the head of the "ruling" family seems to have been that of the tribal religious leader, final judge of disputes, organizer of protection of the inhabitants, or leader of raiding expeditions, rather than that of a despotic chief. Bahrain, long the commercial center of the Gulf, is more complex in political structure and has developed as a stratified conquest chiefdom or state structure since the eighteenth century. In no case is it clear that the economic support of the ruling dynasty was derived wholly from tribute, tax, or port customs, and in fact the chiefs were probably owners of trading and pearling ships themselves in most cases. Such offices as are known to have existed in these petty shaykhdoms, apart from that of the paramount chief, were filled from members of the ruling lineage, prominent merchants or notables, or trusted slaves. In the twentieth century, with the development of the oil industry, administrations of departmentalized bureaucratic structures have developed to deal with the increasing financial, judicial, and commercial problems.

In recent centuries, if not for much longer, maritime activities have dominated these coasts and account in large part for the original development of urban ports in their present locations. With the possible exception of Bahrain and Ras al Khayma, none are self-supporting above a village level of development from subsistence activities possible in their environs alone. The traditional subsistence activities comprise oasis date gardening supplemented by a few fruits, vegetables, and fodder crops; sheep and goat herding in the vicinity of the port towns, and fishing. The towns have functioned most prominently as entrepots and centers of organization of pearling enterprise and commerce, and have many of the features of "ports-of-trade" in relation to the hinterlands or to each other.

The little detailed information that exists on fishing technology in the Gulf dates from the nineteenth century and is covered in a brief paper by MacIvor (MacIvor 1881). The localities, seasonal aspects, boat types, nets and traps, lines and harpoons, and types of marine life taken are summarized in MacIvor's report, but not the economics. He characterized it as the most important industry in the Gulf, next to pearl fishing. Additional scanty information from the writer's brief observations in 1958-59 suggests only that the customary practices continue relatively unchanged, but that the economic organization of fishing would repay investigation. As Harrison indicated for Muscat, there is an intricate specialization of operations among marketers, owners of boats, makers of nets and traps, owners of shrimp traps and fish traps, and fishermen per se, all with customary share divisions of the catch. Fish drying for export from the Trucial Oman, especially Dubai, also deserves description.

Almost the same may be said for date cultivation and shepherd pastoralism. Only for Kuwait from the work of the Dicksons is there any detail on the traditional subsistence activities supporting the development of settlements (H. R. P. Dickson 1949, 1956; V. Dickson 1955). Date cultivation is significant primarily on the Bahrain islands of Manama and Muharraq, and for the Ras al Khayma economy.

Until the present century, however, pearl fishing was the major economic activity of the Gulf. The techniques and work organization of the crews, the seasons, the local marketing and economic organization are in general well recorded (cf. Belgrave 1934; Bowen 1951; Mockler 1886). From every port or fishing village boats with their crews converged upon the banks and sought pearls from June until September or October. The diversity of organization of crews, from parties of free desert tribesmen to slaves, seems to have geographical distribution. Most of the slave crews operated on the southern banks from the Trucial Oman ports, and crews of free tribesmen came from Qatar; Kuwait and Bahrain crews were nominally freemen, sailors or fishermen or parttime shepherds, but the system of paying the crews in advance so enmeshed many in debt, customarily inherited, that a status of debt serfdom effectively tied the divers to boat owners or captains and maintained them as a dependent class.

Boat- and shipbuilding in the Persian Gulf by the hereditary class of specialists, the Baharna, is found in every port of the Gulf, large and small, and the types of craft have been rather extensively described (Bowen 1949; H. R. P. Dickson 1949: 473-83; Johnstone and Muir 1962; Villiers 1940, 1948). A number of distinctive types or styles, found in variable sizes, are constructed, with some tendency for the builders of one port, such as Kuwait, to be best known for the construction of *buums*, while *jalbuuts* are found chiefly at Bahrain. The range of size extends from small fishing boats for offshore use, to moderate-sized coasting vessels, which can negotiate narrow and shallow approaches to the shores, to deep sea ships of 300 or more tons in capacity, which are employed in the long distance trading voyages to India, Southeast Asia, and East Africa. All timbers for construction are imported from India and Africa, and the development of the industry in the Gulf, so distant from its sources of materials, requires explanation. Little is known of the technology, organization of work, and economic relations involved in constructing a Gulf boat or dhow; the vocabulary of shipwrighting was said to resemble Hindi by informants for the writer of this chapter. The structural similarity of Arab sailing craft to those of India is notable.

Maritime trading voyages remain a major economic activity of the Gulf, as of other Arabian ports, in spite of the increasing competition of steam and motor ships and launches since the late nineteenth century. Auxiliary engines are often found in the sailing craft, used primarily to get under way from port. On both sides of the Gulf, sailing, navigation, and trading enterprises seem to have been primarily Arab activities from antiquity. From the hinterlands to the coastal villages of the Gulf, surplus production of various crops and goods was collected at the major Arabian ports by the smaller coasting vessels; these cargoes were then shipped to their major markets in India in the deep draft ships. From the Persian side, wheat and horses or mules were major exports; from Basra, dates; from the Arabian side, horses and clarified butter and dried and salted fish (Pelly 1863). A careful study of the organization of this commerce is needed. At present our knowledge is largely confined to the organization of the trading ship, its crew, ownership, and operation as a joint shares venture (Villiers 1940, 1948). Village crafts are little developed except at Bahrain (pottery, weaving) and Ras al Khayma; urban bazaar crafts are also undistinguished.

Social composition of the populations in the Gulf states is surprisingly heterogeneous. Each "state," in so far as is known, comprises an urban port center, with a larger or smaller hinterland, including a few villages and pastoral groups. By and large, the pastoralists and villagers are tribally organized Sunni Arabs, although some villages, as on Bahrain, are of the nontribal class of Shi'a Baharna. The ports are cosmopolitan, more or less, according to size and location, and include— each dwelling in their own quarters—Baluchis, Iranians, descendants of African slaves (all of whom engage in manual labor), Iranians of Arab descent, Hindu and Muslim merchants from India, shopkeepers, jewelers and craftsmen from India, indigenous Arab merchants, occasional Japanese merchants, and growing enclaves of Europeans and Americans. Nothing is known of guild organization other than the possibility that it existed.

The stratification of the Gulf polities is most marked in Bahrain, where the Sunni Arab merchants, owners of boats, gardens, and other properties form a rather clear controlling class above the laborers, porters, gardeners, fishermen, divers, and craftsmen. Among the latter, the Baharna form the largest class and are Shi'a Muslims. However, for none of the shaykhdoms is the socioeconomic composition very well known in a systematic sense. Lorimer's *Gazetteer* provides an encyclopedic description of Gulf history and society, but little account of integrative mechanisms or structural features (Lorimer 1908-15).

Proximity to the Persian cultural tradition has visibly affected the architecture of the Gulf towns; wind towers are among the most characteristic features of the dwellings and serve as cooling mechanisms during the humid and oppressive summers; they effectively trap and funnel moving air into the rooms below. Otherwise traditional dwellings of the elite are mudbrick or coral-walled compounds, rarely of more than one story, but with high parapets for the secure use of the roofs by women and children. The working classes and casual laborers typically build dwellings of mats or palm branch lattice. The latter, *barastis*, are the most widely distributed. Styles of clothing also reflect contact with India or the Central and North Arabian desert. While members of foreign ethnic groups wear their own styles of dress, two basic styles seem indigenous and reflect at once social status, occupation, and diffusion: the maritime man wears a Madras plaid kilt or *lungi* (of eastern origin) and a loosely wrapped, white headcloth, without hair ropes; a straight-sided, sleeved white or gray gown may be worn when he is not working. A light shawl may be carried over one shoulder or around the shoulders by older men and merchants, an item most characteristic of South Arabian and Yemeni merchants and ruling classes. It is supposed to have traditional implications associated with the Prophet. The second male dress pattern is the northern desert pastoralist's brown, black, or white gown, cloak, and headcloth with hair ropes.

The several chiefdoms of the Persian Gulf rest upon an economic base that in the past consisted in pearling and commerce, primarily developed over a basic but meager subsistence pattern of fishing, small gardening, and shepherding. Sociopolitical development on the Arabian side of the Gulf has also been affected by the controlling and greater power of Great Britain. At the present, the pearl- and trade-based societies are becoming increasingly dependent upon funds derived from oil royalties and to some extent show the development of a class of wage laborers in the oil industry itself. In none of the shaykhdoms where the oil industry has developed, however, do they compose a very large proportion of the working population. While components of the industrial world have established themselves in the Arabian Peninsula (especially oil company production installations and personnel), and the goods and gadgets of industrial production are available in mass, only a little of Western technical skills, science, and managerial experience has been transmitted to the indigenous societies. From observation, however, the peoples of these coastal societies are more interested in learning than the controllers of industrial technology are in teaching.

E. *Central and North Arabia (Saudi Arabia)*

Central and North Arabia comprise the major part of the Arabian Peninsula. Extending from the present boundaries of the Yemen and the southern rim states or sultanates to the cultivated areas of the Levant and Tigris-Euphrates basin, this vast territory is little known ethnographically. In very gross ecological terms it may be divided into the western highlands, the Hejaz and Asir, the southern desert, or Rub' al Khali, and the central portion, including the long wadi and oasis systems of the Nejd, together with the east coast opposite Bahrain, and the northern steppes and desert. Everywhere the rainfall is less than ten inches per year, except perhaps the Asir highlands. Its population, estimated between three and six million (Bullard 1958: 73), is distributed in two patterns, dominated by the pastoral and oasis cultivation habitats. Over much of the area is a thin distribution of pastoral tribes. In the Asir highlands, those of the Meccan area, and in the oasis settlements of the remainder, a sedentary cultivating and urban population is clustered in towns and villages according to the availability of the subsurface water supplies.

The present kingdom of Saudi Arabia has unified the area under a single administration, a process which began in 1902 with the taking of Riyadh by the rising Saudi leader, 'Abdul 'Aziz 'Ibn Saud, and which was completed by him in 1926 when the Hejaz was incorporated into the kingdom. Since the discovery and development of vast resources in oil during the 1930s, the economic security of the state has been reinforced. The brief history of the rise of the Saudi kingdom must include the accompanying and supporting Wahhabi movement, a religiopolitical movement of the order of revivalistic or nativistic phenomena, which has not been fully appreciated in this respect. As in the cases of Zaidi-controlled Yemen and Ibadhi-controlled Muscat-Oman, unity and social order have been maintained by the force of sectarian Muslim organization of the ruling class; however, in the Saudi kingdom, the Wahhabi movement successfully incorporated, for a time, many pastoral tribesmen in its ranks. As in the Yemen, the king is also the religious leader, or imam, of the people. More extensively than in other areas discussed, the traditional sources of law, the Muslim Shari'a, govern social life, implemented by the *'ulema*, and supplemented by kingly decree.

Divided into two vice-royalties, and these into provinces, the Saudi kingdom is ruled by governors appointed from the ruling family or from powerful families closely allied by marriage to the ruling family. The Council of Ministers, which forms the bureaucratic hierarchy, is similarly controlled by members of the ruling family holding the key posts.

Apart from the apparatus of a monarchy, Central and North Arabia present culture patterns which have tended to provide the best-known stereotypes of Arabian cultures: the oasis settlement and the nomadic pastoral tribe, primarily the Bedouin camel specialists. Of all Arabian societies, a few of the pastoralists have received the most attention, the Rwala, Shammar, and Mutair.

The vast desert and steppe expanses of North and Central Arabia dominate this region and are occupied by tribal nomadic pastoral societies who depend chiefly upon the husbandry of sheep and camels for subsistence. Dispersed among them, and living in symbiotic relations, are small communities of the Salubba peoples, who do not appear to have tribal organization. They are hunters and guides and water scouts for the pastoralists and also provide tinkering and carpentry services. They and a number of other peoples (e.g. the Hutaim and Shararat), with tribal organization but no territorial claims or traditional genealogical ideological support, rank as the lowest castes of desert society. Shepherd tribes, such as the Hadidiin, Mawaali, and Muntafiq, rank above these, but below and often in client relationship to the "noble" tribes, the camel pastoralists, the "true" Bedouin. The "noble" tribes of the desert are initially identified and set apart sociologically by the ideological superstructure of the tribal genealogies, which provide an over-all plan of the relationships of the patrilineally organized segments of Bedouin tribal organization. The tribe is the largest territorial unit that acts politically in making war, peace, or alliance in briefly organized confederations. A paramount chief from a hereditary chiefly lineage is recognized by all members, but he has no despotic authority. His full functions remain to be analyzed. The declaration of war and peace, leadership in military expeditions, and carrying out of negotiations with other societies are among them, however. Since the pastoral tribes—mounted, mobile, and well armed—hold the power of attack in the indigenous cultural system, most of the northern oases are under their control. The nineteenth-century Rashidi state, as well as the rise of the present Saudi kingdom, were thus based upon tribal military power, and the leaders of these states are or were of tribal origin.

In its role as a nomadic pastoral society, however, the tribe is composed of parallel segments or clans, each led by a chief. Each segment or clan moves with its herds through the annual regime of grazing in the tribal territory. Summers are spent in camps on the permanent wells, generally near settlements. With the first rains the segments (sections or "clans") move out into their grazing territories in close or open order, as security demands. The ecology of camel pastoralism requires frequent movement, and the capacity of the camel to withstand thirst and to consume dry forage makes it possible to exploit territories beyond the range of sheepherders.

Nomadic movement requires portable equipment, and the household goods of the northern pastoralists are relatively uniform, from the Murra tribes of the northeastern Rub' al Khali northward. The black or brown tent of camel, sheep, or goat hair is ubiquitous and has spread far beyond the North and Central Arabian desert, where it probably originated (Feilberg 1944). Economic status differences are reflected in the size and furnishings of tents. Camel saddles and harnesses and tent equipment such as the interior curtain, coffee hearth, and equipment have been described in detail by many writers (cf. H. R. P. Dickson 1949, Musil 1928).

Camels and other animals are owned individually, but tribal rules of kinship obligations operate to provide access to animals for those in need. The hazards of desert economy and the rather slow reproductive rate of camels—one offspring in two years—make for inequalities, and among the pastoralists' means of increasing their herds or recouping losses is the institution of the raid (Sweet 1965b). As for other pastoral peoples, the mobility of nomadism and the practice of raiding contribute to the development of Bedouin military organization and a warrior class among the tribesmen. Horses have also been bred among the Bedouin for special military uses as well as for export.

The Bedouin encampment typically is composed and aligned in lineages, the smallest unit comprising the single-family tent set among the cluster of patrilineal kin. The oldest male is the leader of the group, and with him are likely to be associated brothers, sons, cousins, and nephews; unmarried women, wives, and widows; and children. While lineage endogamy is considered typical of Bedouin society, chiefs of lineages, sections, and tribes can be seen, from the abundant literature, to use marriage as a means of cementing alliances with chiefs of other units, larger or smaller. A man's marriage to the daughter or sister of another whose rank is above him is tantamount to allegiance and, vice versa, to expecting allegiance.

While the encampment consists of a core of patrilineally related tribesmen, nonmembers are also usually present as protected neighbors, or as herdsmen under customary contract relations to the head of a family group. In a section (clan) or tribal chief's camp, a blacksmith, Salubba guides, and slaves may also be found.

The disputes that arise in Bedouin society are settled by tribal law, administered by recognized judges. The blood feud involves a group of kinsmen to the fifth degree from the victim or murderer called the *khamsa*, and customs surround the vengeance acts in such a way as to promote settlement by payment of camels and equipment in customary equivalences for the life of a man or woman; while the murderer and his kin seek sanctuary with some distant tribe until the matter is settled.

Nominally Sunni or Wahhabi Muslims, the northern tribal pastoralists hold many other beliefs that are not well known. Jinns, or societies of anthropomorphic spirits complementary to human societies, inhabit the earth. Soothsayers are to be found. Myths and legends, as well as poetry and song, are well developed in Bedouin culture and have been collected by a number of scholars (Montagne 1935, Musil 1928a).

While in South Arabia, tribal camel breeders engage in transport work, providing baggage camels and controlling caravan movement themselves, the North Arabian Bedouin tribesmen do not. They sell camels to a guild of town-based camel merchants, the *'aqayl*, whose members move annually among them, buying up the animals the Bedouin are willing to sell. Or the Bedouin may sell a few beasts in the urban market towns of the oases, to which they go regularly to supply and equip themselves for their long grazing treks and raids. Movement of caravans or travelers across tribal territories, however, is controlled by the tribesmen through the custom (general in tribal Arabia from north to south) of the *rafiq* or responsible companion who provides escort and security from predation. The control of caravan routes across North Arabia, and especially the great Meccan pilgrim caravans, has long been one of the sources of tribal income and power.

While North Arabian pastoral tribes are relatively well known from the literature of scholarly travelers, historical and human geographers, and others, no recent studies have been made in the ethnographic sense. Some attention has been given to the cohesive function of parallel-cousin marriage (Murphy and Kasdan 1959) and to the ecology of camel pastoralism (Sweet 1965a, b), but these studies are dependent in the main upon the literature available.

Less well known than the nomadic pastoralists of North Arabia are the oasis settlements. Only two studies of any depth are available, Boucheman's monograph on the Syrian desert caravan town of Sukhne (Boucheman 1937) and Vidal's study of the geography and economy of the oasis of Al Hasa in eastern Arabia (Vidal 1955). Mecca and other cities and towns of Arabia are known in the historical, geographical, and architectural sense, and, in addition to the well-known authorities, the *Encyclopedia of Islam* abundantly provides this type of information.

Sukhne is a small caravan and market town northeast of Palmyra. Its inhabitants are almost all of desert tribal derivation, together with a few long-settled clans. Its chief business has been the supply of camels to Meccan pilgrims starting from Damascus, and its history is one of subordination to the various tribes of the area or to Ottoman governors. The right to supply pilgrimage camels is the crux of struggle between the two parties into which the town divides, under the leadership of the largest "clans." In the dominance of kin group factions, desert costume, diet, and many other traits, Sukhne is clearly allied culturally to desert tribal culture. The houses of mud brick are built by women. Well-irrigated gardens supply dates, fruits, wheat, barley, and maize. Small flocks of sheep and goats and herds of camels are kept. Donkeys are the chief work animal. A few craftsmen, metalworkers, and carpenters, are present to supply their services to pilgrim caravans, as well as specialists in trapping and training hunting falcons, which are in demand by desert tribal chiefs. A chief economic activity of Sukhniotes is the collection and burning of suitable plants from the desert. The ash is then collected for soapmaking factories in Aleppo.

The oasis of Al Hasa in eastern Arabia provides, relative to Sukhne, an example of the contrasts that occur in size, social composition, and productivity of Arabian oasis settlements. Shaped like an L and comprising three great blocks of cultivation, the oasis covers some 180 square kilometers. Vidal estimates its total population at 160,000, living in two large towns, Hofuf and Mubarraz, and in numerous other villages and hamlets scattered through the oasis. The Bani Khalid and the 'Ujman tribes have competed for control of the area, now under the jurisdiction of the Saudi kingdom. Each of the many villages has its headman and its imam and a large proportion of the population are Shi'a Muslims; they are predominately the peasant gardeners, tenants, and artisans.

As a major market center, a weekly market in each town and permanent bazaars provide produce, animals, and goods of both local production and foreign import. Several forms of land tenure apply to the extensive date palm gardens, and Vidal's information provides a checklist or model against which tenure in other areas of Arabia could be compared: *mukumah* land, belonging to high officials, such as the emir or governor of the oasis; *bait al mal*, or government-owned land, often under the administration of an important individual; private individual ownership; multiple ownership of plots within a garden irrigated in common; joint ownership, with division of the harvest by shares, but work in common or under the care of a specialist (*wakil*) (Vidal 1955: 131-34). These categories, as described by Vidal, correspond to the traditional tenures cited earlier, but add details which are, perhaps, peculiar to Al Hasa.

The intricate system of distributing the irrigation water from the springs follows a customary schedule; owners are responsible for following the schedule, and failures to do so will be subject to direct complaint from the next owner in the sequence or complaint to the court of the emir or *qadhi*. As elsewhere in Arabia, there does not appear to be a special functionary or bureaucracy for controlling or overseeing distribution of the water supply. There are no *qanats* in Al Hasa. Animal and hand-lift mechanisms are also used with wells.

Some gardens specialize in date palm cultivattion, but lucerne, rice, and a variety of other vegetables and fruits are usually grown under the palms.

Al Hasa crafts in metalwork and textiles are also important; most of the craftsmen are Shi'a Muslims, and the work is carried out in small shops in the bazaar streets of the larger towns. Coffeepots are the chief manufacture in metal; cloaks are also a Hofuf textile specialization, woven in small shops of two to six looms (hand-operated, horizontal, two-bar looms with up to eight treadles). In style and quality, Al Hasa is famous for its coffeepots and cloaks of fine camel hair. Lime burning, pottery, basketry, leatherworking, and woodworking complete the list of crafts.

Descriptive materials on other oases or cultivated areas can be gleaned from the works of Philby, Musil, and others, but by and large this facet of Arabian culture remains little known.

IV. *Conclusion*

This brief sketch of sociocultural systems in the Arabian Peninsula omits a great deal of known ethnographic detail in the interest of providing an over-all framework to be filled in or altered as future work supplies. Structural variability in Arabia is clearly present, and is tied closely to the spatial relationships of the four habitats. Where cultivable land is predominate, extensive and diverse in production, as in the Yemen, the maximum integration at state level of organization over time as well as area is maintained, regardless of external conditions. But where cultivable habitats are frequently and widely separated by less productive areas, a state scale of organization breaks down easily when environmental or economic calamities occur, as in the Muscat-Oman, unless externally derived resources are available.

This initial attempt at summary generalizations should serve only to stimulate further study of the cultural content and organization of Arabian systems. With the secularization of political organization that is accompanying the response of Arabian systems to spreading industrial technology, and with the increasing sharing of oil subsidy wealth among the polities (to suggest only two factors), an interesting change and expansion of scale of political integration seems to be emerging in all parts of the Arabian Peninsula, but especially in those parts that have in the past century and a half experienced more or less control of their affairs by the former British colonial administration—South Arabia, Muscat-Oman, and the states of the Persian Gulf.

THE ARABIAN PENINSULA:
AN ANNOTATED BIBLIOGRAPHY

Abu Hakima, Ahmad Mustafa
  1965   *History of eastern Arabia, 1750-1800; the rise and develop-*
         ment of Bahrain and Kuwait. Beirut, Khayats. 19, 213 pp.;
         illus., maps, bibliog., index.

         A British-trained Arab historian's account of the rise of Arab
         polities in the Persian Gulf during the eighteenth century.
         Use of Arab chronicles and local tradition enriches the ac-
         count considerably.

American University, Foreign Area Studies
  1971   *Area handbook for the peripheral states of the Arabian*
         Peninsula, Washington, D.C., U.S. Government Printing Of-
         fice. xiv, 202 pp.; map, bibliographies, index.

Ashkenazi, Touvia
  1938   "Tribus semi-nomades de la Palestine du Nord," *Études*
         d'Ethnographie, Tome II, Paris, Librairie Orientaliste Paul
         Geuthner. xvii, 286 pp.; illus., map, charts.

         A monograph summarizing the social and economic aspects
         of culture of the semi-nomadic tribes of northern Palestine,
         who are of mixed derivation—Arab, Kurd, Turkoman,
         Egyptian.

  1948   "The 'Anazah Tribes," *Southwestern Journal of Anthropol-*
         ogy 4: 222-39.

         A description of the tribes and history of the 'Anazah con-
         federation of Bedouin tribes of the Syrian desert, following
         the traditional genealogical plan. Chieftainship and size of
         tribes are considered.

Bacon, Elizabeth E.
  1954   "Types of pastoral nomadism in Central and Southwest
         Asia," *Southwestern Journal of Anthropology 10*: 44-68.

         Rejoinder to Patai (1951), setting forth the similarities and
         differences between nomadic pastoralism in the two areas in
         question.

  1958   "Obok, a study of social structure in Eurasia," *Viking Fund*
         Publications in Anthropology, No. 25, New York, Wenner-
         Gren Foundation for Anthropological Research.

Bacon's monograph, in Part VIII, pp. 123-34, discusses Bedouin tribal organization, distinguishing between the egocentric sliding lineage, or vengeance unit, and the fixed lineage, or "clan."

Belgrave, Charles Dalrymple
1928 "Bahrain," *Royal Central Asian Society Journal 15*: 440-45.

A concise summary on Bahrain before the discovery and development of oil, by the former British adviser to the Bahrain ruler.

1934 "Pearl diving in Bahrain," *Royal Central Asian Society Journal 21*: 450-52.

Economic aspects of pearl diving.

1966 *The pirate coast*, London, G. Bell and Sons. xii, 200 pp.; illus., map, bibliog., index.

A scholarly presentation (fortified with introductory historical chapters and a concluding chapter on the current scene in the Arab states of the Persian Gulf) of the diary of Francis Loch, covering the years 1818-21 of British naval operations against the concurrent Arab expansion in the Persian Gulf. Loch commanded H.M.S. Eden. Belgrave characteristically regards the Arab expansion as "piratical" (cf. Sweet 1964).

Belgrave, James H. D.
1953 *Welcome to Bahrain*, Stourbridge, Worcestershire, Mark and Moody. 154 pp.; illus., map.

An official guidebook by the former Director of Public Relations in Bahrain (son of C. D. Belgrave). Accurate and adequate source for basic data on the people, state structure, economy, and history.

Bell, Gertrude L.
1907 *The desert and the sown*, London, New York; William Heinemann, E. P. Dutton. 16, 347 pp.; illus., map.

A travelogue by a British Arabist, archeologist, and political officer of a trip along the borderlands between cultivating villages and pastoral areas from the latitude of Jerusalem to Aleppo, about the turn of the twentieth century. A potpourri of excellent information and anecdote.

Bent [James] Theodore, and Mabel Bent
1900 *Southern Arabia*, London, Smith, Elder. 10, 455 pp.; illus., maps, appendixes, bibliog.

The Bents, scholarly British travelers, were the first to explore and study parts of southern Arabia. In this volume is the record of their observations in Bahrain, Muscat, the Hadhramaut, Dhufar, Socotra, and the Fadhali and Yafa'i territories near Aden, in the last decade of the nineteenth century. Still useful, and there has been very little since on Socotra.

Blunt, Anne
1879   *Bedouin tribes of the Euphrates*, London, New York; John Murray, Harper & Brothers. 445 pp.; illus., map.

A record of travels among the Shammar Bedouin on both sides of the Euphrates, about contemporary with Doughty's trip. Good observations of Bedouin life of the time, before the intensive penetration of the West.

Boucheman, Albert de
1934a   "Matériel de la vie bédouine, recueilli dans le désert de Syrie tribu des arabes Sba'a," Institut Français de Damas, *Documents d'Études Orientales 3*. 140 pp.; illus.

A monograph on the material household equipment, crafts, and costume among the Sba'a Bedouin of Syria by a French ethnographer and officer of the French Mandate government.

1934b   "Note sur la rivalité de deux tribus moutonnières de Syrie: les 'Mawali' et les 'Hadidiyin'," *Revue des Études Islamiques 1*: 11-58. Maps, charts.

A brief study of political relations between two powerful shepherd tribes of Syria, and of the relations of each tribe with its "satellites." The sedentarization process is discussed, and tribal structure is described.

1937   "Une petite cité caravanière: Suhné," *Institut Français de Damas, Documents d'Études Orientales 6*.

An historical, economic, social, and political study of a small caravan town in the Syrian Desert during the Mandate period.

Bowen, Richard Le Baron, Jr.
1949   *Arab dhows of eastern Arabia*, Rehoboth, Mass., privately printed. 10, 51 pp.; illus., map, figs.

Subtitle: "A dissertation on the sailing characteristics of the lateen-rigged Arab watercraft of the western Persian Gulf, with a discussion of the probable evolution of the lateen rig and a consideration of the development and the construction of the Arab dhow." Types of dhows are reviewed; a very useful discussion, but with some inaccuracies of detail.

Bowen is a civil engineer and was in Arabia as an Aramco employee at the time of his studies.

1951a   "Marine industries of eastern Arabia," *Geographical Review 41*: 384-400.

Fishing, coral rock mining, pearling, and the effects of oil development on labor. Useful information on Arab organization of economic activities.

1951b "The pearl fisheries of the Persian Gulf," *Middle East Journal* 5: 161-80.

An historical, technical, and economic summary of pearling, which is in general accurate and more up to date than Lorimer and Belgrave.

1958 "Irrigation in ancient Qataban (Beihan)," in *Archeological Discoveries in South Arabia*, R. Le B. Bowen, Jr. and Frank P. Albright, Baltimore, The Johns Hopkins Press: 43-147; illus.

Bujra, A. S.
1967a "Political conflict and stratification in Ḥaḍramaut—I," *Middle Eastern Studies 3*: 355-75.

1967b "Political conflict and stratification in Ḥaḍramaut—II: nationalism and the Yemeni revolution: their effects on Ḥaḍramaut," *Middle Eastern Studies 4*: 2-28.

These two papers delineate the stratified character of traditional Ḥaḍramaut society at home and in Indonesia, the emergence of the Sādah and Irshādi factions representing the traditionalist and the egalitarian movements; and, from the unique vantage point of residence in a Ḥaḍramaut village, the course of the Yemeni revolution in 1962-63, together with its effects in the Ḥaḍramaut.

1970 "Urban elites and colonialism: the nationalist elites of Aden and South Arabia," *Middle Eastern Studies 6*: 189-211.

Bullard, Reader, ed.
1958 *The Middle East: a political and economic survey*, 3d ed. London, published by Oxford University Press under the auspices of the Royal Institute of International Affairs. 18, 569 pp.; map.

A reference source for fairly recent statistics and estimates, as well as concisely summarized political history.

Burckhardt, John Lewis
1831 *Notes on the Bedouins and Wahábys*, 2 vols. London, H. Colburn and R. Bently.

A classic by a Swiss explorer for European commercial interests; concerned with the Bedouin of northern Arabia and perceptive on social structure of the tribes.

Bury, G. Wyman
1911 *The Land of Uz*, London, Macmillan. 28, 354 pp.; illus., map.

Adventures and observations in the course of political work in the Aden hinterland. Geographical descriptions are excellent; a good deal of useful information on markets, towns, and settlements not found elsewhere. Some "adventures" are of doubtful authenticity.

1915 *Arabia Infelix, or the Turks in Yemen*, London, Macmillan. 10, 213 pp.; illus., maps.

Bury records a journey in Yemen from Hodeidah to San'a. He went as a "naturalist," after ten years as a British political officer in the Aden Protectorate. Anecdotal, but with clear descriptions of ecological variety and peoples and customs.

Carruthers, Douglas
1910 "A journey in north-western Arabia," *Geographical Journal* 35: 225-48.

Carruthers, a British geographer and naturalist, traveled from Tebuk to Teima Oasis in 1909. Tribal notes of interest on the Beni Shakr and Rwala Bedouin and the Shararat, and geographical notes of ecological significance.

Caton-Thompson, G., and E. W. Gardner
1939 "Climate, irrigation and early man in the Hadhramaut," *Geographical Journal 93*: 18-38.

Geological and archeological discussion of the Hadhramaut in relation to the problem of possible dessication.

Coon, Carleton S.
1943 "Southern Arabia, a problem for the future," *Papers of the Peabody Museum of American Archeology and Ethnology, Harvard University 20*: 187-220. Cambridge, Mass., Peabody Museum. Map.

A synthesis of the then known material on southwestern Arabia, cultural and physical, from Yemen to Dhufar. The continuity of structure is emphasized, with declining scale of organization from west to east.

Dickson, Harold Richard Patrick
1949 *The Arab of the desert; a glimpse into Badawin life in Kuwait and Sau'di Arabia*, London, Allen and Unwin. 648 pp.; illus., drawings, maps.

A monumental encyclopedia on the area designated in the title, filled with personal reminiscences by a British political officer stationed in the area in various places from the first World War. Much of the description refers to the Mutair; accuracy is still in doubt. Sections on the Muntafiq shepherd tribes of Iraq and on pearl diving and dhow building in Kuwait.

1956 *Kuwait and her neighbours*, London, Allen & Unwin. 627 pp.; illus., maps.

An equally monumental encyclopedia and companion to the above volume, but containing largely historical reminiscences. Some information refers particularly to the Ajman Bedouin. The Ikhwan Rebellion is documented from the author's point of view.

Dickson, Violet
1955 *The wild flowers of Kuwait and Bahrain*, London, Allen & Unwin. 144 pp.; illus., drawings, maps.

An ethnobotanical manual with valuable material on grazing vegetation and areas in Kuwait, by the wife of H. R. P. Dickson.

Dostal, Walter
1959 "The evolution of Bedouin life," in *L'Antica Società Beduina*, Francesco Gabrieli, ed., Studi Semitici No. 2, Centro di Studi Semitici, Università di Roma, Roma: 11-34.

Dostal seeks to reconstruct the development of "Bedouinism" from the evidence available in archeological and ethnographic materials. While the milieu in which camel domestication took place cannot yet be established, Dostal argues for the development of camel herding from small-scale patterns to the classical warrior-aristocrat camel specialists of northern Arabia, following the introduction of the horse and its riding equipment and the transfer of the horse usage and equipment to the camel.

Doughty, Charles M.
1936 *Travels in Arabia Deserta*, 2 vols. New York, Random House. 696 pp.; illus.

Doughty's "classic" is written in pseudo-archaic English, meant to give the flavor of Arabic and Arabian desert life. Doughty traveled with a small tribe, the Fuqara, who had recently moved into the territory under Shammar Rashid influence (1870s), and he spent some time in the oasis settlements of the Qasim district.

Eccles, G. J.
1927 "The Sultanate of Muscat and Oman," *Royal Central Asian Society Journal 14*: 19-42. Maps.

A useful historical and geocultural sketch of Muscat and Oman with the details of travel from the Batinah Coast across the watershed and return by two passes to the interior. Eccles was a British officer attached to the Sultan of Muscat and in command of the Muscat Levies; he was escorting the D'Arcy Exploration Company's geological survey of 1925.

Fayein, Claudie
    1957   *A French doctor in the Yemen*, London, Robert Hale. 288 pp.; illus., index.

Dr. Fayein, a French general medical practitioner, spent about a year and a half, 1952-53, in the Yemen, stationed chiefly at San'a, but with considerable freedom of movement. In addition to her medical training, she had had some introduction to Arabic and cultural anthropology, and she states her philosophical position as an atheist and a Marxist. The account is almost wholly personal and anecdotal, but she conveys a sympathetic understanding of the feudal society of Yemen in most of its social aspects and describes the social life of the upper-class harems to good effect. Even though systematic detail is lacking, it is an important contribution to the small body of literature on the Yemen available. (Translated by D. McKee.)

Feilberg, Carl G.
    1944   *La tente noire; contribution ethnographique à l'histoire culturelle des nomades*, København, Gyldendal [also published as: Copenhagen, Nationalmuseet, Skrifter Etnografisk Raekke 2]. 12, 254 pp.; illus.

Construction and distribution of the northern Arabian pastoralists' black tent; its diffusion to Africa and Asia.

Fisher, William B.
    1958   *The Middle East; a physical, social, and regional geography*, 2d ed., London, Methuen.

The most useful geographical survey of Arabia is available in this book by a professional geographer.

Glubb, John Bagot
    1937   "Arab chivalry," *Royal Central Asian Society Journal 24*: 5-26.

A British officer and former commander of the Arab Legion of Jordan describes Bedouin social customs as chivalric, a widespread point of view among the post-World War I British in the Near East.

    1943   "The Sulubba and other ignoble tribes of southwestern Asia," in *The Yezidis, Sulubba, and Other Tribes of Iraq and Adjacent Regions,* Henry Field and John B. Glubb, *General*

Series in Anthropology No. 10, L. Spier, ed., Menasha, Wisc., G. Banta Publishing Co.: 14-17.

A brief and little-recognized sketch of the Sulubba, Sulailat, Hazim, Shararat, Awazim, and Hutaim folk of northern Arabia, who are without tribal organization in some cases and who are the lowest castes in desert society.

Gräf, Erwin
1952 "Das Rechtswesen der heutigen Beduinen," *Beiträge zur Sprach- und Kulturgeschichte des Orients Vol. 5*, Walldorf, Hesse, Orientkunde. 198 pp.; glossary.

A compilation of materials and summary of northern Arabian tribal law and terminology covering theft, inheritance, vengeance, and modes of trial by ordeal and oath.

Great Britain, Admiralty, Naval Intelligence Division.
1920 *A handbook of Arabia: I, general*, London, H. M. Stationery Office. 708 pp.

A geographical and tribal survey, with estimates of populations, herds, and productivity of the time. Still a useful source book for reconstruction.

Guarmani, Carlo C. C.
1938 *Northern Najd: a journey from Jerusalem to Anaiza in Qasim* (Translated by Lady Capel-Cure, introduction and notes by Douglas Carruthers), London, The Argonaut Press, xliv, 134 pp., map.

Guarmani, an Italian, made his journey to Anaiza about 1851, ostensibly in search of horses. He was traveling at the time the Rashid "house" of the Shammar were moving toward the defeat of the early Wahhabi movement. His account contains valuable descriptions of social and economic relations of the desert tribes and people. Carruthers' introduction is also useful in providing background and critical comments on Guarmani's observations and estimates of oasis settlement populations. The significance of horse breeding for export to India among the northern tribes is also indicated.

Hamilton, Robert Alexander Benjamin
1942 "The social organization of the tribes of the Aden Protectorate," *Royal Central Asian Society Journal 29*: 239-48.

A summary of Hamilton's concept of state and tribal confederation structures and social classes in the West Aden Protectorate.

1949 *The Kingdom of Melchior: adventure in South West Arabia*, London, John Murray. 10, 212 pp.; illus., maps.

Personal experiences of a British political officer in the Aden Protectorate during the 1930s, with much useful description of customs and social organization.

Hansen, Henny Harald
1961   "The pattern of women's seclusion and veiling in a Shi'a village," *Folk 3*: 23-42. Illus.

A study by a Danish social anthropologist and member of the Danish Archaeological Bahrain Expedition of 1960, made in the village of Sar, Manama, Bahrain. The meaning of seclusion and veiling in everyday life in a Bahrain village in relation to Quranic prescription.

Harris, Walter B.
1895   *A journey through the Yemen and some general remarks upon that country*, Edinburgh and London, William Blackwood and Sons. 12, 386 pp.; illus., maps, appendixes.

An informed British journalist's journey from Aden to San'a by merchant type caravan, and from San'a to Hodeidah under state escort. Good observations of village and caravanserai scenes, shortly after the Yemeni rebellion.

Harrison, Paul W.
1924   *The Arab at home*, New York, Thomas Y. Crowell. 12, 345 pp.; illus.

Useful general account of the ecological and social types found in eastern Arabia, the Persian Gulf, and Muscat.

1940   *Doctor in Arabia*, New York, The John Day Company. 303 pp.; illus., map.

An American medical missionary's account of experiences and observations of life in Muscat-Oman and the Persian Gulf from about 1900 to 1930. In spite of the style and special pleadings, there is excellent and wide-ranging material on economic activities, maritime and interior communities, change, and folk medicine.

Hartley, B. J.
1944   "Dry farming methods in the Aden Protectorate," in *Proceedings of the Conference on Middle East Agricultural Development*, Cairo, Middle East Supply Centre, Agriculture Report 6: 37-45.

Brief but concise description of cultivation techniques and adaptation in the Aden highlands (Audhali).

Hartley, John
1961   *The political organization of an Arab tribe of the Hadhramaut*, unpublished doctoral thesis, University of London School of Economics. 212 pp.; maps, figs.

The first study by an anthropologist of a South Arabian tribe, the Nahid, who are predominately spate flood farmers and whose political structure is characterized by the author as "bi-cephalous" or dual.

Hay, Rupert
1959 *The Persian Gulf states*, Washington, D.C., Middle East Institute. 17, 160 pp.; illus., map.

This succinct politico-historical account by the British Resident in the Persian Gulf from 1941 to 1949 brings up to its date Arnold Wilson's standard history, from the British point of view.

Henninger, Joseph
1959 "La societé bedouine ancienne," in *L'Antica Società Beduina*, Francesco Gabrieli, ed., Studi Semitici No. 2, Centro di Studi Semitici, Università di Roma, Roma: 29-93.

While Henninger is primarily concerned with the structure of pre-Islamic Bedouin society, he deals extensively with contemporary materials. He distinguishes as Bedouin those nomadic Arab camel pastoralists who have the warrior complex, and whose tribal status is superior to other social units in the desert.

Hess, J.
1938 *Von den Beduinen des innern Arabiens*, Zürich, Niehans. 177 pp.

A topically arranged account, with vocabularies and translations of stories of Bedouin life, taken from 'Utaibi tribesmen.

Hunter, Frederick M., and C. W. H. Sealy
1886 *An account of the Arab tribes in the vicinity of Aden*, Bombay, Central Government Press. 1, 75 pp.; appendixes.

The authors were first and second British Political Residents at Aden in the late nineteenth century. Geographical, historical, and tribal descriptions of the time, which include estimates and sources of tribal income of the 'Abdali (Lahej), Subaihi, 'Akrabi, Fadhali, Haushabi, 'Aulaki, Yafa'i, 'Alawi, Dhala, Wahidi, 'Irqa, Mahra, Kasa'di, Qu'aiti, and Kathiri groups.

Ingrams, Doreen
1949 *A survey of social and economic conditions in the Aden Protectorate*, Eritrea, Government Printer, British Administration. 216 pp.; illus., charts, map.

The only publication approaching an ethnographic survey of the area indicated by the title, by the wife of the British political officer stationed in the Hadhramaut during the late 1930s and '40s.

Ingrams, William Harold

1935   "House building in the Hadhramaut," *Geographical Journal* 85: 370-72.

A brief account of the structure of the multistoried dwellings of the wealthier classes in the ancient cities of the Hadhramaut.

1936   *A report on the social, economic and political condition of the Hadhramaut* (Colonial No. 123), London, H. M. Stationery Office, 177 pp., map.

A comprehensive survey, incorporating traditional history. The tribes, confederations, and organization of the Qu'aiti and Kathiri states are sketched.

1942   *Arabia and the Isles*, London, John Murray. 16, 367 pp.; illus., maps.

An officer in the British Colonial Administrative Service, Ingrams served in Zanzibar and then for some ten years in the Hadhramaut during the 1930s and 1940s. This account of his experiences is primarily concerned with pacifying the feuding tribes. A wealth of observational detail on all aspects of life in the Hadhramaut and Zanzibar. [3d ed. New York, Frederick A. Praeger, 1966. 10, 400 p.]

Jaussen, Antonin J.

1948   *Coutumes des Arabes au pays de Moab*, Paris, Adrien-Maisonneuve (reprint of 1908 edition). 9, 448 pp., illus., map.

A general account of family and household life, tribal organization and relationships, tribal law, economic life, and religion among the tribes east of the Jordan River in the late nineteenth century. Tribal lists of Moab and Negev areas. Mixes seminomads and full nomads.

Jayakar, A. S. G.

1900   "Report on the recent epidemic of cholera in Maskat and Matra, with a few general remarks on the epidemic in Oman," *Great Britain, Government of India, Administrative Report on the Persian Gulf Political Residence and the Maskat Political Residence, 1899-1900*, Bombay.

Apart from the epidemiology, this account sets out a good sociological description of Muscat, its ethnic composition and settlement pattern, and includes data on local medical practices. Jayakar, an "Anglo-Indian," was the Government doctor stationed at Muscat for many years.

Johnstone, T. M.
1961 "Some characteristics of the Dōsiri dialect of Arabic as spoken in Kuwait," *School of Oriental and African Studies, University of London, Bulletin 24*: 249-97.

This article contains a brief conversation between two Dōsiri Bedouin, brothers, which concerns camels, camping, and camel care; a unique document, however brief.

Johnstone, T. M., and J. Muir
1962 "Portuguese influences on shipbuilding in the Persian Gulf," *Mariner's Mirror 48*: 58-63.

Evidence in terms of techniques, from field observations, of diffusion of Portuguese techniques into Arab shipbuilding in the Persian Gulf.

Johnstone, T. M., and J. C. Wilkinson
1960 "Some geographical aspects of Qatar," *Geographical Journal 126*: 442-50. Map.

A brief historical and geological description of the peninsula of Qatar, with up-to-date information on the tribes living there.

Keith, Arthur, and Wilton M. Krogman
1932 "The racial characteristics of the southern Arabs," Appendix I in *Arabia Felix*, Bertram Thomas, New York, Charles Scribner's Sons: 301-33.

A discussion of the "racial affinities" of the southern Arabs, based on gross measurements of head and stature made by Thomas. The similarities to both African and Indian populations are noted, but explanation is speculative.

Kelly, John B.
1964 *Eastern Arabian frontiers*, New York, London; Frederick A. Praeger, Faber and Faber. 319 pp.; tribal lists, glossary, maps, bibliography in footnotes, appendixes of documents of arbitration, index.

A thorough and detailed history of the dispute over territorial claims to the Buraimi Oasis area by Saudi Arabia and the Arab States of the Persian Gulf, from the point of view of British "commitments" and interests in the oil resources. It is based on extensive archival research and knowledgeable travel in the area.

Kennett, Austin
1925 *Bedouin justice: laws & customs among the Egyptian Bedouin*, Cambridge, The University Press. 16, 158 pp.; illus.

Kennett was a British Administration Officer in the Libyan and Sinai areas after the First World War, and his material derives from his experiences. The Sinai material is most comparable to Arabian Bedouin. Somewhat anecdotal, it covers tribal organization, judicial processes of trial, blood payment, debts, land disputes, inheritance, wounds and damages, and the rights of women.

Landberg, Carlo
1901-13   *Études sur les dialectes de l'Arabie méridionale*, 2 vols. in 4, Vol. I, Hadramoût; Vol. II, Datînah; Vol. III, Datînah, Leyden, E. J. Brill.

These volumes contain many texts, with translations which include explicit ethnographic information on a wide variety of customs, crafts, classes, beliefs. Illustrations. Much of the information was recorded in Europe from informants who accompanied Landberg there.

Landen, Robert Geran
1967   *Oman since 1856; disruptive modernization in a traditional Arab society*, Princeton, Princeton University Press. 15, 488 pp.; tables, genealogical charts, maps, bibliographical notes, index.

A deeply documented and scholarly account of the Muscat-Oman Sultanate in its vicissitudes since 1856, under increasing and conflicting pressures from Western powers. It is not clear whether the author has ever visited the Sultanate itself. A good indication of the obstacles to access to archival resources in the bibliographical notes and in the description of those that are accessible.

Little, Otmar Henry
1925   *The geography and geology of Makalla (South Arabia)*, Cairo, Government Press.

Based on a survey trip made in 1919-20 by two English technical experts at the request of the Qu'aiti Sultan. Little's account contains a good deal of economic information on Makalla, its vicinity, and the Wadi Hajir.

Lorimer, J. G.
1908-15   *Gazetteer of the Persian Gulf, 'Oman, and Central Arabia*, 2 vols. in 4 parts, Calcutta, Superintendent of Government Printing, India. Illus., maps.

A monumental historical, geographical, and economic work on the Persian Gulf made available for public use in 1958. Extensive identification, location, and major features of ethnic groups, tribes, and settlements in the Gulf. Primarily political in orientation, and dated to about 1900.

MacIvor, I.
   1881   "Notes on sea-fishing in the Persian Gulf," in *Selections from the Records, no. 181, Administration Report of the Persian Gulf, 1880-81*, Great Britain, Government of India, Calcutta: 54-77.

   A summary by the then Assistant Political Resident of the Persian Gulf on fishing technology and the general economy of fishing in the Gulf. The most detailed description available, with a list of species taken.

Mikesell, Marvin K.
   1955.   "Notes on the dispersal of the dromedary," *Southwestern Journal of Anthropology* 11: 231-45.

   A paper by a geographer on the probably Oman origin of the single-humped camel and its dispersal in the Near East. It was probably domesticated by sedentary peoples.

Miles, Samuel B.
   1881   "Notes on the tribes of 'Oman," in *Selections from the Records, no. 181, Administration Report of the Persian Gulf, 1880-81*, Great Britain, Government of India, Calcutta: 29-44.

   A sketch of Muscat-Oman tribal structure, with a list of 135 tribes, their factional affiliation (Ghafiri or Hinawi), estimated population, districts, and villages. More detailed information on 23 important tribes, including their clans and their economic bases.

   1919   *The countries and tribes of the Persian Gulf*, 2 vols. London, Harrison and Sons.

   Miles was British Political Resident at Muscat during the late nineteenth and early twentieth centuries. This is a compilation of his several papers, largely historical and geographical, and primarily concerned with Muscat-Oman. (It was reprinted, with an introduction by J. B. Kelly, by Frank Cass, London, in 1966.)

Mockler, E.
   1886   "Note on the weights and measures employed in the pearl trade of the Persian Gulf," in *Administrative Report on the Persian Gulf . . . for 1885-86*, Great Britain, Government of India, Bombay: 110-16.

   A valuable essay on the several standards used in the Gulf and on the modes of making up parcels of pearls for sale to foreign markets. The role of competition between Arab sellers and Indian buyers is also noted. Mockler was the British Political Resident at Muscat.

Montagne, Robert

1932   "Notes sur la vie sociale et politique de l'Arabie du Nord: les Šemmar du Neǧd," *Revue des Études Islamiques 6*: 61-79.

Concise discussion of the structure of the Shammar tribes of the Nejd.

1935   "Contes poétiques Bédouins," *Bulletin d'Études Orientales 5*: 33-120. Illus., map.

A collection of Shammar texts with translations, prefaced by a useful history of the Shammar, discussion of tribal structure, economy, and effects of diversifying camel pastoralism with shepherding by groups which crossed the Euphrates to the Syrian Jazira.

1947   *La Civilisation du désert; nomades d'Orient et d'Afrique*, Paris, Hachette, 1947. 270 pp.; illus., figs., map.

Comparative study with Arabian data based chiefly on the Shammar tribes and emirate, but including the Saudi kingdom, shepherd tribes, and the sedentarization process.

Murphy, Robert F., and Leonard Kasdan

1959   "The structure of parallel cousin marriage," *American Anthropologist 61*: 17-29.

An analysis of first-cousin marriage among Bedouin, together with a description of tribal structure as comprising fissioning agnatic lines or patrilineages.

Musil, Alois

1926   *The northern Ḥeǧâz, a topographical itinerary*, New York, American Geographical Society. 16, 771 pp.; illus., map, 15 appendixes.

Journey in the summer of 1910 from Maan to 'Aqaba, south to Madian, thence to Sharma, and Tebuk, with scattered geographical and ethnographic material on the Shararat, 'Imran, Howaitat, Beni 'Atiyah, Bali, and settlements in their territories. This volume is notable for its illustration of the *rafiq* institution, of the conditions of life in the desert in summer (May-July), and for the less cohesive organization of tribal clans in this region than is found in the Syrian Desert.

1927a   *Arabia Deserta, a topographical itinerary*, New York, American Geographical Society. 17, 631 pp.; illus., maps, 8 appendixes.

Musil's journeys of 1908-09, 1912, 1914-15 in northern Arabia, moving largely with the shaykhly clan of the Rwala. The main text is full of ethnographic and ecological information scattered through the diary-form record. Besides the Rwala, information is given on the 'Amarat, Salubba, Fed'an,

Weld 'Ali, and Shararat. Musil was an historical geographer, professor of Oriental studies at Prague.

1927b   *The Middle Euphrates, a topographical itinerary*, New York, American Geographical Society. 15, 426 pp.; illus., maps, appendixes.

Expeditions of 1912 and 1915 to "southern Mesopotamia." Contact with the 'Amarat, 'Akaydat, Gbur, Zafa', Beni Tamin, Dlaym, Zabayd, and Sha'ban. Apart from tribal and clan lists, and locations, there is little ethnographic data.

1928a   *The manners and customs of the Rwala Bedouins*, New York, American Geographical Society. 14, 712 pp.; illus.

The most complete study available of a northern Arabian Bedouin tribal culture. Texts of poems, glossaries, anecdotes, and description based chiefly on material collected in 1908-09 on the paramount chief's clan. Technology, economics, sociology, ideology are covered. Information on social structure and economic organization seems weak in discussion, but not in implication to the skillful interpreter.

1928b   *Northern Neǧd, a topographical itinerary*, New York, American Geographical Society. 12, 368 pp.; illus., map, appendixes.

Journeys in 1915 in the Nefud, recording geographical and cultural information on the tribes: Shammar, Weld Sleyman, Hutaym, Az Zafir, and settlements in their territories. The Rashidi emirate (Shammar) was dominant at the time. Appendixes include histories of the rival chiefly families of Rashid and Sa'ud.

1928c   *Palmyrena, a topographical itinerary*, New York, American Geographical Society. 14, 367 pp.; illus., maps, appendixes.

Journeys of 1908, 1912, 1915, which provide scattered but important information on the Rwala, 'Umur, Fuwa're, Beni Khalid, Mawali, Sba'a, and Hadidiin tribes.

Niebuhr, Carsten

1792   *Travels through Arabia, and other countries in the East* (translated by Robert Heron), Edinburgh, R. Morison and Son.

A classic account by a Danish engineer of travel by a scientific mission from Europe. Sections on Sinai, the Yemen, and the Persian Gulf. Niebuhr's observations in the Yemen have been in part confirmed by twentieth-century visitors.

Oppenheim, Max von

1939-68   *Die Beduinen*, 4 vols. in 5, Leipzig, Otto Harrassowitz, 1939 (Vol. I), 1943 (Vol. II); Wiesbaden, Otto Harrassowitz, 1952 (Vol. III).

Begun by Oppenheim, an historian, Vol. III was completed and edited by Werner Caskel. Primarily ethnohistories of the Bedouin tribes, with information on their locations, annual migrations, and shaykhly families.

Patai, Raphael
  1948 "A survey of Near-Eastern anthropology," *New York Academy of Sciences, Transactions Series 2, 10*: 200-09.

  A survey in terms of the urban-peasant-pastoralist trichotomy of economic and community patterns of the Levant area of the Near East, and a call for more intensive study.

  1951 "Nomadism: Middle Eastern and Central Asian," *Southwestern Journal of Anthropology 7*: 401-14.

  Comparison of North Arabian and Central Asian cultural patterns among nomadic pastoralists, with trait differences emphasized.

  1952 "The Middle East as a culture area," *Middle East Journal 6*: 1-21.

  Generalized "culture traits" that characterize the Middle East as a bona fide culture area.

Pelly, Lewis
  1863 "Remarks on the tribes, trade, and resources around the shore line of the Persian Gulf," *Bombay Geographical Society Transactions 17*: 32-112.

  Covering both Arab and Persian sides of the Gulf, this survey illustrates the role of maritime Arabs in the collection and shipment of products of the Persian side to the Indian markets. Pelly was the British Political Resident in the Gulf at the time.

Philby, Harry St. John Bridger
  1933 *The empty quarter*, London, New York; Constable, Henry Holt. 24, 433 pp.; illus., map.

  Philby's 1932 crossing of the Rub' al Khali Desert, with a few interesting notes on the Murra tribe and its usage of parts of this desert.

  1952 *Arabian highlands*, Ithaca, New York, Cornell University Press. 16, 771 pp.; illus., maps, diagrams.

  Philby's accounts of several journeys made by camel and truck in southwestern Saudi Arabia in the 1930s. Detailed observations cover the topography, economy, settlements, tribes, markets, architecture, dress, customs, and personalities of Asir and the adjacent interior. Full of unsystematically arranged cultural data.

Philby, once a British officer (First World War), became a Muslim and went into private business in Arabia. His extensive travels have been recorded in a series of volumes, only two of which are noted here. All are of great value, but are difficult to use because of the diary arrangement.

Qubain, Fahim I.
1955 "Social classes and tensions in Bahrain," *Middle East Journal* 9: 269-80. Map.

A sociopolitical account of factions and issues in Bahrain society after the Second World War and the development of oil.

Raswan, Carl R.
1936 "Tribal areas and migration lines of the North Arabian Bedouins," *Geographical Review 20*: 494-502.

A short article, with a map of the areas claimed by the major North Arabian Bedouin tribes as their *dirahs*, or customary grazing territories.

1947 *Black tents of Arabia*, New York, Creative Age Press. 16, 206 pp.; illus.

Raswan's romanticized account of life among the Rwala Bedouin in the 1930s. Raswan is a horsebreeder.

Schorger, William D.
1958 "An anthropological frame of reference for research on the Middle East," *Report on Current Research on the Middle East*, Washington, D.C., Middle East Institute: 1-14.

Scott, Hugh
1942 *In the High Yemen*, London, John Murray. 19, 260 pp.; illus., figs., maps.

A British naturalist's account of his visit to Yemen (1938-39) for the British Museum of Natural History. A very useful account, with historical summary, of a trip limited in its range by political controls. Ecological diversity is set out clearly, with the climatic conditions indicated.

Serjeant, R. B.
1949 "The cemeteries of Tarīm (Ḥaḍhramawt) (with notes on sepulture)," *Le Muséon 62*: 151-60.

A discussion of the segregated cemeteries and the socioeconomic classes of Tarim, and of customs associated with the use of the cemeteries.

Serjeant is Professor of Arabic at Cambridge University.

1950 "The Quarters of Tarīm and their Tanṣūrahs," *Le Muséon 63*: 277-84.

The tansurahs are rally-chants of the quarters, which are used on all communal occasions and in times of crises such as fire or flood.

1951　*South Arabian poetry, I: prose and poetry from Hadhramawt*, London, Taylor's Foreign Press. 14, 87 pp. (English introduction); 173 pp. (Arabic texts).

Texts in Arabic and an excellent introductory section on contemporary poetry and song in South Arabia and their sociological contexts. Commercial recordings available are listed.

1953　"Notes on Ṣubaiḥi territory west of Aden," *Le Muséon 66*: 123-31.

A brief account of the Subaihi tribe of the former West Aden Protectorate; they are camel breeders and small cultivators and possess a star calendar.

1957　"The Saiyids of Hadhramawt," London, Luzac.

An historical and functional study of the Saiyid class.

Smith, W. Robertson

1885　*Kinship and marriage in early Arabia*, Cambridge, The University Press. 14, 322 pp. (Reprinted from the 1903 edition with a Preface by E. L. Peters, by Beacon Press, Boston, 1966.)

A classic study of kinship structure and custom in Arabia; its thesis is the priority of matrilineal over patrilineal systems; its chief value is the keen exposition of kinship structured society in this area.

Smith was a nineteenth-century Orientalist who participated in the interest of scholars in this field in reconstructing from documentary evidence the society of early and pre-Islamic times.

Stark, Freya

1936　*The southern gates of Arabia; a journey in the Hadramaut*, London, John Murray. 282 pp.; illus., map, appendix.

Account of a trip from Makalla to the Hadhramaut towns, about 1935, by a well-known literary journalist and Arabist. Useful observations and anecdotes on the harim side of life among the elite.

Sweet, Louise E.

1964　"Pirates or polities? Arab societies of the Persian or Arabian Gulf, eighteenth century," *Ethnohistory 11*: 262-80.

A discussion of the eighteenth-century Arab societies of the Persian Gulf as polities in the process of expansion, in contrast to the British view of their raiding customs as "piratical."

1965a "Camel pastoralism in North Arabia and the minimal camping unit," in *Man, Culture, and Animals: The Role of Animals in Human Ecological Adjustments*, American Association for the Advancement of Science, No. 78, Washington, D.C.:129-52.

1965b "Camel raiding of North Arabia Bedouin: a mechanism of ecological adaptation," *American Anthropologist 67*: 1132-50.

These two papers (1965a, b) discuss, from the literature and from informants' accounts in Kuwait, some of the ecological adaptations characteristic of North Arabian Bedouin societies.

Thesiger, Wilfred P.
1959 *Arabian Sands*, New York, London; Dutton, Longmans. 16, 326 pp.; illus., maps.

Thesiger, a British geographer and explorer, made a number of journeys in South Arabia, with tribesmen, between 1945 and 1950. Scattered ethnographic detail upon the Mahra, Bait Kathir, Rawashid, Manahil, Sa'ar, 'Awamir, Junuba, Wahiba, and Duru—the pastoral tribes along the southern and eastern boundaries of the Rub' al Khali.

Thomas, Bertram Sidney
1929 "Among some unknown tribes of South Arabia," *Royal Anthropological Institute Journal 59*: 97-111.

Observations and speculations on the Hadara group of tribes of the Dhufar region, South Arabia. (Harasis, Bautahara, Mahra, Qarah, and Shahara.)

1931 *Alarms and excursions in Arabia*, London, Indianapolis; George Allen and Unwin, Bobbs-Merrill.

1932 *Arabia Felix: across the "empty quarter" of Arabia*, New York, Charles Scribner's Sons. 29, 397 pp.; illus., appendix by Keith and Krogman (q.v.).

Extensive material on Dhufar, the Qarah, and other Hadara tribes, and on the Bedouin of the southern border of the Rub' al Khali, especially the Rawashid.

1938 "Four strange tongues from South Arabia: the Hadara group," *British Academy, Proceedings, 23*, London, Humphrey Milford. 105 pp.; map.

The Dhufar area tribes and their sections, listed with notes on their interrelations and peculiarities.

Twitchell, Karl S.
   1958   *Saudi Arabia; with an account of the development of its natural resources*, 3d ed. Princeton, Princeton University Press.

   A useful discussion of the scenes in Saudi Arabia since the development of oil.

Van den Berg, L. W. C.
   1886   *Le Hadhramout et les Colonies Arabes de l'Archipel Indien*, Batavia, Java. 7, 292 pp.; illus., map.

   Part One of this book, pp. 9-103, constitutes a description of the Hadhramaut based on interviews with natives who had emigrated from there to the Dutch East Indies. The account is comprehensive, but shows a Saiyid-merchant bias in the informants. Two major omissions are the transport functions of the Bedouin and tribesmen and the saints' cults. The information on commercial practices is not paralleled anywhere.

   Van den Berg was an official in the Dutch Colonial Administration.

Van der Meulen, Daniël
   1947   *Aden to the Hadhramaut: a journey in South Arabia*, London, John Murray. 16, 254 pp.; illus., map, glossary.

   The author served as a Dutch Colonial Administration Officer in the East Indies and as a diplomat in Arabia. This account is of a journey in 1939, before the Second World War and its aftereffects had seriously reduced the resources of the Hadhrami Saiyids and merchants whose wealth derived from the East Indies. This account also precedes the general truce and pacification of the area under W. H. Ingrams. Apart from considerable bias, the account contains many useful observations.

Van der Meulen, Daniël, and Hermann von Wissmann
   1932   *Hadramaut: some of its mysteries unveiled* (translated by M. Barber), London, Luzac.

   A journey in 1931 from Makalla via the Wadi Do'an to the towns of the Hadhramaut valley. Scattered useful observations of customs, settlements, geography.

Vidal, F. S.
   1955   *The oasis of Al-Hasa*, Drahran, Arabian American Oil Company.

   A circumspect geographical and economic study of the highly productive oasis of Al Hasa, in eastern Saudi Arabia. Abundant illustrations, settlement and dwelling plans.

Villiers, Alan John
  1940 *Sons of Sinbad: an account of sailing with the Arabs in their dhows. . . . ,* New York, Charles Scribner's Sons.

  An account of Villiers' voyages with Arab dhows in the Red Sea and Indian Ocean; the major voyage was in a Kuwait-owned dhow from Aden to East Africa, finally returning to the Persian Gulf ports.

  1948 "Some aspects of the Arab dhow trade," *Middle East Journal* 2: 399-416.

  Structure and operation of Arab ships and sea trading in 1938-39, with comment on the successful persistence of this commercial pattern in spite of industrial shipping.

  1952 *Monsoon seas: the story of the Indian Ocean,* New York, McGraw-Hill.

  A well-written, popular account, containing useful observations on Arab sea voyages and trading, from experience. As a well-informed professional seaman, Villiers supplies many technical details and a good discussion of economic organization and changes.

Wilson, Arnold T.
  1954 *The Persian Gulf; an historical sketch from the earliest times to the beginning of the twentieth century* (second impression), London, Allen and Unwin. 13, 327 pp.; appendix, map.

  A useful, standard history of the Gulf area from the British point of view. The appendix ("A Summary of Scientific Research in the Persian Gulf") and the bibliography are especially useful guides.

Wolf, Eric R.
  1951 "The social organization of Mecca and the origins of Islam," *Southwestern Journal of Anthropology* 7: 329-56.

  An interesting interpretation of the "rise of Islam" as a change from a kin-based society to a rudimentary state structure.

Zwemer, Samuel M.
  1900 *Arabia: the cradle of Islam,* 3d ed., revised, New York, Fleming H. Revell. 437 pp.; illus., maps.

  Subtitle: "Studies in the geography, people and politics of the Peninsula with an account of Islam and mission work." Apart from the American missionary's bias, there is much pre-oil and pre-World Wars detail, particularly on Muscat and the Persian Gulf, where Zwemer was stationed in a medical mission station of the American Dutch Reformed Church.

Addenda to Bibliography, 1971

Journal literature on current events accumulates on the Arabian Peninsula, but, with the continued medieval hostility to uncommitted social scientists by the ruling or controlling regimes or established commercial and industrial corporations, the availability of such studies as have been made is very low. A few bona fide anthropologists and linguists are known to have done some research in various parts of the Peninsula, but it is fruitless to cite other than the meager number of titles below.

L.E.S.

Bujra, A. S.
    1967   "Political conflict and stratification in Ḥaḍramaut," *Middle Eastern Studies 3*: 355-75; *4*: 1-28.

Diqs, Isaak
    1967   *A Bedouin boyhood*, London, George Allen and Unwin. 7, 176 pp.

            Autobiographical sketches by a young man of "Bedouin" tribal origin, educated in the Western tradition in Jordan and Saudi Arabian schools and colleges. The anecdotes are stereotypical and sentimentalized, but a sympathetic picture is presented of individuals and social events. The economic background is limited-range shepherding rather than camel nomadism in a state-controlled system.

Hansen, Henny Harald
    1968   "Investigations in a Shī'a village in Bahrain," Copenhagen, *Nationalmuseet, Skrifter, Etnografisk Raekke 12.* 208 pp.; drawings, photographs, map, references.

            An historical and descriptive monograph of the village of Sār (pop. ca. 450), Bahrain Island, Bahrain, based on two months of resident field work under limited conditions in 1960, supplemented by visits and area travels.

            Dr. Hansen was a member of the Danish Bahrein Expedition, and the monograph suitably supports her ethnographic collection for the National Museum of Denmark. Special focus is given her view of the women's pattern of life, material culture, and the customs followed during Ramadan.

Hijazi, A.
    1964   "Kuwait: development from a semitribal, semicolonial society to democracy and sovereignty," *American Journal of Comparative Law 13*: 418-38.

Kuwait, Ministry of Education
  1966 *Archeological investigations in the Island of Failaka*, Kuwait (in Arabic).

Serjeant, R. B.
  1968 "Fisher-folk and fish-traps in al-Bahrain," *School of Oriental and African Studies, University of London, Bulletin 31*: 486-514. Drawings, photographs.

  A detailed "Orientalist" description of the technology and economics of the ḥaḍrah, or tidal fish weirs of Bahrain, replete with annotations and vocabulary. A thorough, scholarly, descriptive essay, though lacking in clarity of organization and analysis.

Winder, Richard Bayly
  1965 *Saudi Arabia in the nineteenth century*, New York, St. Martin's Press. 14, 312 pp.; illus., maps, bibliog., index.

  History of the rise and fall of the nineteenth-century "commonwealth of Wahhabi village puritans," as the background to the formation in the twentieth century of the Saudi monarchy.

CHAPTER 5

Israel

ALEX WEINGROD

Israel is a small, culturally Western nation, situated along the Eastern Mediterranean coast. Although sharing borders with four other Middle Eastern states (Lebanon, Syria, Jordan, and Egypt), there are major cultural differences between Israel and the adjoining nations. Prior to Israel's establishment in 1948, the population included an Arab majority and a Jewish minority. Since 1948, however, this population ratio has been reversed: many Arabs left the country during the 1947-48 war, and, in addition, a large-scale Jewish immigration has subsequently taken place. This population shift differentiates Israel from other Middle Eastern states, and lends it its distinctive sociocultural character.

These population changes are summarized in Tables I and II. Table I shows that in the eighteen-year period between 1947 and 1965, the size of the Jewish group increased by more than 300 per cent, while the Arab population decreased by 60 per cent. Moreover, immigration also

TABLE I

ISRAEL POPULATION

1947-1965 BY RELIGIOUS GROUP*

	1947	1949	1955	1965
Jews	630,000	1,013,900	1,590,500	2,299,100
Arabs	740,000	160,000	198,600	299,300
Muslims		111,500	136,300	212,408
Christians		34,000	43,300	57,100
Others		14,500	19,000	29,808
Total	1,370,000	1,173,900	1,789,100	2,598,400

*From the *Statistical Abstract of Israel 1965*, Table I.

267

resulted in a culturally heterogeneous Jewish population. Prior to 1948, the Jewish group was mainly composed of European-born immigrants. As shown in Table II, since 1948 there has been a large-scale movement of Jews from Middle Eastern and North African countries to Israel; the proportion of European-born immigrants fell from nearly 90 per cent during 1919-47, to less than 45 per cent in 1948-58. Migrations have therefore resulted in a shift from a dual Jewish-Arab society with a homogeneous Jewish population, to a dominant, multiethnic Jewish community with an Arab minority.

These population statistics underscore two key features of Israeli social and cultural structure: the diversity of the population and the rapid changes that have recently taken place. These two themes are emphasized throughout this chapter. The over-all organization of the chapter may be summarized as follows:

Numerous locally organized groups divide Israeli society into a variety of distinctive social units. Each group possesses its own social and cultural organization, in which its unique patterns are expressed. A series of national economic, political, and social institutions also cuts across the society; these institutions provide points of contact and linkage between local groups and, in addition, expose the numerous subgroups to the dominant culture. Set within a small territory, and including a comparatively small population, the various groups interact with one another. This interaction, as well as the new conditions brought about by migration and the formation of the state, have resulted in processes of rapid social and cultural change. Thus, how Israeli society is organized, and the processes and directions of change, are the central problems posed in this chapter.

TABLE II
JEWISH IMMIGRANTS BY
PERIOD AND CONTINENT OF BIRTH*

	1919-1948	1948-1958
Total immigrants	452,306	932,833
Total per cent	100.00	100.00
Europe	87.50	44.50
Middle East	9.70	29.60
North Africa	1.00	25.00
Other	1.80	.90

*[Patinkin 1960: 22.]

A Review of Cultural Antecedents

The emphasis in this analysis is upon contemporary patterns of social organization. However, these patterns cannot be properly understood without reference to recent historic developments. In particular, an analysis of the early twentieth-century Jewish colonization movement is crucial to understanding contemporary Israeli society: this movement shaped many of the present-day Israeli institutions, and certain of its ideals continue to be viable. Although the description that follows is very selective, it does indicate some of the salient features of the colonization culture (Eisenstadt 1954: chap. 3).

The Jewish colonization movement—which began in the 1880s and continued until the establishment of Israel in 1948—was composed primarily of self-selected persons. Most immigrants were young and unmarried, and the majority came from the countries of Eastern Europe. Pre-Revolutionary Russian thought shaped the immigrants' ideals: they "assimilated the humanist-liberal, radical and social democratic traditions of intellectual revolt" typical of pre-Revolutionary Russia, and then transformed these traditions into the guiding principles of the colonization movement (Berlin 1958: 208).

Zionism, socialism, and pioneering were the main emphases in the colonization culture. Zionism stressed the establishment of an autonomous Jewish society: the immigrants believed that the "Jewish problem" would only be solved by the creation of an independent Jewish state. Zionism therefore had political, economic, and cultural implications. The small Jewish community quickly developed its own political institutions; although under Turkish and later British rule, it successfully organized a kind of "quasi-government." To give several examples, a national representative assembly was elected, a clandestine army (the Haganah) organized, and the Jewish Agency formally represented the Jewish community before various international bodies. These national-scale agencies also engaged in important economic activities; public funds were channeled by the authorities into various development projects (for example the purchase of land or financial assistance to new settlements). Such economic planning and development activities were key aspects of the colonization program.

Cultural autonomy—another feature of the Zionist program—is best illustrated by the renaissance of Hebrew: previously limited to sacred use, Hebrew became the settlers' language of conversation, and books and plays were also written in Hebrew. At the same time, however, the colonists never severed their connections with modern European culture. On the contrary: they were closely bound to, and influenced by, political and literary developments in the Western world. Thus although linguistically distinctive, the cultural style of the colonization movement was fundamentally European. It should also be noted that the colonists were secular in outlook: many rejected the orthodox religious tradition and wished instead to create a new type of Jewish secular culture.

The immigrants' socialism rested upon the wish to fashion a Utopian society: a classless, cooperative society, free of social and economic exploitation, represented the immigrants' desired goal. Jews were to fill all economic roles, and the positive virtues of work—and particularly of farming—were stressed; indeed, physical labor and simplicity in dress and possessions were idealized. In addition, national-scale organization and a type of welfare state political-economic system were other dominant features of the emergent Jewish community. These tendencies were best illustrated by the Histadruth, the General Federation of Jewish Workers. The Histadruth organized the various Jewish workers into national unions. In addition, it established major industrial enterprises (particularly in building and transportation) and created a system of social insurance and health clinics. These activities aimed at establishing a worker-controlled, egalitarian economic system; although privately-owned enterprises were also prevalent, the government and Histadruth-directed economic resources were major factors in the new colonization economy.

Pioneering was an expression of both Zionist and socialist ideals. The pioneers, or chalutzim, were persons responsive to national needs—persons who valued public service and who participated in national endeavors. For example groups of pioneers established new farming communities in remote, isolated areas; in this fashion they settled lands claimed by the nascent Jewish state and also contributed to building a worker's economy. Not all of the colonists were pioneers; but the pioneering ethic was influential throughout the Jewish community, and the political elite was dominated by its members.

These features of the colonization culture are important for understanding contemporary Israeli life. However, it should again be emphasized that the ideals described were dominant tendencies and that other value-systems were also present. For example the pioneer-socialist ethic did not embrace the small numbers of Yemenite and Kurdish Jews who immigrated during the early twentieth century and who maintained a separate cultural life; neither did it extend to urban middle-class or orthodox religious elements in the Jewish population. The colonization culture did, however, shape the political and economic institutions that subsequently became dominant in Israel; and it has also continued to be a powerful cultural force, influencing both new immigrants as well as the native Arab population.

The prestate Jewish society was a small, intensely-interacting community, in which the leading institutions (such as the Histadruth or the settlement movements) functioned with a minimum of bureaucratic organization; voluntary groups were dominant during this formative period, and the society was open and highly mobile. As Eisenstadt stresses, the prevailing cultural homogeneity and ideological consensus permitted the rapid absorption of new immigrants (Eisenstadt 1954: 64). Poststate immigration, on the other hand, differed fundamentally from this type of society. Most immigrants who entered Israel following 1948 were not self-selected, but instead were part of mass immigration movements. The newcomers immigrated in family groups, and they included a broad population spectrum (Sicron 1957). Immigration was particularly large during the 1948-51 period, when more than 600,000 immigrants entered the country; since 1951, the yearly rate has been considerably smaller. Unlike the early colonists, these immigrants—including European survivors of World War II and Jews from throughout the Middle East and North Africa—were not drawn by a socialist-pioneering ideology, but rather were fleeing from their former lands or were attracted by the promise of a Jewish state. Moreover, many of the newcomers (particularly from Yemen and from rural areas in Iraq and North Africa) were almost totally unfamiliar with modern Western civilization, while others (from Tunisia and Morocco, for example) had comparatively recent contacts with Western urban ways of life. Most of the immigrants did not share the ideological principles of the earlier colonists, and in many cases they also represented different civilizations. Poststate mass immigration therefore led to increased cultural heterogeneity and produced new conditions of culture contact and change. Although, as was earlier pointed out, small numbers of Middle Eastern Jews had previously immigrated during the prestate period, mass immigration resulted in the emergence of a multiethnic Jewish community.

Population and Ecology

Israel is the smallest state in the Middle East: its length is only 426 miles, and it varies in width from 12 miles (near Petach Tikva) to approximately 70 miles in the southern Negev. The total land area includes 7,993 square miles, of which roughly three fifths is classed as cultivable. Israel's topography is, in general, similar to that of the neighboring countries, and it is usually classed as forming part of the Levant. The northern Galilee region, for example, is similar to highland areas in Syria and Lebanon, and the southern Negev resembles the adjoining Sinai Desert.

Although the total land area is exceedingly small, there are wide internal variations in rainfall, temperature, and altitude. Rainfall is heaviest in the northern and central regions, while there is very little annual precipitation in the southern desert area. The rains are concentrated during the winter months (November through March), and rain does not normally fall during the summer. Temperatures are moderate, ranging from winter low temperatures of 35-40 degrees to summer highs of 85-90 degrees. Temperatures vary between areas, however, and are higher in the southern desert and several northern valleys (e.g. the Jordan and Beth-Shan valleys) than they are along the central coastal strip or in the more hilly zones. Although there are no high mountain areas, the northern Galilee and Jerusalem regions may be classed as hilly regions, while the coastal strip and large areas in the south are plain or plateaulike. In general, rainfall decreases and temperature increases from north to south, and the altitude rises in a general west-east slope.

These differences in topography and climate give rise to numerous small ecological zones. In the northern region, for example, one moves quickly from a narrow coastal strip to more hilly regions, and then to several fertile valleys, followed by the deep depression near the Sea of Galilee. Within each of these zones, distinctive types of agricultural or settlement adaptations have been made: different crops are grown, and the village or town residential patterns may differ. Small in size and exceedingly diverse, these zones lend an irregular pattern to the countryside.

Four larger ecological regions may be distinguished: the northern region, extending from Haifa to the Syrian and Lebanese borders in the north and including both the Western and Upper Galilee; the coastal region, a narrow strip stretching along the Mediterranean from south of Haifa to Ashcalon near the Gaza Strip; the Jerusalem region, including the city of Jerusalem and the nearby hilly zone; and the southern Negev Desert, extending from Beersheba in the north to Eilat on the Red Sea. Although, as has already been noted, these regions include various smaller zones, this division emphasizes some of the key ecological features of the country.

The northern region is typically hilly, although it also includes several fertile valleys and the depression around the Sea of Galilee. This area receives substantial amounts of winter rainfall (annual average rainfall ranges from between 450-600 mm.) and has traditionally been an agricultural center. The main crops grown are cereals, fruit, vegetables, and grapes; cotton and sugar beets have also recently been introduced in several zones. Haifa, a port town with a population of 200,000, is the only urban center in the north. The Haifa area includes extensive shipping facilities and heavy industrial development, as well as light manufacturing and commercial facilities. Other towns in this region include the traditional centers of Acre, Nazareth, Tiberias, and Safad, as well as newer towns such as Affula and Kiryat Shmona. This region includes approximately 25 per cent of the total Jewish population, and 80 per cent of the Arab population.

The coastal region includes the narrow, level plain along the shores of the Mediterranean. This region has mild winters and hot, moist summers, and also receives adequate amounts of winter rain. Citrus groves are extensively planted, and vegetable production and dairying are also well developed. This area includes the heaviest concentration of population—more than 50 per cent of the total population live here. Although it includes roughly 13 per cent of the Arab population, the majority of the population is composed of Jews residing in a series of urbanized communities. An urban cluster centered around Tel Aviv extends from Nathanya in the north to Rechovoth in the south. Tel Aviv, the largest city in Israel, has a population of 400,000. While many of the communities in this cluster are small in size, the net effect of their proximity is the creation of a zone of dense population concentration. This region is Israel's industrial, commercial, administrative, and cultural base; with Tel Aviv at its center, the coastal plain is the hub of the entire country, and other regions are its periphery.

The Jerusalem region extends outward from the coastal plain and includes the city of Jerusalem and the slim band connecting it with the coast. Winters are more severe in this hilly region than along the coast, and the summers considerably cooler. Although a string of new settlements have been established nearby, Jerusalem is, in effect, a city without a hinterland; the limited agricultural activity in this region is mainly based upon fruit cultivation. Jerusalem is the capital of Israel and is the seat of numerous government offices as well as the Hebrew University. A city with a population of 190,000, it is primarily an administrative and educational center, although it also includes some light industrial and commercial enterprises.

. The largest region territorially, but smallest in population, is the Negev: it includes 60 per cent of the total land area, but only 4 per cent of the population. Stretching from north of Beersheba to Eilat on the Red Sea, the Negev includes both areas of arable land and an extensive rocky desert. Rainfall in the northern portions averages 180 mm. per year, while in the south, precipitation rarely occurs. Irrigation agriculture, based mainly upon grains, vegetables, and industrial crops, is widely developed in the zone north of Beersheba, where many new villages have been established. Mineral deposits have also been developed in the Negev, particularly in the Dead Sea area. Beersheba, with a population of 65,000, is the largest town in this region; several small new "development towns" have also been formed. Israel's small Bedouin population is concentrated in this region, mainly in the area south of Beersheba.

As is indicated in this brief summary, the population as a whole is unevenly distributed throughout the countryside: although government policy has aimed at dispersing the Jewish population, the coastal strip is densely populated, while the Negev and parts of the northern region are sparsely settled. Moreover, the Arab population is concentrated in the north, with small pockets in the coastal region and in the south, while the Jewish population is heaviest along the coastal plain. In addition, within the Jewish population, the immigrant groups have frequently become concentrated in different zones. Ethnic trends in Jewish settlement patterns are summarized in Table III.

TABLE III
JEWISH IMMIGRANTS
BY DISTRICT, YEAR, AND PLACE OF BIRTH*

	Europe		North Africa, Middle East		Other	Native	Total
	To-1947	Post-1947	To-1947	Post-1947			
North	8.5	17.2	.5	30.9	4.7	38.2	100.00
Haifa	16.8	26.8	1.3	15.7	4.0	35.4	100.00
Central	9.9	18.3	2.0	27.9	4.0	37.9	100.00
Tel Aviv	21.9	20.0	3.9	12.1	4.9	37.2	100.00
Jerusalem	9.4	8.7	3.7	22.8	5.4	50.0	100.00
South	3.4	13.8	.4	43.0	5.4	34.0	100.00

*Based on the *Statistical Abstract of Israel 1962*: 23.

This table records two different trends. On the one hand, each district includes some proportion of immigrants from both European and Middle Eastern countries, as well as native-born Israelis. For example the proportion of native-born persons is generally the same throughout, with the exception of the Jerusalem district, where it is higher. One may therefore conclude that Jewish settlement patterns do not indicate any gross segregation between immigrant groups and native-born persons, or between immigrants from different world regions. At the same time, however, differences in concentration between the immigrants' groups do exist. The urbanized Tel Aviv and Haifa districts have a high proportion of European immigrants, while the southern district contains a large proportion of Middle Eastern immigrants. Ethnic concentration is particularly striking in new immigrant villages and towns in the northern and southern regions. Most immigrant villages also contain a single ethnic group, and many of the "development towns" have a high proportion of immigrants from North Africa.

It should also be noted that residential separation tends to divide the orthodox religious segments of the Jewish population from other groups. While in most respects the state and its citizens can be characterized as "secular" in outlook, the Jewish orthodox groups constitute a sizable minority. These groups are largely European in origin, and form close neighborhoods in Jerusalem, Bnai Brak, and Nathanya, as well as forming residential clusters in other towns. A number of villages are also composed of orthodox religious Jews. Internal social life in these sections is guided by religious law and custom, and these areas therefore contrast sharply with other neighborhoods.

This analysis of regional topography and national population stresses some of the differences which divide Israel both naturally and socially. While these distinctions are crucial for an analysis of Israeli society, it should also be recalled that the total land area is exceedingly small and that the various regions or cultural groups are closely linked with one another. The sheer smallness of the country gives rise to a condition in which no region is truly remote from others. A well-developed road and rail system links the regions to one another; Beersheba in the south or Haifa in the north are no more than a few hours' travel from either Tel Aviv or Jerusalem. Moreover, none of the regions is extensive in size, and each includes members of the various religious or ethnic groups. The relatively small population also contributes to a sense of cohesion: social networks are often national in scale, joining together members of common interest or occupational groups or kinsmen and persons who share an ethnic tradition. In general, neither ecological differences nor population concentration has given rise to political or cultural "regionalism"; the various regions and groups are tightly linked within the confines of a small nation.

In concluding this section on population and ecology, it is also important to point out that while mass immigration has dramatically changed the character of the Jewish population, the population now includes an ever-larger proportion of younger persons who were born in Israel. As shown in Table IV, 34 per cent of the total population are in the age-group 0-14, and another 23 per cent are in the 15-29 category. This high proportion of young persons has important social, economic,

TABLE IV
POPULATION BY AGE
AND RELIGIOUS GROUP (1965)*

Age	Jews	Arabs	Total
0-14	32.4	50.0	34.4
15-29	23.8	24.2	23.9
30-44	17.9	12.9	17.4
45-64	19.6	8.7	18.3
65+	6.3	4.2	6.0

*Taken from the *Statistical Abstract of Israel 1965*, p. 36.

and political implications. For example, it indicates that internal pressures on the economy for housing and jobs will grow and that new political attitudes and alliances may be formed. What is even more important for present purposes, these figures suggest that Israel is moving into a kind of "postimmigration" period, in which a growing number of persons are born and become socialized in the country itself. Thus while ethnic and cultural divisions will continue to have relevance for all age-groups, the increased number of Israeli-born persons in the population is likely to magnify the range of common symbols and experience and will therefore give new definitions and meanings to the various immigrant ethnic groups.

Local Organization: City, Town, and Village

Israel is a highly urbanized nation: more than a third of the population lives in Tel Aviv, Haifa, and Jerusalem, and Tel Aviv alone includes 18 per cent of the total population. Striking differences in residential patterns exist between Jews and Arabs, however: 83 per cent of the Jewish population lives in cities and towns and 17 per cent in villages; while among the Arab groups the proportions are nearly reversed. Urbanism is, nonetheless, a major force throughout the society, and is influential in all sectors of the community.

Tel Aviv, Haifa, and Jerusalem, all of which are comparatively new cities, are constructurally and architecturally akin to modern Western cities. For example, walled quarters are absent, and the relatively new concrete buildings are based upon recent Western designs. As is typical of immigration conditions, these cities include some neighborhoods of distinct cultural concentration. Residential differences exist between the veteran, prestate population and the more recent immigrant groups. Immigrants have tended to concentrate on the peripheries of most cities—where housing was made available to them by government agencies—while the veteran population has remained in the center or moved to suburban areas. Ethnic clustering of population also occurs; some neighborhoods include a heavy concentration of immigrants (from Yemen or Rumania, for example), while in other areas social class or other criteria form the basis of residence.

These neighborhoods are often zones of intense social and cultural activity. The ethnic residential clusters are a locus for distinctive cultural expression, in regard to such matters as language, dress, or general lifestyle. Artificially created by the pressure of rapid migration, some neighborhoods quickly change their character; the original immigrants move out and become dispersed to other zones, and others replace them.

Urban social organization is based upon four main types of primary groups: family and kinship, age-groups, occupational groups, and voluntary associations. A major point to recognize is that the organization and cultural modes of these groups differ widely between persons from European and Middle Eastern background. In regard to family and kinship, persons of European origin tend to marry at an older age, and also to have smaller families, than do Middle Easterners. Talmon calls urban European families "non-familistic": i.e. they are characterized by the "delegation of functions to other institutions, discontinuity between familial and social roles and atomization of the nuclear family." Among Europeans, the family is not an embracing economic or political unit, but rather "different members of the family participate in different organizations and associations and perform many roles which are independent of their family roles." Talmon adds that "economic continuity, financial assistance and mutual aid" are established between kinsmen, and that "families maintain close relations through frequent visits." In brief, urban European families in Israel are similar to those in other modern Western settings (Talmon 1954: 343-44).

In contrast with European families, Middle Eastern families are typically extended units whose members engage in multiple, family-oriented activities. Although significant differences exist among the Middle Eastern groups (for example, Kurdish and Moroccan families are structurally different), the families in this category are similar in that family ties and activities are extensive (Feitelson 1959, Goitein 1955, Weingrod 1960). Parental authority tends to be strong, and while in recent years joint family traditions have become less binding, family members continue to have mutual responsibilities; they often engage in cooperative household and economic activities, for example. Kinship tends to be traced bilaterally, and well-defined lineages do not exist. Extensive and stable relations are maintained between kinsmen, and, as Talmon comments (1954: 345), the community is "an aggregate of families and within it families of kinsmen tend to cluster and to form united power groups." Thus, among these groups the family is the basic unit of social organization, and family groups have important social, economic, and political functions.

Age-groups, composed of adolescent youngsters, are another important aspect of urban social structure; indeed, "youth culture" is a distinctive feature of Israeli life, and these groups have had important socialization functions. Formally organized age-groups are typically affiliated with national youth movements, most of which are adjuncts of Israeli political parties. The principal aim of the youth movements is to develop a "socialist-pioneering" ideology among its members; some youngsters are actively engaged in national tasks, particularly in the establishment of new agricultural settlements. Youth movements have also recently emphasized more general educational, social, and recreational activities. Membership in these groups is drawn from all sections of the youth population. In addition to these units, informal age-groups and cliques are also widespread. Deviant groups of delinquent youth have also been noted in urban settings. These groups are mainly composed of immigrant youngsters, and their behavior is closely related to problems of immigrant family adjustment to new urban conditions (Eisenstadt and Ben David 1956).

Occupational groups form another important unit of local social organization. Most business and industrial enterprises in Israel are of the usual Western type, in which the organization is extensive, rational, and systematically bureaucratized. Although industrial plant or office work situations have not been studied systematically, several general observations may be offered. Work groups are points of contact and linkage between different segments of the population; in this sense they serve a general integrative function among the disparate elements of urban society. In the hierarchy of work itself, however, the veteran population tends to hold higher income and status positions than do the immigrant groups. This relationship is expected, since most immigrants arrived with little capital and few of the skills required by a modern Western technology. In addition, Europeans as a group also hold higher income and authority positions than do persons of Middle Eastern origin; Europeans comprise a high proportion of persons holding managerial positions, while Middle Easterners include the bulk of unskilled workers. These contrasts are mainly the result of differences in skills (most notably in education) between ethnic groups, although other social factors may also give preference to Europeans (Patinkin 1960: 26, Table IV). Thus although work situations do have an integrative function, they also reflect important income and power distinctions between different groups in the population. It should also be noted that the members of occupational groups are organized within numerous local or national unions and professional organizations. These organizations provide wider contacts among persons sharing common occupational interests.

In describing voluntary associations, Eisenstadt (1956) distinguishes between groups whose functions are purely social and groups having an ideological or political orientation. "Social" groups are widely distributed throughout urban society, and members of these groups form small cliques and circles. In many cases they are based upon common ethnic backgrounds. In addition, immigrants have often formed politically-oriented "landsmanshaften" and national associations. Such associations are frequently concerned with general policy questions; they may form pressure groups, or seek other ways to influence government policy on behalf of their members. Membership in these groups is drawn from the middle-class segments of the immigrant population, particularly persons employed in government or allied agencies, but does not usually include members of the active political elite.

The various primary groups—family and kinsmen, age-groups, occupational groups, and voluntary associations—have important functions in communicating and maintaining cultural traditions. As basic interaction and socialization units, the families transmit different life-styles. Iraqi or Hungarian immigrant families, for example, often converse in their native tongues, have different traditions of diet and dress, and also transmit different ideals and values to their children. The close family ties typical of most Middle Eastern groups are especially important in maintaining these immigrants' cultural traditions. Distinctiveness in cultural content is further reinforced by the close ties existing among persons who share common ethnic backgrounds. Israeli urban life therefore exhibits a large degree of cultural variation—the distinctive customs of the different groups continue to be expressed. At the same time, however, other group contexts—in school or work situations or in youth groups—provide different, more universal types of cultural understandings. For example, the schools impart basic skills and common values, Hebrew is the national language, and all persons share common citizenship requirements. Moreover, the veteran European community continues to retain its cultural dominance; as will later be described in greater detail, Western culture in the broadest sense represents the direction of cultural change.

Before considering local organization in rural areas, it is useful to note some elements of social organization in smaller towns. Studies of new "development towns" and older communities indicate that the primary groups described above are also important in the social organization of smaller towns. P. Cohen (1962) and Katz and Zloczower (1961) describe patterns of ethnic residential concentration in their studies of the town of Rechovoth. This community includes zones of Yemenite and European population concentration—ethnic neighborhoods have persisted for several generations and are the loci for separate forms of social organization and cultural expression. Family organization among these two groups parallels the models outlined earlier; i.e. Yemenite family and kinship groups are tightly organized and undertake joint activities, while family functions are more limited among Europeans. Katz and Zloczower also note that although both European and Yemenite youngsters were members of youth movements, the youngsters were affiliated with different groups; indeed, cliques or peer groups did not normally include members of both ethnic groups. In regard to occupational groups, the ethnic hierarchy of income and status previously described for cities is also prevalent in the town. Voluntary associations, such as friendship or synagogue groups, are also ethnically separate. This almost total ethnic separation may be extreme, and is not necessarily characteristic of all small towns; but in a modified form these patterns of organization are probably typical of many of the smaller communities.

While Israeli urban social organization is similar to other Western cities, rural Jewish communities are significantly different. Most agricultural land is owned by government agencies and is leased to the cultivators. Then, too, with the exception of citriculture, the privately-owned family farm is unknown in Israel. Rather, rural life is organized in village patterns, and the villages themselves have either a communal or cooperative social-economic system.

There were, in 1965, 230 communal villages, or kibbutzim, with a total population of 80,000 persons. Individual kibbutzim vary greatly in size, from less than a hundred persons in new villages to more than a thousand in some older communities. Although the villages include members of all ethnic groups, the overwhelming majority are European or Israeli-born. Kibbutzim are widely scattered throughout the countryside, with many villages located in militarily sensitive border regions. The kibbutz economy is normally based upon intensive farming, but many villages have also established small industrial plants and workshops; the agricultural technology is highly mechanized, and the farming system emphasizes modern production techniques.

What is most distinctive about the kibbutz is its unique form of social and economic organization. The basic social unit in these villages is the commune, or adult membership. Village property is owned and managed by the community as a whole: the agricultural implements, community buildings, and members' dwellings are the property of the commune, rather than of the individual members and their families. Both men and women work—men are mainly engaged in agricultural or industrial activities, while most women are employed in service tasks. Kibbutz members are not directly remunerated for their work, however; salaries are not paid, but rather each member receives "according to his needs." The commune provides its members with a dwelling, clothing, personal effects, as well as educational and recreational facilities. Economic "exploitation"—the hiring of outside, nonkibbutz workers—is also formally forbidden by kibbutz ideology; hiring labor has recently become common in many kibbutzim, however. The kibbutz strives to become a "classless" society, in which private property is eliminated and replaced by communal ownership and controls.

Family life has also been reorganized in the kibbutz. A husband and wife live together in the same room, but kibbutz children typically live in separate children's quarters. The children "spend a few hours every day with their parents and siblings, but from birth on they sleep, eat and study in special children's houses" (Talmon 1954: 348). Although parents have important functions in socializing the young, educational activities are organized within special age-groups directed by teachers and youth leaders. Thus, as Spiro has pointed out (1954), many of the social functions normally attributed to the nuclear family are performed by the commune. Emotional and psychological bonds do unite parents and children, however: Spiro's research in child-rearing practices indicates that the communal system of child rearing results in group-oriented, self-reliant youngsters—although he also notes strains of emotional insecurity within the youth population (Spiro 1958: chap. 16).

Each kibbutz is an autonomous, self-directed community: the villages maintain their own schools, health facilities, recreational areas, and cultural activities. In regard to kibbutz government, important policy decisions are made at general meetings of all kibbutz members. Daily management is entrusted to small, regularly elected committees; the various economic "branches" (vegetable garden, dairy herd, poultry, etc.) are each directed by kibbutz members chosen from among those who have the required skill and experience. Although Eva Rosenfeld (1951) and Talmon (1956) have demonstrated the stratification into elite groups, age-groups, and other social-political divisions in kibbutzim, there is little evidence for a strict separation between these groups (managers and workers, or veterans and newcomers), and the political system appears to be open and fluid (E. Rosenfeld 1951, Talmon 1956).

The kibbutzim are organized into three national political-party affiliated settlement movements; these movements represent village interests in government and government-allied agencies, and also engage in economic and educational activities. As the prime representatives of the "pioneering ideology," kibbutz members are well represented within the national elite; historically, kibbutz membership bore high esteem, and even though kibbutz prestige has diminished in recent years, members of kibbutzim continue to fill important government posts. Kibbutz members are also a part of national social networks—for example age-groups cut across local villages and join youngsters from different communities.

The moshav, the second type of rural Jewish community, is best described as a cooperative village. In common with the kibbutz, the moshav emphasizes cooperation between members, self-labor, and "classlessness." However, while there is similarity in the guiding principles of both types of communities, their social and economic systems are much different.

In the moshav, each family lives in its own home and works its own plot of land. The nuclear family is the basic production and consumption unit: a man and his children work their own fields, and the villagers receive direct remuneration for their crops. At the same time, however, every family is allocated equal resources, and numerous bonds of cooperation join the family groups. For example each family receives the same sized plot of land, equal access to water, and the same opportunities for credit and mechanized implements. This equal division is meant to minimize economic differences among the members and to prevent the formation of separate class or interest groups.

Cooperation in the moshav is expressed through a system of communitywide purchasing and marketing arrangements. The villagers market their produce jointly, and they also contract for agricultural commodities (seed, fertilizer, water, credits, or implements) in common. To cite one example, the village contracts for loans from banks or other financial institutions and then allocates the funds to the individual members. These cooperative arrangements bind the producers to one another and thereby emphasize their mutual interdependence.

The moshav political system reflects democratic principles: general policies are decided during villagewide meetings, and elected committees direct various aspects of community life. However, the administration of communitywide economic affairs is usually entrusted to hired personnel: since all of the villagers are engaged in farming, salaried specialists are required to manage the village's complex cooperative system. In some cases, the specialists (nurses, teachers, mechanics) are members of the moshav community, while in other villages they remain salaried functionaries. Each moshav is an autonomous community, and the villages maintain their own educational, health, and cultural facilities.

Moshavim are small in size, ranging from 70 to 150 families. Although the cooperative social-economic structure is common to all villages, moshavim formed prior to 1948 differ significantly from those communities established following the creation of Israel. The prestate moshavim—which number 85 villages, with a population of approximately 30,000 families—were formed by pioneer groups of European immigrants. These early settlers (the first moshavim were formed in 1921) consciously fashioned the social system earlier outlined. Since 1948, however, new moshavim have been formed by groups of immigrants from European and Middle Eastern countries. Although in some cases these immigrants chose to adopt the moshav pattern, in most cases they were directed to the villages by government planning groups. These latter villages, called moshvei olim (immigrant villages), may be thought of as "administered communities": i.e. they are not autonomous villages, but rather their development is directed by government authorities. Many such communities have recently been formed: in 1965 there were 262 immigrant moshavim, with a population of approximately 97,000 persons.

These two types of moshavim exhibit different developmental features. In a study of several veteran moshavim conducted during 1945-46, Talmon (1952) concluded that moshav members were ranked differently depending upon their excellence in farming, participation in the authority structure, and conformity to group norms; such characteristics were highly esteemed by members of the veteran moshavim. In addition, group formation based upon ethnicity and length of residence in the village (newcomers or veterans) was also evident. However, these distinctions did not usually lead to the formation of opposed factions or interest groups; the social and ideological homogeneity prevalent in most veteran moshavim usually prevented the formation of opposed blocs of settlers. Many of these older villages have become prosperous communities, and in some, cooperative traditions have been replaced by more individualistic practices.

Although the time-depth is brief, patterns of development in immigrant moshavim seem much different. Some of these villages include settlers from different countries (Rumania and Yemen, for example), while in others, and particularly villages formed by immigrants from Middle Eastern countries, the community is dominated by large clusters of kinsmen. These ethnic or kinship groups typically form political factions, and enduring villagewide disputes have been common. Since in most cases the settlers directed to the villages had no previous farming experience, groups of veteran Israeli instructors were assigned to each new village. These instructors, and the planning authorities they represented, managed the villages' financial and organizational system, and also taught new farming skills to the immigrants. Some immigrant villages have in recent years become economically viable communities, while in others, factional disputes and planning errors have retarded community development (Weingrod 1962, Willner 1969).

Patterns of local organization in Israeli Arab villages are, of course, much different. Arab villages follow traditional Middle Eastern forms of social organization; although behavior patterns have changed considerably during the past several decades, the traditional norms continue to be powerful. In addition, the large-scale flight of Arabs from Israel during 1947-48 has led to a general population reorganization. In many instances, entire communities fled and did not return, while in others several segments of a village left or joined another community.

The normal agricultural cycle in Arab villages is based upon a two-crop system: winter crops are mainly grains, while summer crops include vegetables, grains, and fruits. In some areas olive cultivation is also widespread. In the traditional village economy—still prevalent in some communities—there is little "occupational specialization and the family [expends] much energy in time consuming building, in supplying water and fuel, in milling and the like" (H. Rosenfeld 1958: 1128). Modernization and economic specialization have increased during the past several decades, and with a quickened pace since 1948; a modern agricultural technology has been introduced and, in addition, a growing number of villagers have found employment in surrounding rural areas or in nearby cities and towns.

The patrilocal extended family is the basic unit of village social organization. Composed of a man and his wife, their married sons and their families, and the unmarried sons and daughters, the extended family forms a joint residence and economic unit. According to traditional norms, the father "owns all capital and controls the labor power of all under his roof. ... Sons work for the father on his land, with his flock, or in some craft" (H. Rosenfeld 1958: 1127). Although a woman leaves her father's residence at marriage, close emotional and jural ties continue to link her with her father's household. Paternal control tends to be complete and authoritative, but interpersonal tensions, caused by the sons' desire for greater independence or by rivalry between the brothers, may divide the family members.

Extended families are joined into named patrilineal lineages (*hamula*). Villages are normally composed of a number of lineages, and lineage heads hold informal and often formal authority positions. Henry Rosenfeld notes (1958: 1127) that the "lineages are mainly involved with matters of factionalism and the power structure." Political factions are normally based upon the maximal lineage, and the opposition between these groups may unite the various subunits.

In regard to local government and administration, lineage heads often dominate the community councils and wield important powers within the village. The village mukhtar, or several such officials, traditionally represents the village before government personnel. Local village councils have also been formed by the Israeli government, and these groups now have the responsibility for formulating communitywide policies. National political party activity also encompasses the Arab villages, and, as will later be described in greater detail, this new type of affiliation has further altered the traditional authority structure.

In common with Arab villagers, the traditional forms of Bedouin social and political organization have also undergone widespread transformation. Marx notes that Israeli Bedouin society is "comprised of the meager remnants of larger units which split up and dispersed in many directions at the time of the establishment of the State. They are to a great degree cut off from their kinsmen across the borders . . ." (Marx 1958: 17). The tribal groups have been allocated grazing zones in the Negev region, and their nomadic movements are tightly controlled by government officers; traditional warfare and raiding have been almost completely eliminated. Moreover, although the traditional camel and sheepherding activities are still maintained, the Bedouin are "gradually moving toward sedentarization and permanent agriculture" (Marx 1958: 17). In brief, recent political and economic developments have almost completely changed the conditions of Bedouin life.

The key local units in Bedouin social organization are the nuclear and extended family and the lineage. Economic cooperation joins family members, and families as well as kinsmen form common residence groups. Economic and political roles are differentiated in regard to age and sex—men are active as herders, in farming, or the new government-sponsored occupations; while women care for the tent or household. Respect and authority are granted to family elders, who are influential in framing lineage and tribal policy. Lineage members also have important mutual responsibilities; for example, "Usually it is the *hamula* which pays ransom and the *hamula* which avenges the blood of its sons," and lineage endogamy is preferred (Marx 1958: 27).

The tribes, which are based upon real or fictive common descent, compose the main political units of Bedouin society. The tribes traditionally guaranteed the members security by strength and force of arms; alliances and confederations of tribes held domain over large grazing areas and thereby guaranteed their members' rights and possessions. More recently, the tribal functions have diminished appreciably, as government control has put an end to tribal violence. Marx also observes that, with the imposition of tranquillity and tight external control, the sheikh's powers have grown increasingly authoritarian; since the sheikh has become, in effect, a government agent, "more real power is concentrated in his hands and whereas he was once the leader solely in times of need, he is now the person who controls the daily political and economic affairs of the tribe" (Marx 1958: 30).

Although city, town, and village have been analyzed separately in this section, it is important to emphasize that urbanism has a pervasive influence throughout the society. A kind of urban life-style has been maintained in the veteran kibbutzim and moshavim: the school systems in these villages are on a par with many urban schools, health services are excellent, and films and various cultural performances are regularly scheduled. Moreover, the mass media of radio, newspapers, and, most recently, television spread their messages throughout the society—to the Arab villager as well as the kibbutznik. In addition, the wide-ranging social networks of contact and communication that characterize Israeli society also bring city and village nearer to one another. Urban influences are thus widespread, and, indeed, the distinctions between "urban" and "rural" are slight.

National Organization: Patterns of Stratification

National political and economic institutions have major roles within Israeli society. As was noted earlier, the smallness of the country's size and population limits the development of local or regional interests and magnifies the importance of national institutions. Then, too, the colonizing groups were ideological advocates of national planning and state-directed projects; this philosophy, which continues to be influential, has resulted in the wide proliferation of national agencies. Moreover, not only is it true that government and allied national agencies possess broad economic and political strength but also that no other groups of comparable power are present within the society: there are neither separate economic interests nor regional or ethnic groups to constitute sources of major independent power. National institutions therefore dominate the political and economic system, and their influence is pervasive.

The formal structure of government may briefly be described as follows: Israel is a parliamentary democracy, similar in certain respects to the British system. The Knesset, or parliament, a unicameral body composed of 120 members, is the supreme legislative group; indeed, "it not only legislates, but also checks on the government and its administration, and reviews and exercises a considerable degree of direction of domestic and foreign affairs" (Kraines 1961: 49). Election to parliament is determined by proportional representation from political party lists; i.e. the percentage of votes a party receives determines the number of seats it receives in the Knesset. Governments are formed by the party, or coalition of parties, which possesses a parliamentary majority. Since the first election in 1949, no single party has received a majority, and the governments have therefore all been party coalitions. A Prime Minister heads the government, and the various governmental responsibilities are divided among the members of his cabinet. Elections are normally held every four years, unless the government falls, and parliament dissolves, in the interim. A President is also elected by the Knesset; his term of office lasts five years, and his duties are mainly symbolic and advisory. Although Israel does not have a written constitution, the government framework has been largely unchanged since the formation of the state. However, the political system has reflected both continuity and relative instability. Mapai, the largest political party, has been the dominant group in all of the governments formed since 1948, but eleven different governments were formed during this period, and national elections were held five times.

Government activities have had widespread social and economic consequences. Although a Jewish "quasi-government" functioned during the mandatory period, the emergence of the state signaled a major elaboration of government activities. Basic government services—such as fiscal direction and postal and police operations—were begun, while economic, military, and foreign affairs activities became much more extensive. An independent judiciary and a system of social service administration were established. In brief, an entire state structure began to function. Moreover, the great wave of immigration following the establishment of Israel also led to an increase in government activity. The "welfare state" political philosophy characteristic of the colonization period extended to the new immigrants as well. Most immigrants arrived in the country without financial resources, and the state assumed responsibility for providing them housing, employment, health, and educational facilities. The government also undertook responsibility for economic direction; financial controls guided the economy generally, and, in addition, government expenditures in housing and industrial development were very extensive. These economic activities, and the allied progressive social legislation, maintained a high level of employment and also guaranteed a minimum standard of living. Government-directed educational and army activities also had important social and cultural consequences. Universal elementary education provided both immigrant and Israeli-born youngsters with educational skills and understandings; an extensive secondary school system was also established, and university attendance reached 20,000 students in 1965. The Israeli Army has been another critical social framework. Army forces include both a large core of professionals and a much larger active reserve. In addition to its military activities, the army has also developed an explicit social and cultural program; army service has provided a training ground for immigrant youths, and the army has also undertaken numerous educational and public service tasks.

All these activities, which have continued since 1948, have had different, and in a sense, contradictory, results. The government has provided a well-defined national administrative and judicial system; although lack of experience has at times resulted in inefficient operation, the governmental framework has generally operated smoothly. State-directed programs have also led to broad-range economic development, and the majority of immigrants have been absorbed within the economy. At the same time, the growth of government institutions has resulted in increased bureaucratization and also has injected new rigidities into the social and economic structure. The bureaucratically-organized government agencies exercise authority in many spheres of life. Dependence upon these agencies has been particularly acute for new immigrants, who were required to deal with government agencies in regard to housing, employment, or local services. Bureaucrat-immigrant relations often became a source of tension, and frequently resulted in discontent or apathy. Moreover, the formalization of government power has also contributed to the cleavages between different segments of the population, particularly between new immigrants and the veteran population.

Other nationally organized groups, most notably the Jewish Agency and the Histadruth, also possess wide political and economic powers. Formally responsible for immigrant absorption (including housing and the establishment of new agricultural settlements), the Jewish Agency has filled many functions paralleling those of the government. Histadruth activities are also numerous and complex, including the organization of workers into trade unions, the operation of the country's largest medical system (Kupath Cholim), large-scale industrial and commercial enterprises, banking facilities, publishing, cultural activities, and others. As is the case for the government and the Jewish Agency, Histadruth activities are centrally directed and bureaucratically organized. Although the interests of these three groups sometimes conflict, their policies are usually accommodated to one another, mainly through the political party system. In effect, the elite corps of these groups constitutes the Israeli equivalent of an "establishment": including both technicians and ideologists, and with a preponderance of Europeans, these groups control and manage broad economic and political forces.

Political party organization is another distinctive feature of the Israeli social structure. Political life is extremely vigorous, and the parties, most of which originated in the prestate Zionist movement, are engaged in a broad spectrum of activities: in addition to the usual political work, the parties also "operate daily and weekly newspapers in various languages ... engage in economic enterprises, operating banks, insurance companies, agricultural settlements, theatres, housing developments, health and welfare institutions, sports clubs and youth groups" (Kraines 1961: 62). Not only are party activities diverse but the number of political parties is also very large: as many as 26 parties have entered lists in national elections. This splintering of the electorate, coupled with the wide array of party activities, has led to intense political activity and to the politicization of many features of daily life. The web of party links allows for the coordination of activities throughout the society, but it also places a premium upon party membership and allegiance, and thereby has become another source of social rigidity.

The large number of political parties notwithstanding, political power has crystallized around a smaller number of parties. Neither sectional nor ethnic and occupational groups (such as farmers or businessmen) have organized large, successful political parties; rather, the dominant parties are all national groups, although they are themselves composed of coalitions of interests. The parties range from a small Communist Party on the extreme left to the orthodox religious groups on the far right. Mapai, a "social-democratic" party, is the largest single group, and has received between 30 and 40 per cent of the total vote. Other smaller parties of the left include Mapam and Achdut Avoda, both of which draw their main support from the kibbutzim and urban workers. The Liberal Party and Heruth stand somewhat to the right of center, and include roughly a third of the electorate. The remaining third of the voting population is divided among the various religious parties and other small splinter groups. Interestingly, the continuous large-scale immigration has not substantially affected the balance between the parties; immigrants have been drawn to all of the major parties, and their proportional strength has not changed dramatically during the past decade. On the other hand, political leadership has been dominated by European or Israeli-born persons, and immigrants from Middle Eastern countries have been underrepresented within the political elite.

Political party branches are organized locally throughout the country; an estimated quarter of the eligible voters are members of political parties. However, the direction of political affairs—both locally and nationally—is usually centrally controlled by the national party leadership. The major function of the larger parties is the direction of government and allied national institutions: party cadres hold key leadership positions within the government, Jewish Agency, Histadruth, as well as in other large economic enterprises. This "interlocking directorate" of party personnel permits the mobilization of broad forces throughout the society. The parties formulate programs ranging over broad areas of public life, and the party-linked institutions become vehicles for carrying out the directives. Clashes of interest and personality may take place, but the party system has become a major coordinating network throughout the society.

The judiciary, the second branch of government, is an independent body. The legal system is a composite of different traditions—including Ottoman Law, regulations and ordinances retained from the British mandate period, legislation passed by the Knesset, and religious law. Both secular and religious court systems have been established. The secular courts deal with civil and criminal matters, while the religious courts have jurisdiction over "personal matters"—marriage, divorce, and inheritance. Jewish, Muslim, and Christian courts have been constituted, and they determine legal issues on the basis of traditional religious precedent. Control of marriage and divorce by religious courts has been an issue of continuing political controversy; this system, which originated during Turkish rule, has nonetheless been retained since the state's establishment.

Although political participation extends to all sectors of the population—all citizens may vote, and legal guarantees of civil liberties are effectively maintained—certain restrictions have at various times been placed upon the Arab population. Since 1949, military government regulations have been enforced in zones of Arab population concentration in the northern and southern regions. At one time, evening curfews were enforced in Arab villages, and special passes required in order to travel to other sections of the country (these restrictions were lifted in 1962). Arabs are not conscripted to serve in the army (Druzes may serve, however). The military government system is officially considered to have been a necessary, if unfortunate, security measure, in view of the continuing tensions between Israel and the Arab states. Its general sociological effect, however, has been to limit contact between the Jewish and Arab populations, and thereby to reinforce the social and cultural distinctions between these groups.

Israel's economic situation exhibits a number of special features. The country itself is comparatively poor in natural resources: there are no extensive areas of rich farmlands, and the existing mineral and oil deposits are relatively small (with the exception of the Dead Sea zone). Furthermore, as was earlier emphasized, the post-1948 mass immigration led to a sudden growth in population; thus, not only were natural resources limited but in addition the economy faced the difficult task of absorbing a large number of additional unselected immigrants. Problems of economic absorption were further compounded by the fact that most immigrants had formerly been employed in commerce and craft work—occupations "which did not conform with Israel's economic structure and development needs" (Sicron 1957: 119). Moreover, the continuing friction between Israel and her neighbors separated the country from its natural markets and also forced a heavy expenditure in an extensive military program. At the same time, however, the economy has each year received massive foreign financial grants and loans; indeed, as Patinkin emphasizes, this continuing dependence upon foreign assistance is the "most distinctive characteristic of the Israeli economy" (Patinkin 1960: 47).

For many immigrants, entering the economy required difficult social and psychological adjustments: the new occupations were mainly in relatively menial, unskilled tasks, and the immigrants needed to master new skills and adjust to a new, often lower, social status. Nevertheless, most immigrants have been successfully integrated into the economy; although unemployment has been a continuing problem, and some proportion of employment is artificially generated by government spending, the majority of immigrants have become engaged in productive work. Israel's economic growth during the past decade has been rapid; Patinkin writes that "the overall picture" is one of "almost continuous growth in GNP," and, what is more, that this economic development is "to a significant degree ... the result of the increasing efficiency with which the economy operated" (Patinkin 1960: 58, 70). Per capita income has also increased, although unevenly, for all sectors of the population, and personal consumption is on a par with many economically advanced countries. On the other hand, the artificial nature of the economy is well illustrated in an analysis of the labor force: nearly 30 per cent of the labor force is employed in service occupations, while 21 per cent is employed in manufacturing, 17 per cent in agriculture, 12 per cent in commerce, and the remaining 20 per cent in various other occupations (Patinkin 1960: 41). This concentration of persons in service tasks—

mainly in government and related employment—is greater than in most advanced countries and constitutes one of the main structural problems of the economy.

With the exception of grains, fodder, and meat, which are mainly imported, Israeli agriculture is self-sustaining. Indeed, the severe food shortages and rationing which took place during the early 1950s have in recent years been replaced by surplus crops of vegetables, eggs, and dairy products. This extensive agricultural development is primarily the result of heavy government investment in new farming communities. Since 1956, however, government investment policies have veered away from agriculture and have instead been directed to new industry, housing, communication, and transportation. Local Israeli industries are mainly new, and they are relatively small in scale. The economy produces a wide variety of consumption and production products—including construction materials, textiles, household items, machine assembly goods, and the like. However, most raw materials, as well as large machinery, are imported from abroad; these include, for example, timber, oil, iron and steel manufactures, aircraft, shipping, and other items (*Statistical Abstract of Israel 1961*: 279-80). Since Israel's establishment, the country's import-export ratio has been heavily out of balance, with imports far outstripping exports. The principal hard-currency earners are citrus exports, tourism, polished diamonds, chemicals, and manufactured goods. The recurring balance-of-payments crisis has been met by foreign government and private loans, German reparations payments, and funds contributed to Israel's development by supporters in Jewish communities throughout the Western world. Thus, in effect, the rapid development of the economy, as well as the growth of per capita income and personal consumption, has in large measure been made possible by continuous large-scale foreign economic support. Even though the economic system is modern in format and technology, and employment levels have continued to be high, the economy's dependence upon outside economic assistance has not been significantly reduced.

As was stressed earlier, the government's role in economic development has been extensive. The government (and allied national groups) is not only a major employer, it has also tightly controlled fiscal activity and has itself built new industrial plants as well as extending loans for the development of others. Investment policies have, in addition, sought to disperse factories—and thereby the population—throughout the countryside; for example, the "development towns" and villages recently built in the peripheral northern and southern regions have developed as government-sponsored and -directed communities. Thus public rather than private funds have been the primary levers in economic expansion;

while some local private investment has occurred, most funds have been channeled through government agencies. Moreover, government appointed managers—what Eisenstadt has called "government entrepreneurs"—rather than private corporations or managers, wield considerable economic influence. This concentration of economic power in government hands has important political meanings: political interests may, at times, influence economic policies, and political party affiliation may become an important factor in allocating positions or resources. Even though government-sponsored development programs have had notable success, the coupling of political and economic interests within the governmental structure has been another source of rigidity.

In both the present and in previous sections of this chapter, reference has frequently been made to differences in status between the various segments of the society. In the section on "Local Organization," occupational differences between Europeans and Middle Eastern immigrants were noted, for example, while in this present section on "National Organization" the higher status political offices of Europeans were also observed. These two perspectives of local and national level can now be combined and systematically explored by considering the pattern of Israeli social stratification.

In general, the pattern of social stratification within the Jewish population is one in which Europeans, including both veterans and immigrants, hold the higher prestige and income positions, while the Middle Eastern immigrants and veterans tend to fill lower positions. This typical pattern can be observed in an analysis of levels of income, occupation, education, and political leadership. Hanoch's study of income differentials reveals that significant disparities exist between the European and Middle Eastern segments. For example, while the median family income of European immigrants in 1959 was I£343, the median income for Middle Easterners was I£259 (Hanoch 1961: 68). Since, as was noted earlier, Middle Eastern families tend to be larger than European families, the per capita differences are even greater. Hanoch's research also shows that while the real income for all segments of the population has risen, European incomes rise more rapidly than do those of the Middle Easterners. Both the income rise for all groups and the continued disparities are significant facts; on the one hand, the population as a whole is better housed and better fed, yet affluence has grown unevenly. These differences are, of course, reflected in an analysis of occupation; for example 30 per cent of European males were classed as "administrative and managerial" in the 1965 census, while only 15 per cent of the Middle Eastern immigrants were in the same category; conversely, 36 per cent of the Middle Easterners were classed as "construction workers" in contrast to 19 per cent among Europeans. A similar pattern can be observed in regard to education; for example, 69 per cent of secondary school students were born to European parents, 23 per cent to Middle Eastern parents, and the remaining 8 per cent to Israeli-born parents (*Statistical Abstract of Israel 1966*: 315). Concerted educational and scholarship programs have in recent years resulted in a higher proportion of Middle Eastern youngsters attending secondary school and university —yet the disparities remain considerable.

Although comparable statistics do not exist in regard to political leadership, the high government, political party, army, or trade union positions also tend to be dominated by the European segment of the population. Lower echelon posts are held by Middle Easterners, and there is also some evidence that political leadership may be a particularly promising route of social mobility. Even though higher education and political participation may provide "mobility ladders," a clear pattern of ethnic stratification can be said to characterize the Jewish population.

Contrasting the Arab with the Jewish sectors also indicates wide disparities. Detailed statistical information is not available in all categories for the Israeli Arab population. The data on education, however, show that roughly 50 per cent of the adult Arab population has received no schooling, and only 1 per cent has had university training; while among Jews 11 per cent received no education, and 10 per cent have had university training (*Statistical Abstract of Israel 1966*: 612). Although the percentage of Arab youngsters who attend primary and secondary schools has grown rapidly, it continues to be less than the percentage for the Jewish population. An analysis of income and occupation figures would undoubtedly reveal similar differences as well as analogous changes; the income of the primarily village Arab population falls below that of the Jewish population, even though Arab incomes have grown rapidly during the past two decades.

What general conclusions may be drawn regarding Israeli social stratification? First, it seems clear that all segments of the population have benefited from the general rise in income and the adoption of universal education. In this sense, the entire population has enjoyed a rise in living standards. Second, within the Jewish population a close correlation exists between social class and ethnicity: Europeans hold the higher-income, higher-class positions, while Middle Easterners are in lower-class positions. Third, large-scale differences separate the Jewish from the Arab community, and although there has been a notable rise in income and education among Arabs, the predominately village-based Arab population continues to be distinct from the mainly urban Jewish population. Some of the implications of this status hierarchy will be discussed in the following section.

Social and Cultural Change

Rapid social and cultural change is a distinctive feature of Israeli society: the formation of the state, the subsequent mass immigration, the flight of the Arab population—these events have created new and fundamentally different social and cultural conditions. Moreover, social interaction between members of the major population groups (veterans-immigrants, Europeans-Middle Easterners, Jews-Arabs) has produced widespread change within each group. Israel's small size and population also enhance its sensitivity to change; economic, cultural, or political developments quickly flow through the entire society, influencing all sectors of the population.

For purposes of analysis, it is useful to examine the various population groups separately. To begin with, the veteran European population has itself experienced many critical changes during the past two decades. It will be recalled that during the prestate colonization period the Jewish community was characterized by a high degree of consensus and social cohesiveness, an emphasis upon national service, and by informally organized, "open" systems of leadership. However, as Eisenstadt has emphasized, the formation of the state "completely transformed the whole social scene," bringing with it a "growing formalization, bureaucratization, and loss of cohesiveness of the various primary groups" (Eisenstadt 1954: 124). In brief, the familiar pattern of a lessening of solidarity following independence characterized the Israeli experience. The life style of the veteran population changed from an emphasis upon "simplicity" and national service to a greater interest in personal consumption. Indeed, it is fair to conclude that this segment (both in the cities as well as in the kibbutz and the moshav) has become increasingly more middle class in behavior and attitude. These developments have been accompanied by changes in the relative political influence of different interest groups; for example the pioneer moshav and kibbutz groups lost some political power, while urban workers, professionals and government technicians gained in strength. As in other industrial states, these (and other) interest groups compete for economic benefits, frequently rejecting the government's appeals for national solidarity (Eisenstadt 1967).

These changes have not been total and all-embracing: the older pioneering ideology continues to be influential, and national service goals are voiced by the political leadership. However, this traditional Israeli ideology has in recent years been challenged by the more technical or "pragmatic" view characteristic of the younger generation. Advanced scientific and technical training is highly valued among this segment of the population.

Although itself changing in numerous ways, the veteran European segment has continued to be the dominant social and cultural force in the society. The major political and cultural institutions generally reflect the ideals and interests of this group; indeed, strenuous efforts have been made during the past two decades to alter the immigrants' ideals and behavior in order to better conform with those of the veteran European population. The school curriculum and army service have been geared toward socializing immigrant youngsters in a European, or Western, tradition. This program of cultural reform has had mixed results: many of the immigrants have successfully adopted new cultural traditions, while the response of others has been one of ambivalence or frustration. What is important to note, however, is that although the population has changed greatly, Israel's cultural tradition has continued to be typically Western (Weingrod 1966).

Immigration has, of course, led to strikingly new conditions for the various immigrant groups. Immigrants flowing into the country needed to learn a new language and set of cultural meanings, adopt new types of occupations, and adjust to political and social systems different from their own. The government immigration agencies assisted the immigrants in many important ways—by providing housing, making jobs available, organizing occupational training programs and adult education courses. Yet since they were dependent upon these agencies for essential needs and services, part of an immigrant's adjustment also included learning how to deal with these large, bureaucratically organized groups, and how, if possible, to manipulate them.

Eisenstadt's studies of immigrant absorption indicate that adjustment to the new Israeli conditions depend upon such variables as the immigrants'. predispositions to change, their identification with Jewish society, the nature of their primary group relations, the continued effective functioning of immigrant elites, and the nature of the communications networks operating between the immigrants and the receiving society (Eisenstadt 1954: chap. 6). Stable family groups predisposed to accept the Israeli norms were likely to experience rapid absorption, whereas groups which had negative predispositions to change and unstable primary-group ties might become disorganized and were only loosely tied to the receiving society. Or, to cite another instance, open communications networks between the immigrants and the new society led to an understanding of the new cultural norms, while communications blocks led to misunderstanding and deviant behavior. Eisenstadt also points out that, in common with other immigration situations, the immigrants tended to adapt quickly to new economic conditions, while their cultural traditions retained their preimmigration forms (Eisenstadt 1954: 166-72). In general, some segments of the immigrating groups became associated with and dispersed throughout the veteran society, while many others maintained a separate, distinct social and cultural organization.

These developments pertain to immigrant groups generally. In addition, immigrants from Middle Eastern countries also entered into intense culture contact situations. For these immigrants (from Yemen, Iraq, or Morocco, for example), the contrasts between their traditional culture and the Israeli norms were very great; to cite several instances: physical labor in the traditional culture was generally shunned, participation in public life was restricted to males, and parental control extended over broad areas of conduct. Daily informal contacts with members of the dominant Israeli culture tended to challenge these traditional patterns of behavior—in the new society men were expected to perform physical tasks, the Israeli emphasis upon equality for women offered new roles for females, and youngsters were encouraged to assert their independence from their parents. In addition to this situational exposure to Israeli norms, the Middle Eastern youngsters in particular were the object of the school and army programs of cultural reform. Thus, for example, while serving in the army the youngsters were separated from home and family influences and were subjected to intense cultural pressures.

These various contacts have resulted in a reorganization of the immigrants' traditional social relations. Among the more important developments has been the general separation between generations. The Middle Eastern youngsters—who adapted more quickly to the new Israeli conditions, and who were also part of the special training programs—became culturally differentiated from their parents. In many instances, the youngsters were relied upon by their elders as "interpreters" and cultural guides; while in other cases the differences between the generations led to conflict and misunderstanding. The extended family ties also were loosened: close residential and economic cooperation between families was no longer the norm, and, instead, the individual nuclear families acted as more distinct units. Many immigrant women also entered the labor force; under the influence of new cultural models, and with separate sources of income, they have become more independent. These changes have also tended to weaken the position of the family "patriarch"; male family authority has progressively diminished. These changes notwithstanding, it should also be added that while under stress the Middle Eastern primary groups continue to be vital centers of social interaction.

The present stratification of Israeli society, in which Europeans occupy the higher-class positions, and Middle Easterners are in lower-class posts, has been a continuing source of tension. While on the one hand there has been an ideological emphasis upon immigrant absorption, the close association between social class and ethnicity has meant that the European and Middle Eastern groups continue to be distinct from one another. Among Middle Easterners, feelings of discrimination and prejudice are common; in a more general sense, from their lower-class perspective they may become disaffected by a lack of total participation in the society. Without minimizing these problems, it should also be noted that the growing number of Israeli-born Middle Eastern youngsters and of immigrants who have found satisfying economic or political positions now have an increasing "stake" in the society and are more tightly bound to it than was formerly the case.

Turning next to a consideration of change in Arab village communities, the main trends appear to be rapid population growth, economic development, the weakening of extended family relations and patriarchal control, and the introduction of new forms of political activity. The general expansion and modernization of the national economy has provided new occupational possibilities to the villagers. For example both seasonal and permanent work opportunities are available in the vicinity of Arab population concentrations; moreover, the agricultural technology has become mechanized, and government and allied national groups have sponsored some local industrial activity and cooperative undertakings. This economic growth has given employment to villagers who had little or no land, and the increased agricultural efficiency allows landowning families to divert some of their labor to other activities. Thus Israeli Arabs have increasingly become part of an industrial economy.

Economic growth has led to greater economic and cultural heterogeneity. Different economic interest groups have arisen, and the numerous contacts with the national economy have more closely tied the villages to urban ways of life. In effect, the villages are more attuned to, and affected by, economic or cultural developments on a national scale. Then too, these changes have altered primary-group relations: extended family ties have become more tenuous, and strict patriarchal control over family matters has also lessened.

The new political conditions have also led to important internal changes. Political power no longer resides in the village, but is rather concentrated within the Israeli state political apparatus; as a consequence, the power of local leadership depends upon contacts and influence among the Jewish bureaucracy. At the same time, the various Israeli political parties have also campaigned for support among the Arab villagers, and party groups have been formed at the village level. These activities have opened new avenues of social mobility, since they offer positions and enhanced status to more mobile persons.

Even though economic and political participation may provide links between Jews and Arabs, the Israeli Arab community continues to be in an ambiguous position. Abner Cohen's remarks well summarize this situation:

> Time is only accentuating the dilemma for the . . . villagers, rather than easing or resolving it. The more these villagers are economically absorbed within Israeli society and the more material benefits they gain from it, the more they feel the hostility between the two fronts, and the more drawn they become, at least emotionally and culturally, to the surging Arab nationalist movement [A. Cohen 1965: 19].

In brief, the dilemmas of the Arab minority are far from being resolved.

In summary, the major population segments—the European veterans, immigrants from European and Middle Eastern countries, and the local Arab population—all exhibit new social and cultural features as they react to novel conditions and to one another. Viewed as a whole, contemporary Israeli society appears culturally diverse, as the various ethnic and religious groups compose separate subcultures. Indeed, the formation of a culturally heterogeneous, ethnically-oriented society has been the major structural change of the past two decades. However, the veteran European community has retained its political and cultural dominance, and "Westernization" marks the direction of cultural change. The European sector is, in effect, the high prestige group within a system of ethnic social stratification, while the Middle Eastern groups hold lower-class positions. At the same time, the range of cultural universals also tends to grow, and ties do link the various ethnic groups; these links are particularly significant for the increasing numbers of Israeli-born youngsters. The continued growth in the economy and increased educational training for Middle Eastern groups may result in more widespread social mobility and the growing importance of class rather than ethnic affiliation. The Arab minority, although experiencing a rising living standard, continues to have an ambiguous position. The prognosis is, therefore, for a society in which Western norms will retain their dominance and become even more widely distributed, but within which separate forms of ethnic and religious group organization will also be retained.

Postscript

This chapter was first drafted in 1962 and later revised in 1966. Now, writing in the spring of 1970, it already needs substantial updating. The major new event, of course, was the Arab-Israel war of June 1967, and the warfare that still continues. The war, and the ceaseless political and military crises that followed, have brought about a series of rapid social, economic, and political changes. Indeed, certain of the primary structural issues that have confronted Israeli society since its inception appear, at least for now, to be relegated to secondary importance; while the social forces that had their inception with the 1967 war seem to have turned the social structure in new directions.

Looking back at Israel's brief history between 1948 and June 1967, it is probably fair to state that military security, immigrant absorption, economic development, and the formation of a viable democratic polity were the key problems that the Israeli society faced. It is also fair to conclude that with the exception of the first, these problems are no longer felt to be—and in fact no longer are—principal issues. The central concerns of the society are no longer, for example, increasing agricultural productivity or assimilating Jews from Middle Eastern countries. Rather, since the June 1967 war a single issue has dominated all others: namely, whether or not, and under what conditions, peace can be established between Israel and the Arab states. Moreover, since there has not been peace but rather constant warfare, Israeli society has become, in effect, a kind of "crisis society." Some of the consequences of this new condition will be briefly sketched out below.

It should not be surprising to find that since the 1967 war social relationships among the varied segments of the Jewish society have become increasingly solidary, while social relationships between Jews and Arabs (both within Israel and in the occupied areas of Jordan, Syria and Egypt) are not merely "ambiguous" but rather tense and overtly hostile. The experience of the war itself has had the effect of driving the varied segments of the Jewish society closer together. The war energized and involved all groups in the population, and the experience stands symbolically for their incorporation within it. Moreover, external conflicts have led to greater internal cohesion. It is as if the "first law of conflict theory"—that conflicts between subgroups diminish when they face a common foe—has here literally become effective. To return again to a primary illustration, it appears that the previous sense of division and prejudice that frequently characterized relationships between Middle Eastern and European Jewish groups has greatly diminished. This is not to say that the objective features of the stratification system have changed; Europeans continue to have higher incomes and to monopolize prestige posts, just as they formerly did. Yet the experience of crisis and warfare has clearly developed new feelings of common loyalties and solidarity between groups. Indeed, it may be fair to conclude that these recent experiences have had the effect of more fully absorbing or assimilating the various immigrant groups—and the Middle Eastern segments in particular—within the fabric of the Jewish society.

Turning to Jewish-Arab relationships, the political-military crisis has nearly sealed these groups off from one another. In the days immediately following the June war, many Jews were hopeful that a rapprochement between Arab and Jew might soon become possible. That optimism has now vanished. To be sure, in places such as Jerusalem, Jews and Arabs can now, for the first time since 1948, mingle and interact within the city. Jews and Arabs trade in one another's shops, and a growing number of Arabs are employed in Jewish-owned construction or industrial enterprises. Yet these encounters are, at best, strained and formal, and commonly they involve deep suspicion and mistrust. In the West Bank and Gaza regions relationships are, of course, those between military occupation forces and an occupied civilian population, and they are expectedly hostile. Within Israel itself, social ties between Jews and Arabs have similarly become strained; the loyalties and allegiance of the Israeli-Arab population is being severely tested, and sizable numbers of Arabs are drawn to the cause of Arab nationalism. In brief, if the post-1967 period has strengthened ties within the Jewish society, it has also brought a deep deterioration in relationships between Jews and Arabs.

It may be useful also to indicate briefly some recent changes in economic and political organization. Those structural features that have characterized the Israeli economy during the past two decades—a heavy foreign trade deficit, the high proportion of persons employed in service occupations, tight government regulations over the economy, as well as a growing number of government-owned industries—have persisted in the post-1967 period. Moreover, in this war economy an ever-increasing proportion of economic resources have been allocated to military expenditures. The government's defense industries have greatly expanded as more sophisticated military equipment is manufactured locally. Not surprisingly in a war economy, employment levels have been high, and inflationary pressures also have been strong. Finally—and this is perhaps the most significant point—under the current pressures the capacities of the economy seem to have become more fully developed. The work force has itself become more professional and competent, the scale of industrial enterprises has grown significantly, and real progress has been made in organizing sophisticated systems of production and organization. To sum up briefly: in response to the military crisis the Israeli economy has become thoroughly modern and industrial, and, indeed, can be characterized as becoming "postindustrial."

In regard to political organization, the most significant development has been the formation of a "national unity" coalition government, which includes nearly all of the political parties. The Labor Party still dominates this coalition (as it has all governments formed since 1948), but for the first time the coalition includes representatives of the Heruth, a more nationalist and ideologically antisocialist group. Formally, the opposition is limited to small or splinter parties or to vocal groups outside the party system who may disagree with and protest government policies. The level of political activity and debate continues to be intense; the war situation has not curtailed the society's democratic process. It is significant, too, to note that the veteran European-born leadership is being replaced by a somewhat younger, Israeli-born elite group.

To conclude this brief postscript, attention should now be given to outlining some features of Israel as a "crisis society." The term "crisis society" refers to a society at war. Since June 1967, there has been an unending stream of violence and of events that signal continuing tension and violence. Nearly each day, and at times from hour to hour, there are reports of casualties, fatalities, new clashes, threats of even larger-scale conflicts, and so forth. To be sure, these are not new events in the Middle East: there have been repeated acts of violence along the borders since 1948, and little progress has ever been made toward resolving Arab-Israeli political tensions. In this sense, Israeli society has been in crisis since its inception. Yet the post-1967 conditions are more extreme in comparison with the past 20 years. It is for these reasons that Israel can be termed a "crisis society."

What are the consequences of these crisis conditions? Some have already been mentioned, and others may be briefly indicated here. First, as was suggested earlier, the persisting crisis has magnified solidarity within the Jewish society. Warfare itself, the recurrent training exercises that draw large segments of the population out from their civilian occupations and into military ranks, the widespread feeling of a small nation outnumbered by its enemies—these conditions have had the effect of increasing national solidarity. There is reason to suppose that this will persist for as long as the crisis continues.

Second, crisis conditions have also further developed the power and scope of national institutions and nationwide social networks. Earlier it was pointed out that since its formation Israeli society has had a distinctive national level cast to it. It is hardly surprising to find that during a period of warfare—an eminently national undertaking—these tendencies have progressed even further. The rapid growth of the military industries has added to the centralization of the economy, and the communications of information and rumor spread with amazing speed across the entire social system. As both of these examples suggest, national events and issues have a pre-eminent importance. The crisis conditions seem to have pulled the 2,300,000 or so Jewish population closer into the centers of national life.

Finally, the post-1967 crisis has also given greater influence to the military elites. Once again, this is certainly an expected outcome of a protracted war. As the crisis continues and, indeed, escalates further, the professional army corps receives higher esteem and greater influence over political and economic policies. However, there are no indications that political controls have shifted from civilian to military hands. The army officers are themselves members of wide-ranging civilian social networks, and, moreover, at the cabinet and lower governmental levels civilian personnel continue to exercise superior authority.

In conclusion, what the long-range outlook is for a "crisis society" is yet uncertain. The critical question is when and how the crisis—the war —will end. Should it continue, will today's solidarity turn inevitably into a closing of dissent and an authoritarian regime, the economy become a miniature "military-industrial complex," and the army corps gain greater influence? Or, alternately, will the essentially democratic format remain strong in the face of a long-lasting war, and the society learn to cope with war while it continues to be creative socially and culturally? If the crisis ends, will new forms of relationships be created between Arabs and Jews, and some of the older tensions within the Jewish society reassert themselves? Writing in the spring of 1970, it is surely not possible to predict the shape that Israeli society is taking. For the moment, the unanswered question is how that society will respond to the continuing crises of war.

ISRAEL:
AN ANNOTATED BIBLIOGRAPHY

Bachi, Roberto
    1958   "Trends of population and labour force in Israel," in A.
          Bonné, ed., *The Challenge of Development*, Jerusalem, Jeru-
          salem Post Press: 41-80.

          Professor Bachi, the dean of Israeli demographers, summar-
          izes the development of the Jewish population from the nine
          teenth-century colonization period until the mid-1950s. This
          article is particularly useful since it assembles summaries of a
          large number of demographic studies (for example, regarding
          marriage, intermarriage, fertility, spread of Hebrew, labor
          force participation, occupational structure, and others).

Berlin, Isaiah
    1958   "The origins of Israel," in Walter Z. Laqueur, ed., *The Mid-
          dle East in Transition*, London, Routledge and Kegan Paul:
          204-21.

          This brief, discursive article traces some of Israel's East Euro-
          pean cultural roots: Berlin shows why and how contempo-
          rary Israel continues to reflect the East European background
          of its veteran population. The article is important since it
          emphasizes this relationship with skill and clarity.

Bernstein, Marver
    1957   *The politics of Israel; the first decade of statehood*, Prince-
          ton, Princeton University Press. 360 pp.

          Bernstein surveys various features of Israeli government—the
          party system, the cabinet and president, public administra-
          tion, government and economic development, local govern-
          ment, and welfare legislation. The framework is somewhat
          formal, and the sources limited, yet the author has a fresh,
          critical. perspective, and the book presents information in
          many key areas.

Cohen, Abner
    1965   *Arab border-villages in Israel: a study of continuity and
          change in social organisation*, Manchester, Manchester Uni-
          versity Press.

          A detailed comparative analysis of social change in Arab villages situated in the Israeli "Triangle." This excellent study focuses upon the shifting bases of village solidarity and on the relationships between village political organization and the Israeli political structure, and also clarifies the ambivalent position of the Israeli Arab minority.

Cohen, Erik
1969 "Mixed marriage in an Israeli town," *Jewish Journal of Sociology 11*: 41-50.

In this study, the only analytic discussion of Arab-Jewish marriages that is currently available, Erik Cohen provides information and insight regarding intermarriage in its Israeli social contexts.

Cohen, Percy S.
1962 "Alignments and allegiances in the community of Shaarayim in Israel," *Jewish Journal of Sociology 4*: 14-38.

Deshen, Shlomo A.
1965 "A case of breakdown of modernization in an Israeli immigrant community," *Jewish Journal of Sociology 7*: 63-91.

Eisenstadt, Shmuel Noah
1954 *Absorption of immigrants*, London, Routledge and Kegan Paul (also published in 1955 by The Free Press, Glencoe, Illinois).

Eisenstadt's book—the first large-scale sociological study of aspects of Israeli society—includes both theoretical and descriptive material: the author proposes a sociological theory of immigration and immigrant-absorption, and then presents research data drawn mainly from pre- and post-state Jewish colonization in Israel. The analysis of the pre-state society is particularly useful, as is the description of change brought about by the formation of the state. The sections on post-state processes of immigrant absorption present a good model for analysis—but the data themselves are only partly presented. As yet the only general study of immigrant absorption in Israel, this book is a good beginning for continued intensive research.

1956 "The Social conditions of the development of voluntary associations—a case study of Israel," *Scripta Hierosomylitana 3*: 104-25 (Jerusalem, at the Magnes Press, Hebrew University).

1958 "Israel," in Arnold M. Rose, ed., *The Institutions of Advanced Societies*, Minneapolis, University of Minnesota Press: 384-443.

In this general essay, Eisenstadt analyzes some of the main Israeli institutional systems—the family, economics, politics, and cultural values. Although some of the material is also contained in other works, the essay is particularly useful as it relates the various institutions within the total national context.

1967   *Israeli society*, New York, Basic Books.

This comprehensive volume is an updating of Eisenstadt's and his colleagues' work through the mid-1960s. The chapters on social, economic, political, and cultural organization bring together a mass of sociological documentation. Although in part clumsily pieced together, the book is the best current reference to Israel society.

Eisenstadt, Shmuel Noah, and Y. Ben David
1956   "Intergenerational tensions in Israel," *International Social Science Bulletin 8.*

Etzioni, Amitai
1959   "Alternative ways to democracy: the example of Israel," *Political Science Quarterly 74*: 196-214.

Etzioni asks the question: Is continuous one-party domination consonant with democracy? His consideration of Israeli politics suggests that it may be, since the parties themselves are composed of conflicting interests, are "centrist" and therefore express broadly-based views, and also enter into coalitions with groups representing other views. This is an important analysis, although perhaps too optimistic regarding the flexibility of a single-party dominated society.

Fein, Leonard J.
1967   *Politics in Israel*, Boston, Little, Brown.

In this well-written, carefully-presented study of contemporary Israeli politics, Fein draws together material regarding the political culture and distribution of power in Israeli society. The author analyzes the changing character of the society and the political parties, relations between parties, government, and policy, and, more generally, the links between "society" and "politics." A first-rate analysis of the present-day political scene.

Feitelson, Dina
1959   "Aspects of the social life of Kurdish Jews," *Jewish Journal of Sociology 1*: 201-16.

Descriptive of Kurdish Jews prior to their immigration to Israel, this article provides important ethnographic background material regarding a little-known Middle Eastern Jewish group. The data include descriptions of household and family groups, the life-cycle, occupational and authority roles, and relations with the non-Jewish Kurdish population.

Frankenstein, Carl, ed.
1953 *Between past and future; essays and studies on aspects of immigrant absorption in Israel*, Jerusalem, Henrietta Szold Foundation for Child and Youth Welfare. 335 pp.

The thirteen articles collected in this volume present data on different facets of immigrant absorption: for example social policy in the absorption of immigrants, descriptions of new community formation, educational problems among Middle Eastern immigrants, and the acculturation of Yemenite groups. The articles are of uneven quality—some are in loose, "diary-type" form; while others present the results of more systematic research. This volume provides an introduction to several key features of the "Israeli reality"—both in terms of the immigrant groups themselves and also regarding the cultural norms of Israeli researchers and the veteran society generally.

Goitein, Shelomo Dov
1955 "Portrait of a Yemenite weavers' village," *Jewish Social Studies 17*: 3-26.

Goldberg, Harvey
1967 "FBD marriage and demography among Tripolitanian Jews in Israel," *Southwestern Journal of Anthropology 23*: 176-91.

One of a series of excellent articles regarding continuity and change among a Middle Eastern immigrant group.

Halpern, Ben
1961 *The idea of the Jewish state*, Cambridge, Harvard University Press.

This first volume in a series on the development of Israeli society is written mainly from a historical perspective: Halpern examines the European origins of Zionism and Israel, and then traces the political development of the Jewish community in Palestine-Israel. The book successfully examines a vast amount of material—in regard to the Zionist movement, the political maneuvering surrounding the "Palestine question," and recent events in Israel's political history. This book is very helpful for understanding the origins and growth of Israel.

Hanoch, G.
1961 "Income differentials in Israel," *Fifth Report, 1959 and 1960, Falk Project for Economic Research in Israel*, Jerusalem, Falk Project for Economic Research.

Israel
 1949 *Statistical abstract of Israel*, Jerusalem, The Government Printer.

Each year the government statistical bureau summarizes a wealth of data in these volumes. The data include, for example, statistics on population, settlement, migration, national income and expenditure, labor force, foreign trade, government finance, education, etc. Although the categories are not fully comparative from year to year—the recent volumes tend to be more complete—the *Abstract* is an invaluable source of basic information.

Katz, Elihu, and Awraham Zloczower
 1961 "Ethnic continuity in an Israeli town," *Human Relations 14*: 293-327.

The authors analyze European and Yemenite youngsters in a small town in relation to their family and peer group ties and activities. The conclusions suggest a large measure of "continuity"—and therefore have important implications in the analysis of Israeli society.

Kraines, Oscar
 1961 *Government and politics in Israel*, Boston, Houghton Mifflin.

This book presents a concise description of the Israeli system of government. The major areas covered include the legislative process, government structure, law and public administration, civil liberties, local government, and political party activity. Primarily descriptive rather than analytic, the book is a helpful compendium of material regarding Israel's government.

Marx, Emanuel
 1958 "Bedouin Society in the Negev," *New Outlook* (Tel Aviv) *2, no. 1*: 17-24; *2, no. 2*: 25-31.
 1967 *Bedouin of the Negev*, Manchester, Manchester University Press; New York, Praeger.

This is an important contribution to studies of the Bedouin and nomadic peoples in general. Marx's anthropological study concentrates particularly upon questions of domestic group and tribal organization, although the general ecological and political setting is also described. This cogent study presents important ethnographic detail, as well as making important theoretical contributions.

Matras, Judah
 1965 *Social change in Israel*, Chicago, Aldine Publishing Company.

Through the skillful use of demographic data, Matras presents a highly sophisticated analysis of social change in contemporary Israel. Such important questions as changes in family formation, occupational structure, and in the basis of electoral support are carefully analyzed. This study lends an excellent view of the changing structure of the Israeli community.

Minkovitz, Moshe
1967 "Old conflicts in a new environment; a study of a Moroccan Atlas Mountains community transplanted to Israel," *Jewish Journal of Sociology 9*: 191-208.

A brief case study of political conflicts in a transplanted Moroccan community.

Patai, Raphael
1953 *Israel between East and West; a study on human relations*, Philadelphia, Jewish Publication Society. 348 pp.

Patai examines the European—Middle Eastern "clash of cultures" in Israel, and then makes the case for greater cultural understanding. The book contains valuable information regarding Middle Eastern Jewish groups, as well as material describing non-Jewish communities in Israel. The conceptual and background data are useful—but now limited by events since the 1950s.

Patinkin, Don
1960 *The Israel economy; the first decade*, Jerusalem, Falk Project for Economic Research in Israel. 155 pp.; charts, 45 tables.

This excellent essay presents a balanced, well-documented analysis of Israel's economic development. Drawing upon extensive data collected by government agencies and the Falk Project for Economic Research, Patinkin emphasizes such issues as relations between immigration, labor force, and employment; the growth in national product; inflation and dependence upon foreign capital. The analysis is sober and questioning throughout—Patinkin sees both the expanding economy as well as the still uncertain foundations upon which it is constructed. The tables and charts are an important source of basic population and economic information.

Rosenfeld, Eva
1951 "Social stratification in a 'classless' society," *American Sociological Review 16*: 766-74.

Rosenfeld, Henry
1958 "Processes of structural change within the Arab village extended family," *American Anthropologist 60*: 1127-39.

Rosenfeld considers family, household, and marriage relations in an Israeli Arab village. The study takes a several-generation perspective, and thereby both describes the traditional system and also indicates changes within it. The emphasis upon potential points of conflict in the system helps the reader to understand various features of village life.

Seligman, Lester G.
1964 *Leadership in a new nation; political development in Israel*, New York, Atherton Press. xvi, 141 pp.

In this slim volume, Seligman, a political scientist, analyzes the orientations and policies of the political-party elites.

Shuval, Judith T.
1963 *Immigrants on the threshold*, New York, Atherton Press.

Based upon large-scale questionnaire sampling, Shuval's social-psychological study details the states of mind and conditions of immigrants to Israel in 1949 and 1950. The author examines such important questions as the relations between ideology and predisposition to change and the effect of concentration-camp experience upon the immigrants' adjustment to Israeli conditions, and also documents the difficulties and frustrations of the mass immigration period.

Sicron, Moshe
1957 *Immigration to Israel, 1948-1953*, Jerusalem, Falk Project for Economic Research in Israel. 124 pp.; 72 tables.

Part of the publication series of the Government Central Bureau of Statistics and the Falk Project for Economic Research, this book analyzes the demographic features of the mass immigration that followed the establishment of Israel. The data analyzed include the relative volume and intensity of immigration; age, sex, and family structures of the immigrants; participation in the labor force; and occupation prior to migration. The data are reliable and clearly presented; they provide an excellent base for considering many problems of immigrant absorption.

Spiro, Melford
1954 "Is the family universal?" *American Anthropologist 56*: 839-46.

1956 *Kibbutz: venture in Utopia*, Cambridge, Harvard University Press.

This community-study analysis of a kibbutz (communal settlement) describes how this distinctive type of society is established and then maintained. Spiro examines such themes as the social history of the kibbutz, the kibbutz family, stratification in a "classless society," the communal settlement within Israeli society, and the political ideology of the settlement. The view provided is insightful and well presented; it suffers somewhat, however, by a lack of comparative perspective, particularly in regard to political ideology and the dynamics of internal community organization. Nevertheless, this monograph makes a major contribution to Israeli studies.

1958   *Children of the Kibbutz*, Cambridge, Harvard University Press.

A companion to the earlier general monograph on the kibbutz, this study focuses upon the socialization process in a "non-family" situation. The analysis follows kibbutz children through a series of developmental stages—from earliest infancy experience and training, through school, and finally adult membership in the commune. The observations are perceptive, and there is an excellent blending of theory with observation. The analysis is well documented, and provides a rather complete image of socialization, its achievements and problems, in kibbutz society. (Written with the assistance of Audrey G. Spiro.)

Talmon, Yonina
1952   "Social differentiation in co-operative communities," *British Journal of Sociology 3*: 339-57.

This study of veteran moshavim (cooperative villages) includes an analysis of the moshav system, as well as preliminary findings regarding the bases for social differentiation in cooperative villages. Since the research was conducted in 1946, it provides an interesting base for comparison with more recent developments in veteran communities, and also between these villages and new-immigrant moshavim.

1954   "The family in Israel," *Marriage and Family Living 16*: 343-49.

1956   "Differentiation in collective settlements," *Scripta Hierosylmitana 3*: 153-78. (Jerusalem, at the Magnes Press, Hebrew University).

Part of a larger research program in collective settlements, this article reports on a comparative study of stratification. Talmon argues that although differences in authority and lifestyle do exist between kibbutz members, these do not tend to cystallize into opposed interest groups; moreover, certain authority roles are regularly reallocated, and the system thereby retains flexibility.

Weingrod, Alex
  1960   "Change and continuity in a Moroccan immigrant village in Israel," *Middle East Journal 14*: 277-91.
  1962   "Administered communities: some characteristics of new immigrant villages in Israel," *Economic Development and Cultural Change 11*: 69-84.
  1965   *Israel: group relations in a new society*, New York, Frederick A. Praeger for the Institute of Race Relations.

      This book deals mainly with cultural variation and stratification—relationships between the various immigrant-ethnic groups, and between Arabs and Jews. A general view of the social and cultural structure of contemporary Israel.

  1966   *Reluctant pioneers: village development in Israel*, Ithaca, Cornell University Press.

      An analysis of the development of a Moroccan immigrant village, seen from the perspectives of the immigrants as well as the government settlement authorities. The pattern of development of a single new village is traced in detail, and more general conclusions are drawn following comparisons with other immigrant villages.

Weintraub, Dov, and F. Bernstein
  1966   "Social structure and modernization: a comparative study of two villages," *American Journal of Sociology 71*: 509-21.

Willner, Dorothy
  1969   *Nation building and community in Israel*, Princeton, Princeton University Press.

      A generally excellent, well-documented study of Israeli settlement institutions and the immigrants' responses to their new conditions. The author's analysis of the settlement groups is especially rich in detail.

Index